AFRICAN HISTORICAL DICTIONARIES
Edited by Jon Woronoff

1. *Cameroon,* by Victor T. LeVine and Roger P. Nye. 1974. *Out of print. See No. 48.*
2. *The Congo,* 2nd ed., by Virginia Thompson and Richard Adloff. 1984. *Out of print. See No. 69.*
3. *Swaziland,* by John J. Grotpeter. 1975.
4. *The Gambia,* 2nd ed., by Harry A. Gailey. 1987.
5. *Botswana,* by Richard P. Stevens. 1975. *Out of print. See No. 70.*
6. *Somalia,* by Margaret F. Castagno. 1975.
7. *Benin (Dahomey),* 2nd ed., by Samuel Decalo. 1987. *Out of print. See No. 61.*
8. *Burundi,* by Warren Weinstein. 1976. *Out of print. See No. 73*
9. *Togo,* 3rd ed., by Samuel Decalo. 1996.
10. *Lesotho,* by Gordon Haliburton. 1977.
11. *Mali,* 3rd ed., by Pascal James Imperato. 1996.
12. *Sierra Leone,* by Cyril Patrick Foray. 1977.
13. *Chad,* 3rd ed., by Samuel Decalo. 1997.
14. *Upper Volta,* by Daniel Miles McFarland. 1978. *Out of print. See No. 74.*
15. *Tanzania,* by Laura S. Kurtz. 1978.
16. *Guinea,* 3rd ed., by Thomas O'Toole with Ibrahima Bah-Lalya. 1995.
17. *Sudan,* by John Voll. 1978. *Out of print. See No. 53.*
18. *Rhodesia/Zimbabwe,* by R. Kent Rasmussen. 1979. *Out of print. See No. 46.*
19. *Zambia,* 2nd ed., by John J. Grotpeter, Brian V. Siegel, and James R. Pletcher. 1998.
20. *Niger,* 3rd ed., by Samuel Decalo. 1996.
21. *Equatorial Guinea,* 2nd ed., by Max Liniger-Goumaz. 1988.
22. *Guinea-Bissau,* 3rd ed., by Richard Lobban and Peter Mendy. 1996.
23. *Senegal,* by Lucie G. Colvin. 1981. *Out of print. See No. 65.*
24. *Morocco,* by William Spencer. 1980. *Out of print. See No. 71.*
25. *Malawi,* by Cynthia A. Crosby. 1980. *Out of print. See No. 54.*
26. *Angola,* by Phyllis Martin. 1980. *Out of print. See No. 52.*
27. *The Central African Republic,* by Pierre Kalck. 1980. *Out of print. See No. 51.*
28. *Algeria,* by Alf Andrew Heggoy. 1981. *Out of print. See No. 66.*
29. *Kenya,* by Bethwell A. Ogot. 1981.
30. *Gabon,* by David E. Gardinier. 1981. *Out of print. See No. 58.*
31. *Mauritania,* by Alfred G. Gerteiny. 1981. *Out of print. See No. 68.*
32. *Ethiopia,* by Chris Prouty and Eugene Rosenfeld. 1981. *Out of print. See No. 56.*

66. *Algeria,* 2nd ed., by Phillip Chiviges Naylor and Alf Andrew Heggoy. 1994.
67. *Egypt,* 2nd ed., by Arthur Goldschmidt, Jr. 1994.
68. *Mauritania,* 2nd ed., by Anthony G. Pazzanita. 1996.
69. *Congo,* 3rd ed., by Samuel Decalo, Virginia Thompson, and Richard Adloff. 1996.
70. *Botswana,* 3rd ed., by Jeff Ramsay, Barry Morton, and Fred Morton. 1996.
71. *Morocco,* 2nd ed., by Thomas K. Park. 1996.
72. *Tanzania,* 2nd ed., by Thomas P. Ofcansky and Rodger Yeager. 1997.
73. *Burundi,* 2nd ed., by Ellen K. Eggers. 1997.
74. *Burkina Faso,* 2nd ed., by Daniel Miles McFarland and Lawrence Rupley. 1998.
75. *Eritrea,* by Tom Killion. 1998.

Historical Dictionary of Burkina Faso

Second Edition

Daniel Miles McFarland
and
Lawrence A. Rupley

African Historical Dictionaries, No. 74

The Scarecrow Press, Inc.
Lanham, Md., & London
1998

SCARECROW PRESS, INC.

Published in the United States of America
by Scarecrow Press, Inc.
4720 Boston Way
Lanham, Maryland 20706

British Library Cataloguing in Publication Information Available

Library of Congress Cataloging-in-Publication Data

McFarland, Daniel Miles.
    Historical dictionary of Burkina Faso /
  Daniel Miles McFarland and Lawrence A. Rupley.—2nd ed.
      p.   cm.—(African historical dictionaries ; no. 74)
    Rev. ed. of: Historical dictionary of Upper Volta (Haute Volta),
1978.
    Includes bibliographical references and index.
    ISBN 0–8108–3405–7 (cloth : alk. paper)
    1. Burkina Faso—History—Dictionaries.   I. Rupley, Lawrence.
II. McFarland, Daniel Miles. Historical dictionary of Upper Volta
(Haute Volta) III. Title. IV. Series.
DT555.517.M44   1998
966.25—dc21
                                       97–30169
                                          CIP

ISBN 0-8108-3405-7 (cloth : alk. paper)

Contents

Editor's Foreword

When the first edition of this book was published, nearly two decades ago, Burkina Faso (then Upper Volta) could fairly be regarded as poor but promising. Very sadly, it is now even poorer and what promise remains appears in the people, who are, as the author says, "hardworking, resourceful and adaptable." Alas, since the economy has wilted — indeed, almost literally so — there is not much hope for them in Burkina Faso. They must go abroad to find work and send money back to those who stay behind. But despite long periods abroad in neighboring countries, the people remain closely attached to their homeland. Yet, even now, if the political situation could be improved, something might be done. Here too, after eight regimes since political independence in 1960, most of them military, none of them very democratic, there is not much hope left. This is not a very happy prognosis and one can only pray that it will prove as mistaken as the earlier one.

Nonetheless, Burkina Faso is an important part of West Africa. It is one of the larger nations, with a substantial population. And it borders six other countries, many of them in similar straits. To understand what is happening in this country, and the whole region, it is useful to have an updated historical dictionary. Like the earlier edition, this one provides essential information in the form of a chronology, introduction and dictionary. The latter contains entries on numerous persons, places and events, political parties and other organizations, features of the economy, society and culture. It reaches far back into history to trace the evolution from the precolonial, to the colonial, to the independence periods and then takes stock of the present state of affairs. Some of this is summed up in the appendices or illustrated in the maps. The bibliography, particularly extensive, suggests further reading.

It was not easy to find authors for this volume, neither the first nor the second edition. There are not many specialists dealing with Burkina Faso. Thus, we were lucky twice over. The foundation was laid by Daniel Miles McFarland, formerly professor of African Studies at James Madison University. His special interest is the Volta River region and the peoples who live there. It has now been built upon by Lawrence

Rupley, who has taught in both West and East Africa and lived in Burkina Faso in the latter 1980s. That Dr. McFarland was particularly interested in the historical and political side, and Dr. Rupley in the economic and financial ramifications, has broadened and strengthened this new *Historical Dictionary of Burkina Faso*.

Jon Woronoff, Series Editor

Preface

Daniel McFarland's first edition was published in 1978. From that time until the early 1990s, he updated many of the entries and collected new materials. Due to family health considerations he felt unable to see this second edition through to completion. I agreed to undertake the project in 1995 with complete access to Professor McFarland's collected materials. I spent time at the Indiana University Africana Library later in 1995 working on bibliographic entries and searching out news items covering the past half dozen years.

Writing about a country which has changed its name poses frequent challenges in a book of this kind. I have tried to use the name that was correct at the time, where a specific historical period is implied. Otherwise I intended to use "Burkina Faso". In the bibliography an English translation of French titles is included in the majority of cases.

It is hard to know how specific one should be with references to sources when one has a hundred-page bibliography attached! As well as specific references cited elsewhere, I have made significant use of Robin Sharp's *Burkina Faso: New Life for the Sahel?: A Report for Oxfam* (1990). For some recent statistics I relied on the Economist Intelligence Unit's *Country Profile: Niger, Burkina Faso 1994–95*. And the 1984 edition of *Muslim Peoples: A World Ethnographic Survey* edited by Richard V. Weekes has provided useful background on a number of Burkina's major ethnic groups. Over and over I have been impressed at the care with which Professor McFarland's research was done, and thank him for that. I benefitted in a major way from the availability of Samuel Decalo's bibliography on Burkina Faso published by Clio Press in 1994.

As Professor McFarland wrote in 1977, this book is based on the pioneer work of Henri Labouret, Louis Tauxier, Elliott P. Skinner, Françoise Héritier-Izard, Michel Izard and Myron Joel Echenberg. It is an honor to stand in their shadow. I want to repeat his acknowledgement of support from Raymond Dingledine, Paula W. See, Ronald Carrier and his associates in the James Madison University history department, and for the loyal patience shown by his family, especially Anne S. McFarland, throughout the project. Janis Pivarnik collected materials from far and wide. The work was supported by generous grants from James Madison University and the Madison College Foundation.

For this second edition, thanks go to Nancy J. Schmidt, Africana Librarian at Indiana University in Bloomington, Indiana, for encouragement and assistance. Thanks also to Nancy Heisey, Joanne M. Zellers of the Library of Congress African Section, Greg Finnegan, Phil Horst, and to John Grimley for assistance with the maps. I am particularly grateful to all the Burkinabè friends and colleagues from whom I learned during my 1985–1990 stint in Burkina. A partial list would include Papa Job, Somfida, Sibidou, Justin, Hippolyte, Sophie, Maurice, Samuel, Helene, Thomas, Martin, Michelene and Jean.

I am grateful to my family and friends for their patience and support, and for their advice on French translation from time to time.

Lawrence Rupley
Akron, Pennsylvania
July 1997

A Note on Spelling

Anyone who has written about West Africa knows the problems posed by spelling African nouns. Each European language approaches the problem differently. Arabic and local usage also introduce complications. For American readers, diacritical marks are often a mystery of unfathomable proportion. As Burkina Faso is now a francophone nation, French renderings are preferred in most cases in this book. George Peter Murdock's *Africa: Its Peoples and Their Cultural History* has influenced the spelling of major ethnic groups. Many entries in this Dictionary include alternate spellings. *Cartes Routière* published by the Institut Géographique du Burkina, by Michelin, and by Texaco, and the United States Board on Geographic Names gazetteer for Upper Volta/Burkina Faso were references for place name spellings. "Chute" for waterfall, "falaise" for cliff or escarpment, "mare" for lake or marsh, and "mont" or "pic" for hill are often used because that is the way they appear on maps of the area most likely to be used.

Abbreviations and Acronyms

AAOF	Archives of French West Africa, Dakar
ABP	Agence Burkinabè de Presse
ADB	African Development Bank
AFP	Agence France Presse
AHV	Archives Nationales de la Haute-Volta/Burkina Faso
ANSOM	Archives Nationales, Section d'Outre-Mer, Paris
AOF	Afrique Occidentale Française
AV	Alliance Voltaïque
AVP	Agence Voltaïque de Presse
AVV	Autorité des Aménagements des Vallées des Voltas
BADEA	Arab Bank for Economic Development in Africa
BAGF	*Bulletin de l'Association des Géographes Français,* Paris
BBF	Brasseries du Burkina Faso
BCAF	*Bulletin du Comité de l'Afrique Française,* Paris
BCEAO	Banque Centrale des États de l'Afrique de l'Ouest
BCEHS	*Bulletin du Comité d'Etudes Historiques et Scientifiques de l'Afrique Occidentale Française,* Paris
BIAO	Banque International pour l'Afrique Occidentale
BIB	Banque Internationale du Burkina
BICIA	Banque Internationale pour le Commerce, l'Industrie et l'Agriculture du Burkina
BIFAN	*Bulletin de l'Institut Français d'Afrique Noire,* Dakar *Bulletin de l'Institut Fondamental d'Afrique Noire,* Dakar
BND	Banque Nationale de Développement
BSAP	*Bulletin de la Société d'Anthropologie de Paris*
BSG	*Bulletin de la Société de Géographie,* Paris
BSGAOF	*Bulletin de la Société de Géographie de l'Afrique Occidentale Française*
BSGC	*Bulletin de la Société de Géographie Commerciale,* Paris
BSLP	*Bulletin de la Société de Linguistique de Paris*

BUMIGEB	Bureau des Mines de la Géologie du Burkina
CARDAN	Centre d'Analyse et de Recherche Documentaires pour l'Afrique Noire, Paris
CATAF	Centre d'Affectation des Travailleurs Agricoles et Forestiers
CATC	Confédération Africaine des Travailleurs Croyants
CCIAB	Chambre de Commerce, d'Industrie et d'Artisanat du Burkina
CDR	Committees for the Defense of the Revolution
CEA	*Cahiers d'Etudes Africaines,* Paris
CEAO	Communauté Economique de l'Afrique de l'Ouest
CEDESA	Centre de Documentation Economique et Sociale Africaine
CEDRES	Centre d'Etudes, de Documentation et de Recherches Economiques et Sociales, University of Ouagadougou
CEFA	Comité d'Etudes Franco-Africain
CESAO	Centre d'Etudes Economiques et Sociales d'Afrique Occidentale, Bobo Dioulasso
CFA	Colonies Françaises d'Afrique; Communauté Financière Africaine
CFAO	Compagnie Française de l'Afrique Occidentale
CFTC	Confédération Française des Travailleurs Chrétiens
CGT	Confédération Générale du Travail
CGTB	Confédération Générale des Travailleurs Burkinabè
CHEAM	Centre des Hautes Etudes Administratives sur l'Afrique et l'Asie Modernes
CIDESA	Centre International de Documentation Economique et Sociale Africaine, Brussels
CILSS	Comité Permanent Interétats de Lutte contre la Sécheresse dans le Sahel
CINAFRIC	Société Africaine de Cinéma
CMRPN	Comité Militaire de Redressement pour le Progres National
CNEC	Centre National d'Entrainement Commando, Pô
CNR	Conseil National de la Révolution
CNRS	Centre National de la Recherche Scientifique, Paris
CNTB	Confédération Nationale des Travailleurs Burkinabès
CODESRIA	Conseil pour le développement de la recherche economique et sociale en Afrique, Dakar
CSB	Conféderation Syndicale Burkinabè
CSP	Conseil de Salut du Peuple
CVRS	Centre Voltaïque de la Recherche Scientifique, Ouagadougou (later CNRST)
ECA (UNECA)	United Nations Economic Commission for Africa

ECOWAS	Economic Community of West African States (CEDEAO)
EDF	European Development Fund
EDI	*Etudes et Documentation Internationales,* Paris
EEC	European Economic Community (sometimes EC)
ENFOM	Ecole Nationale de la France d'Outre-Mer
EV	Entente Voltaïque
EVOL	*Etudes Voltaïques,* Ouagadougou
FAC	Fonds d'Aide et de Coopération, France
FAO	Food and Agriculture Organization of the UN
FEANF	Fédération des Etudiants d'Afrique Noire en France
FESPACO	Festival Panafricain du Cinéma de Ouagadougou
FIDES	Fonds d'Investissement pour le Développement Economique et Social
FP	Front Populaire (Popular Front)
GAP	Groupement d'Action Populaire
GJA	Groupements de Jeunes Agriculteurs (Young Farmers)
GRAAP	Groupe de Recherche et d'Appui pour l'Autopromotion Paysanne
GSV	Groupe de Solidarité Voltaïque
IBRD	International Bank for Reconstruction and Development (World Bank) (BIRD)
IDEP	Institut Africaine de Développement Economique et de Planification, Dakar
IDERT	Institut d'Enseignement et de Recherches Tropicales
IFAD	International Fund for Agricultural Development
IFAN	Institut Fondamental d'Afrique Noire (once Institut Française d'Afrique Noire), Dakar
IHEOM	Institut des Hautes Etudes d'Outre-Mer
ILO	International Labor Organization
IMF	International Monetary Fund
INADES	Institut Africain de Développement Economique et Social, Abidjan
INAFA	National Institute for Adult Literacy and Training
INBF	Imprimerie National du Burkina Faso (National Printing Office)
IOM	Indépendants d'Outre-Mer
ISEA	Institut de Science Economique Appliquée
ISHA	Institut des Science Humaines Appliquées, Bordeaux
ITCZ	Inter-tropical Convergence Zone
JAOF	*Journal Officiel de l'Afrique Occidentale Française*
JOB	*Journal Officiel du Burkina*
JOHV	*Journal Officiel de la République de Haute Volta*

JORF	*Journal Officiel de la République Française*
JSA	*Journal de la Société des Africanistes,* Paris
LIPAD	Ligue Patriotique pour le Développement
MBDHP	Mouvement Burkinabè de Droits de l'Homme et de Peuples (Burkinabè Movement for Human Rights)
MDV	Mouvement Democratique Voltaïque
MFOM	Section Outre-Mer of the National Archives; once the Archives of the Ministry of Overseas France
MIFAN	*Mémoires de l'Institut Français d'Afrique Noire,* Paris and Dakar
MLN	Mouvement Africain de Libération Nationale
MNP	Mouvement National des Pionniers
MNR	Mouvement National pour le Renouveau
MPD	Movement of Progressive Democrats
MPEA	Mouvement Populaire de l'Evolution Africaine
MPV	Mouvement Progressiste de la Volta
MRP	Mouvement Républican Populaire
MSA	Mouvement Socialiste Africain
NA	*Notes Africaines,* Dakar
NDVOL	*Notes et Documents Voltaïques,* Ouagadougou, Paris
OAMCE	Organisation Africaine et Malgache de Coopération Economique
OAU	Organization of African Unity
OCAM	Organisation Commune Africaine et Malgache
OCAMM	Organisation Commune Africaine, Malgache et Mauritienne
OCCGE	Organisation de Coordination et Cooperation pour la Lutte contre les Grandes Endemies, Bobo Dioulasso
OCRS	Organisation Commune des Régions Sahariennes
ODP/MT	Organisation pour la Démocratie Populaire/Mouvement du Travail
OECD/OCDE	Organization for Economic Cooperation and Development
OFNACER	Office National des Céréales, Burkina Faso
OGPT	Office Général des Projets de Tambao
ONATEL	Office National de Télécommunication
ORD	Organisme Régional de Développement, Burkina
ORSTOM	Office de la Recherche Scientifique et Technique Outre-Mer, Paris
ONSL	Organisation Nationale des Syndicats Libre
OXFAM	Oxford Committee for Famine Relief
PAI	Parti Africain de l'Indépendance
PAP	Parti d'Action Paysanne

PCEHS	Publications du Comité d'Etudes Historiques et Scientifiques de l'Afrique Occidentale Française, Paris
PCRV	Parti Communiste Révolutionnaire Voltaïque
PDU	Parti Démocratique Unifié
PDV	Parti Démocratique Voltaïque
PFA	Parti de la Fédération Africaine
PNUD	Programme des Nations Unies pour le Développement (UN Development Program, UNDP)
PNV	Parti National Voltaïque
PPD	Programme Populaire de Développement
PRA	Parti du Regroupement Africain
PRL	Parti Républicain de la Liberté
PRN	Parti du Regroupement National
PSEMA	Parti Social d'Education des Masses Africaines
PSP	Poste Santé Primaire/Primary Health Post
PTV	Parti Travailliste Voltaïque
RAN	Régie du Chemin de Fer Abidjan-Niger
RCD	*Renseignements Coloniaux et Documents*, Paris
RDA	Rassemblement Démocratique Africaine (African Democratic Rally)
RDCA	Renseignements et Documents Publiés par le Comité de l'Afrique Française
RES	*Revue d'Ethnographie et de Sociologie*, Paris
RETP	*Revue d'Ethnographie et des Traditions Populaires*, Paris
RMAOF	*Revue Militaire de l'A.O.F.*
RPF	Rassemblement du Peuple Français
RVOL	*Recherches Voltaïques*, Ouagadougou, Paris
SAFGRAD	Semi-Arid Food Grain Research and Development
SAMAB	Autonomous Union of Burkinabè Magistrates
SATP	Syndicat Autonome des Travaux Publics
SCOA	Société Commerciale de l'Ouest Africain
SEDES	Société d'Etudes pour le Développement Economique et Social
SELAF	Société d'études linguistiques et anthropologiques de France
SHSB	Société des Huiles et Savons du Burkina
SIAO	Salon International des Artinisat de Ouagadougou
SNEAHV	Syndicat National des Enseignants Africains de Haute Volta (National Union of African Teachers)
SONACIB	Société Nationale d'Exploitation et de Distribution Cinématographique du Burkina
SOREMIB	Burkina Mining, Research and Exploitation Co.
TNB	Télévision Nationale du Burkina

TOM	Territoires d'Outre-Mer
TPC	Tribunaux Populaires de Conciliation (Popular Conciliation Courts)
TPR	Tribunaux Populaires de la Révolution
UAM	Union Africaine et Malgache
UCB	Union de Communistes Burkinabès
UDA	Union Démocratique Voltaïque
UDEAO	West African Customs Union
UDIHV	Union pour la Défense des Intérêts de la Haute Volta
UDJV	Union Démocratique de la Jeunesse Voltaïque
UDV	Union Démocratique Voltaïque
UFB	Union des Femmes du Burkina
UGEB	Union Générale des Etudiants Burkinabè
UGTAN	Union Générale des Travailleurs d'Afrique Noire
UIPL	Union des Indépendants du Pays Lobi
ULC	Union des Luttes Communistes
UMOA	Union Monétaire Ouest Africaine
UNAB	National Union of Burkinabè Elders
UNDD	Union Nationale de Defense de Démocratie
UNEP	United Nations Environment Program
UNFPA	United Nations Fund for Population Activities
UNHCR	United Nations High Commission on Refugees
UNI	Union Nationale des Indépendants
UNPB	National Peasants Union of Burkina
UNRV	Union pour la Nouvelle République Voltaïque
UPV	Union Progressiste Voltaïque
UST	Union Syndicale des Travailleurs
UV	Union Voltaïque
WARDA	West Africa Rice Development Association
WFP	World Food Program
WHO	World Health Organization (Organisation Mondiale pour la Santé, OMS)

25.4 mm. = 1 inch
0.3048 m. = 1 foot (3.208 feet = 1 meter)
1.609 km. = 1 mile

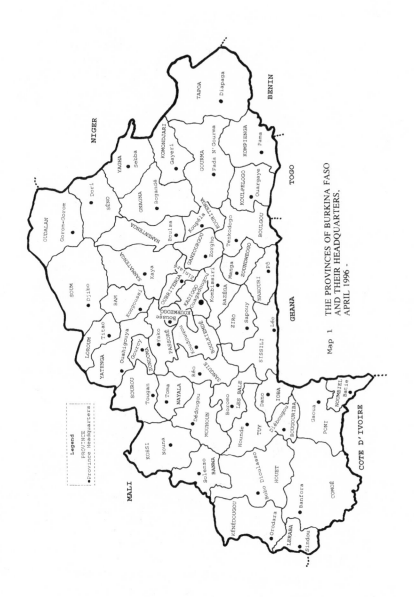

NIGER

MALI

OUDALAN

SOUM

GOROM-GOROM

Djibo

SÉNO

Dori

YAGHA

Sebba

GNAGNA

Bogandé

NAMENTENGA

Boulsa

KOMONDJARI

Gayeri

GOURMA

Fada N'Gourma

TAPOA

Diapaga

BENIN

LOROUM

Titao

BAM

Kongoussi

SANMATENGA

Kaya

YATENGA

Ouahigouya

KOURITENGA

Ziniaré

GANZOURGOU

Koupéla

KOURWEOGO

BOUSSE

OUBRITENGA

Ouagadougou

KADIOGO

Kombissiri

Koudougou

BAZÈGA

Manga

ZOUNDWEOGO

Tenkodogo

KOULPELOGO

Ouargaye

KOMPIENGA

Pama

TOGO

SOUROU

Tougan

ZONDOMA

Gourcy

Yako

PASSORÉ

BOULKIEMDÉ

SANGUIE

Réo

ZIRO

Sapouy

Manga

NAHOURI

Pô

BOULGOU

KOSSI

Nouna

NAYALA

Toma

MOUHOUN

Dédougou

BALE

Boromo

LES BALE

Hounde

TUY

SISSILI

Léo

GHANA

BANWA

Solenzo

KÉNÉDOUGOU

Orodara

HOUET

Bobo Dioulasso

COMOÉ

Banfora

LÉRABA

Sindou

IOBA

Dano

Dissin

BOUGOURIBA

Diébougou

PONI

Gaoua

NOUMBIEL

Batie

CÔTE D'IVOIRE

Map 1   THE PROVINCES OF BURKINA FASO
AND THEIR HEADQUARTERS,
APRIL 1996 -

Legend

PROVINCE
● Province Headquarters

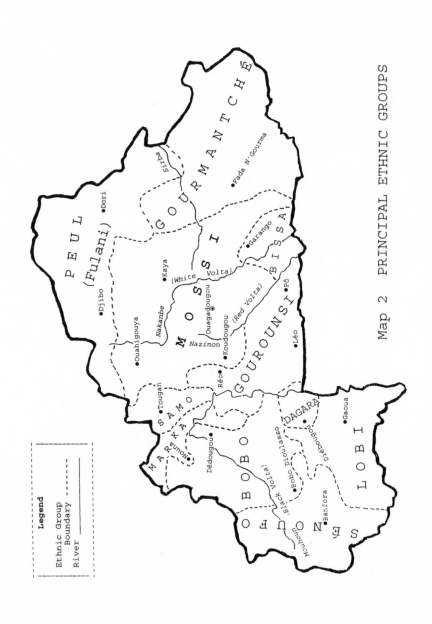

Map 2 PRINCIPAL ETHNIC GROUPS

Legend

Ethnic Group
Boundary -------
River ———————

PEUL
(Fulani)

GOURMANTCHÉ

MOSSI

BISSA

GOUROUNSI

MARKA

SÉ

BOBO

DAGARA

LOBI

SÉNOUFO

Dori

Djibo

Ouahigouya

Nakanbe

Kaya

Siriba

Fada N'Gourma

Garango

(White Volta)

Ouagadougou

Koudougou

(Red Volta)

Pô

Léo

Nazinon

Réo

Tougan

Nouna

Dédougou

(Black Volta)

Bobo Dioulasso

Diébougou

Gaoua

Banfora

Mouhoun

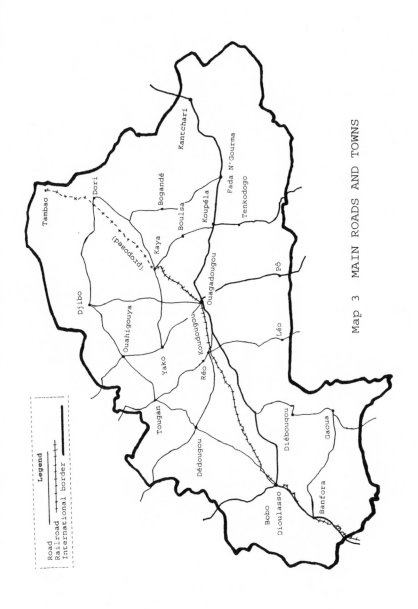

Map 3   MAIN ROADS AND TOWNS

Legend

Road
Railroad
International border

Tambao
Dori
Kantchari
Bogandé
Boulsa
Kaya
(proposed)
Koupéla
Fada N'Gourma
Tenkodogo
Djibo
Ouahigouya
Ouagadougou
Koudougou
Réo
Yako
Pô
Léo
Tougan
Dédougou
Diébougou
Gaoua
Bobo Dioulasso
Banfora

List of Major Ethnic Groups
Burkinabè Peoples

MOSSI (Molé, Moshi)

Birifor
Dagari (Dagarti)
Gourma (Gourmantché)
Gurensi
Konkomba
Kusasi
Nankana
Ouagadougou
Tallensi
Tenkodogo
Wilé (Wala)
Yarsé
Yatenga
Zandoma

SENUFO

Gouin (Guin)
Karaboro
Komono
Minianka
Nafana
Nanerge
Turka (Tourka)
Tussian
Tyéfo (Tiéfo)
Wara

LOBI

Dorosie (Dokhosie)
Dyan (Dian)
Gan
Kulango
Lobi-Dagari
Tegessie (Téguessié)
Tusyan
Vigye (Vigue)

HABÉ

Bobù (Bwa)
Bobo Fing (Black Bobo)
Bobo Gbè (White Bobo)
Bobo Oulé (Red Bobo)
Déforo
Nienige

MANDE

Boron
Busansi (Bissa, Bisa, Boussancé)
Dafing (Marka)
Dioula
Gan
Léla
Marka
Samo
Samogho
Sia (Sya)

GOUROUNSI

Awuna
Builsa
Frafra
Isala (Sissala)
Kasena
Nounouma (Nunuma)
Sissala
Vagala

NINISI (Tengabissi)

Dogon
Fulse (Foulse)
Kibsi
Kipirsi
Kurumba (Akurumba)
Lilsé
Nioniossé (Nyionyiose,
    Nyonyosé, Nioniossé)

OTHERS

Fulani (Fulbe, Peul)
Liptako
Maransé
Silma Mossi
Songhai
Tuareg (Touareg)
Yarsé
Zerma (Zaberma)

Chronology

ca. 700   The Proto-Mossi settled in the Dallol Bosso area west of modern Niamey, Niger. This early kingdom might now be called Diamaré I.

11th cent.   Historians Delafosse and Dim Delobsom date the Mossi states from the eleventh century. The Bobo-Fing move into the bend of the Black Volta.

ca. 1050   Delafosse gives this as date for the start of Oubri's reign. Oubri is fifth in the Nakomsé line of Mossi founding fathers.

1076   The Almoravids conquered ancient Ghana.

1090   Delafosse gives this date for the death of Oubri, fighting the Kipirsi, at Koudougou.

13th cent.   Historian and administrator Tauxier says the Mossi states were founded in the thirteenth century. Modern theory places formation of Mamprusi by Nedega (Bawa) at about 1400. About the beginning of the thirteenth century, Berber pressure forced the Proto-Mossi to the Niger river where they founded a new kingdom of Mindji or Diamaré II.

ca. 1204   Diaba Lompo founded Gourma.

ca. 1250   The Proto-Mossi crossed the Niger and formed Diamaré III in the area of modern Torodi.

ca. 1329   Timbuktu town was ransacked and destroyed by a group of Mossi during the reign of Mansa Musa of Mali. This date is listed from 1328 to 1338 by different authorities. From 1336–80 a Gourma ruler, Banydoba, made frequent raids north against the Fulani and south against the Tomba. Around 1350 the Lobi, Koulango and Gan moved into their present locations (Delafosse). Africanist Labouret suggests a date four centuries later.

ca. 1400   The Mossi chiefdom of Boursouma was founded in the area of modern Ouahigouya.

15th cent.   The Samo move into area along the Sourou river.

ca. 1422	The Mossi began to move west from Diamaré III toward the junction of the White and Red Voltas. About 1433 the Mossi attacked the area of modern Mali.
ca. 1465	Sonni Ali of Songhai (1464–1492) began his campaigns south of the bend of the Niger. At about the same time the Nakomsé expansion north from Tenkodogo probably began. In 1469–70 fighting between Sonni Ali and the Mossi was reported in the bend of the Niger.
ca. 1480	J. D. Fage says the Mossi states of Mamprusi and Dagomba formed in modern Ghana. The Yatenga Mossi attacked Walata (modern Mali).
1483	Sonni Ali of Songhai defeated the Mossi under Yatenga Naba Nasséré in the battle of Kobi near Lake Débo in modern Mali. In 1488 Sonni Ali campaigned in the Niger bend against Mossi forces. There were reports in Portugal that the king of the Mossi might be the long-sought Prester John. In November 1492 Sonni Ali died and was replaced as Songhai king by Askia Muhammad.
ca. 1495	Historian Michel Izard suggests this date for the creation of Oubri's kingdom of Ouagadougou, while J. D. Fage selected 1515. The area between the White and Red Voltas was ruled by the Nakomsé by this time.
1497–98	Mohammed Touré of Songhai (1493–1528) raided into Yatenga and captured many slaves. Many Songhai raids occurred over the next decade.
16th cent.	The migration of the Yarsé began. Large groups of Mande from the west began to settle the valley of the Black Volta.
1533	From Benin the Portuguese tried to make contact with the Mossi. In 1537 Askia Ismaail of Songhai (1537–1539) raided Gourma for slaves. In 1549 Askia Daoud raided into the area of modern Burkina; frequent Songhai raids continued until 1591.
ca. 1540	Michel Izard suggests that the kingdom of Yatenga was started by Yadega.
1591	12 Mar. Battle of Tondibi, 56 kms from Gao, was a decisive defeat for Askia Ishak II's (1582–1591) Songhai army by Moroccan forces. Ishak retreated into Gourma and was killed.
ca. 1596	Delafosse says that the Samo, Samogho and Sia moved into the Black Volta valley.
ca. 1680	The Turka moved into the area west of the Komoé. Around 1690 the Koulango began settling along the Black Volta north of Bouna. 1690 marked the beginning of Ibrahima Saidou's reign in Liptako until 1714. Around

	1700 the Komono moved into the border area of now Burkina Faso and Côte d'Ivoire.
1714	Famagan (Famara) Ouattara founded the Gouiriko (Gwiriko) empire about Bobo Dioulasso. In 1715 the Bobo began to settle along the Bougouriba.
1754	Naba Kango of Yatenga was forced into exile soon after his reign began by the usurper, Wobgho I. In 1757 Naba Kango returned with a Bambara army and regained power in Yatenga; the first known firearms and gunsmiths came to Yatenga.
ca. 1770	The Dyan and Lobi began to settle along the west bank of the Black Volta. Delafosse gives a much earlier date of 1350. In 1790 the Wilé crossed the Black Volta into area near Diébougou. In 1800 the Birifor moved into their present area along the Black Volta. (Delafosse gives 1690).
1809	Abdullah, brother of Usuman dan Fodio of Sokoto, raided Gourma. Liptako became an emirate of the Sokoto Caliphate in 1810.
1815	The Ouattara of Kong raided deep into Lobi country north of Gaoua; attacks continued into the 1890s. In 1820 the Dagari (Dagaba) crossed the Black Volta and settled along the Bougouriba according to Labouret. Delafosse's date is 1700.
1825–34	Civil War in Yatenga. Four sons of Naba Sagha competed for the throne and ruled briefly during these years. During 1832–39 the Zogoré famine in now northern Burkina Faso depopulated wide areas.
ca. 1826	Djilgodji became a part of the Fulani Macina empire of Shaikh Amadu. In 1835 the Bobo Dioula rebelled against the Ouattara.
1848–51	Rissiam lost territory to Yatenga. In 1850 Kong forces raided across Dagari, Dyan and Gan lands in southwest Burkina. Mamadou Karantao founded Ouahabou (Wahabou).
1853	2 July. Heinrich Barth entered modern Burkina Faso on his trip from Say to Timbuktu. He was in Dori 12–20 July, and Aribinda 25–26 July.
1856	About this time the Zerma (Zaberma) under Alfa Hano entered the Gourounsi area.
1871	Moro Naba Koutou died. After a dispute of several months, Koutou's son Al-hassan became Naba Sanem and son Boukary was exiled from Ouagadougou.
1880	Ouahabou attacked the Wilé and the Dyan.
1883	The Zerma occupied Sati for their headquarters. Zerma

leader Alfa Gazari was wounded at Gouro Hill, near Sourgou, by the Kipirsi, and later died. In 1885 a Bobo, Ko and Kipirsi coalition defeated the Zerma under Babatu at Safané.

1885   Baogho became the thirty-eighth Yatenga Naba. This started civil war in Yatenga between Baogho, head of the house of Yemde, and the house of Tougouri.

1886   24 Sep. Gottlob Adolf Krause became the first recorded European to reach Ouagadougou.

1888   Tiéba of Kénédougou (Sikasso) attacked the Samogho village of Diomo and several Turka villages.

5 Feb. On his way from Niéllé to Kong, Louis Gustave Binger crossed the Léraba into modern Burkina Faso. He crossed the Komoé 16 March, and arrived at Bobo Dioulasso on 19 April, which he describes as five villages. On 8 June he crossed the Red Volta west of Dakaye, then visited with Boukary Koutou at Banema for a week. On 15 June, Binger arrived in Ouagadougou where he remained until 10 July. He returned via Boukary Koutou's camp and Gourounsi country en route to Salaga.

19 Apr. Kurt von François crossed Busansi (Bissa) country and reached Zourma, on the Mossi frontier.

1889   Moro Naba Sanem died. Boukary Koutou's troops surrounded Samambili village and forced the electoral college to select him as Naba Wobgho.

1890   10–16 Aug. Dr. François Crozat was in Bobo Dioulasso, then Lanfiéra, and reached Ouagadougou 17 September. On 18 August the Territory of French Soudan was established.

1891   Tiéba conducted a campaign against Turka villages.

9–14 Mar. Parfait Louis Monteil crossed Burkina Faso via Bobo Dioulasso, Lanfiéra, Ouagadougou. He was ordered to leave the country by Moro Naba Wobgho. In Dori on 23 May he signed a treaty with the Liptako ruler. He reached Say on 19 August.

1892   Tiéba campaigned in southwest Burkina Faso. He destroyed Péni and attacked Noumoudara in December.

Apr. Al-Kari's jihad in Samo country began. It lasted more than two years until the French ended it.

1893   A Zerma campaign against the Samo failed. Gourounsi troops revolted against the Zerma east of Koudougou. Hamaria became the resistance leader.

26 Jan. Tyèba (Tiéba) was poisoned during the battle of Bama, northwest of Bobo Dioulasso. His brother,

Babèmba, became the Sikasso ruler and continued attacks to the south and west of Bobo Dioulasso.

1894   May. French forces were defeated by Al-Kari's Marka forces near Boussé, but then defeated and destroyed the Marka army in the battle of Boussé. During much of 1894 there was fighting between Babatu and Hamaria in the area about Léo.

June. After Yatenga Naba Baogho was wounded at Thiou and died at Sim, Bagaré became Naba Boulli.

1 July. George Ekem Ferguson, a Fante in the Gold Coast service, arrived in Ouagadougou. The next day he signed a treaty of protection with Moro Naba Wobgho. Some authorities say December.

1895   Jan. Henri Alexis Decoeur for France and Quernheimb von Carnap for Germany competed in collecting treaties with the Gourma. Bantchandé accepted French protection for Gourma.

9 Feb. Emile Chautemps, French Minister of Colonies, ordered protectorates established over the Mossi, Lobi and Gourounsi. Soudan Lieutenant Governor Louis Albert Grodet ordered Commandant Georges Mathieu Destenave to collect treaties in the Voltaic lands. In May Destenave signed a treaty of protection with Yatenga Naba Boulli (Bagaré).

16 June. French West Africa was created: Senegal, Guinea, Soudan and Ivory Coast at first.

10 July. Destenave was attacked near Yako. He was in Djilgodji, and Liptako in October.

Nov. Yatenga Naba Boulli (Bagaré) was forced from Ouahigouya by Sidiyete's forces. From Bango he called for French help to regain his capital.

1896   Babèmba, Faama of Sikasso, attacked the Turka and Karaboro in the area west of the Falaise de Banfora.

24 May. Lieutenants Paul Voulet and Jean-Marie Chanoine at Macina were ordered to take Sati and Ouagadougou before the English could. On 30 July they left Bandiagara to conquer Mossiland.

July. The Aulliminden Tuaregs ravaged the Oudala.

8 Aug. Samory's son, Sarantyé Mory, tried to arbitrate between Babatu and Hamaria.

10 Aug. In the battle of Sim, Voulet and Yatenga Naba Boulli (Bagaré) defeated Sidiyété Ouedraogo. Voulet had Boulli installed as ruler of Yatenga.

27 Aug. Voulet occupied Yako, then Ouagadougou.

Moro Naba Wobgho and most of the inhabitants fled. On 7 September the French repulsed a counter-attack that Wobgho organized from Posomtenga.

26 Sep. Hamaria for the Gourounsi and Voulet for the French signed a treaty in which the French recognized Hamaria as "King of the Gourounsi"

19 Oct. Mané was captured by Voulet. In November Voulet arrived at Ouahigouya, then attacked the Samo village of Ouilé. He raised Ouidi Sidibé's siege of Sourou. He had Karamoko Ba executed for conspiracy. Meanwhile, forces under Sidiyété had again captured Ouahigouya from the French ally, Naba Boulli. In December Voulet campaigned in Yatenga against Sissamba guerillas under Sidiyété, and recaptured Ouahigouya. After his December return to Ouagadougou, the French and Wobgho fought at Kombissiri. The Mossi were defeated and Wobgho retreated into Busansi country.

1897   15 Jan. In negotiations, Wobgho's brother, Mazi, was offered the Mossi throne by Voulet. Prince Mazi was then found dead after rumors circulated that he would accept the throne from the French.

17 Jan. Destenave arrived at Louta to begin a campaign against rebellious Samos.

21 Jan. Voulet proclaimed the deposition of Moro Naba Wobgho. Mamadou II, youngest brother of Wobgho, was elected successor. As Naba Sigiri, he accepted a French protectorate.

1 Feb. Captains Joseph Baud and L. Vermeersch were in Fada N'Gourma to establish French control and put down a revolt against Fada Chief Bantchandé.

7 Feb. Voulet and Chanoine reached Tenkodogo where they were confronted with an English force under Captain Donald Stewart. Voulet and Stewart agreed to allow their home governments to settle claims to Busansi country.

10 Feb. The Samo resistance to the French was partially broken with the fall of Yaba.

17 Feb. Voulet's and Baud's forces successfully supported Bantchandé against the pro-German Yacom-Bato at Bilanga. Voulet left for Paris.

5 Mar. Chanoine joined the Gourounsi under Hamaria. They attacked the Zerma under Babatu, and administered a bloody defeat. The Zerma army retreated toward Léo, and the French inflicted another defeat on them.

29 Mar. A British force under Francis B. Henderson, in Lobi country, was attacked by Sarantyé Mory at Dokita. The British retreated.

30 Mar. The French began a fort at Ouahigouya to protect Boulli.

17 Apr. Baud (French) and Thierry (German) signed a commitment at Pama to allow their home governments to settle boundaries in the area. On 20 April Scal and Stewart signed a temporary boundary agreement at Yariba (modern Ghana).

22 Apr. Captain Cazemajou signed a treaty with Karamokho Moktar Karantao to grant French protection. The Bwa (Bobo) and French under Caudrelier and Hugot fought at Mansara.

23 Apr. Destenave reached Aribinda, where the ruler, Ahmet-Tafa, asked for French protection.

May. The French campaigned between Koupéla and Tenkodogo against Wobgho's supporters. In May Samory Touré's campaign into Burkina Faso began.

4 May. Captain G. M. Cazemajou signed a treaty with Diébougou and began a French base. Destenave arrived at Yagha, and sent Capt. Betbeder to Say.

11 May. Vermeersch reached Konbobiri in Gourma, and on 26 June Henri-Etienne Bretonnet (1864–1899) reached Kadjar in Gourma.

13 May. Commandant Caudrelier established a French post at Boromo. In June he destroyed Ouarkoye.

6 June. In the battle of Diagourou the French defeated a group of Tuaregs who had been raiding northeast of Dori. Captain Minvielle was killed. On 9 July Destenave left Aribinda for Bandiagara.

17 June. Wobgho and a few followers were defeated south of Tenkodogo by a French patrol under Lt. Abbat. Wobgho escaped into the British zone. On 23 June French forces under Captain Hugot defeated Babatu at Doucé (Dousse) in modern Ghana.

23 July. Germany and France signed an agreement in Paris which determined the northern border of Togo. Germany gave up its claims to Gourma.

July. In latter July Samory gathered the three wings of his army at Darsalami, near Bobo Dioulasso. Samory's army laid siege to Noumoudara, chief village of the Tiéfo; one of Samory's sons, Sekou Touré, was killed.

Aug. Cazemajou recruited porters in Yatenga and several of the porters died. This touched off a new revolt against Yatenga Naba Boulli's rule.

8 Aug. French forces under Captain E. Bouland occupied Lakosso village west of Gaoua. On 11 September Commandant Caudrelier signed a treaty with Baratou Ouattara to place all of Lobi under French protection. On 25 September French forces under Caudrelier occupied Bobo Dioulasso.

Oct. French forces under Commandant Destenave and Lieutenant Naudet campaigned in Yatenga against Sidiyété Ouedraogo's Sissamba rebels, to restore the authority of Boulli (Bagaré). On 15 December many of Sidiyété Ouedraogo's chief officers surrendered to the French at Guibou and paid homage to Boulli (Bagaré). The Chief of Ouro, the Sagha claimant to the Yatenga throne, submitted to Destenave at Tougouya; later the French recognized him as heir to Naba Boulli.

1898   18 Jan. The French defeated resistance at Bagassi, west of Boromo, near the modern railroad.

23 Jan. Shortly after Wobgho, under British protection at Namori in Mamprusi, renewed the Ferguson treaty with the British, French forces began to occupy the Busansi (Bissa) lands south of Tenkodogo to prevent British occupation there.

2–9 Feb. At Gourcy, Boulli (Bagaré) was installed again as Yatenga Naba under French protection.

5 Mar. Destenave met with Molex, Resident of Gourma, in the Yamga region to discuss Dahomey-Mossiland borders. By June, the French controlled the Volta basin north of eleven degrees.

May–June. French occupied the area around Banfora.

14 June. The French and British finally agreed to a boundary which gave Mossi and Lobi lands to the French and split the Gourounsi lands roughly at the eleventh degree of north latitude.

21 June. British Lt. Colonel Henry Northcott and Naba Wobgho, not knowing that Europe had agreed the Mossi rule question, began a march north to restore Wobgho to power. On 30 June they reached Kombissiri, a day's march from Ouagadougou. There French forces claimed that Britain had recognized French rule over Mossiland. As Northcott and Wobgho retreated, they received official

news of the Franco-British border agreement. This ended Wobgho's hopes for a restoration of power.

13 Aug. Troops under Sergeant Pinault left Ouahigouya for a new campaign in Samo country.

29 Sep. Samory Touré was captured in the Ivory Coast and exiled to Gabon, where he died in 1900.

1 Nov. Captain Chanoine awarded medals to several people in Ouahigouya who had aided the French, and then the same in Ouagadougou. He recruited porters for an expedition to Chad. From Koupéla he crossed Gourma to Say, and joined Voulet in Niger on 2 January 1899. They never reached Chad.

1899   13 Jan. Lieutenant Bouticq assumed command of the campaign to crush Samo resistance.

20 Jan. The Chief of Ouro died. He was Sagha pretender to the Yatenga throne, whom the French recognized as Boulli's heir. A week later Yatenga Naba Boulli died. On 4 February Koudougou, a younger brother of Naba Boulli and a member of the Tougouri faction, was selected as Naba Ligidi.

Feb.–Apr. Resistance developed in Yatenga against the new Yatenga Naba. On 22 April Captain Bouticq began a campaign against the rebels. On 19 May Bouticq returned to Ouahigouya after having routed rebel forces in the Boussouma hills.

17 Oct. Bobo Dioulasso became a military post with a commanding officer responsible to the Governor General of French West Africa. French Soudan became Upper Senegal and Middle Niger.

1900   22 Jan. The White Fathers established a mission at Koupéla. On 25 June they, under Guillaume Templier, established a mission at Ouagadougou.

20 Feb. Forces under Captain Bouvet from Ouahigouya continued the campaign against Samo resistance.

13 Apr. The French Parliament passed a requirement that civil government expenses in French protected areas must be borne by the local people.

1901   Feb. The French government ordered an end to domestic slavery in West Africa. The system was tolerated by officials for some time after this.

1902   Unusual Lobi ruins were discovered in the Gaoua area by Lieutenant Schwartz and Maurice Delafosse.

Jan. Sidiyété Ouedraogo, leader of the Yatenga Sissamba

forces, was captured in Kipirsi country. On 12 February Yatenga Naba Ligidi died after a reign of only three years. He was succeeded by a nephew, Kobgha, grandson of Naba Tougouri.

1 Oct. Upper Senegal and Middle Niger became the Territories of Senegambia-Niger, capital at Kayes.

1903   Native rulers in French West Africa were authorized to collect taxes, on commission. In November a new system of native justice was established for French West Africa.

15 Sep. Captain Noiré opened a school at Ouahigouya. On 12 November Sidiyété Ouedraogo and other Yatenga exiles were pardoned.

11 Nov. Father Thévenoud began his mission to the Mossi.

1904   18 Oct. Senegambia-Niger was abolished and replaced by Haut-Senegal and Niger with administration at Bamako. The Government General of French West Africa was established at Dakar.

19 Oct. James O'Kinealy, for the British, and Ferdinand Verlaque, for France, exchanged maps at Léo. They showed their frontier posts on the border of Haut-Senegal and Niger and the Gold Coast along the 11th parallel north latitude from German Togoland to the Black Volta.

26 Dec. Ouagadougou's military commander announced plans for a secular public school.

1905   16 Feb. Moro Naba Siguiri died. On 27 February sixteen-year-old Saidou Congo, son of Naba Siguiri, became Moro Naba Kom II.

25 Mar. The White Fathers dedicated the church which they had built at Ouagadougou. On 6 May Ouagadougou commander Capt. G. E. Lambert tried to close the White Fathers' mission school.

June. Village, district and cercle courts were established in Haut-Senegal and Niger. Chiefs were granted police and judicial power subject to appeal to cercle courts.

1906   A rebellion against French taxes took place in the Turka area. The French administration ordered the White Fathers to curtail their educational work in Burkina Faso. In July the French set up a system of property registration for West Africa.

1907   The French undertook extensive reorganization of districts and principalities in the Upper Volta area. East of the White Volta the territory was divided into the cercles of

Kaya, Dori, Fada N'Gourma and Tenkodogo. Between the Black and White Voltas were the cercles of Ouagadougou, Koudougou and Ouahigouya. West of the Black Volta cercles were formed around Bobo Dioulasso, Dédougou, Gaoua and Batié.

12 July. A native medical service was organized in the Upper Volta area by the French.

1908   A period of severe famine occurred.

During 1908–10 widespread resistance to French rule began in the Kipirsi area west of Ouagadougou and was most evident in the Muslim areas. The French removed many uncooperative chiefs.

1910   24 Aug. A postal, telegraph and telephone service was organized for Haut-Senegal-Niger.

1911   1 Jan. Niger military territory was detached from Haut-Senegal. The military districts of Bobo Dioulasso and Timbuktu were abolished.

1912   17 Feb. The French began to register all men in French West Africa aged 20 to 28 for possible military or labor service in "la force noire". In October enlistment quotas for the "Armée Noire" were established.

16 Aug. A reorganization of village justice system took most criminal jurisdiction from chiefs.

28 Sep. France and Germany released a declaration on boundary between Togo and French territories.

10 Nov. The Mossi areas were combined in a single Cercle du Mossi, which lasted until 1921.

3 Dec. The first White Sisters arrived in Ouagadougou. They established a carpet-making workshop where many young girls were trained.

1913   Mar. Lieutenant Governor Marie-François-Joseph Clozel of Haut-Senegal-Niger visited Ouagadougou by the first automobile to enter that town.

1914   A famine due to drought began, with deaths of at least a fifth of the population in present-day Burkina.

May. A call for a *jihad* against the French circulated among the Muslims in the bend of the Black Volta. It was rumored that a *Mahdi* was coming to liberate the blacks from white rule.

2 Aug. Mobilization orders reached Ouagadougou a day before Germany declared war on France. Troops from Fada took Sansanné-Mango, German Togo, after a forced march of 200 kms. Togoland Germans surrendered to the French and British on 22 August.

2 Sep. Yatenga Naba Kobgha died. His successor was Naba Tougouri (Tiguiri).

1915   27 Feb.–1 Mar. The Almamy of Safané, Chief of Ouahabou, and other Muslims in the Black Volta bend received long prison terms for the *jihad* plot.

27 Apr. Hamaria was arrested and sent to prison.

17 Nov. Bouna village council announced that it would resist military recruitment and the people forced a team of recruiters under Administrator Maguet to withdraw. The revolt quickly spread through the Black Volta bend.

27 Nov. In the battle of Bondoukuy, Maubert, Resident of Bobo Dioulasso, and Sibiri Coulibaly, French-supported Chief of Bondoukuy, were besieged by Bwa and Marka insurgents for more than a week before they escaped. The insurgents took the town.

29 Nov. Administrator Jules Brévié arrived in Dédougou to investigate the insurrection.

5–19 Dec. Nounou, a Marka village loyal to the French, was attacked by insurgents. It was finally relieved by forces under Captain Henri Labouret. On the 23rd the Marka repulsed the French in the battle of Yankasso; Jules Brévié was present.

1916   13 Feb. The French from Dédougou began to crush the revolt of the Marka and Bwa in the Black Volta bend.

13 Mar. Tuareg insurgents near Dori attacked a French squadron under Capt. Fourcade. In June Tuareg resistance collapsed after Yamboli defeat.

12 May. French troops under Captain Cadence occupied Koudougou as unrest spread into the Gourounsi and Kipirsi areas. On 12 June Molard's forces captured Houndé. Peace had returned to most of Burkina Faso by the end of July.

1917   18 Mar. A monthly 120 francs was allotted to families of Africans killed or who died of illness in French service. As of 7 December a new native legal code was promulgated for French West Africa.

1918   11 Jan. Military service registration was required of all males aged 18 to 35 in West Africa. Many fled to Gold Coast to escape military recruitment.

11 Nov. World War I ended in Europe.

1919   1 Mar. A presidential decree provided for the colony of Upper Volta to be separated from Haut-Senegal-Niger. Gaoua, Bobo Dioulasso, Dédougou, Ouahigouya, Ouagadougou, Dori, Fada N'Gourma and Say would be administrative centers for the new colony, with Ouagadougou the capital. On 16 May Frédéric Charles Édouard Alexandre Hesling was appointed Lieutenant Governor of Upper Volta, then Councils of Native Notables were created to advise cercle commandants.

28 June. The Treaty of Versailles divided Togoland between France and England.

21 Oct. A draft of three years for all physically fit males in French West Africa was instituted at the end of July. Upper Volta was assigned a quota of 5600 recruits for the 1920 draft, larger than for any of the other parts of French West Africa.

24 Oct. A presidential amnesty was announced for all acts committed before 19 October 1919.

25 Oct. A head tax of from 1 to 3 francs was imposed on all natives of Upper Volta.

9 Nov. A September decree established the administration of Upper Volta under a Lieutenant Governor, Secretary General and a Council. Lieutenant Governor Édouard Hesling came to Ouagadougou and began an intense year-long building program using *banco* (mud bricks).

1920   1 Jan. The bureaus and services of government at Ouagadougou were activated. *L'Hotel du Gouvernement* was opened on 29 February, one of many which had been started only in mid-November.

14 Mar. French citizens in Upper Volta voted for a delegate to the *Conseil Supérieur des Colonies.*

31 Mar. Hesling instructed commandants to see that the human rights of native women be protected and that ancestral traditions be modified in a progressive evolutionary way.

19 Apr. A postal system was established; to deliver to each cercle headquarters twice monthly.

22 May. The first colony administrative council meeting was held. A budget of 5,102,225 francs was approved.

July. A Primary and Professional School was established to prepare candidates for the Ecole William Ponty, and a school for bridge builders was established, both in Ouagadougou.

20 Oct. The Cercle of Ouahigouya was separated from the Cercle of Mossi.

4 Dec. Haut-Senegal-Niger became French Soudan.

1921	Hesling reorganized the judicial system, giving chiefs jurisdiction in some minor cases. In June Tenkodogo was again made a cercle headquarters.
1922	1 May. Father Joanny Thévenoud became Bishop of Ouagadougou. On 26 June Hesling issued a decree creating a girls' school at Ouagadougou.
1923	1 Mar. The Cercle of Mossi became Cercle of Ouagadougou. On 26 May a head tax was placed on all Europeans and *assimilés* in Upper Volta. *L'Association d'Anciens Combatants* (Association of Retired War Veterans) of Upper Volta was established on 1 July.
1924	27 Jan. A meteorite landed in Upper Volta.
	1 Feb. The Saria agricultural station was created in Koudougou Cercle. Sale of alcohol to natives was banned 20 February, and on 22 March the native legal system for French West Africa reorganized.
	25 Apr. All animals from French Soudan or Niger were to be inspected upon entry into Upper Volta. In early May a formal education system was begun.
	26 Aug. The native head tax was raised, with the tax on Fulani, Hausa and Yarcés up to 11 francs; all mining activities were taxed as of 22 October.
1925	31 Mar. A three-year vocational school was established in Ouagadougou to train fitters, cabinet makers, blacksmiths and carpenters. An automobile licensing system was instituted 26 May.
	22 Oct. All official government travel to be via Côte d'Ivoire, to connect with the railroad from the coast which had reached Niangbo.
1926	The American Assemblies of God opened missions at Ouagadougou, Kaya and Yako.
	11 Mar. Lt. Governor Hesling appointed Moro Naba Kom an officer in the Legion of Honor. In April a tax of 1.50 francs per kilogram was placed on the sale of kola nuts. At the end of October all males not drafted into military service were made liable for service on public works projects. In late December the Cercle of Say, except the canton of Botou and territory around Téra and Yatacala, was transferred to Niger, effective 1 January 1927.
1927	1 Jan. Bobo Dioulasso and Ouagadougou became Mixed *Communes* of the First Degree, entitled to administration by a mayor, six French and six native notables and a

municipal commission. Lt. Governor Hesling's administration ended 7 August.

1928   A five-year plague of locusts began. Destruction of crops
caused widespread famine. The world economic depression began to be felt. On 13 January Alberic Auguste
Fournier became the Lieutenant Governor of Upper Volta.

1930   8 Dec. Congregation of the Black Sisters of the Immacu-
late Conception was founded for Mossi women.

1931   The Baloum Naba visited the Colonial Exposition at Vincennes and returned to Ouagadougou as an enthusiastic
advocate of Western culture.

1932   11 Apr. The Moro Naba wrote Blaise Diagne protesting
the possibility that the colony of Upper Volta might be
abolished and Mossiland annexed to the Ivory Coast.
However, following a 3 September decree, the colony of
Upper Volta was abolished on 31 December. The Cercle
of Ouahigouya, part of Dori, and part of Dédougou were
annexed to French Soudan. The rest of Dori and the Cercle of Fada were added to Niger. Most of Upper Volta became the Upper Ivory Coast.

1933   12 Mar. Lt. Governor Dieudonné François Joseph Marie
Reste officially arrived in Ouagadougou.

1934   1 Jan. Railroad service from Abidjan opened to Bobo
Dioulasso.
The Bobo Nana Vo movement in western Upper Volta
protested government requisitions of food and animals. A
16 August meeting of chiefs under the leadership of Dim
Delobson denounced Christian missionaries for subvert-
ing traditional culture.

1936   19 Jan. Cathedral of Ouagadougou was dedicated.

1938   1 Jan. Upper Ivory Coast became a single administrative
unit under a Resident-Superior stationed at Ouagadougou:
Edmond Jean Louveau.

1939   Thousands died in an epidemic of meningitis.
3 Sep. World War II began in Europe. Two days later two
sons of the Moro Naba volunteered to serve in the French
forces against Germany.

1940   18 June. With the collapse of allied forces in northern
France, de Gaulle's radio appeal was carried in Upper
Volta for the battle to continue beyond France. French
West Africa Governor General Léon Cayla said he would
abide by the armistice and support the French Vichy gov-
ernment.

22 June. Edmond Jean Louveau, Upper Ivory Coast chief administrator, telegraphed his support for General de Gaulle, and encouraged his officials to follow suit. Numbers of French soldiers left Bobo Dioulasso to join de Gaulle's resistance movement; some people crossed into Gold Coast. The early July British fleet attack on French ships at Oran, Algeria, turned many French officials against the British cause. British ships and aircraft also bombarded Dakar harbor.

22 July. Edmond Louveau and the High Commissioner for French West Africa, Pierre François Boisson, met at Bobo Dioulasso to discuss obligations to Vichy or de Gaulle. Louveau was ordered to Dakar, imprisoned in Bamako and Algiers, then taken to France on 24 December to be tried for treason.

23–25 Sep. British and de Gaulle's Free French forces failed to take Dakar. On 27 October de Gaulle set up Free French government in London.

1941   Aug. Six Europeans were killed by Hamallists at Bobo Dioulasso.

16 Sep. The Moro Naba petitioned the Lieutenant Governor of the Ivory Coast and High Commissioner at Dakar for the re-creation of Upper Volta as a separate colony. The petition was rejected.

11 Oct. Louveau was sentenced to life at hard labor. He escaped from prison in December, 1943, and joined de Gaulle's forces in Algiers.

1942   12 Mar. Moro Naba Kom II died at Ouagadougou. On 23 March Moro Naba Sagha II began his reign and pledged full allegiance to the Vichy government.

2 May. The ordination of the first three Voltaics as Catholic priests took place at Koumi Seminary.

June. High Commissioner Pierre François Boisson toured Upper Volta. In November he announced French West Africa's allegiance to the provisional French government at Algiers. In November the Allied invasion of North Africa began.

1944   30 Jan. Brazzaville Conference on the future of French Africa convened. The 6 June invasion of Normandy marked the start of France's liberation.

1945   The Mossi organized the *Union pour la Défense des Intérêts de la Haute Volta* (later the *Union Voltaïque*) to press to re-create Upper Volta.

8 May. World War II ended in Europe. On 21 October

delegates were elected to the Paris Constituent Assembly to establish the Fourth French Republic. The Baloum Naba ran from the Mossi area of Ivory Coast. He was defeated, 12,900 votes to 13,750 for Houphouët-Boigny.

1946   Jan. The French colonies became *La France d'Outre-Mer* (Overseas France).

20 Feb. Arbitrary house arrest, collective fines and non-judicial sanctions were ended in Overseas France and freedom of assembly established on 13 March. On 11 April the *Loi Houphouët-Boigny* ended forced labor in French West Africa.

30 Apr. Native customary law was abolished in French West Africa. On 7 May the status of "subject" was abolished and all people in Overseas France became citizens (not necessarily voters). In June election to second Constituent Assembly, Houphouët-Boigny ran unopposed.

1 Sep. The *Mouvement Progressiste de la Volta* (MPV) was founded at Bobo Dioulasso, by Sanou Sonny and Traoré Bakary. Following the July petition by Moro Naba Sagha and his court to re-create Upper Volta, the Minister of Overseas France replied sympathetically on 3 September.

27 Sep. Freedom of the press was established in Overseas France. On 5 October wage-earners, veterans and property-owners were given the vote in Overseas France. On 13 October the French Constitution of 1946 was adopted by a narrow referendum margin. It created a Council of the Republic and Assembly of the French Union.

18–21 Oct. A Bamako Conference organized a West African political party called the *Rassemblement Démocratique Africain* (RDA).

2 Nov. An election was held for members of the French National Assembly of the Fourth Republic. The Ivory Coast was authorized three deputies. Ouëzzin Coulibaly, Bobo, Philippe Zinda Kaboré, Mossi, and Félix Houphouët-Boigny were elected.

15 Dec. Following the establishment of Territorial Assemblies for the colonies of Overseas France on 25 October, the first elections for West Africa (1946–1952) were held.

1947   24 May. Philippe Zinda Kaboré died suddenly at Abidjan a short time after making a violent speech in Ouagadougou denouncing the Moro Naba.

4 Sep. The French National Assembly reconstituted Upper

Volta as a separate territory, and Administrator Gaston Mourgues was assigned to reorganize Upper Volta with its 1932 territories.

1948   29 Apr. Albert Jean Mouragues became Governor.

21 June. In elections for Upper Volta's first Territorial Assembly and delegates to the French National Assembly it was charged that the French Socialists through Governor Mouragues favored the *Union Voltaïque* (UV) over RDA. Henri Guissou, Mamadou Ouédraogo and Nazi Boni were elected to go to Paris. In September Upper Volta delegates led in the formation of the *groupe des Indépendants d'Outre-Mer* (IOM), an anti-Communist group of African deputies in the French National Assembly.

1949   Jan. Elections selected Upper Volta's first General Council. The *Union Voltaïque,* the Mossi party, won most of the seats.

16 Sep. Bishop Thévenoud of Ouagadougou died.

21 Dec. Thomas Sankara was born in Yako.

1950   The French National Assembly passed a law to provide equality in recruitment, pay and promotion to Europeans and Africans in Overseas France.

1951   In May a new law greatly broadened the franchise in Overseas France. In June Henri Guissou, Joseph Conombo, Nazi Boni and Mamadou Ouédraogo, all IOM members, were elected to French National Assembly.

1952   The Union of the Traditional Chiefs of Upper Volta was organized under leadership of the Moro Naba.

The March elections for the Territorial Assembly (1952 to 1957) were a defeat for the RDA by the *Union Voltaïque* with the *Rassemblement du Peuple Français* (RPF), party of the Yatenga Naba and Michel Dorange, becoming the chief opposition to the Moro Naba's UV. In April Johannes Roland Pré became Governor of Upper Volta, and in December the French National Assembly passed a Labor Code for Overseas France prescribing equal pay, a 40-hour week, paid holidays, trade union rights.

1953   The Grand Mosque was built in Ouagadougou; much building occurred in the larger towns. In February an IOM conference convened at Bobo Dioulasso. Nazi Boni and Dr. Joseph Conombo were the leading Voltaic figures. Léopold Senghor of Senegal attended. Later in February, Salvador Jean Etcheber became Governor of Upper Volta.

1954   The May fall of Dien Bien Phu in Vietnam marked the

beginning of the end of the French empire. The full-scale Algerian revolution began in October.
In June Dr. Joseph Conombo became Secretary of State for the Interior in the Mendès-France government in Paris. In December Robert Buron, Overseas France minister, and Conombo took part in opening the Ouagadougou-Abidjan railroad line.

1955   18 Nov. After becoming a *commune de moyen exercice* in 1953, Ouagadougou became a full commune, entitled to elect a municipal government.

1956   2 Jan. In elections for the National Assembly in Paris, Nazi Boni, now head of the non-Mossi western party *Mouvement Populaire d'Evolution Africaine* (MPEA), Henri Guissou and Dr. Joseph Conombo, leaders of a new group called the *Parti Social d'Education des Masses Africaines* (PSEMA), and Gérard Kango Ouédraogo, a Yatenga Mossi who supported the Gaullists, were elected.
29 Feb. Bishop of Koupéla Abbé Yougbaré became the first African Catholic bishop in French Africa.
In June the *Loi Cadre* introduced universal suffrage and a single electoral roll for Overseas France. The Federation of West Africa was liquidated and Upper Volta became a territory. The CATC, *Confédération Africaine de Travailleurs Croyants,* organized in Ouagadougou. And in November the first municipal elections were held in Bobo Dioulasso and Ouagadougou. The *Parti Démocratique Unifié* (PDU), a union of PSEMA and RDA, won by large margins in both. Joseph Ouédraogo was elected mayor of Ouagadougou.

1957   6 Mar. Ghana became the first colony in West Africa to gain independence from a European power.
In March the French National Assembly agreed to set up Executive Councils selected by territorial assemblies in each overseas territory. In the election, the PDU got 37 seats; the *Mouvement Démocratique Voltaïque* (MDV) of Dorange and Gérard Kango Ouédraogo, 26; the *Mouvement Populaire Africain* of Nazi Boni, 5; and 2 independents.
17 May. Ouëzzin Coulibaly became Vice President of the Council and organized Upper Volta's first African government with Cabinet of 7 PDU members and 5 MDV. One of the Cabinet's first acts was to visit the Moro Naba.
12 Sep. At Bobo Dioulasso Dr. Joseph Conombo announced an end to the union of PSEMA and RDA.

12 Nov. Moro Naba Sagha II died. Moussa Congo, age 27, became Moro Naba Kougri on 28 November.

5 Dec. The *Groupe de Solidarité Voltaïque* (GSV) elected Nazi Boni President of the Territorial Assembly over Moussa Kargougou, the RDA candidate supported by Ouëzzin Coulibaly, 37–31. In mid-December Dr. Joseph Conombo called upon the Coulibaly government to resign after a vote of no confidence. The Territorial Assembly adjourned until a government reorganization could occur.

1958   11 Jan. Maurice Yaméogo and other MDV members changed party membership to give Coulibaly a majority. On the 25th the MDV ministers resigned from Coulibaly's Cabinet. The Assembly approved a new RDA-controlled Cabinet with Maurice Yaméogo elevated to Minister of Interior. In late April Laurent Bandaogo, RDA of Tenkodogo, was selected President of the Territorial Assembly over Nazi Boni, GSV of Dédougou, 38 to 32.

May. An attempt was made on Nazi Boni's life.

1 June. General de Gaulle became French premier. Félix Houphouët-Boigny, RDA leader in West Africa, became a de Gaulle Minister of State. In August de Gaulle met with Upper Volta representatives at Abidjan to discuss a Franco-African Community.

7 Sep. Ouëzzin Coulibaly died in Paris, where he had gone for medical treatment at the end of July.

In late September Upper Volta overwhelmingly approved de Gaulle's Franco-African Community and Constitution of the Fifth French Republic. A day later Guinea became the first territory of French West Africa to gain independence.

The Constitution of the French Community was promulgated in early October, with the right of self-determination guaranteed to each territory. Vice Presidents of Councils of Government in the Territories now became Presidents of the Councils of Ministers. On 20 Oct. Maurice Yaméogo was elected in Upper Volta.

17 Oct. French army prevented Moro Naba Kougri and followers from taking over the government.

26 Oct. RDA conference in Ouagadougou called for new elections, a new Constitution and membership in the Mali Federation. In December Modibo Keita of Soudan sought Voltaic support for the Federation; the Moro Naba called

for a union government of Upper Volta and supported federation.

9 Dec. Maurice Yaméogo organized a government of unity with 7 RDA and 5 *Parti du Regroupement Africain* (PRA) ministers.

11 Dec. Upper Volta became an autonomous republic within the French Community with Maurice Yaméogo as premier and Paul Masson as High Commissioner.

18 Dec. In Paris, Yaméogo told General de Gaulle that Upper Volta favored close cooperation with Ivory Coast over membership in a West African federation. Two days later the Moro Naba announced his opposition to the Mali Federation.

29–30 Dec. Federalists from Senegal, Soudan, Dahomey and Upper Volta met at Bamako, Soudan. Yaméogo did not attend.

1959   14 Jan. A Federal Constituent Assembly met at Dakar and on the 17th the Federation of Mali was proclaimed. Yaméogo, opposed to a federation, headed the Upper Volta delegation. The Upper Volta delegation took an oath to uphold it, but Yaméogo later denied this. On 28 January the Territorial Constituent Assembly ratified the Constitution of the Mali Federation and gave Yaméogo full powers for three months.

3–4 Feb. Maurice Yaméogo attended the first meeting of the Executive Council of the French Community in Paris, and the second in March. Its final meeting was in December.

28 Feb. Republic of Upper Volta constitution was approved by a rump session of Constituent Assembly with most westerners absent. Mali Federation membership was not part of Constitution. On 15 March the "anti-federalist" constitution was approved by referendum. Only the area west of the Black Volta opposed.

24 Mar. Ali Barraud of Bobo Dioulasso and Nazi Boni of Dédougou were present at the inauguration of the Mali Federation in Dakar.

4 Apr. A protocol of economic cooperation and a joint agreement on operation of the Abidjan-Niger railroad were signed with the Ivory Coast.

6 Apr. French West Africa was formally dissolved. In June Upper Volta joined other former members in a Customs Union and agreement to divide property of the colo-

nial administration. On 7 April Niger, Ivory Coast and Upper Volta formed the *Conseil de l'Entente Sahel-Benin* (Council of Entente). Dahomey joined prior to first meeting 29 May.

19 Apr. Assembly elections gave Yaméogo's RDA 64 seats, the PRA 7, and MDV 4. Yaméogo was elected President of the Council of Ministers on 25 April. In late August Yaméogo dismissed Mayor Joseph Ouédraogo and his Ouagadougou municipal council.

5 Oct. Nazi Boni, Laurent Bandaogo and others who opposed Yaméogo and supported the Mali Federation organized the *Parti National Voltaïque* (PNV). On the 7th Yaméogo ordered PNV dissolved; opposition then organized the *Parti Républicain de la Liberté* (PRL). On 3 January 1960 demonstrators pulled down the Upper Volta flag in Dédougou and replaced it with Mali's. Yaméogo outlawed the PRL on the 7th.

26 Oct. Radio Haute Volta began transmission. Television on a limited scale followed in 1963.

11 Dec. The Territorial Legislative Assembly became the National Assembly and Yaméogo became Chief of State and President of the Republic of Upper Volta. *"Fière Volta de mes aieux"* by Abbé Robert Ouédraogo became the national anthem.

1960   Many African countries became independent during 1960: Togo on 27 April; Dahomey on 1 August; Niger on 3 August; Upper Volta on 5 August; and Cote d'Ivoire on 7 August. Upper Volta joined the United Nations on 20 September.

9 Mar. Upper Volta and Côte d'Ivoire signed a convention on labor migration from Upper Volta.

4 June. President Yaméogo and the other Council of Entente leaders demanded independence outside the French Community. Yaméogo became a great hero. In late June Nazi Boni and other opposition leaders wrote to Yaméogo suggesting that all the people be invited to help build the country. Five of the six writers were arrested on 2 July. Nazi Boni escaped to Mali before capture. The five arrested were released in November.

11 July. Maurice Yaméogo and Michel Debré signed an accord to withdraw Upper Volta from the French Community. Yaméogo returned to a tumultuous welcome at Ouagadougou on 15 July. Via radio President Yaméogo denounced French High Commissioner Paul Masson on

21 July. The independence agreement was ratified on 27 July.

23 Sep. Republic of Soudan became Republic of Mali and withdrew from the French Community, ending the dreams of a Mali Federation.

24–26 Oct. Yaméogo attended the Abidjan Conference of French-speaking African countries. At the Francophone Brazzaville Conference in December Yaméogo became identified with the moderate group.

27 Nov. Of those voting, 99.5 percent approved a new Constitution for Upper Volta. On 8 December Yaméogo was elected President by the Voltaic National Assembly. Dr. Joseph Conombo was elected Ouagadougou mayor later in the month.

1961–62 The Schweeger-Hefel excavations in the Mengao region of Kurumba found Nioniosse remains dating to about 1315.

1961 5–6 Jan. The Council of the Entente met; Yaméogo began a term as its president.

24 Apr. France and Upper Volta signed an agreement of cooperation. It was revised in 1986.

8–12 May. Yaméogo attended the Monrovia Conference of African States; he visited Accra for discussions with Nkrumah 21–22 May. On 8 June Ghana and Upper Volta agreed to end customs barriers. Agreement lasted less than three years.

July. Yaméogo visited Israel and signed treaty of aid, cooperation and friendship.

9 Sep. The *Union Africaine et Malgache* (UAM), which had been formed in March, established a Defense Council to be located at Ouagadougou.

1962 In late January Yaméogo attended the Lagos Conference of "Monrovia" States to discuss a permanent organization. Mali President Modibo Keita visited Upper Volta in March; Upper Volta joined the West African Monetary Union in May.

31 July. Yaméogo met President Nkrumah near the Ghana border and they drove together to Tenkodogo for a conference. On return trip two days later an attempt was made on Nkrumah's life in Ghana.

1963 10–14 Mar. The heads of state of UAM met in Ouagadougou. Yaméogo was elected to head that organization for a year. In early May Upper Volta became a member of the International Monetary Fund; the Organization of

African Unity was established in Addis Ababa later that month.

1964   24 Apr. The National Assembly passed a law limiting workers' activities and outlawing strikes.

1965   10–12 Feb. The French-speaking African heads of state met in Mauritania and established the *Organisation Commune Africaine et Malgache*.

3 Oct. Yaméogo was reelected President with 99.98 percent of the vote cast. After divorcing an earlier wife, Yaméogo married 22-year-old former beauty queen Nathalie Félicite Monaco Adama on 17 October. On the 6 November return from their honeymoon, the President and his new wife received a cool reception in Ouagadougou.

1 Nov. Mass abstention from the legislative election polls protested against Yaméogo, as did a boycott of municipal elections on 5 December.

28 Dec. Council of the Entente met and discussed common nationality among the four Entente states.

30 Dec. The government announced an austerity budget with higher taxes and sharp cuts in salaries of government employees. The next day Minister of Interior Denis Yaméogo broke up a meeting of the nation's leading labor chiefs. Labor leaders called for a 3 January general strike.

1966   1 Jan. President Yaméogo declared a state of emergency. On 2 January he placed troops around all public buildings and warned government workers against general strike participation.

3 Jan. A general strike began. Mobs attacked UDV-RDA party headquarters and National Assembly. Army Chief of Staff Lt. Colonel Sangoulé Lamizana assumed power and Maurice Yaméogo resigned.

4 Jan. Colonel Lamizana organized a military government. Labor leaders ended the general strike and announced support for him. Constitution was suspended and National Assembly dissolved. New Cabinet had seven military and five civilians.

28 Jan. Municipal councils in the principal towns were replaced by groups responsible to Lamizana. On 31 January he selected a 41-person consultative committee to replace the National Assembly.

1 Feb. Colonel Lamizana visited with President Houphouët-Boigny in Abidjan. On 17 February Lamizana

announced an austerity budget similar to Yaméogo's budget of 30 December.

21 Sep. All political activities were outlawed. On 12 December the Supreme Council of the Armed Forces announced its intent to rule for four years.

26 Dec. Former President Yaméogo failed in an attempt at suicide.

1967   22 Apr. Lt. Colonel Lamizana promoted to General. On 9 September Lamizana announced arrest of persons said to have plotted government overthrow. On 9 December the government confiscated the property of many former Yaméogo officials.

1968–74   Period of Sahelian drought.

1968   21 Jan. General Joseph Ankrah of Ghana made a state visit to Ouagadougou; Lamizana reciprocated in August. Lamizana attended April West African economic summit at Monrovia. Upper Volta joined the resulting West African Regional Group.

30 Apr. The Syndicate of the Traditional Chiefs, led by Moro Naba Kougri, asked for a restoration of the powers of chiefs. On 5 August the Upper Volta government gave the Moro Naba the rank of Commander of the Voltaic National Order, the first such official recognition of the Mossi ruler.

5 June. Former first lady Félicité Yaméogo was given a suspended sentence for plotting against the government.

1969   5 Apr. Lamizana promised that civilian rule would be restored by November 1970.

28 Apr. Embezzlement trial of former President Yaméogo began. On 8 May he was sentenced to five years hard labor and fine of over one hundred thousand dollars. He was released in August 1970 on the tenth anniversary of independence.

May. Nazi Boni died in an automobile accident while still in exile.

15 Sep. Beginning of a failed strike by civil servants for higher pay. The government took over all Catholic elementary schools on 1 October.

14 Nov. Former National Assembly president Begnon Koné convicted of embezzlement; five years' hard labor. Released with Yaméogo in August 1970.

19 Nov. Aliens without residence permits were required to leave Ghana within two weeks.

1970   29 May. Lamizana announced new Constitution and renewal of political activities. Constitutional referendum
held 14 June. 98.41 percent support (one quarter ab-
stained). The President would be the oldest army officer
with the highest rank; one third of Cabinet to be military.
After four-year transition period President to be elected
for five-year terms by direct universal suffrage. In first
general elections since 1965 in December UDV-RDA
(Yaméogo's old party) won 37 National Assembly seats.
PRA got 12, the MLN 6, and independents 2.

1971   13 Feb. Gérard Kango Ouédraogo, head of UDV, was
elected Premier by the National Assembly, 47–10.

16 May. Entente Council of Heads of State met in Ouagadougou.

3 Oct. President Lamizana, on his first official visit to
France, requested an increase in French assistance for development of the Volta valleys and a higher education
center in Ouagadougou.

1972   Feb. President Lamizana visited Egypt and pledged support to Egypt in its struggle against Israel.

Mar. Third Festival of African Cinema was held in Ouagadougou. It was billed as a rally against colonialism and
cultural alienation.

20–22 Nov. French President Pompidou, in Upper Volta,
announced partial cancellation of debts owed France by
French-speaking African countries.

1973   Jan.–Feb. Crisis created by civil service strike.

There were harsh drought conditions in 1973 in northern
Upper Volta, especially in Gorom-Gorom area north of
Dori. Antoine Dakoure, Minister of Agriculture, was appointed head of a committee to coordinate relief efforts for
all the West African Sahel areas. Many Malian nomads
crossed into Upper Volta in search of water. President
Lamizana visited Paris in June and October to request
more aid for Sahel drought areas. A September Sahel nations heads of state conference in Ouagadougou set up a
committee to combat drought in the Sahel (CILSS),
Lamizana as Chairman. They also requested a ten year de-
lay to settle external debts.

18 Oct. Upper Volta broke diplomatic relations with Israel.

Dec. The National Assembly voted to censure Premier
Gérard Ouédraogo. Joseph Ouédraogo, Ali Barraud and
Joseph Conombo led the opposition.

1974   8 Feb. The army dismissed Premier Ouédraogo, suspended the Constitution, dissolved the National Assembly. Lamizana became premier and minister of justice in a government of national renewal.

21 Feb. U.N. Secretary-General Kurt Waldheim attended a drought control meeting at Ouagadougou.

30 May. Lamizana abolished all political parties and established a one-party system under the *Mouvement pour le Renouveau* (Movement for Renewal). He announced that Upper Volta would be divided into 10 departments, each under a military prefect. In July Lamizana appointed the 65-member CNR (National Consultative Council for Renovation).

24 July. The chairman of the national committee to distribute foreign relief aid, Maj. Johnny Ouédraogo, was arrested for corruption.

31 July. An agreement was signed to exploit Tambao manganese deposits. In September the French offered to help finance construction of a university at Ouagadougou.

4 Sep. Tuareg refugees in the north complained of their treatment by the government in the drought area. A boundary commission met to discuss border disputes in the Upper Volta-Mali Oudalan area, along the Béli river in extreme northern Upper Volta. Voltaic Minister of Interior, Capt. Charles Bambara, touched off a crisis by saying that his government could close the border to herdsmen who watered their cattle in the disputed area.

Dec. An onchocerciasis (river blindness) control program was initiated, including aerial spraying.

4 Dec. Presidents Lamizana and Moussa Traoré met to discuss border disputes in the Béli river area. Agreed to use peaceful means to resolve disputes. On 14 December Malian troops ambushed a Voltaic truck near Djibo. Two days later a Voltaic Sergeant Kossoube was killed in the area. On the 26th four West African heads of state ordered a truce. A mediation commission was established to settle the dispute on 30 December.

1975   7–8 Mar. Lamizana attended Francophone African Conference in Bangui. Upper Volta joined Economic Community of West African States at a May meeting.

3 June. New border clashes between Mali and Upper Volta forces occurred in the Béli River area. On 13 July an agreement was reached in the dispute.

Dec. Upper Volta began its first official census. Published

in 1978, it showed population of 5,638,203. On 8 December Lamizana announced a two-year deadline for all Upper Volta businesses to "Voltaïze" 51 percent of their stock "in vital sectors" to the government. On 17–18 December a general strike to demand wage increases and return to civilian government paralyzed the country.

1976   4 Jan. Upper Volta and Cuba established diplomatic relations. On 28 January the first sugar refinery went into full production at Banfora.

29 Jan. President Lamizana dissolved his government after two months of labor crisis. On 9 February a new Cabinet was announced with an increase in civilian ministers. Zoumana Traore, leader of a major union, joined the Cabinet. Saye Zerbo was removed as Minister of Foreign Affairs.

17 Mar. The general strike ended.

10–11 May. Lamizana attended the Paris summit of French and African leaders.

23 July. Mamadou Sanjo was dismissed as Finance Minister for criticizing the budget. On 25 August a national game park was established at Pô.

5 Oct. A 32-member commission appointed in April proposed a referendum on a new constitution for March and presidential elections in May 1977.

5 Nov. The five protocols to establish ECOWAS were signed at Lomé, Togo.

1977   14 Jan. A "Government of National Unity" took office; old political alliances were represented; only 4 of 20 Cabinet members were military. In March a special commission recommended a 7-year Presidential term and multiparty system.

1 Mar. National teachers' union (SNEAHV) called a 48-hour strike to protest salaries. On 14–16 March the entire government traveled by train to Bobo Dioulasso, stopping at major towns en route.

1 Oct. Official ban of May 1974 on political parties was lifted; seven parties allowed to resume. On 27 November referendum voters approved by 97.75 percent draft Third Republic constitution. It provided for a democratic, secular republic, an elected president and 57 National Assembly delegates, five-year terms, and three political parties.

1978   29 Mar. Ghana and Upper Volta agreement to build two hydro-electric dams on the Black Volta.

30 Mar. Lamizana began his presidential candidacy. Macaire Ouedraogo, Joseph Ouédraogo and Joseph Ki-Zerbo demanded that he run as a civilian. In 30 April National Assembly election: 28 seats to UDV-RDA, 13 to UNDD, 9 to UPV, 6 to PRA and 1 to UNI. Turnout was 40 percent of registered voters.

14 May. Presidential elections. Turnout 35 percent of registered voters. Aboubakar Sangoulé Lamizana of UDV-RDA received 425,000, Macaire Ouedraogo of UNDD 275,000, Joseph Ouédraogo of RDA 165,405 and Joseph Ki-Zerbo of UPV 158,237. Since no one received the required 50 percent, the two highest ran again 28 May. Turnout of 44 percent elected President Lamizana 711,722 over Macaire Ouedraogo 552, 956.

9 June. Gérard Kango Ouédraogo was elected National Assembly Speaker over Joseph Ouédraogo, 29 to 28.

22 June. Sangoulé Lamizana was sworn in as President of Third Republic. Government of National Unity was dissolved on 1 July.

7 July. By 29 to 1 and 27 abstentions Dr. Joseph Issoufou Conombo (UDV-RDA) was elected Premier by National Assembly. His 16 July government included only two military cabinet members.

15 Sep. Upper Volta and Ghana agreed on demarcation of their 380 km. border.

24 Sep. Lamizana began a ten-day visit to France and Germany in search of aid. 1979 foreign aid reached a record US $116 million, 70 percent of the government budget.

1 Nov. Joseph Ki-Zerbo, leader of the UPV, resigned from the National Assembly.

1979   3 Feb. The major labor unions launched a campaign against the Lamizana government. On 24 February, opposition groups demonstrated in Ouagadougou.

21 Mar. Government announced a joint venture with France to encourage cotton production (SOFITEX).

20 Apr. Former President Maurice Yaméogo and President Lamizana met privately in Ouagadougou.

23 May. Two leaders of the Voltaic Organization of Free Unions (OVSL) were arrested for inciting revolt. Week-long protest strikes paralyzed Ouagadougou and forced their release.

26 May. President Lamizana attended the West African

Monetary Union meeting which opened the Central Bank of West African States in Dakar. He met French President Giscard d'Estaing in June.

28 May. The National Assembly recognized the UDA-RDA, UNDD, and UPV as the three legal parties. In November Joseph Ki-Zerbo's UPV became the Voltaic Progressive Front (FPV).

5 July. Lamizana denounced demands by unions and appealed in vain for national unity.

10 Dec. President Lamizana acknowledged Upper Volta's dependence on foreign aid for survival.

1980   1 Jan. Unions began a general strike against the government. Most public services were closed.

8 Feb. The heads of state of Togo, Niger and Upper Volta met in Bobo Dioulasso. Ghanian President Hilla Limann paid an April state visit.

22 Apr. Premier Joseph Conombo appealed to foreign nations to save the people and livestock of northern Upper Volta from starvation. Pope John Paul II visited Ouagadougou on 10 May and called on the world to support the peoples of the Sahel.

1 Oct. A strike of school teachers became a general strike in early November. After surviving a National Assembly no confidence vote by a 33–24 margin, the Lamizana government ordered an end to all marches and demonstrations on 12 November. On 22 November teachers agreed to return to work after Lamizana agreed to their salary demands.

25 Nov. Col. Saye Zerbo led a "colonel's coup" against Lamizana. The Constitution of 1977 was suspended. An attempted counter coup by the riot police on behalf of Lamizana failed. The CMRPN, *Comité Militaire de Redressement pour le Progrès National,* was established (31 members and Col. Zerbo as Chairman). Customary chiefs backed it.

8 Dec. A 16-member Cabinet was established under Saye Zerbo and the CMRPN. He awarded teachers most of their October and November demands.

1981   16 Jan. Foreign Minister Felix Tientarboum announced that the Libyan attempt to transform its embassy into a "people's bureau" was unacceptable.

13 Mar. An all-weather road from Kongoussi to Djibo was opened.

1 May. Col. Zerbo outlined the Military Committee's development priorities and warned that labor unions must accept constraints on their actions and speech. Compulsory military service was announced. The next day trade unions held a mass demonstration against the government and demanded more pay and a freeze on food prices. On 6 June Col. Zerbo suspended a number of union members for their participation in illegal protest strikes. On 18–19 August three of the four Voltaique trade unions met in Bobo-Dioulasso and warned the government against taking away the rights of unions.

Sep. Col. Zerbo appointed Captain Thomas Sankara Secretary of State for Information. On 15–24 September Zerbo visited Togo, Benin, Niger, Mali.

1 Oct. Work began on the railroad line to Kaya which, in time, should continue to Tambao.

1 Nov. Col. Zerbo ordered an end to strikes as "a luxury". The *Confédération des Syndicats Voltaïques* (CSV) was dissolved by the CMRPN after Soumane Touré called for a general strike in December. Touré went into hiding.

1982   14 Feb. The CMRPN partly lifted its ban on strikes.

12 Apr. Thomas Sankara, Blaise Compaoré and Henri Zongo resigned from the CMRPN and were arrested.

14–16 Apr. A strike to protest suppression of the right to strike, the banning of the CSV, and the arrest order on Soumane Touré was unsuccessful. On 1 May the major trade unions demanded a return to constitutional government.

9–18 Sep. CSV leader Soumane Touré was arrested in Léo, and 82 public service employees were tried for taking part in April's illegal strike.

21 Sep. British Steel was contracted to furnish the rails for the 98-km. Ouagadougou-Kaya railroad. On 30 September six ministerial changes were made. In early October Col. Saye Zerbo visited Libya.

7 Nov. Col. Gabriel Yoryan Somé led an officers' coup (Upper Volta's sixth) which deposed Saye Zerbo. The group formed the *Conseil de Salut du Peuple* (CSP). On 9 November Surgeon Major Jean Baptiste Ouédraogo was appointed Head of State and Col. Gabriel Yoryan Somé continued as Army Chief of Staff. On 16 November the CSP pensioned off 21 senior army officers who supported President Lamizana.

8 Dec. The 36th Moro Naba, Kougri, died. He began his reign in 1957. His son, Ousmane Congo, succeeded him as Moro Naba Baongo.

24 Dec. *Confédération des Syndicats Voltaïques* (CSV) was restored to legal status by the CSP.

1983

10 Jan. Thomas Sankara was named Premier by CSP.

17 Jan. Nigeria announced the expulsion of foreigners, including thousands of Voltaics.

Feb. Prime Minister Thomas Sankara made a trip to Libya; Libyan leader Qadaffi visited Ouagadougou in April.

28 Feb. A coup attempt against the CSP failed. An anti-government plot was uncovered on 1 March. Several leaders of the *Front Progressiste Voltaïque* (FPV) were arrested and charged.

7–12 Mar. Sankara attended New Delhi Conference of Nonaligned Nations; he met Fidel Castro, Samora Machel and Maurice Bishop. On 26 March he gave a major speech to CSP-sponsored mass rally.

20–26 Apr. Head of State Ouédraogo visited Ghana, Benin and Niger.

15 May. Sankara gave a major speech to CSP-sponsored rally in Bobo Dioulasso. French President Mitterrand's top advisers held conferences with President Ouédraogo.

17 May. President Ouédraogo purged his government of pro-Libyan and anti-French elements and dissolved the Council for the Salvation of the People (CSP). Prime Minister Thomas Sankara and Jean-Baptiste Lingani were arrested. Sankara was imprisoned in Ouahigouya. Zongo and Compaoré evaded arrest. Zongo subsequently surrendered. Compaoré returned to Pô, Sankara's previous command, and organized resistance. On 18 May the Libyan chargé d'affaires was asked to leave Upper Volta.

20 May. Students demonstrated in Ouagadougou for the release of Sankara and Lingani. Minister of Youth and Sports Ibrahima Koné and Soumane Touré, leader of the *Confédération des Syndicats Voltaïques* (CSV), were arrested for inciting the students.

25 May. Col. Gabriel Yoryan Somé was appointed Secretary-General of National Defense. On 27 May Head of State Jean Baptiste Ouédraogo promised a future return to civilian government and release of all political prisoners.

30 May. Under pressure from Pô troops under Compaoré,

Sankara and supporters were released from prison, Sankara to Ouagadougou house arrest.

9 June. A Libyan radio station began beaming pro-Sankara broadcasts into Upper Volta.

10 June. Sankara and Jean-Baptiste Lingani were re-arrested, but soon released as a result of new threats from troops at Pô. From June through August Compaoré continued to resist in Pô.

18 June. The main arms depot in Ouagadougou was blown up, causing widespread damage and injury.

4 Aug. A coup freed Sankara and others, and overthrew the Ouédraogo regime. The *Conseil National de la Révolution* (CNR) took power with Sankara as president and Compaoré as minister of state to the presidency. Sankara called for mass Committees for the Defense of the Revolution (CDRs).

5 Aug. A decree established a new country-wide territorial division of 30 provinces, under high commissioners, and 250 departments, under prefects, with local government divided into districts and villages, effective on 15 September.

6 Aug. Libya's Qaddafi sent congratulations to Sankara, then a Libyan aircraft arrived with aid. Sankara requested Libyan authorities to cease aid.

8 Aug. Former Secretary-General of National Defense Col. Gabriel Yoryan Somé and paratroop Major Fidel Guebré were captured and shot.

18 Aug. The purpose of the Committees for the Defense of the Revolution (CDRs) was explained by national chairman Major Abdoul Salam Kabore.

24 Aug. Thomas Sankara formed a government with Compaoré as Minister of State, Lingani, National Defense, and Arba Diallo, Foreign Affairs.

9 Sep. Followers of former President Saye Zerbo attempted a coup. On 13 September more than fifty officers were dismissed from the armed forces and gendarmerie. Also on that date workers took over Voltéléc, the national electric company.

16 Sep. Captain Sankara made a state visit to Mali. It was announced that the Mali-Upper Volta border dispute would be submitted to the International Court of Justice.

22 Sep. Captain Sankara made a trip to Niger. On 30 September he met Ghanaian Head of State Flight Lt. Jerry Rawlings at Pô.

2 Oct. Sankara presented his "Political Orientation Speech" on behalf of the National Council of the revolution (CNR). On 9 October women held a mass pro-Sankara march in Ouagadougou. In a September speech in Dori and his 2 October speech, Sankara promised a new place for women in Voltaic society.

12 Oct. Joseph Ki-Zerbo, former president of the National Assembly Joseph Ouédraogo, former President Maurice Yaméogo, and former Head of State Col. Saye Zerbo were placed under house arrest.

24 Oct. It was announced that CDRs were to be set up in all places of work. On 27 December, the head of the secondary school teachers' union warned against making trade unions subordinate to CDRs.

31 Oct. Upper Volta was elected to a two-year term on the U.N. Security Council.

4–8 Nov. Joint military exercises—Operation Bold Union—were held with Ghana near Pô; Sankara and Rawlings observed them.

9 Nov. A Revolutionary Solidarity Fund was established to provide rural famine relief.

21 Dec. Angolan President Eduardo dos Santos met with Sankara in Ouagadougou.

1984   3 Jan. Following their establishment on 19 October 1983, the People's Revolutionary Courts began trials of leaders of the Zerbo and Lamizana regimes, on live radio. Former President Sangoulé Lamizana was acquitted on charges of embezzlement.

19 Jan. The CNR transferred tax collection from local chiefs to CDRs instead. In early February the CNR decreed an end to all tribute payments and obligatory labor to traditional chiefs.

31 Jan. U.N. Secretary-General Pérez de Cuéllar visited Ouagadougou. On 11–12 February Ghanaian Head of State Flight Lt. Jerry Rawlings visited.

20–21 Mar. The National Union of African Teachers of Upper Volta (SNEAHV) leadership, associated with Joseph Ki-Zerbo's banned FPV, called a teachers' strike. Next day, CNR dismissed 1,500 teachers.

31 Mar. Sankara did official visits to Algeria, Mauritania, and Saharan Arab Democratic Republic.

8 Apr. Land was distributed in Ouagadougou for housing construction. On 26 April Sourou Valley irrigation project

was launched to irrigate 16,000 hectares (39,500 acres) of land near Ouagadougou.

3 May. Col. Saye Zerbo was convicted of embezzlement and fraud and sentenced to 15 years' imprisonment.

27 May. Scheduled visit of Sankara to Côte d'Ivoire was canceled; several alleged coup plotters were arrested. Seven, including former Ouagadougou mayor Col. Didier Nobila Tiendrebéogo, were tried and executed on 11 June. It was alleged that the plotters had links to exile Joseph Ki-Zerbo.

12 June. National Defense Minister Jean-Baptiste Lingani accused France and the United States of interference in Upper Volta's internal affairs.

23 June. Sankara began an African trip, including Ethiopia, Angola, Mozambique, Congo, Madagascar and Gabon. In July he visited Rumania and Eastern Europe in search of financial aid. The Chinese-built stadium was opened in Ouagadougou.

12 July. Compulsory military service was instituted.

3 Aug. The CNR granted amnesty and release from house arrest for former President Maurice Yaméogo and former Premier Dr. Joseph Issoufou Conombo.

4 Aug. During anniversary celebrations, the Republic of Upper Volta was renamed Burkina Faso: "land of incorruptible (upright) people." A new flag and national anthem were adopted. An agrarian reform law nationalized all land and mineral wealth.

19 Aug. Thomas Sankara dissolved his Cabinet in a controversy with the League for Patriotic Development (LIPAD), and excluded LIPAD from the 31 August Cabinet. A number of leading LIPAD members were subsequently arrested on 28 October.

22 Sep. A day of solidarity with housewives was proclaimed in Ouagadougou; men were encouraged to go to market and prepare meals. On 25–30 September in Cuba Sankara was awarded Cuba's highest honor.

1 Oct. CNR announced that drought, winds, and grasshoppers had created catastrophic conditions across northern Burkina. The CNR launched a 15-month Popular Development Program, and abolished the long-standing head tax on rural Burkinabè.

4 Oct. Sankara addressed the U.N. General Assembly Session in New York and called for a greater voice for the small nations in world economic decisions.

27–29 Oct. Sankara became chairman of ECOWAS at its meeting in Bamako, Mali. Also in Bamako on the 29th, Sankara became president of the CEAO in the midst of a scandal over missing CEAO money.

5–9 Nov. Sankara visited the People's Republic of China, and attended Organization of African Unity meeting in Addis Ababa, Ethiopia, 12–15 November.

25 Nov. Start of 15-day campaign to immunize all Burkinabè under age fifteen against meningitis, yellow fever and measles; 2.5 million immunized.

3 Dec. A national conference of the CDR voted to deduct a month's pay from top civil servants and military officers and a half month from other civil servants to help pay for development projects.

11 Dec. Burkina Faso declined to attend the Conference of France and African States.

31 Dec. Sankara announced suspension of all residential rents for 1985 and start of a massive public housing construction program.

1985   Heavy rains for the first time in several years produced enough food to feed Burkinabè. Campaign was launched to plant 10 million trees in 1985.

28 Jan. Several major unions denounced the CNR's social and economic policies. Several union leaders were suspended from their jobs.

1 Feb. Sankara launched the "Battle for the Railroad" to lay the rails on the Ouagadougou-Kaya roadbed with voluntary labor.

11 Feb. Moro Naba Baongo and President Thomas Sankara held a brief meeting.

12 Feb. Sankara attended a meeting of the Entente Council in Yamoussoukro, Côte d'Ivoire, despite the prior day's explosion that destroyed rooms reserved for the Burkinabè delegation.

1–8 Mar. A national conference on women's emancipation in Ouagadougou drew 3,000 attendees.

17–23 Mar. Joint military maneuvers were held with Ghana. In April a Ghana-Burkina joint commission met to explore integration of the two countries.

3 Apr. The International Court of Justice began studying the Burkina-Mali border dispute.

31 May. Three soldiers were killed in explosion of ammunition depot at Goughin (Ouagadougou) military camp in what may have been a coup attempt.

9 June. Burkina Faso began work on the Kompienga Dam project, which was opened in early 1989.

July. Joseph and Josephine Ki-Zerbo, in exile since October 1983, received two-year sentences by the People's Revolutionary Court in Ouagadougou for tax evasion and illicit enrichment.

4 Aug. An all-female mass parade emphasized steps toward equality for women at the second anniversary of CNR. A partial amnesty was announced for Jean Baptiste Ouédraogo, Saye Zerbo and Gérard Kango Ouédraogo.

12 Aug. Sankara dissolved his government, and announced reorganized Cabinet on 31 August.

10 Sep. At special meeting of the Entente Council in Yamoussoukro, Côte d'Ivoire, Burkina refused to join in condemning international terrorism.

9–11 Dec. Libya's President Qaddafi, accompanied by a 450-man bodyguard, visited Ouagadougou.

10–20 Dec. Population census was undertaken. On 14 December Burkina Faso census takers took count in four villages along the Malian border.

25 Dec. Fighting broke out along the Burkina-Mali border in the Agacher area north of Dori. Burkina conducted air attacks on Sikasso, and Mali an air raid against Ouahigouya. This war lasted five days; total casualties of 100 reported. Cease-fire signed on 29 December. Burkina released Malian war prisoners on 3 January 1986.

1986 All restrictions against contraception were abolished.

3 Jan. Former President Saye Zerbo and National Assembly leader Gérard Kango Ouédraogo were released from prison to house arrest.

8 Jan. Provisional census results gave total Burkina Faso population of 7.9 million.

17 Jan. Sankara and Mali's Moussa Traoré met in Côte d'Ivoire to end border disputes.

Feb.–April. Literacy campaign was conducted in nine indigenous languages. 35,000 people involved.

4 Feb. Cooperation agreements between France and Burkina Faso were signed in Paris, replacing those dating from 1961. In late March the West African Economic Community summit met in Ouagadougou.

3 Apr. The Burkinabè People's Tribunal convicted three former CEAO officials of embezzlement.

4 Aug. Sankara announced a five-year plan for national economic self-sufficiency.

6 Aug. CNR changed names of White Volta to Nakanbe, Red Volta to Nazinon, and Black Volta to Mouhoun.

14–16 Aug. A Ghana-Burkina joint committee agreed to require study of both English and French.

18 Aug. The Government was dissolved to show that ministers were servants of the people. Compaoré, Major Jean-Baptiste Lingani and Capt. Henri Zongo were appointed Coordinators of Burkina Faso and mandated to act for President Sankara.

27 Aug. Nicaraguan President Daniel Ortega arrived in Ouagadougou for a state visit. On 3 September Sankara addressed the Eighth Summit of Nonaligned Countries in Harare, Zimbabwe.

23 Sep. Togo claimed that Burkina and Ghana aided an attempted coup in Togo.

6–12 Oct. Sankara visited the Soviet Union. On his return trip he visited Qaddafi in Libya. On 8–9 November he visited Cuba and Nicaragua.

17–18 Nov. French President Mitterrand visited Burkina. Sankara denounced French ties to apartheid South Africa.

22 Dec. In International Court of Justice ruling on border dispute, Burkina received Béli eastern zone and Mali the western "four village" zone.

Dec. U.N.-assisted program had brought river blindness effectively under control in Burkina.

1987   The Poura gold mine re-opened in 1984. Together with subsequent mining activity in the north and Sebba regions, 1987 marketed gold production of 2.6 tons yielded US$38 million in export revenues. Smuggled gold was estimated at 4 tons annually.

8 Mar. Sankara addressed International Women's Day celebration in Ouagadougou. On 11 April he launched the National Peasants Union of Burkina.

30 May. Soumane Touré, leader of the Burkinabè Workers' Confederation and LIPAD was arrested.

15 July. Air Burkina established regular service to Accra, Ghana.

10 Aug. Sankara visited Qaddafi in Libya.

2 Oct. Sankara spoke in Tenkodogo on the fourth anniversary of "Political Orientation Speech". In an 8 October speech Sankara suggested national elections for a council of 120 members.

15 Oct. The Movement of Progressive Democrats (MPD) was founded by Hermann Yaméogo and others.

15 Oct. Sankara and 13 associates were killed in a coup led by his closest aides, Blaise Compaoré, Jean-Baptiste Lingani and Henri Zongo. The Compaoré-led Popular Front dissolved the CNR.

27 Oct. A Koudougou rebellion led by Capt. Boukary Kaboré, loyal to Sankara, failed and he fled to Ghana.

1988   Following improved grain production in 1986 and 1987, poor rains caused 1988 harvests to fall.

8–10 Jan. Compaoré addressed a national meeting of mass organizations, which adopted 36 motions for new direction. Throughout 1988 some austerity measures were lifted to gain legitimacy with urban dwellers and civil servants. By year-end a new presidential palace was under construction.

21 Jan. Heads of State of Ghana and Burkina Faso met in Tamale, Ghana.

18 Mar. The Committee for the Defense of the Revolution (CDR) was formally dissolved.

July. Compaoré renewed Sankara's commitment to continue building the rail line to Tambao. Line of 105 km. was completed to Kaya northeast of Ouagadougou by end of 1988.

4 Aug. Togo President Eyadema visited Burkina.

23 Aug. A reshuffle reduced the civilian representation in the Cabinet. A week later President Compaoré launched a campaign against "laziness" and "amateurism" in the public sector.

Sep. Compaoré paid a 6-day visit to North Korea.

15 Oct. Celebrations marked the first anniversary of the Popular Front; 120 convicts were released.

Nov. Burkina Faso and Libya signed a cooperation agreement. Burkina Faso recognized PLO-proclaimed Palestinian state. In December Compaoré attended Franco-African Summit, Burkina's first since 1983.

28 Dec. Seven supporters of Boukary Kaboré, accused of murdering the officer who defeated him at Koudougou, were executed.

1989   Good 1988 rains led to best-ever 1989 harvests.

Jan. Compaoré visited Togo. Malian and Burkina provincial authorities discussed border matters.

15 Apr. Government created *Organisation pour la Démocratie Populaire/Mouvement du Travail* (ODP/MT) to rally all groups in the Popular Front.

25 Apr. In a major cabinet reshuffle, Compaoré named

Clément Oumarou Ouédraogo, of the *Burkinabè Union of Communists* (UCB), to the new post Minister of Co-ordination of the Popular Front.

17 June. Blaise Compaoré was elected president of the 19-member executive committee of the Popular Front. Lingani was named first deputy chairman and Zongo second deputy chairman. The make-up of the Popular Front had not been previously announced.

3 Aug. Head of State Compaoré amnestied more than twenty political detainees and reduced sentences of more than 150 common law prisoners.

3 Aug. Bernard Lédéa Ouedraogo was named co-winner of the 1989 "Africa Prize for Leadership for the Sustainable End of Hunger". Ouedraogo founded the Six "S" Association (*Se Servir de la Saison Sèche en Savanne et au Sahel*) in 1976, the grassroots self-reliance movement in Burkina Faso.

20 Sep. Minister of Defense Jean-Baptiste Lingani and Economic Promotion Minister Henri Zongo were accused of plotting against Compaoré and executed.

20 Oct. Burkina announced intent to undertake IMF-World Bank 1991–93 Structural Adjustment Program.

25 Dec. The Government announced foiling of another coup attempt with numerous arrests.

1990   15–18 Jan. Ministers of education of nine Sahel countries called for increased international aid to help provide a general basic education for all by the year 2000. On a five-nation West African tour, Pope John Paul launched an appeal for the drought-threatened Sahel on 25 January.

1–4 Mar. Seven political organizations were represented at the first Popular Front congress, which called for a draft constitution within six months. Clément Oumarou Ouédraogo was confirmed as Minister-delegate to the Popular Front coordination committee, the number 2 post in the regime. Capt. Arséne Ye Bognessan, Secretary for organization, and Capt. Gilbert Diendéré, Secretary for defense and security, kept their posts. MPD founder Hermann Yaméogo, son of first president of Upper Volta and political "moderate", was appointed to the executive committee of the Popular Front.

Mar. The Popular Front hailed Nelson Mandela's release by the South African government.

19 April. Clément Oumarou Ouédraogo lost the portfolio of Minister-delegate to the Popular Front co-ordination

committee and his place on the executive committee. He had been dismissed as general secretary of the ODP/MT on 14 April. Marc Christian Roch Kaboré replaced him as Secretary for political affairs and second in command.

3 May. Arséne Ye Bognessan was appointed chairman of 104-member constitutional commission. October draft constitution provided for multiparty system and President elected by universal adult suffrage.

23 May. Capt. Laurent Sedego was dismissed from the Cabinet. He and other officers were dismissed from the army to reinforce army discipline.

July. The Popular Front co-ordinating committee suspended Hermann Yaméogo's MPD from the Popular Front due to an alleged internal MPD crisis.

10 Sep. Compaoré appointed second in command Marc Kabore as Minister of state without portfolio.

Nov. Alain Yoda's Union of Social Democrats (UDS) became tenth political party. Another new party was the Movement for Tolerance and Progress (MTP), led by Emmanule Nayabtigungu Congo Kabore, former general secretary to CNR government and cabinet.

Dec. 2400-delegate constituent assembly met in Ouagadougou; adopted draft constitution, with referendum in March (actually held 2 June) 1991. Elections for seven-year presidential term and 4-year assembly terms to be held in late 1991.

1991   A major demographic survey, between the 1985 and planned 1995 census, was carried out in late 1991.

Jan. Of the 16 political groupings, seven were members of the Popular Front. Thirty-one political parties were officially recognized by mid-year.

2 Mar. Idrissa Ouédraogo from Burkina Faso won the main prize for his film "Tilai" at FESPACO which began in Ouagadougou on 23 February.

Mar. The congress of ODP/MT adopted Blaise Compaoré as its official presidential candidate, and replaced its Marxist-Leninist ideology with a commitment to free enterprise policies. Ram Ouédraogo, leader of the Green Union for the Development of Burkina (UVDB), was the first declared presidential candidate. Hermann Yaméogo, now president of the Alliance for Democracy and Federation (ADF), announced his intent to run for President.

April. Civil conflict in Liberia escalated in 1990. The Compaoré government openly supported Charles Taylor's rebel National Patriotic Front of Liberia (NPFL) and initially refused to join the ECOWAS-sponsored military monitoring group (ECOMOG) sent to Liberia in mid-1990. Relations with some ECOWAS members deteriorated amid claims that a Burkina vessel took Libyan weapons to Taylor and that Burkina had trained some of Taylor's forces. It was announced in April 1991 that Burkina would contribute a contingent to ECOMOG.

April. Official amnesty was granted for the alleged perpetrators of the December 1989 coup attempt. In May the rehabilitation of former President Maurice Yaméogo was announced. Also in May plans to include Thomas Sankara in a shared "national heroes" memorial with Daniel Ouëzzin Coulibaly, Philippe Zinda Kaboré, and Nazi Boni were announced by the Compaoré government.

11 June. A new constitution took effect after referendum approval on 2 June. It was endorsed by 93 percent of voters (49 percent of electorate).

On 16 June the Council of Ministers was dissolved and a transitional government appointed, including Compaoré as interim president. In July the ODP/MT, President Compaoré's party, rejected opposition requests for a national conference to deal with the political reform process, and threatened reprisals if the new constitution were jeopardized. The transitional government was modified to include more representation from outside the Popular Front. In mid-August Hermann Yaméogo and two other ADF members resigned from the transitional government only weeks after being appointed.

3 Sep. After eight years in exile, Joseph Ki-Zerbo returned to Burkina to attend the conference of the National Convention of Progressive Patriots/Social Democratic Party (CNPP/PSD).

7 Oct. A peaceful demonstration of about ten thousand people called for a national conference. A demonstration of some 3,000 on 30 September had clashed with Compaoré supporters.

13 Oct. The African Democratic Assembly (RDA), one of the oldest parties in Burkina, selected Gérard Kango Ouédraogo as its presidential candidate. He was the fifth declared candidate. On 18 October the five opposition candidates decided to boycott the presidential election unless Compaoré called a national conference.

1 Dec. Presidential election was held. It was boycotted by opposition parties, and fewer than one quarter of registered voters participated. Blaise Compaoré was elected President (of IVth Republic).

9 Dec. Political tensions culminated in attacks in which opposition leaders Clément Oumarou Ouédraogo, head of *Parti du travail du Burkina* (PTB), was killed and Tall Moctar was wounded. Both were important in the 20-party Confederation of Democratic Forces (CFD) that organized the boycott of the presidential election.

1992

12 Jan. Under threat of another opposition boycott, parliamentary elections were put back to 24 May. During January Compaoré rehabilitated some 4,000 persons who had been punished for political or trade union activity since 1983.

12 Feb. President Compaoré visited Mali to discuss border delimitation matters.

20 Feb. The Compaoré-proposed National Reconciliation Forum (380 delegates) was suspended by the government after only two weeks. Compaoré constituted the third transitional government in 8 months on 27 February; Hermann Yaméogo and some other opposition members rejoined it.

4 Apr. Only 27 of Burkina's 61 political parties registered for the 24 May general elections for the 107-member National Assembly.

Apr. From 1990 onward, conflict between Tuareg rebels and government forces in Mali and Niger caused refugees to enter Burkina. The refugees represented a burden to Burkina, and the potential for renewed rebel attacks to Mali and Niger.

24 May. President Blaise Compaoré's ODP/MT won 78 of 107 seats in the National Assembly election and five other parties that supported the President won six more. An abstention rate of nearly 65 percent was recorded. On 15 June Compaoré dissolved the transitional government and inaugurated the newly elected National Assembly. He appointed Mr. Youssouf Ouédraogo, a forty-year-old economist, as the new Prime Minister.

20 June. The new cabinet formed by Prime Minister Youssouf Ouédraogo included seven political parties. The ODP/MT had 13 ministers, and parties close to the presidential majority had 4 of the 29 total. Arséne Ye Bognessan,

president of ODP/MT and former national coordinator of the CDRs, became Speaker of the National Assembly.

June. According to the Burkinabè Movement for Human Rights (MBDHP), soldiers conducted a punitive expedition in Fada N'Gourma after an altercation between a soldier and a civilian.

10–11 Sep. Malian President Oumar Konaré visited Burkina for discussion of economic cooperation, the northern Mali Tuareg issue, sub-regional security, and joint administration of border areas. Niger had recently arrested a number of persons because of Tuareg rebellion attacks.

Dec. The government, trade unions and private sector representatives began a series of negotiations to define a "social charter".

1993   In late 1992 and early 1993 there was resurgence of social tensions, partially related to government austerity measures linked to IMF-World Bank structural adjustment program. University of Ouagadougou students boycotted classes in late 1992 and January 1993. During protests of reduced scholarship grants and payment arrears, about 15 students were injured. Arrears were paid.

Jan. The freeze in public-sector salaries since 1987 was lifted; worker negotiators thought the adjustments unfavorable in light of inflation.

20 Jan. President Compaoré visited Mali and stated his support for the April 1992 peace plan between the Malian government and the main Mali Tuareg movements. He stressed that non-signer Tuareg leader Rhissa Ag Mohame was not in Burkina.

Jan.–Mar. Austerity prompted some labor unrest, but it was limited by lack of trade union cohesion. A three-day strike in March by the *Confédération générale du travail burkinabé* (CGTB) had little success. The CGTB withdrew from the "social charter" negotiations.

Mar.–May. The National Assembly approved proposals to establish an appointed consultative chamber (*Chambre des Représentants*) with 120 members, three-year terms as provided for in the 1991 constitution.

May. Following a CNPP-PSD split, six of its parliamentary members joined Joseph Ki-Zerbo's new *Parti pour la démocratie et le progrès*.

June. President Compaoré paid his first official visit to France.

16 June. Two Bobo Dioulasso newspaper journalists received six-month prison terms, the first since democratic institutions were restored in 1992.

23 June. Côte d'Ivoire and Burkina experts met to establish a border demarcation commission.

Mid-1993. Compaoré hosted negotiations between the Togolese government and opposition. A Burkinabè military contingent went to Togo; Burkina contributed to an international diplomatic mission to oversee Togo's August presidential election.

3 Sep. A cabinet reshuffle reduced the number of ministers from 29 to 25.

15 Sep. Maurice Yaméogo, first president (1959–1966) of then-Upper Volta, died. He had lived mostly since 1966 in Côte d'Ivoire. He asked to return, and died on the plane back to Ouagadougou.

Oct. Diplomatic relations with Israel, severed in 1973, were re-established.

Dec. Long-time Côte d'Ivoire President Houphouët-Boigny died.

1994 Jan. Prime Minister Youssouf Ouédraogo reshuffled his cabinet again.

12 Jan. Burkina Faso was one of 13 francophone African countries where the CFA franc was devalued by 50 percent against the French franc (and thus other major international currencies). The rate had been unchanged since 1948 at CFAFr 1 = Ffr .02 (1 Ffr = 50 CFAFr). Under that system, CFA Franc zone countries were required to deposit about two-thirds of their foreign exchange reserves with the French Treasury, and in return received guaranteed convertibility into French francs. Devaluation was a French government decision, strongly supported by the IMF; the French government offered to cancel the official debt owed to it by ten CFA countries, including Burkina (it was halved in the others).

Because the exchange rate was determined by forces affecting the French franc, the CFA franc had been overvalued in recent years, thus hurting Burkina's export competitiveness. Indeed, Burkina's livestock exports increased markedly in the first half of 1994 after the devaluation. But devaluation also raised the cost of imports of finished goods and of inputs for local producers, and increased the expectations of inflation (any seller with power to do so would raise prices). And the devaluation instantly doubled the size of Burkina's external debt in local-currency terms.

In anticipation of likely domestic protests and inflation, the Burkina government immediately imposed temporary retail price controls on certain imports; increased public and private salaries and education scholarships; reduced customs tariffs on imports; increased guaranteed producer prices for cotton and rice; lowered tax rates; and urged government agencies to reduce operating expenses. The 1994 inflation rate was held to 24.7 percent.

2 Feb. Diplomatic relations with Taiwan, severed in 1973, were restored, and the Taiwanese government announced agriculture and medical assistance. Soon thereafter the People's Republic of China suspended official relations.

Feb. Negotiations between the government of Niger and Tuareg leaders took place in Ouagadougou.

20 March. Prime Minister Youssouf Ouédraogo resigned from the government. Negotiations between the government and the unions following the January devaluation did not reach agreement. The unions had asked for 40–50 percent wage increases. Marc Christian Roch Kaboré, member of the cabinet since 1989, was named Prime Minister. On 6 April the CGTB called a 3-day general strike following meetings with Kaboré at which the government offered salary increases of 6–10 percent to help cushion the end of price controls.

April. President Compaoré visited France for cooperation discussions with President Mitterrand and Prime Minister Edouard Balladur. Established diplomatic relations with South Africa in May.

19 June. Compaoré met with 600-women Koudougou conference to hear their grievances. He urged traditional, religious and state leaders to combat the exclusion of women, and pledged 500 million CFA to the Fund to support women's remunerative activities. Established in 1990 with UNDP support, the Fund had already given 2,000 loans with a 90.5 percent repayment rate.

June. Heads of state of Burkina, Mali and Niger met with Col. Qaddafi in Libya to discuss regional (Tuareg) security issues. In late July Mali, Burkina, and the UN High

Commission on Refugees (UNHCR) reached an agreement regarding repatriation of refugees from Burkina to Mali.

13 July. An agreement was signed by the governments of Burkina and Côte d'Ivoire to privatize the Abidjan-Ouagadougou-Kaya railway line in May 1995.

Aug. Burkina denied any involvement in arms trafficking to Liberia, and denied a July claim that 3,000 Burkinabè mercenaries were fighting alongside Charles Taylor's NPFL.

27–29 Aug. Prime Minister Mahamadou Issoufou of Niger visited Burkina Faso to discuss mounting insecurity and conflicts. Agreement was reached to speed demarcation of the Niger-Burkina border and to revise the 1964 border protocol.

5 Sep. Due to concern about possible reprisals from Algerian Islamic fundamentalists, the opposition Social Democratic Party (PSD) called on the government to reconsider taking in 20 Muslims expelled from France (19 Algerian, 1 Moroccan).

14 Oct. Renewed clashes in Mali's Tuareg zone led to a fresh inpouring of Tuareg refugees (and some from Niger) to three camps in Burkina. The total of some 25,000, most women and children, had grown by four times in three months. By year-end UNHCR estimated the total at nearly 50,000. The main refugee camp was near the Mali border north of Djibo.

Nov. Compaoré visited France (and also attended Franco-African summit).

1995   12 Feb. Municipal elections were held in the major towns (more than 10,000 inhabitants and budget at least CFA 20 million). Compaoré's supporters won absolute majorities in 26 of the 33. Participation was over 75 percent of those registered to vote; fewer than 10 percent of the eligible registered.

Mar. A U.N. delegation visited to investigate arms proliferation in Burkina, Chad, Mali and Niger.

May. A private consortium of French, Belgian, Ivoirien and Burkinabè interests began operating the Abidjan-Ouagadougou-Kaya railway line.

11 June. Lt.-Col. Ibrahim Traoré became armed forces Chief of Staff. The Cabinet was expanded to 25 from 23.

July. Compaoré met with recently-elected French President Jacques Chirac in Côte d'Ivoire.

Aug. *Bloc socialist burkinabè* leader Ernest Nongma Ouédraogo was imprisoned for six months for allegedly insulting the head of state.

1996   Jan. A UN Development Program (UNDP) conference of African economy and finance ministers was held in Ouagadougou.

Following negotiation with Muslim leaders the government decided to allow mosques to re-open. They were closed following violent clashes and two deaths in April 1995.

Feb. The presidential party, the *Organisation pour la Démocratie Populaire/Mouvement du Travail* (ODP/MT), and nine parties grouped around it formed a new political party, the *Congrès de Démocratie et Progrès* (CDP). Arséne Ye Bognessan, former leader of the ODP/MT, became the CDP's president.

Following the merger, Prime Minister Marc Christian Roch Kaboré was named "Special adviser to the president." Kadre Désiré Ouédraogo, former deputy governor of the Central Bank of West African States (BCEAO), was immediately named prime minister. A few minor cabinet changes were also announced.

Mar. The UN Food and Agriculture Organization announced that a decline in cereal grain production had put some 700,000 people in Burkina's northern provinces under threat of famine.

Niger, Burkina Faso and the UN High Commission on Refugees (UNHCR) signed an agreement to repatriate refugees from Burkina to Niger.

5 Apr. Finance Minister Zéphirin Diabré announced the adoption of a new enhanced structural adjustment facility with the International Monetary Fund for the period 1996–1998. The first structural adjustment program covered 1993–1995.

24 Apr. In anticipation of parliamentary elections to be held in 1997 the National Assembly adopted legislation to create fifteen new provinces, making a total of 45, effective immediately.

May. It was announced that 4,000 people had died in a meningitis epidemic since the beginning of 1996.

6 Jun. The Burkinabè government withdrew its diplomatic recognition of the Sahraoui Arab Democratic Republic (Western Sahara). This was the first occasion in recent years in which any African country "de-recognized" Western Sahara.

July. President Compaoré visited France and discussed the planned Franco-African summit to be held in Burkina Faso.

The National Assembly voted to increase Burkina's Value Added Tax (VAT) from 15 to 18% in January 1997. The increase was intended to replace reduced customs duties agreed within the West African Economic and Monetary Union (UMOA).

24 July. The number of National Assembly deputies was increased from 107 to 111.

Aug. The government launched a campaign to promote its borrowing internally rather than from foreign lenders. The funds were to be used for village-level microproduction. Finance and Economy Minister Diabré also appealed for an increase in private investment.

9 Oct. The cabinet adopted the draft budget for fiscal 1997 which included total expenditure of CFAFr 363.958 billion, 64% of which was to be financed from internal sources.

The Burkina government received a grant of CFAFr 117 billion from the European Development Fund to finance a 1996–2000 program focused on road infrastructure, rural development, good management of public affairs, decentralization, culture, and a water supply project for Ouagadougou.

26 Oct–2 Nov. The Salon International des Artinisat de Ouagadougou (SIAO) artisan and craft fair was held in Ouagadougou with numerous countries represented.

4–6 Dec. The nineteenth French-African Summit meeting was held in Ouagadougou in the new conference center and VIP chalets located in "Ouaga 2000." Twenty-six heads of state attended, and 45 African countries were represented.

17 Dec. The National Assembly authorized the state to reduce its ownership in the national air transport company, Air Burkina, from 66% to 25% of the shares. Other ownership shares will be held by private Burkinabè investors, the West African Development Bank, Air Afrique, and 3% by Air Burkina staff.

1997   Jan. The Burkina Faso motto of "La Patrie ou la Mort" was replaced by "Unité, Progrès, Justice."

2 Jan. President Blaise Compaoré officially launched a CFAFr 5 billion public borrowing campaign aimed at mobilizing resources from internal private savings. The funds

are intended to finance rural development and the micro-business sector.

3 Jan. The Belgian Prime Minister, Mr. Jean-Luc Dehaene, paid a three-day visit to Ouagadougou.

6 Feb. Leadership of the Burkinabè public media was reshuffled. Mr. Issaka Sourwema was made head of Sidwaya, Mrs. Aine Koala became director of Burkinabè National Television, and Mr. Rodrigue Barry became Burkinabè Radio Broadcasting director.

10 Feb. Ouagadougou University students decided to end their two-week-old strike as a gesture of good faith following the government's announcement that four student leaders would be released. But on 13 February the students decided to resume the strike. The students were demanding direct aid to non-grant-receiving students instead of loans, a direct bus link to the campus, and health care for all students.

12 Feb. The National Assembly revised the law to set up the national election commission (CNOE). The new text reduces to ten the representatives of political organizations, whereas the previous one (adopted in November 1996) had two representatives from each party. Traditional and religious communities, trade unions, the supreme court and the Faso moderator will be represented in the 25 CNOE members. Additionally, the CNOE president and vice president will now be elected by secret ballot by the commission members, rather that the CNOE president being appointed by the president of the Supreme Court from among magistrates.

A spokesman for the main opposition party, the *Parti pour la démocratie et le progrès* (PDP), denounced the "non-independent and non-permanent" character of the revised CNOE, and said that "the government continues to monopolize the essential aspects of the commission."

14 Feb. The government announced postponement of parliamentary elections from 27 April to 11 May 1997 for technical reasons, including revision of the electoral roll to take place between the 5th and 30th March.

22 Feb.–1 Mar. The 15th Pan African Film Festival (FESPACO) was held in Ouagadougou.

5 Apr. Immigration problems were the concern of discussions during the first meeting of the Côte d'Ivoire-Burkina Faso cooperation commission. Nearly half the immigrants living in Côte d'Ivoire are Burkinabè.

11 May. Elections for the National Assembly, originally scheduled for 27 April 1997, were held, with approximately a 50% turnout. President Compaoré's party, the *Congrès de Démocratie et Progrès* (CDP), won 101 of the 111 parliamentary seats. Some voter registration cards were reportedly held for pickup at the polling places because they were late in being distributed. However, the cards themselves contained the information as to the polling place at which the voter was to present himself or herself.

10 June. Prime Minister Kadre Désiré Ouédraogo formed a new government with a cabinet increased from 26 to 29 members. ADF leader Hermann Yaméogo was not included in the new cabinet, and the PDP's Joseph Ki-Zerbo declined an invitation to join it. Arsène Yé Bongnessan gave up his post as president of the National Assembly to become Minister of State in the Office of the President.

Introduction

The country of Burkina Faso is located in the heart of West Africa, bordered on the north and west by Mali, on the east by Niger, and on the south by Benin, Togo, Ghana and Côte d'Ivoire. The area of the country is 274,200 square kilometers. Six West African countries are larger, twelve are smaller. The American state of Colorado is of comparable size. Twenty years ago only Ghana and Nigeria in West Africa had more people. However, according to the UN Fund for Population Activities, Burkina's estimated 1996 population of 10.6 million was exceeded in West Africa by Nigeria, Ghana, Côte d'Ivoire, Cameroon, and Mali. Burkina's population is similar to that of Greece or Portugal and somewhat larger than the American state of Michigan.

Burkina Faso has a diverse population, The Sénufo, Habé, Lobi and Mande live mostly in the western part of the country. Some of these have never organized states, while others have seen several polities come and go. The center and southeast have been the location of four major and other minor Mossi states which have dominated a varied group of Gourounsi and Ninisi peoples. The northeast, north of Aribinda and Dori, in the Sahel, has seen the Tuareg, Fulani and Songhai pass to and fro in search of water and pasture for their herds. Hausa, Yarsé and Dioula merchants have trudged the dusty byways selling their kola and salt and buying what they could. Zerma have come aslaving, desolating the land and exterminating whole villages. Marabouts have come in the name of Allah, and missionaries in the name of Christ. The French came, and tied divergent peoples together within the borders of one state.

The country is a plateau, drained mostly to the south by the Volta system. In Burkina the river names were changed in 1986. The Mouhoun (former Black Volta), Nakanbe (White Volta), and Nazinon (Red Volta) each flow separately in Burkina Faso. They all eventually join the Volta River in Ghana, as does the Pendjari/Oti. The country was the upper Volta river system's namesake prior to its renaming as Burkina Faso in 1984. A part of Gourma is drained toward the Niger, as is a bit of the northwest via the Bani. Half the Sikasso Plateau gives its waters through the Komoé and across Côte d'Ivoire to the Gulf of Guinea. The average

1

altitude of the plateau is about 400 meters. Mount Téna Kourou at 749 meters, in the far southwest corner, west of Banfora and adjacent to the Mali border, is the highest point in the country. The lowest land is in the bogs of the Arly Reserve in the far southeast on the Benin border.

The economy of the country is based on rain-fed subsistence agriculture and livestock herding. The soil is mostly sterile laterite. Drought is a recurrent and constant fact of life, as the 1970s and early 1980s again reminded us; the driest years of the twentieth century occurred in 1982/83 (see FAMINE). Millet, sorghum, maize, fonio, cassava, sweet potatoes, peas, beans, peanuts, rice and yams are the basic foods. Cotton, sheanuts, peanuts and sesame seeds are cash crops and provide some export revenue. Cotton has alternated with gold as Burkina's largest export in recent years. Above Ouagadougou Zebu cattle thrive beyond the reach of the tsetse fly. Although no longer the largest item, livestock is still an important export. Below the capital small Ndama and Lobi cattle, relatively resistant to the fly, furnish a meager supplement to the wealth of their owners. Sheep, goats, pigs and poultry are raised primarily for local consumption.

There are small amounts of antimony, marble, zinc, graphite, bauxite, tin and iron in the ground of Upper Volta. Commercial gold mining resumed in 1984 after having been suspended in 1966; official production of 3.7 tons in 1988 made gold Burkina's largest export, but it fluctuated by 50 per cent during the next several years. Smuggled gold was estimated at 4 tons annually. Prospecting and research on deposits of phosphates is intended. There are major deposits of manganese and limestone at Tambao in the remote extreme northeastern corner of Burkina Faso, and an international mining consortium was organized in 1974. Transport is the main constraint. The Ouagadougou-Kaya rail line opened in the late 1980s, but still ends some 200 km. short of Tambao. However, manganese exports began in 1993. There are plans for a cement works at nearby Tin Hrassan, and a dam at Tin Akof.

Until recently all of Burkina's electricity required imported petroleum fuels. In 1988 a hydroelectric dam project was completed at Kompienga, and was designed to meet approximately one-quarter of Burkina's power needs. A second hydroelectric project was begun in the early 1990s at Bagré. Noumbiel has been proposed as the location of a hydroelectric and irrigation dam on the Mouhoun River east of Gaoua, with expected generating output equal to Kompienga and Bagré combined. Consideration has also been given to the viability of extending the Ghanian electricity network into Burkina.

Upper Volta/Burkina Faso became politically independent in 1960. The country's limited power in international trade and limited resource base in the face of rapidly rising expectations, as in most of the Third World, left Burkina's political leaders with little room for maneuver.

Since 1960 there have been three civilian leaders and five military ones, and two of the three civilians first came to power in military uniforms. The creation of Upper Volta in 1919, its abolition in 1932, and re-amalgamation in 1947 left a considerable residue of border ambiguity between Mali and Burkina. Outbreaks of fighting in 1974–1975 and 1985 resulted, but considerable diplomatic efforts to avoid conflict have been made in more recent years.

The economic prospects for Burkina Faso are bleak by conventional standards. The resource and production base has been small, giving rise to a persistent structural deficit in international trade, and Burkina is relatively densely populated. Every year thousands leave the country to seek employment in neighboring countries, especially Ghana and Côte d'Ivoire. The economy generates little capital for financing industrial expansion. Literacy rates are low, and the imbalance of global economic power against poor countries works to Burkina's disadvantage.

At the same time, the people of Burkina—hardworking, resourceful, adaptable—are the country's greatest resource. Survival has been due in part to self-reliance efforts that range from land reclamation contour ridging to well-digging to tree-planting. Survival is due to remittances from emigrants working abroad, and to emergency food aid by international governmental and non-government organizations.

Survival is due to support by the Burkina government of these and other measures, and its recognition of the seriousness of the problems that confront the country. A populist government from 1983 to 1987 captured the imagination of many younger persons throughout Burkina Faso and Africa as it insisted that material poverty was not synonymous with lack of dignity for people. And concerted efforts can make an impact: by the early 1990s Burkina ranked third in sub-Saharan Africa in the proportion of the population with access to installed safe water supplies.

The Dictionary

Within the Dictionary, cross references to other entries are indicated by *quod vide,* abbreviated as: (q.v.).

-A-

ACACIA. Several varieties of spiny shrubs and thorn trees which are common in Burkina Faso (for example, *acacia albida*). These trees are a source of gum arabic, khaki dye, tannin, building materials and fire wood.

ACULO. Grusi-speaking group along the Ghana-Burkina Faso border around the village of Prata.

AFRICAN DEMOCRATIC RALLY. *see* RASSEMBLEMENT DEM-OCRATIQUE AFRICAIN (RDA)

AGACHER (Akchar). Also known as the Oudalan (q.v.) region. A region of nomadic cattle people. This dune area in the Béli (q.v.) river valley along the Mali-Burkina Faso border is some 200 km. north of Ouagadougou (q.v.). It is about 160 km. long and 15 km. wide. It is thought to have deposits of manganese (q.v.), titanium, gas and oil. In 1974–1975 Mali tried to have the border moved south 10 km. so that the Béli would be within Mali borders. While awaiting the International Court of Justice ruling on that dispute, fighting broke out along the Burkina-Mali border in December 1985 in the Agacher area north of Dori (q.v.) and a five-day war ensued. When the International Court of Justice ruled in December 1986, Burkina received the Béli eastern zone and Mali the western "four village" zone.

AHMADIYYA. The most recent of the Muslim *tariqas* (q.v.) or broth-erhoods of West Africa.

ALBY, MARIE-MAXIMILIEN-GUSTAVE, 1855–1920. French administrator. Born in Marseilles, he entered military service in 1874, and saw service in Tunisia in 1881. He then became a colonial administrator and held assignments in Tahiti, Guinea and Dahomey. In 1894 he was sent into the hinterland of Dahomey to make contact with the Mossi (q.v.). Alby crossed Busansi (q.v.) territory and reached the outskirts of Ouagadougou (q.v.) early in 1895. When the Moro Naba (q.v.) refused him entry into the capital, Alby returned to Dahomey by way of Pama (q.v.). He later saw service in Madagascar and Indochina, and retired in 1910.

ALEXANDRE, GUSTAVE (sometimes PIERRE G.), 1896–1954. French priest. Born near Lille and educated at its seminary, he joined the White Fathers (q.v.) order. Assigned to Ouagadougou (q.v.) as a teacher in 1923, he began work on his two volume dictionary and a grammar of Moré (q.v.) which he completed ten years later. At various times he taught at Manga, Pabré, Guilongou and Bam (qq.v.). His health forced him to return to France 1933–1936, and again in 1938. He was a military chaplain in Tunisia during World War II, after which he returned to Lille and supervised publication of a new edition of his dictionary and grammar by IFAN in 1953.

ALKAALI (Alkali). A magistrate in an Islamic court.

AL-KARI. *see* DEME, AHMADU

AMARIYA. *see* HAMARIA

AMMAN, CAPTAIN. French officer who was commandant at Ouagadougou and at Ouahigouya (qq.v.) around 1898 when the French were establishing control over the Mossi (q.v.).

AMORO. *see* OUATTARA, AMORO

ANIMISM. *see* RELIGION, TRADITIONAL

ANTONETTI, RAPHAEL-VALENTIN-MARIUS. French administrator. Governor, Saint Pierre and Miquelon, 1906–1909; Lieutenant Governor, Senegal, 1914–1915; Lieutenant Governor, Upper Senegal-Niger, 1915–1918; Lieutenant Governor, Ivory Coast, 1918–1924; Governor General, French Equatorial Africa, 1924–1934. He was in charge of the Voltaic area during much of World War I.

ARBOUSSIER, HENRI JOSEPH MARIE D'. French administrator. Graduate of the Ecole Coloniale in 1898. He served much of his career in West Africa. He spoke Arabic, Fulani (q.v.) and Bambara. He was appointed head of the Cercle (q.v.) of Ouagadougou (q.v.) in 1911 and in this position became a close friend of the Moro Naba (q.v.). When World War I began, d'Arboussier quickly recruited a troop of Mossi (q.v.) from the Ouagadougou area and helped take northern Togo from the Germans. Later he was Governor of New Caledonia, 1923–1925, and Resident Commissioner in the New Hebrides, 1921–1923, and 1925–1929.

ARIBINDA. 14°14′N 0°52′W. Town in northern Burkina Faso (q.v.) in Soum province (q.v.) midway between Djibo and Gorom-Gorom (qq.v.). Ancient engravings and remains of post-neolithic peoples have been found in the area. There are many Fulani (q.v.) cattle-breeders in the area and also Songhai and Tuareg (qq.v.) nomads. Barth (q.v.) was in the area in the latter part of July 1853, reporting that he saw elephants and buffalo. The Aribinda Kurumba (q.v.) rulers signed a treaty with the French under Destenave (q.v.) in 1897.

ARLY NATIONAL PARK. A National Park in Burkina Faso (q.v.) located 225 km. southeast of Ouagadougou (q.v.) on the border with Benin (formerly Dahomey). The Pendjari River (q.v.) separates Arly from the Pendjari Reserve in Benin. Water buffalo, lions, hippopotami, wild boar, elephants, antelope and baboons are reported on both sides of the river.

ARNAUD, ROBERT, 1873–1950. French administrator and author. Born in Algiers, he served as Commandant of the Cercle (q.v.) of Ouagadougou and was Inspector of Administrative Affairs in Upper Volta, 1924–1929. He was acting Lieutenant Governor after Hesling (q.v.) left in 1927. Arnaud wrote a number of novels about French colonial life under the pseudonym Robert Randau.

ART. The Bobo (q.v.) are known for their wooden sculpture of cocks, buffalo and antelope, and they produce interesting bronze castings. The Lobi (q.v.) make metal objects, pendants and three-legged wooden stools that are distinctive. The Sénufo are famous for their face and helmet masks, especially the "bird-woman" mask. Their carved doors and rhythm instruments and their statuettes are fine examples of African art. The Mossi (q.v.) produce bronze figurines which depict scenes in daily life and masks. Art in northern Burkina Faso (q.v.) resembles the famous Dogon and Bambara art of Mali.

ASAWAD DESERT. The area south of the bend of the Niger below Timbuktu and Gao and north of 14° north latitude. Tuareg, Fulani and

Songhai (qq.v.) inhabit this dry area, which is mostly in Mali. The area was known to the Hausa (q.v.) as Gourma (q.v.).

ASSEMBLEE DE L'UNION FRANÇAISE (ASSEMBLY OF THE FRENCH UNION). The representative body of the French Union, created by the French Constitution of 1946. It met at Versailles and its functions were purely advisory. Eight persons from Upper Volta served in this assembly between 1948 and 1958.

ASSEMBLEE TERRITORIALE DE LA HAUTE VOLTA (TERRITORIAL ASSEMBLY). Created in 1946 as part of the movement to liberalize the French colonial system by giving people in the French Union territories some representation. Three functioned in Upper Volta between 1946 and 1959.

ASSIMILATIONIST THEORY, FRANCOPHONE. This dates from 1848 when the French National Assembly granted French citizenship to inhabitants of French colonies. It inspired Louis Faidherbe, a French naval infantry captain who assumed leadership of Senegal in 1854. His vision was the assimilation of West Africa into a growing and reforming French empire, including European culture. The assimilationists believed that an African elite would first adopt French language and European culture, such adoption would spread more widely, and Africans might ultimately become full citizens of the French or Belgian mother country.

ASSOCIATION SIX-S. *see* SIX-S

ATTIE, NADER LOUIS. Member of the Third Territorial Assembly, 1957–1959. He was a member of the *Mouvement Démocratique Voltaïque* (MDV) (q.v.) political group from Koudougou (q.v.). He was also briefly a member of the Senate of the French Community, created under the Constitution of the Fifth French Republic in September 1958.

ATYULO. Small group near Léo (q.v.) and the Ghanian border.

AUBARET, ANDRE. Member of the Third Territorial Assembly, 1957–1959 from Kaya (q.v.). He was a member of the Grand Council of *Afrique Occidentale Française* (AOF), and the *Parti Démocratique Unifié* (q.v.).

AUTOCHTONES. Indigenous or very early settlers.

AUTORITE DES AMENAGEMENTS DES VALLEES DES VOLTAS (AVV). The Volta (q.v.) Valley Authority is a scheme to resettle 400,000 to 800,000 people on land cleared of river blindness by the World Health Organization (WHO) onchocerciasis program (q.v.).

AWUNA. One of the Gourounsi (q.v.) groups who live in the border area between Ghana and Burkina Faso.

-B-

BA, OUSMANE. He was born in 1919 at Bafoulabe, Soudan (Mali), and was a graduate of the African School of Medicine and Pharmacy at Dakar. A leader of the labor movement in West Africa, he became active in the *Rassemblement Démocratique Africain* (RDA) (q.v.) after 1947. He was a Minister in the Council of Upper Volta from May 1957 to December 1958, when he was dismissed by Maurice Yaméogo (q.v.), president of the Council of Ministers, because of a disagreement over joining the Mali Federation (q.v.). Bâ returned to the Soudan where he was active in politics until 1968.

BA, YOUSSOUF. Fulani (q.v.), born in Mali, he was interpreter to the French government and adviser to Naba Kom II (q.v.) between the two world wars.

BABATU (Babato, Baba), ?–1901. Also Mahama dan Issa. The third and last leader of the Zerma (q.v.) in Gourounsi (q.v.) country. His forces were divided by the rebellion of Hamaria (q.v.), and he never recovered from the defeat at Gandiaga (q.v.) (modern Ghana) in March 1897. He died in Yendi, Dagomba.

BABEMBA. King or Faama of Kénédougou (q.v.) or Sikasso from 1893 to 1898. He was a brother and successor to Tiéba Traoré (q.v.). Throughout his reign he conducted frequent raids into the area south and west of Bobo Dioulasso (q.v.). In 1898, when the French tried to force a garrison on Sikasso, Babèmba committed suicide.

BABOLO. Tributary of the Komoé (q.v.) southeast of Banfora and north of the border with Côte d'Ivoire. Very few people live in the area and a forest reserve is located there.

BADEMBIE, NEZIEN. Army officer. Commander of Gendarmerie under Lamizana (q.v.) in 1980. He supported Saye Zerbo (q.v.) in November 1980 coup against Lamizana and was minister of interior in the *Comité Militaire de Redressement pour le Progrès National* (CMRPN) (q.v.) government. Badembie was killed just after the November 1982 coup.

BADOT, JEAN. Voltaic ambassador to the Soviet Union beginning in 1974.

BAFING. Local name for the Black Volta (Mouhoun [q.v.]) west of Dédougou (q.v.).

BAGARE (Bakaré). *see* BOULLI

BAGHIAN, USMAN. Imam (q.v.) of Ouagadougou (q.v.) at the time of Moro Naba Wobgho (q.v.). He was host to Krause, Binger and Crozat (qq.v.) when these Europeans visited the Mossi (q.v.) capital 1886–1890.

BAGRE (Bagéré). 12°32′N 1°22′W. Location of a second hydroelectric project, begun in the early 1990s and situated on the Nakanbe (q.v.) southeast of Ouagadougou (q.v.).

BAGUE. Another name for the Sourou river (q.v.), one of the chief tributaries of the Black Volta (Mouhoun [q.v.]).

BALIMA, SALFO ALBERT, 1930– . Lawyer. Born at Tenkodogo (q.v.) and educated in France. Ministry of Foreign Affairs, 1958, and its secretary general, 1960–1961. International Labor Office, 1959. Secretary-general of the Union Africaine et Malgache, 1961–1963. Director of the Department of Labor, Manpower and Vocational Training 1963–1965. Political Cabinet of the UN secretary-general 1965–1970. United Nations Development Program representative in Bangui 1971–1973. Economic counselor to the President 1973. Former president of the Upper Volta-UN Association, and secretary-general of the National Commission to UNESCO. Balima has authored several scholarly articles.

BALLOT, MARIE PAUL VICTOR, 1853–1939. Born in Martinique and educated in France, he was resident to Porto Novo, 1887–1888, 1889–1891. He was lieutenant governor of Dahomey from 1891 until 1900 where he played a major role in leading the movement to claim Gourma (q.v.) for France.

BALOUM NABA. Mossi (q.v.) Palace intendant. One of the chief lieutenants of the Moro Naba (q.v.).

BAM. Province of which Kongoussi (q.v.) is the chief place.

BAM, LAKE. 11°23′N 1°31′W. One of the few permanent lakes in francophone West Africa, it is located north of Ouagadougou (q.v.) on the Nakanbe (White Volta) (q.v.).

BAMA. Village a short distance northwest of Bobo Dioulasso (q.v.). In 1893 the Faama of Sikasso (Kénédougou [q.v.]) died near here while on a raid.

BAMBARA, CHARLES HOUNSSOUHO, 1938– . Military officer and politician. Educated in Ouagadougou, Senegal, and St. Cyr, France. He held several positions in Lamizana's (q.v.) government. Bambara was chief of the Military Cabinet in 1970, and appointed interior minister in early 1974. As head of the Voltaic delegation at a Border Commission meeting between Mali and Upper Volta in September, 1974, he angered the Malian delegation by statements about the use of wells in a disputed area by Malian herdsmen. He was then demoted to minister of information. Bambara became Minister of Posts and Telecommunications in the Comité Militaire de Redressement pour le Progrès National (q.v.) government 1980–1982. He was dismissed from the armed forces in 1982.

BANAKELEDAGA. 11°19′N 4°20′W. An agricultural experimental station is located here, near Bobo Dioulasso (q.v.).

BANBOU. 11°19′N 3°37′W. A forest reserve south of Houndé. There are several forest reserves in this area.

BANCOVILLE. Name that the French often used for Ouagadougou (q.v.) after Lt. Gov. Hesling (q.v.) rebuilt the town with *banco* (mud bricks) in 1920.

BANDAOGO, LAURENT. Voltaic political leader. A member of several coalitions against Yaméogo (q.v.), Bandaogo was a member of the Grand Council of French West Africa, 1948–1957, represented Tenkodogo in the Territorial Assembly (q.v.), 1948–1959, and was president of the Territorial Assembly in 1958–1959.

BANEMA. Town near the Red Volta where Boukary Koutou, later Moro Naba Wobgho (q.v.), lived in exile while his brother was Moro Naba (q.v.). Boukary conducted slave raids into Gourounsi (q.v.) country from here. Binger (q.v.) visited Boukary here twice in the summer of 1888.

BANFORA. 10°38′N 4°46′W. Important town on the railroad (q.v.) southwest of Bobo Dioulasso (q.v.), and headquarters of Comoé province (q.v.). There is an agricultural experimental station here. It is a center for the sale of peanuts (q.v.), rice (q.v.), shea-butter, sesame and livestock. Bricks are manufactured here. The sugar refinery,

SOSUCO, Burkina's first, was opened here in 1975 and is the largest industry in the country. The Cascades of Banfora are nearby, and the Komoé (q.v.) river rises in the neighborhood. Banfora's population in 1985 was about 17,000.

BANFORA, FALAISE OF. Scarp between Banfora and Bobo Dioulasso (qq.v.) in southwest Burkina Faso (q.v.). The railroad (q.v.) climbs the cliff just north of Banfora and follows the line of it some 85 km. to Bobo Dioulasso. The scarp is one of erosion in siliceous sandstone and averages about 150 meters in height.

BANGRE. A small ethnic group in Burkina Faso.

BANGUEL DAO. 14°03′N 0°09′W. Hills north of Dori (q.v.) just to the west of the road to Gorom-Gorom (q.v.). They rise to 392 meters.

BANH. (Ban) 14°05′N 2°27′W. Frontier post 20 km. from the Mali border and 50 km. north of Ouahigouya (q.v.).

BANQUE CENTRALE DES ETATS DE l'AFRIQUE DE l'OUEST (BCEAO). *see* FRANC ZONE

BANTCHANDE (Bancandi, Band-Chandé). Chief of Fada N'Gourma (q.v.) who claimed to be the 23rd successor to Diaba Lompo (q.v.), founder of the Gourma (q.v.) dynasty. He was ruler at Fada N'Gourma (1892–1911) at the time the Europeans first arrived. Unable to establish his control over rebellious subjects, he accepted French protection by a treaty signed on 20 January 1895 with Henri Decoeur (q.v.). In February 1897 French troops under Baud and Voulet (qq.v.) helped him defeat rebels under Yacom-Bato (q.v.). Bantchandé had first gained power in 1892 by the assassination of his brother Naba Yentougoury.

BAOBAB. The *Adansonia digitata* is a tree common to all of Africa. It is also called a monkeybread tree. It has bell-like flowers which hang from the tree in late July and early August. Its ground-up leaves provide a flour that can be made into a calcium-rich sauce. Its fruit has a lemon taste and can also be made into a seasoning powder for cooking.

BAOGHO (Baogo). The 38th Yatenga Naba. He served as ruler of Yatenga (q.v.) from 1885 to 1894. A son of Naba Yemdé (q.v.), he was chief of Zogoré before becoming Yatenga Naba. Soon after he assumed power the sons of Naba Tougouri (q.v.) began a civil war which lasted for the rest of the century. Baogho lived at Sissamba (q.v.) until 1892, when he moved to Ouahigouya (q.v.). He appealed to the French for support in 1894, but he refused to allow the French to mediate between the factions in the rebellion. Baogho collected an army to restore order in his kingdom and attacked the rebels at Thiou (q.v.), where he was killed.

BAONGO, 1954– . The 37th Moro Naba (q.v.). Born Ousmane Congo, the son of Moro Naba Kougri (q.v.) became ruler of the Mossi (q.v.) in 1983 after the death of his father in December 1982.

BAOULE. Another name for the Kou (q.v.). This river is one of the upper tributaries of the Mouhoun (Black Volta) (q.v.). It rises southwest of Bobo Dioulasso (q.v.) and flows northeast until it is joined by the Sourou (q.v.), which flows southward out of Mali.

BARABOULLE (Baraboulé). 14°12′N 1°51′W. Located northwest of Djibo (q.v.) it is one of the two original Fulani (q.v.) chiefdoms (the other was Djibo). It was founded by people who came from the area of Douentza, Mali.

BARANI. 13°10′N 3°53′W. A Fulani (q.v.) town in northwestern Burkina Faso not far from the Mali border. In the 1870s Dian Sidibé (q.v.) established his rule here, and after his death he was replaced by his brother, Ouidi. (See SIDIBE.) Ouidi became an ally of the French against the Samo, Bwa and Marka (qq.v.) of the area.

BARIBA (Barba, Bargu). People who are related to the Yoruba of Nigeria and who live mostly in northern Benin today. A few of them live among the Gourma (q.v.) in southeast Burkina Faso (q.v.).

BARKA. Small Mande (q.v.) ethnic group in western Burkina Faso.

BARRAUD, DR. ALI, 1918– . Physician and political leader from Bobo Dioulasso (q.v.). He was one of the founders of the *Parti Démocratique Voltaïque* (PDV) in 1948. While in the Territorial Assembly (q.v.), 1957–1959, he was associated with the *Parti Démocratique Unifié* (PDU) (q.v.), and was also a member of the Grand Council of French West Africa (*Afrique Occidentale Française*, AOF). His strong support of the Mali Federation (q.v.) in 1959 placed him in opposition to Yaméogo (q.v.). In 1971 Barraud became minister of public health and population, but his opposition to Premier Gérard Ouédraogo (q.v.) caused him to resign in January 1974. The first deputy secretary-general to the *Union Démocratique Voltaïque*

(UDV-RDA) (q.v.) 1970–1974, he became UDV-RDA leader in 1977.

BARRY, DJIBRINA, 1947– . Economist, born in Ouahigouya. Educated in Ouagadougou and Rheims, France, Barry taught at Ouagadougou Technical College, University of Ouagadougou, and National School of Administration. He later became the secretary-general of the Chamber of Commerce, Industry and Crafts, minister of trade, industrial development and mines 1980–1982, and minister of energy and mines 1982.

BARSALOGHO. 13°25′N 1°03′W. Village in Djilgodji (q.v.).

BARTH, HEINRICH, 1821–1865. German explorer who was born in Hamburg and educated in Berlin. With British support, he crossed the Sahara in 1850 and spent more than four years in the Soudan. On 24 June 1853 he set out from Say and crossed the area of modern Burkina Faso (q.v.). He crossed Yagha (q.v.) country, was in Liptako (q.v.), Dori area from 12–20 July, and in Aribinda (q.v.) on 25–26 July. From there he went on to Hombori and to Timbuktu. Barth's five-volume *Travels and Discoveries in North and Central Africa* is one of the greatest books in travel literature.

BASGHA. Holy day of the Mossi (q.v.). On this day the Moro Naba (q.v.) remembers his ancestors and makes offerings at their graves.

BASSANO, EMILE. He was appointed minister of information in the military government in February 1976.

BASSOLET, FRANÇOIS DJOBY. Journalist. He was born at Réo (q.v.) in 1933. His father was chief of the Gourounsi (q.v.). A graduate of a journalism school in Paris, he served on the staff of *Carrefour Africain* (q.v.) and as director of information for the Voltaic government. He authored a history of Upper Volta, *Evolution de la Haute Volta de 1898 au 3 janvier 1966,* which was published in 1968. Bassolet was a member of the *Parti du Regroupement Africain* (PRA) (q.v.) until it was dissolved in 1979, when he joined Joseph Ki-Zerbo's *Union Progressiste Voltaïque* (UPV) (q.v.). He was a member of the National Assembly 1978–1980 during the Third Republic (q.v.).

BASSOLETH, BLAISE. Political leader. He was a member of the Council of the Republic (q.v.), 1958–1959, during which period he represented Koudougou (q.v.) in the Territorial Assembly (q.v.) as a member of the *Mouvement Démocratique Voltaïque* (MDV) (q.v.) party.

He became secretary-general of the *Parti du Regroupement Africain* (PRA) (q.v.). In 1970 he was appointed executive assistant in Lamizana's (q.v.) cabinet.

BATAILLE DU RAIL. The project to lay the rails on the roadbed from Ouagadougou to Kaya (en route to Tambao) (qq.v.) with voluntary labor. Sankara (q.v.) launched the "Battle for the Railroad" in February 1985.

BATIE. 9°53′N 2°55′W. Village 64 km. southeast of Gaoua (q.v.) near the Mouhoun (Black Volta) (q.v.) and the borders of Ghana and Côte d'Ivoire. It is a market for peanuts and shea (qq.v.) nuts, and a sleeping sickness clinic is located there.

BAUD, JOSEPH MARIE LOUIS, 1864–1904. French soldier. He was born at Annecy-le-Vieux and attended Saint Cyr. His first assignment was in Indochina. In 1893 he was sent to Dahomey, where he distinguished himself as an explorer of the hinterlands. From July 1893 to March 1894 he toured the upper part of modern Benin, going on to Say, on the Niger, in January 1895. Baud and Vermeersch (q.v.) were then sent on a mission to reconnoiter the Volta area north of the Germans in Togo and the British in the Gold Coast. They left Carnotville (modern Benin) on 26 March 1895, crossed to the Komoé (q.v.), and descended to Grand Bassam, which they reached 12 June 1895. The Baud-Vermeersch team were then sent to occupy Gourma (q.v.) for France. They left on that mission in January 1897. They were joined by Voulet (q.v.) at Tigba, 17 February, and successfully supported Bantchandé (q.v.) against his enemies at Bilanga two days later. Wounded fighting pillagers at Dendi, on the Niger in October, Baud was returned to France in March 1898. Baud saw service in China during the Boxer campaign in 1900. In 1903 he was assigned to Madagascar, where he died on Christmas day, 1904.

BAWA. *see* NEDEGA

BAZEGA. Province with Kombissiri (q.v.) as its headquarters.

BELI RIVER. Line of intermittent marshes and swamps in the extreme northeast of Burkina Faso along the Mali border. Waters from the Béli flow into the Goroual (q.v.) in Niger. A border dispute in this area resulted in clashes between troops of Mali and Upper Volta in late 1974 and mid-1975. There was a five-day war in December 1985 following allegations of improper census taking by Burkina in Malian territory. In December 1986 the International Court of Justice ruled, and

Burkina received the Béli eastern zone and Mali the western "four village" zone.

BELLA (Bellah). Nomadic herdsmen who live in the Béli (q.v.) River area. They are mostly serfs of the Tuareg (q.v.) in the area.

BELLEHEDE. An intermittent stream which, during the nineteenth century, divided the Muslim states of Macina, Djilgodji (q.v.) and Sokoto.

BEMBA. *see* BURICIMBA

BERE. 11°50′N 1°09′W. Small village southeast of Kombissiri (q.v.) which was visited by Gottlob Krause (q.v.) in August, 1886.

BEREGADOUGOU. 10°46′N 4°45′W. National fishery station near Banfora (q.v.). Also the 717 meter peak which dominates the Banfora Plain.

BERNARD, PIERRE. *Union Voltaïque* (UV) delegate from Bobo Dioulasso (q.v.) in the first Territorial Assembly (q.v.), 1947–1952. He was president of the Assembly in 1950.

BILHARZIA (schistosomiasis). *see* HEALTH

BINGER, LOUIS GUSTAVE, 1856–1936. French administrator and explorer. Binger was born at Strasbourg, Alsace. He joined the French army in 1874, and in time was sent to Senegal, where he learned Bambara and joined Faidherbe's staff. In September 1887 he began his famous trip through the bend of the Niger. Before the end of the month he had reached Samory's (q.v.) camp before Sikasso. He was in Kong (Côte d'Ivoire) on 20 February 1888. In April Binger visited Bobo Dioulasso, and he reached Ouagadougou (qq.v.) in June. There he was unsuccessful in his attempts to get the Moro Naba to accept French protection. From the Mossi (q.v.) capital he went south to Salaga (Ghana), and he returned to Kong by January 1889. The great journey was completed when Binger reached Grand Bassam on the Guinea coast on 20 March 1889. In 1893 Binger became the first Lieutenant Governor of Côte d'Ivoire, a position he held until 1895. After he returned to France he had great influence on French colonial policy.

BINGO. *see* GOURMA or FADA N'GOURMA

BIOUNGO. A Mossi (q.v.) principality to the east of Tenkodogo (q.v.).

BIRIFOR. Molé-speaking people who live near the Ghana-Burkina Faso border, mostly in the area near Diébougou, Gaoua, (qq.v.) and the Mouhoun (Black Volta) (q.v.).

BISSA (BISA). *see* BUSANSI

BITTOU. 11°06′N 0°08′W. Caravan stop below Tenkodogo (q.v.) in Busansi (q.v.) territory, Boulgou province (q.v.). The French built a post here in early 1898 to keep the British out. In the legends of Rialle (q.v.) and Nyennega (Yennega) (q.v.), Rialle lived near Bittou.

BLACK VOLTA (MOUHOUN). *see* VOLTA RIVER

BLE. Small group living in the village of Blédougou (10°35′N 5°16′W) in the Sindou (q.v.) area of southwest Burkina Faso. They belong to the Mande (q.v.) language group.

BLENI. 11°34′N 5°03′W. Village in western Burkina Faso near the border with Mali. Here in the 1860s the army of Kénédougou (q.v.) under King Daula Traoré was defeated by the army of Gouiriko, Tiéfo and Bobo Dioula (qq.v.). The king lost his wife, a sister, and his son, Tiéba Traoré (q.v.), the future Faama of Sikasso, to the allies, who carried the royal family into captivity.

BOBO (Bwaba, Bwa). People who live in the provinces of Mouhoun and Houet (qq.v.) in western Burkina Faso (q.v.) and in the bordering area of Mali. They are closely related to the Mande (q.v.). The name "Bobo" is derived from a Mande word which is a facetious term meaning "a mute person" or a "stammerer." The Bobo call themselves "Bwanu" (singular) and "Bwaba" (plural), and their language "Bwamu." The Bobo are divided into several groups: 1) White Bobo, Bobo Gbè or Kian (Tian); 2) Red Bobo, Bobo Oulé or Tara; 3) Black Bobo, Bobo Fing or Boua. The Dioula (Dyula) Bobo, Niénigé and the Lila or Kadenba are closely associated groups.

BOBO DIOULASSO. 11°12′N 4°17′W. The second city of Burkina Faso and headquarters of Houet (q.v.) province (and formerly chief place of Hauts Bassins Département). It is 320 km. from Ouagadougou (q.v.) and 790 km. from Abidjan. Its elevation is 433 meters. It is an ancient Dioula (q.v.) trade center on the route from Djenne to Kong and Begho. Slaves, kola nuts (q.v.) and gold were once the chief commodities in its markets. Today cotton, peanuts, shea (qq.v.) butter, cattle and sisal are the most important concerns of its merchants. Louis Binger (q.v.) visited Bobo Dioulasso in 1887, followed by Crozat (q.v.) in 1890, Monteil (q.v.) in 1891, and the French army in 1897. The railroad (q.v.) from Abidjan reached the village in 1934, and for two decades the place flourished as the most important commercial center in the area of modern Burkina Faso. Since Independence in 1960, however, Ouagadougou has overshadowed Bobo Dioulasso. Today the city is serviced by an international airport, the railroad and a fine network of roads (q.v.). It is an important processor of agricultural products. There are many interesting tourist attractions in the area.

Two Burkina-based development training organizations, *Centre d'Etudes Economiques et Sociales d'Afrique Occidentale* (CESAO) and *Groupe de Recherche et d'Appui pour l'Autopromotion Paysanne* (GRAAP) (qq.v.), are both based in Bobo Dioulasso. *L'Organisation de Coordination et Cooperation pour la Lutte contre les Grandes Endemies* (OCCGE) (q.v.) was organized in 1968.

BOGANDE. 12°59′N 0°08′W. Market town on the route between Fada N'Gourma and Dori (qq.v.). It is the headquarters of Gnagna province (q.v.).

BOLON. Small Mande (q.v.) group in the area of Orodara (q.v.), southwest of Bobo Dioulasso (q.v.).

BONDE, BAGNAMOU, 1934– . Born in Boni, district of Houndé. He attended primary school at Houndé, 1943–1946, and secondary school in Bobo Dioulasso (q.v.), 1946–1950. He joined the French army and served in Indochina and Algeria. From 1962 to 1963 he received officers' training at Melun, France, after which he returned home to join the police forces, 1964–1966. He served as minister of justice for Lamizana (q.v.) from January 1966 until 1970, and again beginning October 1974.

BONDOUKUY (Bondukoui). 11°51′N 3°46′W. Town on the highway between Bobo Dioulasso and Dédougou (qq.v.). The Catholics (q.v.) built a mission here in 1913. Bitter fighting took place here between Bwa and Marka (q.v.) insurgents and French supporters in November and December 1915 and in 1916.

BONGARE. 13°46′N 0°37′E. Border town southeast of Dori (q.v.) on the Niger border.

BONGHO. *see* BAONGO

BONGNESSAN, ARSENE YE. Army officer. A close associate of Blaise Compaoré (q.v.), Capt. Arsène Yé Bongnessan became national coordinator of the Revolutionary Committees after the Popular Front (q.v.) government took power in 1987.

BONI, NAZI, 1912–1969. Political leader and author. He was a Bwa (Bobo Oulé), born near Dédougou (q.v.). He attended primary school at Ouagadougou, and then studied at the prestigious William Ponty Normal School in Dakar. From 1931 to 1941 he taught school in Ouagadougou (q.v.), and spent the years of World War II in Abidjan. After the war he returned home and entered political life, affiliating in the beginning with the *Union Voltaïque* (UV). Boni served as a deputy for Bobo Dioulasso (q.v.) in the French National Assembly, 1948–1960, and the Territorial Assembly (q.v.) of Upper Volta during most of the same period. He was president of the Territorial Assembly briefly in 1957–1958.

During his political career Boni was leader of the opposition to Mossi (q.v.) and *Rassemblement Démocratique Africaine* (RDA) (q.v.) domination of the country. In 1955 he left the UV and founded the *Mouvement Populaire de l'Evolution Africaine* (MPEA) (q.v.). He helped organize several parties and coalitions designed to check the allies of Houphouët-Boigny in Upper Volta. He supported joining the Mali Federation (q.v.) and attempts to keep French West Africa united, and he did his best to organize an opposition to Yaméogo—all in vain. Boni was defeated in the 1959 elections, and was forced into exile when Yaméogo (q.v.) gained power. While away from home in Mali and in Senegal, he completed a novel, *Crepuscule des temps anciens* (The Twilight of Former Times), a story of his people, the Bwa in the Dédougou area, and the revolt of 1916. In 1966 Boni was allowed to come home again, after his enemy was removed from power, but the military government restricted his political activities. He was killed in an automobile accident at Konkoulgou, 40 km. west of Ouagadougou, in May 1969.

BORGO AIRPORT. The international airport of Ouagadougou (q.v.).

BORODOUGOU CLIFFS. Caves of troglodytes (primitive cave dwellers) 14 km. out of Bobo Dioulasso (q.v.). There are a number of interesting rock engravings located here.

BOROMO. 11°45'N 2°56'W. A town 159 km. east of Bobo Dioulasso on the highway to Ouagadougou (qq.v.). The Mouhoun (Black Volta) (q.v.) is a short distance east of town, and the railroad (q.v,) a few kilometers north. A French post was established here in Gourounsi (q.v.) country in May 1897. It is a center for the shea butter trade and was headquarters of a cercle prior to 1983. A game reserve is just east of Boromo, and elephants were sometimes still seen as recently as 1990.

BORON. Branch of the Dioula (q.v.) in the Bobo Dioulasso (q.v.) area.

BOSSORA. 11°43′N 4°05′W. A village 70 km. north of Bobo Dioulasso (q.v.) on the right or east side of the Mouhoun (Black Volta) (q.v.). Here the Ouattara (q.v.) royal family of Kong went into exile when Samory (q.v.) destroyed their city in 1897.

BOTOU. 12°40′N 2°03′E. Town on the Niger border in Tapoa province (q.v.) at almost equal distance between Kantchari (q.v.) and Say.

BOUGOURIBA. Province in southwest Burkina of which Diébougou (q.v.) is the headquarters.

BOUGOURIBA. Tributary of the Mouhoun (Black Volta) (q.v.) which rises in the area below the Falaise of Banfora (q.v.) and drains Lobi and Bobo (qq.v.) country between Gaoua, Houndé and Bobo Dioulasso (qq.v.). It has its highest water between July and October. Interesting ruins are located in its basin.

BOUKARY KOUTOU. see WOBGHO; MORO NABA

BOULGOU. Province in southeastern Burkina of which Tenkodogo (q.v.) is the headquarters.

BOULKIEMDE. Province located west of Ouagadougou (q.v.) of which Koudougou (q.v.) is the headquarters.

BOULLI (Bagaré, Bangré, Patougou-Naba Bakharé). The 39th Yatenga (q.v.) Naba. He was a son of Yatenga Naba Tougouri (q.v.) and leader of a rebellion of the sons of Naba Tougouri against their cousin, Yatenga Naba Baogho (q.v.). After Baogho was killed at Thiou (q.v.), Bagaré was proclaimed ruler by his followers. Taking the name, "Boulli," the new Yatenga Naba signed a treaty of protection with the French and held his throne only with French support. He died on 27 January 1899 and is buried at Somniaga (q.v.).

BOULSA (Bulsa). 12°53′N 0°59′W. Tradition says it was founded by the *kourita* (q.v.), a son, of Naba Oubri (q.v.). It was the seat of one of the ancient Mossi (q.v.) principalities and is headquarters of Namentenga (q.v.) province. Lying east of Ouagadougou (q.v.), it was once located on important trade routes.

BOUNA (Bona). 12°01'N 3°15'W. Marka (q.v.) village which resisted the Ouahabou and Zerma (qq.v.) forces in 1885 and French army recruiters in November 1915. Yissou (q.v.), one of the leaders of the revolt against the French, lived here. It is 14 km. south of Safané (q.v.).

BOURGES, YVON, 1921– . French administrator and politician. Governor (q.v.) of Upper Volta, 1956–1958. He was born in Paris and educated in Paris, Metz and Rennes. Bourges joined the civil service in 1944 and the colonial service in 1948. He held assignments in both Equatorial and West Africa, reaching the posts of governor of Upper Volta and then high commissioner of Equatorial Africa under the Fifth Republic in the period just before African independence. After returning to France he was elected to the National Assembly and was a minister in several Cabinets.

BOURSOUMA. 13°30'N 2°24'W. Mossi (q.v.) province whose traditions date the formation of the town from the end of the fourteenth century. This means that it is one of the oldest villages in Yatenga (q.v.).

BOUSMA. see BOUSSOUMA

BOUSSANCE, BOUSSANGA (Bissa). see BUSANSI

BOUSSE. 13°06'N 3°23'W. Muslim center near the border of Mali in northern Dafina (q.v.). The village was capital of Al-Kari's state of Marka (q.v.) Muslims at the start of the French period. French forces under Captain Bonaccorsi attacked and sacked the town on 1 July 1894. Al-Kari was killed during the battle.

BOUSSE. 12°39'N 1°53'W. Town about 50 km. northwest of Ouagadougou on the highway to Ouahigouya (qq.v.). It was the headquarters of a cercle prior to 1983.

BOUSSOU. Town northwest of Yako (q.v.).

BOUSSOUMA (Bousma, Busuma). 12°55'N 1°05'W. There are several places in Burkina Faso which use this name, but the most important is the town located just to the south of Kaya (q.v.) and east of Mané (q.v.) near the Boussouma Hills. The town was founded by a son of Moro Naba Koudoumie (q.v.) in the mid-sixteenth century and it became the seat of one of the most powerful Mossi (q.v.) principalities. Often at odds with its neighbors, it fought many wars with Ouagadougou (q.v.). Monteil (q.v.), in May 1891, was the first Frenchman to reach the area. Early in 1899 the area was the scene of bitter last-ditch fighting against the French.

BOUSSOUMA HILLS. Highlands between Kaya (q.v.) and Tikaré to the west. They are about 110 km. north of Ouagadougou (q.v.). Their highest point is about 510 meters.

BRAAHIMA, SEYDU. Leader of the jihad of Usman dan Fodio of the Sokoto Caliphate about 1809. He was the first emir of Liptako (q.v.), ca. 1809–1816.

BRETONNET, HENRI-ETIENNE, 1864–1899. French naval officer. After service in the French Congo, the French expedition up the Niger, and the campaigns to take Dahomey, he was attached to the Monteil (q.v.) expedition in 1895 in Côte d'Ivoire. He took part in the campaign against Samory (q.v.). In late 1896 Bretonnet joined Baud and Vermeersch (qq.v.) in their attempt to take the hinterland of Dahomey ahead of the Germans and British. After a subsequent transfer, he was killed in fighting in 1899.

BUILSA. Grusi people who live along the Ghana-Burkina Faso border. Their area was the center of Zerma (Zaberma) (q.v.) power at the end of the nineteenth century. They are often identified with the Gourounsi (q.v.).

BUR. A noncompulsory initiation practiced in western Burkina among men and women. The ceremony is intended to bring health and success and membership in a secret society or club.

BURICIMBA (sing. buricino). Lineage of Diaba Lompo (q.v.) of Gourma (q.v).

BURKINA FASO. "Land of upright people". The country was renamed by the *Conseil National de la Révolution* (CNR) (q.v.) government on 4 August 1984 one year after assuming power. The name is coined from Moré and Dioula, and "Burkinabè" from Peul (Fulani).

BUSANSI (Bisa, Bisano, Bissa, Boussancé, Busanga). Intrusive Mande (q.v.) who settled the area along the Nakanbe (White Volta) (q.v.) below Tenkodogo (q.v.) by 1300. Some live across the border in modern Ghana and Togo. According to some traditions, Rialle (q.v.), progenitor of the Nakomsé (q.v.) line of Mossi (q.v.) rulers, was Busansi.

BUSU. A division of Yatenga (q.v.).

BUSUMA. *see* BOUSSOUMA

BWA (Bwanu [sing.] and Bwaba [pl.]). Bwamu *see* BOBO

-C-

CAISSE DE SOLIDARITE REVOLUTIONNAIRE (Revolutionary Solidarity Fund, CSR). Established in November 1983 to channel voluntary contributions to provide family relief to the rural population. By mid-1985 nearly 500 million CFA francs had been collected.

CARNAP-QUERNHEIMB, LIEUTENANT KARNAP VON. German officer. He entered the area of modern Burkina Faso (q.v.) in January 1895. Taking the chief of Pama (q.v.) for the paramount chief of all Gourma (q.v.), von Carnap signed a treaty with the chief placing all Gourma under German protection. He also signed treaties in Matiakoali and Kankantiana.

CARREFOUR AFRICAIN (African Crossroad). From 1959 it was the official newspaper of the *Union Démocratique Voltaïque* (UDV-RDA) (q.v.) published at Ouagadougou (q.v.) during the early period of independence. Later it was published by the government information service as a French-language magazine bi-monthly, then weekly by the mid-1980s.

CATHOLICS. Catholics entered the Voltaic area with the French in 1896. The White Fathers (Pères Blancs) (q.v.) founded their first mission at Koupéla (q.v.) in 1900 and at Ouagadougou (q.v.) in 1901. The White Sisters (Soeurs Blanches) arrived a decade later. Father Joanny Thévenoud (q.v.) began his work in Ouagadougou in 1903. Catholicism in Burkina Faso is a tribute to his indefatigable work in behalf of his religion (q.v.). Soeur Marie-André du Sacré-Coeur aggressively fought to change the status of women in Burkina Faso. Abbé Yougbaré (q.v.) became the first African Catholic bishop in West Africa when he was consecrated Bishop of Koupéla on 29 February 1956. In April 1960 Abbé Paul Zoungrana (q.v.) was made an archbishop and later Zoungrana became a cardinal, also firsts for West Africa. The Catholic church has played an extremely important role in the modernization of Burkina Faso.

CAUDRELIER, PAUL CONSTANT, 1858–1914. French officer. Born in Strasbourg, he attended Saint Cyr and was commissioned in the marines in 1881. Assigned the responsibility of occupying the valley of the Black Volta from the Sourou (q.v.) to Bouna (Côte d'Ivoire), he left San (Mali) early in May 1897, established a post at Sono (q.v.), near where the Sourou enters the Black Volta north of Dédougou (q.v.), and took Boromo (q.v.) on 13 May. He destroyed Ouarkoyé (q.v.) on 2 June and troops under his command had completed his mission by the end of the year. In June 1908 Caudrelier was promoted to general and placed in command of all troops in West Africa. He was killed early in World War I while fighting near the Meuse.

CAZEMAJOU, MARIUS GABRIEL, 1864–1898. French officer. Born in Marseille, he attended the Polytechnique and was commissioned an officer in the Engineers. He was under the command of Caudrelier (q.v.) during the occupation of the Black Volta area in 1897. In August of that year he recruited porters in Yatenga (q.v.) for an expedition to Say and Lake Chad. On the trip many of the porters died, causing uprisings in Yatenga. This same expedition disturbed the British, who felt they had prior claim to the area east of Say. Cazemajou was killed on 5 May 1898 in a skirmish near Zinder.

CEDRES ETUDES: REVUE ECONOMIQUE ET SOCIALE BURKIN-ABE. Journal published by the *Centre d'Etudes, de Documentation et de Recherches Economiques et Sociales,* Faculty of Economic Science and Management, University of Ouagadougou (q.v.), beginning in 1977.

CENTRE D'ETUDES ECONOMIQUES ET SOCIALES D'AFRIQUE OCCIDENTALE (CESAO) (West African Center for Economic and Social Studies). The CESAO, based in Bobo Dioulasso (q.v.), is a nongovernment development training organization (NGO) (q.v.) which was started by a Catholic missionary order with long experience in Burkina. It began publication of *Construire Ensemble* in 1973.

CENTRE VOLTAIQUE DE LA RECHERCHE SCIENTIFIQUE (CVRS). Research agency in Ouagadougou (q.v.) founded in 1950 which published materials on Voltaic social sciences and history. The CVRS published *Notes et Documents Voltaïques* (q.v.), *Recherches Voltaïques* (q.v.), and *Travaux et Mémoires du CVRS*. The CVRS later became the Centre National de Recherche Scientifique et Technologique (CNRST). CNRST publications include *Science et Technique: Revue semestrielle de la Recherche au Burkina* (*Série: Sciences Sociales et Humaines*).

CERCLES. Unit of government used by the French in West Africa. Cercles were divided into subdivisions. There were 118 cercles in French West Africa at one time. A commandant was in charge of each cercle. After World War II there were 10 cercles in Upper Volta. Their headquarters were in Bobo Dioulasso, Gaoua, Tougan, Koudougou, Dori, Ouahigouya, Ouagadougou, Kaya, Fada N'Gourma and Tenkodogo (qq.v.). The Constitution (q.v.) of 1970 divided the country into eight departments and 44 cercles. In September 1983 a new system divided the country into 30 provinces (q.v.) under high commissioners, and 250 departments under prefects, with local government divided into districts and villages.

CFA FRANC. *see* FRANC CFA and FRANC ZONE

CHAMBRE DES REPRESENTANTS. Established in May 1993 by the *Assemblée des Députés du Peuple* (National Assembly) as an appointed consultative second chamber of the Assembly as provided for in the 1991 constitution. It had 120 members appointed for 3-year terms.

CHANOINE, CHARLES PAUL JULES, 1870–1899. (Chanoine's given name is listed as Jean Marie in some sources.) Born in Paris, son of an officer who was later to be a general and minister of war, he attended Saint Cyr, was commissioned, and assigned to the Soudan in September 1895. He was second in command to Voulet (q.v.) on the expedition which conquered Mossiland in 1896–1897, directing the campaign to help Hamaria against Babatu (qq.v.) in the Gourounsi (q.v.) area. In 1898 Chanoine was appointed to serve with Voulet on the disastrous Central African Expedition. In November he crossed northern Upper Volta recruiting porters for the march to Lake Chad. He joined Voulet at the beginning of 1899 and they both were killed in the Zinder area in July.

CHERON, E. GEORGES, 1882–1971. French administrator who spent much of his career at posts in West Africa. He served in the Soudan from 1902 to 1915 and again from 1920 to 1937. He was commander of the cercles (q.v.) of Bobo Dioulasso, Banfora, and Kaya (qq.v.). He authored several publications on the peoples of western Upper Volta.

CHRISTIANITY. *see* CATHOLICS, PROTESTANTS

CICATRICES. Decorative scarifications used by a number of ethnic groups. The distinctive scars, *cicatrices,* of the Mossi (q.v.), two series of three lines cut across the cheek, date from Oubri's (q.v.) time, about 1495.

CINEMA. In recent years Burkina Faso (q.v.) has acquired an international reputation in filmmaking. The biennial *Festival Panafricain du Cinéma de Ouagadougou* (FESPACO) (q.v.) has led some to nickname Ouagadougou (q.v.) "the Hollywood of Africa." Since 1986, despite formidable problems in securing finance and film distribution arrangements, Burkina has been producing two full-length feature films a year. Burkinabè directors have won a number of film prizes and increased recognition by international audiences for films such as "Tilai", "Yaaba", "Wend Kuni", "Zan Boko". See IDRISSA OUE-DRAOGO and GASTON JEAN-MARIE KABORE.

CIRANBA. *see* GOUIN

CLIMATE. Most of Burkina Faso (q.v.) lies within a tropical savannah (q.v.) zone (Sudano-Guinean and Sudano-Sahelian), with the area north of Djibo and Dori (qq.v.) in the Sahel (q.v.) zone. The climate is coolest from May to December, and hottest from March to May. Temperatures range from 6.8° to 12.8°C (44°–55°F) in January to 40.2° to 48.2°C (104°–119°F) in the hot season. It is dry from November to February. Most of the rain falls in July, August and September. Rainfall is highest in the southwest and lowest in the northeast, and ranges from approximately 500 mm. to 1,145 mm. annually. Variability of rainfall is characteristic, and drought has been a periodic feature of life in Burkina.

CLITORIDECTOMY (female circumcision). Female circumcision was outlawed in Burkina by the Sankara *Conseil National de la Révolution* (CNR) (q.v.) regime.

COAT OF ARMS. The Coat of Arms of Upper Volta, adopted in 1961, consisted of a shield with RHV on the national colors of black, white and red, representing the three Voltas. White horses stand on each side of the shield, with spears behind and hoes beneath the shield. The motto was Unité, Travail, Justice.

COEFFEE, ROBERT. Born about 1912 in Ouagadougou (q.v.). He joined the French army in 1932 and was a soldier for 25 years. He was secretary of state for defense and veterans in the Lamizana (q.v.) government, 1966–1970.

"COLONEL'S COUP". The 25 November 1980 coup that ousted Lamizana (q.v.) led by Col. Saye Zerbo (q.v.).

COMITE MILITAIRE DE REDRESSEMENT POUR LE PROGRES NATIONAL (CMRPN) (Military Committee for the Enhancement of National Progress). The 31-member CMRPN was established 25 November 1980 following the "colonel's coup" (q.v.) against Lamizana (q.v.) led by Col. Saye Zerbo (q.v.). Bademble Nezien (q.v.) was minister of the interior, Felix Tientarbourn (q.v.), foreign affairs, and

Charles Bambara (q.v.), information. It ruled until Zerbo was overthrown on 26 November 1982.

COMITE PERMANENT INTERETATS DE LUTTE CONTRE LA SECHERESSE DANS LE SAHEL (CILSS). In 1973 eight Sahel nations (Cape Verde, Chad, Gambia, Mali, Mauritania, Niger, Senegal, Upper Volta) established the CILSS, an intergovernmental committee to combat drought in the Sahel (q.v.), headquartered in Ouagadougou (q.v.).

COMITES DE DEFENSE DE LA REVOLUTION (CDRs) (Committees for the Defense of the Revolution). Mass organization to mobilize support for *Conseil National de la Révolution* (CNR) (q.v.) programs and to draw people into political activity in neighborhoods, towns, villages, workplaces, schools, and army units. Created by the CNR immediately following the 4 August 1983 revolution. Patterned on the Ghanian People's Defense Committees, Abdul Salam Kaboré (q.v.) was the first national chairman, and Pierre Ouédraogo (q.v.) the second. The CDRs ceased to function following the 15 October 1987 overthrow of the Sankara (q.v.) government; they were formally dissolved on 18 March 1988. A large number of committees were created within the CDR, such as the *Comité Populaire Activité Jeunesse,* CPAJ (Youth Activities Committee) of the CDR.

COMMUNAUTE ECONOMIQUE DE L'AFRIQUE DE L'OUEST (CEAO). Customs union organization of francophone West African states created in 1973 by Côte d'Ivoire, Mali, Mauritania, Niger, Senegal and Upper Volta. Headquartered in Ouagadougou (q.v.), it replaced the West African Customs and Economic Union (UDEAO). Its activities to promote trade, regional economic development, and specific development projects were supported by a regional corporation tax and it operated a Community Development Fund. Within Burkina the CEAO is perhaps best known for the trial and conviction in April 1986 of the top three CEAO officials for embezzlement (the Senegalese secretary-general Moussa Ngom, Ivoirien director Mohamed Diawara, and Malian director Moussa Diakité) by the Burkinabè People's Revolutionary Court. In 1995 the CEAO was replaced by a new monetary union, the *Union Economique et Monétaire de l'Afrique de l'Ouest* (UEMOA) (q.v.).

COMMUNAUTE FINANCIERE AFRICAINE (CFA). *see* FRANC ZONE and FRANC CFA

COMMUNAUTE FRANÇAISE. An association of French colonies and dependencies in a French Community established by the Constitution of the Fifth French Republic in 1958. In 1960 the French Constitution was amended to allow members to become independent and still retain membership in the Community.

COMOE. Province with Banfora (q.v.) as its headquarters.

COMOE. *see* KOMOE

COMPAORE, BLAISE, 1951– . Military officer and politician. Son of a Mossi (q.v.) chief, he was born in Ouagadougou (q.v.) and received military training in Yaoundé, Cameroon. His wife, Chantal, was the niece of then-president Houphouët-Boigny of Côte d'Ivoire.

Compaoré served in the Para-commando Regiment at Dédougou (q.v.) 1977–1981. He first met Thomas Sankara (q.v.) at parachute school in Rabat, Morocco in early 1978. As commander of the National Training Center for Commandos (CNEC) in Pô, Compaoré was the leader of the 4 August 1983 march on Ouagadougou that overthrew the *Conseil de Salut du Peuple* (q.v.) regime and brought the *Conseil National de la Révolution* (CNR) (q.v.) to power. He was then minister-delegate to the president (Sankara's chief lieutenant in the CNR regime) 1983–1987, and minister of justice 1985–1987. In August 1986 Compaoré, Jean-Baptiste Lingani and Henri Zongo (qq.v.) were appointed coordinators of Burkina Faso.

Compaoré led the coup of 15 October 1987 in which Sankara and 13 of his associates were killed, and led the Popular Front (q.v.) regime. He became president of the Front's Executive Committee in June 1989. Lingani and Zongo, the remaining two officers who organized the August 1983 CNR coup with Sankara and Compaoré, were summarily executed in September 1989 with the after-the-fact allegation that they were plotting against Compaoré.

After considerable jockeying with opposition parties, a new constitution was adopted in June 1991. The *Organisation pour la Démocratie Populaire/Mouvement du Travail* (ODP/MT) (q.v.) adopted Blaise Compaoré as its official presidential candidate in 1991, and also replaced its Marxist-Leninist ideology with a commitment to free enterprise policies. In the December 1991 presidential election, boycotted by all the opposition parties, Compaoré won with an electoral turnout of 25 percent. In the May 1992 National Assembly elections Compaore's ODP/MT won three-quarters of the seats.

Internationally, Compaoré held numerous meetings with Mali's leaders on border demarcation. In December 1988 he attended the Franco-African summit, Burkina's first since 1983. During the 1990s Compaoré increasingly assumed a role as a regional mediator, promoting negotiations between the Togolese government and opposition and between

Tuareg (q.v.) rebels and the authorities in Niger and Mali. That role has not been always clear to all Economic Community of West African States (ECOWAS) (q.v.) members, particularly in relation to the Liberian civil conflict in 1990. The Compaoré government supported the rebel National Patriotic Front of Liberia and initially refused to join the ECOWAS-sponsored military monitoring group amid accusations that Burkina Faso was involved in arms trafficking from Libya and training mercenaries. Troops from Burkina were sent to Burundi in 1993 as part of the Organization of African Unity peacekeeping force. The 1996 Franco-African summit was held in Burkina.

The Sankara regime's quest for self-reliance was abandoned by the Compaoré administration; one of its first moves was to ease restrictions on the import of fruit and vegetables. Despite the fact that Burkina was not as debt-distressed as many other third-world countries, the Compaoré government agreed in 1991 to pressures from international donors and creditors to introduce a three-year Structural Adjustment Program (SAP) and its accompanying austerity, which was backed by the International Monetary Fund and World Bank.

CONFEDERATION AFRICAINE DES TRAVAILLEURS CROYANTS (CATC). Catholic labor union organized in 1956 and headed by Joseph Ouédraogo (q.v.) at one time. It played an important role in political affairs in the period after independence. Also see *Confédération Française des Travailleurs Chrétiens* (CFTC).

CONFEDERATION FRANÇAISE DES TRAVAILLEURS CHRETIENS (CFTC). Catholic labor union directed by Joseph Ouédraogo (q.v.) after 1953. In 1956 it became the *Confédération Africaine des Travailleurs Croyants* (CATC) (q.v.).

CONFEDERATION NATIONALE DES TRAVAILLEURS BURKINABE (CNTB). A trade union (q.v.) group led by Emanuel Ouedraogo.

CONFEDERATION NATIONALE DES TRAVAILLEURS VOLTAIQUES (CNTV). A trade union (q.v.) group.

CONFEDERATION SYNDICALE VOLTAIQUE (CSV), later Conféderation Syndicale Burkinabè (CSB). The largest most radical trade union (q.v.) movement in the country. Soumane Touré, its leader after 1978, was closely linked to the Ligue Patriotique pour le Développement (q.v.), was often imprisoned, and supported the Popular Front (q.v.) coup in 1987.

CONGO, OUSMANE. *see* BAONGO

CONGRES DE DEMOCRATIE ET PROGRES (CDP). A political party formed in early 1996 by merger with President Compaoré's *Organisation pour la Démocratie Populaire/Mouvement du Travail* (ODP/MT), of nine parties grouped around it. Arséne Ye Bognessan, former leader of the ODP/MT, became the CDP's president. The other parties included the CNPP/PSD, the PDR, the MDS, the UDS, the GDR, the RSI, the PPU, and UDPB, the PACT/LS, and parts of the BSP and the GDP. This left only four "solitary" parties in the 107-member National Assembly: the PDP of Joseph Ki-Zerbo (9 seats), Hermann Yaméogo's Alliance for Democracy and Federation (ADF) which supported Compaoré's program (5 seats), the *Rassemblement Démocratique Africaine* (RDA) of Gérard Kango Ouédraogo (4 seats), and the PSB of Benoit Lompo (1 seat).

CONOMBO, DR. JOSEPH ISSOUFOU, 1917–. Moaga physician and political leader. Born in Kombissiri (q.v.), he attended elementary school in Ouagadougou (q.v.), the White Father's School, William Ponty and finally the Medical School at Dakar. He served during World War II in the French army in North Africa, France and Germany. Returning to Upper Volta after the war, he entered medical practice and played an active role in founding the *Union Voltaïque*. He represented his country in the French National Assembly, 1951–1959, and in 1954–1955 he was under secretary of state for the interior in the Mendes-France French government. Conombo was mayor of Ouagadougou from 1960 to 1965, and became director of public health in the military government from 1966 to 1968. In October 1969 he was tried and acquitted of charges of financial misappropriation. In 1971 he became minister of foreign affairs in the Gérard Ouédraogo (q.v.) government, but resigned that post in December 1973 when he was one of the three opposition leaders which led the National Assembly to vote to censure Prime Minister Ouédraogo. As a *Union Démocratique Voltaïque* (UDV-RDA) (q.v.) leader he was elected premier in July 1978 by the National Assembly and served until the Lamizana (q.v.) government was overthrown in November 1980. Conombo was placed under house arrest until he was granted amnesty in August 1984 by the Sankara (q.v.) government.

CONQUIZITENGA. *see* KONKISTENGA

CONSEIL DE LA REPUBLIQUE. The Council of the Republic was created by the French Constitution of 1946. Seven persons from Upper Volta served in this group as representatives from their country between 1947 and 1960.

CONSEIL DE L'ENTENTE. *see* ENTENTE, COUNCIL OF

CONSEIL DE NOTABLES INDIGENES. A Council of Native Notables was established in each cercle during the colonial period for advisory purposes only.

CONSEIL DE SALUT DU PEUPLE (Council for the Salvation of the People, CSP). Government established following the 7 November 1982 coup led by Col. Gabriel Yoryan Somé (q.v.) which deposed Saye Zerbo (q.v.), which briefly called itself *Conseil Provisoire de Salut du Peuple* (CPSP). Surgeon Major Jean Baptiste Ouédraogo (q.v.) was appointed head of state. In late November Jean-Baptiste Lingani became permanent secretary, and Thomas Sankara (qq.v.) became prime minister in January 1983. Sankara, Lingani and others were arrested in May 1983 when President Ouédraogo purged his government of pro-Libyan and anti-French elements and dissolved the CSP. The Ouédraogo regime was overthrown on 4 August 1983 when the *Conseil National de la Révolution* (CNR) (q.v.) came to power.

CONSEIL NATIONAL DE LA REVOLUTION (CNR) (National Council of the Revolution). Governing body formed by Sankara (q.v.) and others upon taking power on 4 August 1983. It was dissolved after the 15 October 1987 coup.

CONSEIL NATIONAL POUR LE RENOUVEAU (National Consultative Council for Renewal). A council of 65 members appointed by President Lamizana (q.v.) in July 1974 with consultative role to the military government.

CONSTITUTION. In February 1959 the Republic (q.v.) of Upper Volta Constitution was approved by a rump session of the Constituent Assembly with most representatives from western Upper Volta absent; it was approved by a referendum on 15 March 1959. Mali Federation (q.v.) membership was not a part of the constitution. It was suspended in January 1966 when Lt. Colonel Sangoulé Lamizana (q.v.) assumed power and Maurice Yaméogo (q.v.) resigned.

The Constitution of 1970 established the Second Republic which ran from 22 February 1971 to 8 February 1974. It provided that the head of state should be the highest-ranking officer of the armed forces; the prime minister should be chosen by the majority party of an elected National Assembly; the prime minister should select his Cabinet from members of the National Assembly and army.

The Constitution of 1977 established the Third Republic which ran from 22 June 1978 to 25 November 1980. It provided for direct universal suffrage by all citizens over the age of 35; for National Assembly members to be elected for five-year terms; for the president to be elected for a seven-year term; for a limit of three political parties; for a restoration of the traditional roles of chiefs.

The Constitution of 1991 which established the Fourth Republic took effect 11 June 1991 after approval by referendum. In addition to the President and National Assembly, it provided for the establishment of an appointed consultative *Chambre des Représentants* with 120 members.

CONSULTATIVE CONSTITUTIONAL COMMISSION. In March 1970 President Lamizana (q.v.) submitted a draft Constitution to a commission made up of leaders of various unions, religions, professional groups and traditional chiefs. The Commission rejected that draft and presented a counter-proposal. Lamizana announced a revised draft at the end of May which voters approved on 14 June 1970.

COTTON. One of the most important features of the French development program of Burkina Faso was the production of cotton. Lieutenant Governor Hesling (q.v.) dedicated much of his energies to the growing of cotton in the 1920s. The results were disappointing. However, cotton production increased 20-fold between 1960 and 1983. By the early 1990s cotton was grown over an area of some 165,000 hectares, mostly in the southwest, raw cotton was Burkina's largest export, and its production doubled in the three years 1985–1988. The main Sofitex (q.v.) textile mill is located in Koudougou (q.v.).

COULIBALY, AUGUSTIN-SOUDE, 1933– . Poet and author. Born in Tin-Orodara, Haut Bassin, he attended secondary school in Abidjan, 1946–1950, and journalism school in Strasbourg in 1962. Between 1955 and 1968 he mimeographed four novels and a number of poems. Employed in the Ministry of Justice in Ouagadougou (q.v.) 1966–1971, Coulibaly was founder and director of the *Cercle d'Activités Littéraires et Artistiques de Haute Volta* 1967–1969. A collector of traditional oral literature of Upper Volta, his best known work is *Les Rives du Tontombili,* a play about the daily life of a country boy.

COULIBALY, DANIEL OUEZZIN, 1909–1958. Political Leader. Born at Nouna (q.v.), in Bobo-Fing territory near the Mali border, he was educated at William Ponty, graduated first in his class, and served on the faculty there from 1935 to 1942. After leaving William Ponty and Senegal, he moved to Côte d'Ivoire, became a close friend and collaborator of Houphouët-Boigny, and became a dominant voice in the *Rassemblement Démocratique Africaine* (RDA) (q.v.). He was elected twice to the National Assembly and once to the Senate from Côte d'Ivoire. In 1956 and early 1957 he joined Joseph Conombo,

Joseph Ouédraogo, Christophe Kalenzaga (qq.v.) and others in the organization of the *Parti Démocratique Unifié* (PDU) (q.v.). In March 1957 he was elected to the Upper Volta Territorial Assembly (q.v.) from Banfora (q.v.). The PDU won a narrow victory, and Coulibaly was called upon to form the first African government for his homeland. In addition to the responsibilities of trying to manage the affairs of Upper Volta, he still continued his role as one of the leaders of RDA. Just three weeks before the referendum on de Gaulle's constitution, Coulibaly died. Maurice Yaméogo (q.v.) assumed his position as head of the government of Upper Volta.

COULIBALY, MME OUEZZIN. Wife of Daniel Ouëzzin Coulibaly (q.v.). Née Makoukou Traoré. Yaméogo (q.v.) appointed her to his Cabinet after he assumed control of the government, so she became the first woman to hold a Cabinet position in any West African government. She was also elected a member of the Senate of the French Community.

CREMER, JEAN HENRI, 1880–1920. Physician and anthropologist. Born and attended school in Brive, France. He was a graduate of the University of Paris and medical school. In 1908 he studied tropical medicine at Greenwich, England. After a trip around the world as a ship's doctor, Cremer joined the French colonial service and was assigned to Kouri (q.v.) as the local physician. He learned Bambara, Fulani (q.v.) and Bobo (q.v.) languages. Transferred to Dédougou (q.v.), he was attached to units dealing with the insurrection in the bend of the Black Volta in 1915 and 1916. After the war he continued to practice medicine, but he also began to compile a large collection of folklore and linguistic information from all over western Upper Volta. Cremer died suddenly at Ouahigouya (q.v.) early in January 1920. His materials were later edited and published by the colonial government and Maurice Delafosse (q.v.).

CROZAT, DR. FRANÇOIS, 1858–1892. Naval physician. After receiving his medical degree at Lyon in 1886, Crozat was assigned to West Africa and in 1890 accompanied Captain Quiquandon to the court of the Faama of Sikasso, Tiéba. From there he was sent on a mission to the Mossi (q.v.) capital at Ouagadougou (q.v.). Crozat left Sikasso on 1 August 1890, went by way of Bobo Dioulasso, Ouarkoyé and Lanfiéra (qq.v.), reaching Ouagadougou on 17 September. He spent two weeks in the Mossi capital, where he was received by Naba Wobgho (q.v.), and was back in Sikasso by 20 November. Two years later Crozat died of a fever at Tengréla, near Banfora (q.v.).

-D-

DA. 12°02'N 3°09'W. A Marka (q. v.) village in the hills southeast of Safané on the Boromo (qq.v.) road. It was once famous for its fetish and was a place of pilgrimage for animists. It was destroyed during the revolts of the First World War (q.v.), 25 April 1916.

DAFINA. The section in the upper bend of the Mouhoun (Black Volta) and Sourou (qq.v.) river valleys where the Dafing, Samo and Fulani border the Bobo (qq.v.) lands.

DAFING (Dafi). The southern Marka (q.v.). A branch of the Mande (q.v.) people. Many of them are Muslims. The term means "black lips," because some of the women of the area dye their lips blue. The Marka probably began to move into this area at the time of the fall of Songhai (q.v.).

DAGARI (Dagaba, Dagara). Molé-speaking peoples who live on each side of the Mouhoun (Black Volta) (q.v.) along the borders of Ghana and Burkina Faso. Those in Burkina Faso began to move into the area about 1820. Most of them live between Diébougou (q.v.) and Boura. They are closely related to the Lobi (q.v.).

DAKOURE, ANTOINE, 1936– . Military officer and government minister. Born at Tampoui, near Ouagadougou (q.v.), he was educated at a local seminary and at St. Louis in Senegal. Dakoure attended a military school for officers, 1960–1962 and for military engineers, 1962–1964. Returning to Upper Volta, he served as aide-de-camp and then head of the military cabinet for President Yaméogo (q.v.). Under Lamizana's (q.v.) military rule he served first as secretary of state for information 1966–1967, then as minister of agriculture 1968–1974. Dakoure was a key figure in the Lamizana government, and headed the CILSS (q.v.) drought control program for the Sahel (q.v.) nations 1973–1975. He became minister of planning from 1974 to 1976. He was opposed to "politicians" running the government. A member of the Brandt Commission on Development Questions in 1977, he was appointed ambassador to Belgium and the United Kingdom, 1981–1983.

DAMIBA, PIERRE CLAVER, 1937– . Economist. Born in Koupéla (q.v.), he graduated from the Center for Economic and Banking Studies in France. He served as director of planning 1962–1966, minister of planning and public works 1966–1971, and *Mouvement de Libération Nationale* (MLN) (q.v.) member of the National Assembly and economic adviser to the president 1971–1972. Damiba was managing director of the *Caisse Nationale des Dépôts et des Investissements* in Ouagadougou (q.v.) 1972–1975, and president of the West African Development Bank in Lomé 1975–1981. Damiba was special adviser for African affairs at the International Finance Corporation, Washington, DC, 1982–1983, and became regional director of the UNDP Africa Bureau in 1983.

DARGOL. Tributary of the Niger that rises east of Dori (q.v.) in Burkina Faso and crosses part of Niger to reach the Niger River.

DARIGMA. A dependency of Yatenga (q.v.).

DARSALAM, DIALLO. Representative of Tougan (q.v.) and member of the *Mouvement Démocratique Voltaïque* (MDV) (q.v.) in the Third Territorial Assembly (q.v.). He was minister of public health in Coulibaly's (q.v.) government, and also held the post of inspector of primary instruction for a time. In 1966 he replaced Yaméogo (q.v.) as leader of the *Union Démocratique Voltaïque* (UDV) until his death in a car crash in June 1969.

DARSALAMI. 11°03′N 4°22′W. Dioula village southwest of Bobo Dioulasso (q.v.) and just above the Falaise of Banfora (q.v.) or Dingasso. Binger (q.v.) stopped here on 8–17 April 1888, and Samory (q.v.) collected his forces here in July 1897.

DAWEMA. Eighth Moro Naba (q.v.). He ruled at the end of the sixteenth century, lived and died at Saponé (q.v.) and was known as a very cruel king. He spent most of his reign fighting the Busansi and Yako (qq.v.). He was a son of Naba Kouda (q.v.).

DECOEUR, HENRI ALEXIS, 1855–1900. French officer. He was a member of the corps of General Dobbs which was charged in 1893 with the exploration of the hinterland of Dahomey. Baud and Vermeersch (qq.v.) were his associates. In 1895 they disputed the rights of the Germans, Gruner and von Carnap (qq.v.), to establish claims in the Gourma area (q.v.). In January 1895 Decoeur signed a treaty with the chief of Pama (q.v.), and on 20 January he signed a treaty with Bantchandé (q.v.) at Fada N'Gourma (q.v.). Later assigned to Senegal, he died at Dakar in 1900.

DEDOUGOU. 12°28′N 3°28′W. Headquarters of Mouhoun province (q.v.) and located on the main road from Bobo Dioulasso to Ouahigouya (qq.v.). It is 160 km. NNE of Bobo Dioulasso, and about 30 km.

south of where the Sourou (q.v.) joins the Mouhoun (Black Volta) at the top of its great bend. Dédougou is the chief place of the Bobo-Fing, and was the center of much violence during the Bwa revolt in 1915–1916. It is famous for its pottery and wood carvings, and is a center for growing and processing peanuts (q.v.) and shea-kernels.

DEFEROBE (DEFORO). Habé (q.v.) group much like the Dogon and Bobo (q.v.). The Déférobé live north of the Mossi (q.v.) along the Mali border and to the west of Liptako (q.v.).

DELAFOSSE, MAURICE. French administrator and author. In 1902 Delafosse was one of the French discoverers of unusual Lobi (q.v.) ruins in the Gaoua (q.v.) area. His books include a 1912 history and survey of Haut-Sénégal-Niger (q.v.) and a major work on the Mandingo language published in 1929.

DELAVIGNETTE, ROBERT, 1897–1976. French administrator. Born near Dijon, educated at the Ecole Coloniale, he joined the colonial service in 1920. In 1922 he was assigned to Niger and later to Ouagadougou and Banfora (qq.v.). He served eight years in Upper Volta and Niger, and he gained a reputation as "the best colonial administrator of his generation." Returning to France in 1936, Delavignette worked at the Colonial Ministry for a year before becoming director of the school which trained colonial administrators. After World War II he served briefly as High Commissioner of Cameroun, 1946–1947. Returning to France, he became a distinguished professor at the National School for Overseas France. Delavignette is author of several books and articles on French colonialism.

DEME, AHMADU (Al-Kari), ca.1845–1894. Marka (q.v.) Muslim leader. Born in Boussé (q.v.). Studied at Lanfiéra (q.v.) and Macina. He made the pilgrimage to Mecca about 1885, and returned home to organize a jihad against his non-Muslim neighbors, the Samo (q.v.). His crusade was beginning to be successful when the French arrived and put an end to Al-Kari's activities. He was killed in a French attack on Boussé, 1 July 1894.

DEME, MAMADU, ca. 1894. Brother of Al-Kari (Ahmadu Demé [q.v.]). Mamadu made the pilgrimage to Mecca with Ahmadu, and the brothers were allied in their jihad against their pagan neighbors. Mamadu became the almamy, or military leader of the Boussé (q.v.) forces, with headquarters at Koumbara (q.v.), near the Sourou River (q.v.). After his brother was defeated and killed, Mamadu tried to escape, but he was killed by the Samo (q.v.). Another brother, Sarku Demé, escaped to join the forces of Babatu (q.v.) in Gourounsi (q.v.) country and went on to fight for Samory (q.v.) after that.

DEPARTMENT. The Constitution (q.v.) of 1970 divided Upper Volta into eight departments and 44 cercles, with each department under a prefect appointed by the central government. In 1974 two more departments were created and all were placed under military officers. The departments and their chief places were: Center (Ouagadougou), Volta Noire (Dédougou), Hauts Bassins (Bobo Dioulasso), Est (Fada N'Gourma), Nord (Ouahigouya), Centre-Ouest (Koudougou), Sahel (Dori), Centre Nord-Plateaux (Kaya), Centre Est (Tenkodogo), and Sud Est (Gaoua). In March 1976 Lamizana (q.v.) announced that the military prefects would be replaced by civilians. In September 1983 a new system divided the country into 30 provinces under high commissioners, and 250 departments under prefects, with local government divided into districts and villages.

DESTENAVE, GEORGES MATHIEU, 1854–1928. French officer. Graduate of Saint Cyr in 1881. Appointed Resident at Bandiagara in 1894, Destenave became the overall leader of the French forces in the conquest of the upper basin of the Volta River between 1894 and 1898. He saw more of Upper Volta during the period of occupation than any other French officer. He was military commandant of Chad from 1900 to 1902, and he served in World War I as a general.

DIABA LOMPO (Jaba Lompo). Founder of the Mossi (q.v.) kingdom of Bingo or Fada N'Gourma (q.v.). There is no agreement on a date, but it may have been the beginning of the thirteenth century. Diaba Lompo was undoubtedly related to the founders of the other Mossi kingdoms, but the exact relationship is not clear. He was a son, a maternal uncle or a cousin of Ouédraogo (q.v.), founder of Tenkodogo (q.v.).

DIABRE, ZEPHIRIN. Politician. Diabre became minister of the economy, finance and planning in March 1994 in the cabinet of Marc Christian Roch Kaboré (q.v.). He had been minister of industry, trade and mines.

DIALLO, ARBA. Politician. Leader of *Ligue Patriotique pour le Développement* (LIPAD) (q.v.), associated with the *Parti Africain de l'Indépendance* (PAI) (q.v.). The LIPAD was one of the two primary civilian political groups that helped make up the *Conseil National de la Révolution* (CNR) (q.v.) coalition. Diallo was minister of foreign affairs in the Sankara (q.v.) government from August 1983 until 19

August 1984 when the first CNR cabinet was dissolved and the LIPAD was removed from the CNR. Diallo was arrested in late 1984 and released in early 1985.

DIAMARE I (Kingdom of Rozi). Abkal Ould Aoudar's *Aguinnass Afriquia,* 1410, tells of a proto-Mossi state east of modern Niamey (Niger) along the Dallol Bosso with a capital called Rozi. This kingdom lasted from the eighth to the twelfth centuries. It ended when the Mossi (q.v.) were forced westward to the banks of the Niger by Berbers.

DIAMARE II (Kingdom of Mindji). This early Mossi (q.v.) kingdom was founded in the twelfth century. It was located on the east side of the Niger between the modern towns of Niamey and Say in the area of Kouré. Diamaré II lasted only a short time and dissolved when a famine (q.v.) forced the people to cross the Niger in search of food.

DIAMARE III. After crossing the Niger from Mindji about 1132 A.D., the early Mossi (q.v.) spread out into the area between the Sirba and Goroubi (qq.v.) rivers (the Torodé area of modern Niger) and founded a third kingdom. From here they gradually infiltrated the whole region that the Hausa (q.v.) called Gourma (q.v.).

DIAN. *see* DYAN

DIANRA. 13°06′N 3°10′W. Samo (q.v.) village near Tougan (q.v.) and not far from the Mali border. President Lamizana (q.v.) was born here.

DIAPAGA. 12°04′N 1°47′E. Headquarters of Tapoa province (q.v.). A town located in eastern Burkina Faso near the Parc National du W (q.v.). The park headquarters for Burkina Faso are located here.

DIEBOUGOU. 10°58′N 3°15′W. A town located just south of the Bougouriba River (q.v.) on the road from Bobo Dioulasso to Léo (qq.v.). It is the headquarters of Bougouriba province (q.v.) and is an important market town. The French took the town in May 1897, and for a long time they maintained a military base here.

DIENDERE, GILBERT. Military officer. Diendéré was an orderly of Blaise Compaoré (q.v.) who became head of national security after Compaoré replaced Sankara (q.v.) as head of state in 1987. He became commander of the National Training Center for Commandos (CNEC) in Pô (q.v.).

DIM (plural DIMDAMBA). King's son. Also see DIMA.

DIM DELOBSOM, A. A. Educated in French schools, he was employed by the French government at Ouagadougou (q.v.), where he distinguished himself by his diligence in the Bureau of Finances in the 1920s. He interested himself in Mossi (q.v.) history and published several important books. *L'Empire du Mogho-Naba,* 1932, and *Les Secrets des Sorciers Noirs,* 1934, both got fine reviews. In 1934 Dim Delobsom was leader of an attack on the activities of Catholic missionaries (q.v.) in behalf of Voltaic women because he felt such activities destroyed traditional culture. He was transferred out of Ouagadougou, but was appointed chief of Sao district by the Moro Naba (q.v.).

DIMA. Autonomous Mossi (q.v.) principalities. Authorities differ on the names of the autonomous principalities, but some of the important ones were Boussouma, Mané, Riziam (Rissiam), Yako, Téma, Boulsa (qq.v.) and Konkistenga (Conquizitenga). A ruler of one of these principalities was a dim (pl. dimdamba).

DIMDAMBA. *see* DIM

DINDERESSO. 11°14′N 4°22′W. Forest reserve just north-west of Bobo Dioulasso (q.v.) along the Kou (Baoulé) (q.v.) river.

DIONOUGA. 14°33′N 1°57′W. Frontier post 70 km. northwest of Djibo (q.v.) on the Mali frontier.

DIOULA (Dyoula, Dyula, Juula). Mande (q.v.) traders, sometimes called Wangara (q.v.), Mandigos or Malinké. By the fifteenth century they had established trade routes from Djenne to Begho. Two of their more important markets were Kong and Bobo Dioulasso (q.v.). Binger (q.v.) listed five major Dioula families as Da'ou, Kérou, Barou, Touré and Ouattara (q.v.).

Mande-Tan is a Mande language subgroup used as a commercial *lingua franca* in western Burkina Faso (q.v.).

DJERMA. *see* ZERMA

DJIBA (Guiba). Village south of Ouagadougou (q.v.). When the oldest son of the Moro Naba (q.v.) reached the age of ten, he was sent here and installed as Djiba Naba. This was the traditional place where the crown prince lived until he was called to be Moro Naba.

DJIBO. 14°06′N 1°38′W. Fulani (q.v.) town 200 km. north of Ouagadougou (q.v.) which is an important market for cattle, sheep and goats. Tradition says Sambo Nana of Douentza (Mali) founded Djibo in the second half of the sixteenth century. The state of Djilgodji (q.v.) developed from Djibo in the seventeenth century. It is headquarters of Soum province (q.v.).

DJILGODJI (Djelgodji, Gilgoji, Jelgoji). Area about Djibo (q.v.). Name of the Fulani (q.v.) state founded in the seventeenth century. From 1826 to 1897 the area was under the control of Macina. The Kurumba (q.v.) have been in the area longer than the Fulani.

DO. The protecting spirit of the Bobo (q.v.). The Bobo society of masks is dedicated to Do. The masks are used in elaborate agricultural and funeral ceremonies.

DOKITA. 9°49′N 2°58′W. Birifor (q.v.) village in the panhandle of Burkina Faso below Gaoua (q.v.) and near the Mouhoun (Black Volta) (q.v.). In 1897 Samory's (q.v.) son, Sarantyé Mory (q.v.), attacked the village and carried off many women. The English tried to help the Birifor defend the village, but were forced to retreat across the Mouhoun (Black Volta) to Wa after their supplies were exhausted.

DORANGE, MICHEL. Merchant, political leader and former French officer. He served in the Territorial Assembly (q.v.) three times between 1948 and 1959 as a representative of Ouahigouya (q.v.). He was a strong Gaullist and supporter of the Yatenga Naba against the Moro Naba (q.v.). Dorange and Gérard Kango Ouédraogo (q.v.) organized the *Progressiste Voltaïque,* the Voltaic section of the Gaullist RPF, in 1952 and later merged with the *Mouvement Démocratique Voltaïque* (MDV) (q.v.). In 1957 Dorange joined the Coulibaly (q.v.) government as minister of interior.

DORI. 14°02′N 0°02′W. Important Fulani (q.v.) center and headquarters of Séno province (q.v.) located in northeast Burkina Faso near the meridian of Greenwich. The area around Dori is called Liptako (q.v.). Barth (q.v.) was here in July 1853. He reported the town to be an extremely dry and uncomfortable place. Monteil (q.v.) signed a treaty with the chief of the town on 23 May 1891, and Destenave (q.v.) reconfirmed that treaty in October 1895. Many different people come and go in the market. Tuaregs and Songhai and Hausa (qq.v.) are commonly seen there. The livestock fair is famous, and the market is known for the decorated blankets traded there. There is an intermittent lake or marsh north of town and hills southwest on the Kaya (q.v.) road. Rainfall averages 567 mm. per year. Dori is called Wendu or Winde by the Arabs.

DOROSIE (Dorossié, Dorobé). A group of people who may have come to their present location from modern Ghana about 1650. They live in the area around Lakosso, west of Gaoua (q.v.). Binger (q.v.) visited their area in March 1888, and called the region Dokhosie. They fought hard against the *sofa* (q.v.) of Samory (q.v.) in 1897. They were often attacked by the forces of Kong.

DOULOUGOU (Dulugu). The 24th Moro Naba (q.v.). Son of Sagha I (q.v.) and his wife, Poko. He opened his reign, about 1795, with a raid against the Busansi (q.v.) for slaves. Later he fought a long war with Boussouma (q.v.) and Mané (q.v.) in which he was finally killed. He was the first Moro Naba to convert openly to Islam (q.v.), though he continued to conduct the ceremonies of the traditional religion (q.v.). He appointed Mustafa Baghian as first imam (q.v.) of Ouagadougou (q.v.), and he built a mosque for his capital. Three of his sons ruled after him.

DOULOUGOU. 11°59′N 1°28′W. An important town in the early history of the Nakomsé Mossi (q.v.). Moumde, son of Oubri (q.v.), by tradition, defeated the Ninisi (q.v.) here and established his rule over the district.

DOUNA. 14°39′N 1°44′W. Frontier post 80 km. north of Djibo (q.v.). Prehistoric archaeological discoveries have been made in the area.

DOUROULA. 12°35′N 3°18′W. Village located in the northern part of Dafina (q.v.), just to the northeast of the bend of the Mouhoun (Black Volta) (q.v.). It was founded by some of the first Marka (q.v.) who came from modern Mali. It was the home of Mamadou Karantao (q.v.). From here Mamadou set out on his jihad against the pagan Bobo, Samo and Kô (qq.v.). He later established a state around Ouahabou, southwest of Boromo (qq.v.).

DROUGHT. *see* FAMINE

DRY SEASON. The period from November to May. The winds during this period are predominantly dry harmattan off the Sahara which blow across Burkina Faso from the north east.

DYAN (Dyan, Dianne, Janni). Lobi-speaking people who crossed the Mouhoun (Black Volta) (q.v.) into the Diébougou (q.v.) area about 1770.

DYULA. *see* DIOULA

-E-

L'ECLAIR. Ouagadougou (q.v.) newspaper of the *Mouvement de Libér-ation Nationale* (MLN) (q.v.) published by Joseph Ki-Zerbo (q.v.) and school teachers in the 1970s.

ECONOMIC COMMUNITY OF WEST AFRICAN STATES (ECOWAS). ECOWAS was created on 28 May 1975 at Lagos, Nigeria. Membership includes Benin, Burkina Faso, Côte d'Ivoire, The Gambia, Ghana, Guinea, Guinea-Bissau, Liberia, Mali, Mauritania, Niger, Nigeria, Senegal, Sierra Leone, Togo, and Cape Verde (which joined in 1977). Its principal objective was the establishment of a customs union and a common market to promote the free movement of people and goods within West Africa. The rival trading interests of member states and the existence of other regional organizations with similar aims have slowed progress toward the initial ECOWAS objectives. International trade between ECOWAS members had actually fallen from $2.3 billion in 1981 to $2 billion in 1990.

In a major departure from its principal objectives, ECOWAS acted as a regional peacekeeper in the Liberian civil war in 1990–1993 through its monitoring group ECOMOG. As a result of the higher profile within West Africa that the Liberian involvement brought, ECOWAS decided to adopt a permanent regional conflict resolution role. A new treaty to replace that of 1975 was signed by all members in July 1993. In March 1996 the central bank governors of ECOWAS states initialled an agreement for a West African Monetary Agency (WAMA).

EDUCATION. Burkina Faso's richest resource is its people—who are well regarded for their diligence, resourcefulness and adaptability. However, the lack of reading, writing and a basic education is a severe constraint for the illiterate 80-85 percent of Burkinabè, with the rate for women still above 90 percent.

In fact, the government has made sustained efforts to improve literacy rates. From 1983 to 1988 more than a thousand schools were built by townspeople and villagers, and the numbers in secondary schools more than doubled. In the 13 years 1975–1988, some 340,000 people were given literacy training. But current expenditure rates would still mean 100 years before all children would find a school place.

In 1989 only 35 percent of the relevant age group were enrolled in primary school, and 7 percent in secondary, which was a decline from some previous years. The government target was to raise it to 40 percent by 1996. The student-teacher ratio worsened from 47:1 in 1975 to

55:1 in 1989. Many students who joined the "Opération Alpha" literacy campaign were keenly motivated, but there is still a serious lack of printed material in local languages to sustain new readers. Overall, the illiteracy rate is probably increasing due to population (q.v.) growth.

The University of Ouagadougou (q.v.) began as a university in 1974. In 1987 there were 3,850 university students, of whom 80 percent held government scholarships. However, the Structural Adjustment Program begun in 1991 cut the proportion of government funding. The Polytechnical University in Bobo Dioulasso (q.v.) opened in 1995.

EFFORT POPULAIRE D'INVESTISSEMENT (Popular Investment Effort, EPI). Monetary deductions from salaries of government employees and civil servants, introduced by the *Conseil National de la Révolution* (CNR) (q.v.) to be used to fund development projects.

EGLISE APOSTOLIQUE. Dissident group of fundamentalist Protestants (q.v.) in Upper Volta/Burkina Faso who split from the Assemblies of God in 1957.

ENTENTE, COUNCIL OF. A regional agreement between Benin, Côte d'Ivoire, Niger and Burkina Faso to coordinate and promote joint policy on economic development, trade and investment. Houphouët-Boigny proposed this group in lieu of the projected Mali Federation (q.v.) when French West Africa was formally dissolved in April of 1959. Togo joined in 1966. Through the Council, Côte d'Ivoire gave some support and aid to the other members.

ENTENTE VOLTAIQUE. One of the earliest political groups in Upper Volta. It was founded by Henri Guissou and Joseph Conombo (qq.v.) as the Voltaic branch of the *Rassemblement Démocratique Africaine* (q.v.), and was also called the *Union pour la Défense des Intérêts de la Haute Volta*. It split in 1954. In the beginning the *Entente Voltaïque* had the support of most of the traditional chiefs.

ETCHEBER, SALVADOR-JEAN. Governor (q.v.) of the Soudan, 1952–1953, and of Upper Volta, 1953–1956.

ETUDES VOLTAIQUES. Publications issued by the Centre IFAN-ORSTOM in Ouagadougou from 1950 to 1959, new style, 1960–1964. Publications included articles and documents on Upper Volta. It was replaced by *Recherches voltaïques* in 1965.

EXPORTS. In the early 1990s the principal exports of Burkina Faso were raw cotton (q.v.), gold (q.v.), livestock, *karité* (shea [q.v.] nuts), hides and skins, sesame seeds, and human labor. Remittances from Burkinabè workers abroad were equivalent to more than two-thirds of export earnings (and more than one-half of official aid) in the 1980–1985 period. France, the ECOWAS countries, and Taiwan (cotton) were the three largest destinations for Burkina's merchandise exports.

-F-

FADA N'GOURMA. 12°04′N O°21′E. Headquarters and chief town of Gourma (q.v.) province and an important market. In Hausa (q.v.) the name means "place where one pays the tax". The people who live in the area call Fada "Noungu". Located on the watershed between the Niger and the Nakanbe (White Volta) (q.v.), Fada is 219 km. east of Ouagadougou (q.v.) and 323 km. southwest of Niamey. It is on the main road between the two capitals. Diaba Lompo (q.v.) created Fada (or Bingo) at the beginning of the thirteenth century. The French reached the town in January 1895, and the Gourma ruler of the time, Bantchandé (q.v.), accepted French protection. From 1933 to 1948 Fada N'Gourma was in Niger. From 1970 to 1983 it was the headquarters of a department.

FAGA. Intermittent stream, a tributary of the Sirba (q.v.). It is formed in the hills between Dori and Kaya (qq.v.) and joins the Sirba near the border of Burkina Faso and Niger.

FAMA. A king.

FAMINE. Famine is a fact of life for the peoples of the Sahel (q.v.). During the reign of the 16th Moro Naba Zanna (q.v.) at about the end of the seventeenth century a great famine occurred. The Zogoré famine of 1832–1839 resulted in thousands of deaths and many people moved out of the northern areas of Burkina Faso. The Kobgha (q.v.) famine began in 1914 and may have killed a fifth of the population of the area of modern Burkina Faso. In 1928 a five-year plague of locusts (q.v.) began which caused widespread famine. Famine resulted from six years of drought during the 1940s. A long drought that began in 1968 led to famine during the 1972–1975 years. In 1973 the Sahel nations set up a committee to combat drought in the Sahel, *Comité Permanent Interétats de Lutte contre la Sécheresse dans le Sahel*. After a respite in the late 1970s, drought occurred again in the early 1980s. The driest years of the twentieth century occurred in 1982–1983. Good rains brought good harvests in 1985–1986, 1989, and 1992–1993, but there were still food deficits in 1988, 1990, 1991, and 1995. Traditionally, farmers in northern Burkina Faso tried to store a three-year grain supply to cope with periodic drought.

FARAMANA. 12°03'N 4°40'W. Frontier village between Burkina Faso and Mali. On 4 December 1974 President Lamizana (q.v.) and President Moussa Traoré of Mali met here and agreed to use peaceful means to resolve their border disputes in the Agacher Region (q.v.) along the Béli River (q.v.).

FARFIGUELA FALLS. Falls on the Komoé (q.v.) near Banfora (q.v.). The drop is some 67 meters.

FASO DAN FANI. Cotton fabric traditionally woven in narrow strips on hand looms and sewn together to make a piece of cloth.

During the Sankara (q .v.) regime's focus on cultural authenticity, a factory-made facsimile was produced in Burkina which became obligatory dress for civil servants and for official occasions.

FERGUSON, GEORGE EKEM, 1864–1897. A Fante, born in Anomabu, Gold Coast, son of a local Methodist minister, Ferguson attended school in Sierra Leone and entered the service of the Gold Coast government in 1881. He traveled the interior of the Gold Coast as a surveyor, cartographer and negotiator of treaties. He signed a treaty with Moro Naba Wobgho (q.v.) in Ouagadougou (q.v.) on 1 July 1894. Ferguson was killed by the *sofa* (q.v.) of Samory near Wa (modern Ghana) in April 1897.

FEROBE. A Fulani (q.v.) clan.

FESTIVAL PANAFRICAIN DU CINEMA DE OUAGADOUGOU (FESPACO). Biennial Pan-African Film Festival of Ouagadougou (q.v.) which began in 1969. *FEPACI Info/FEPACI News* is published by the Federation of Pan-African Film Makers.

FETE AY (Tin Edia). 14°40'N 0°34'W. Highest point in the northeastern part of Burkina Faso 498 meters. The peak is a short distance west of the Mare de Oursi (q.v.) in the Dandéfanga Hills.

FLAG. The official flag of Upper Volta was adopted on 9 December 1959. The colors of the horizontal tricolor of black, white and red represent the three Voltas. The Burkina Faso (q.v.) flag was adopted on 4 August 1984. In the middle of two horizontal bands, red above and green below, is a five-pointed gold star.

FO. 11°53'N 4°31'W. Site of paleolithic archaeological discoveries. The village is northwest of Bobo Dioulasso (q.v.), across the Mouhoun (Black Volta) (q.v.), on the highway to Faramana (q.v.) and San (Mali).

FONDS D'INVESTISSEMENT POUR LE DEVELOPPEMENT ECONOMIQUE ET SOCIAL (FIDES). The Investment Fund for Economic and Social Development was established by the French government following World War II. It was to help finance large increases in expenditure on public works such as ports, airports, roads (q.v.), public buildings and dams in the francophone African countries. In fact, the largest part of the public works funding came not from France, but from African taxes. It was succeeded by the *Fonds d'Aide et de Coopération* (FAC) (French Fund for Aid and Cooperation).

FONIO. A dry-weather-tolerant crabgrass (*Digitaria exilis*) with seeds that are used as a cereal.

FOREIGN AID AND DEBT. Burkina Faso has received substantial aid inflows in recent years. Aid has been as grants, which help reduce the balance of payments deficit, and as concessional loans. Grants accounted for three-quarters of official development assistance in 1992. Following the devaluation of the CFA franc (q.v.) in 1994, the French government offered to cancel the official debt owed to it by Burkina Faso.

Burkina Faso's lack of natural resources imposed a natural constraint on investment projects in the 1970s. The country was therefore saved from overborrowing in the 1980s and consequently was not one of the World Bank's "debt-distressed" Sub-Saharan African countries in the early 1990s. However, the government has sometimes had difficulty in meeting debt-service payments. The Paris Club creditors agreed to a 1991 debt rescheduling as well as a restructuring of debt service falling due in 1993–1995.

In 1991 at the urging of the International Monetary Fund and World Bank Burkina undertook a three-year Structural Adjustment Program (SAP). The goals agreed were to achieve Gross Domestic Product (GDP) growth of 4 percent, limit inflation to 4 percent, eliminate all debt service payment arrears by the end of 1991, reduce the balance of payments current account deficit to 14 percent of GDP, and restore fiscal balance. The program sought increased agricultural production, extended private sector production, improved investment incentives, tax reform, and enhanced public-sector management and human resource development.

In late 1992 and early 1993 there was a resurgence of social tensions, partially related to the government's austerity measures linked to the structural adjustment program.

FOULSE (Fulse, Foulga, Foulsé). *see* KURUMBA

FOURNIER, ALBERIC-AUGUSTE. Lieutenant governor (q.v.) of Upper Volta from January 1928 to December 1932.

FOUSSET, LOUIS-JACQUES-EUGENE. French Colonial administrator. He was secretary-general of Upper Volta under Lt. Governor Hesling (q.v.) and acting head of the government in Hesling's absence. From 1931 to 1935 Fousset was lieutenant governor of Soudan, and in 1935–1936 he was governor of Martinique.

FRA. (Frafra, also Atyulo [q.v.]) Small group south and east of Léo (q.v.), along the Ghana-Burkina Faso border.

FRANC CFA. The currency of the seven west African *Communauté Financière Africaine* nations and the six central *African Coopération Financière en Afrique centrale* nations.

FRANC ZONE. This financial organization is made up of most of the French speaking African states. Although the franc zone had evolved by 1939, treaties were signed in 1962 and redefined in 1972 with the francophone states in central Africa and in 1973 in West Africa. The *Banque de France* guarantees the money issued by the regional central banks, which in turn must hold at least 65 percent of their reserves in the French treasury. Its principal features are freedom to transfer funds throughout the zone, convertibility of the different currencies and fixed exchange rates.

The *Banque centrale des états de l'Afrique de l'ouest* (BCEAO) based in Dakar is the regional central bank for Benin, Burkina Faso, Côte d'Ivoire, Mali, Niger, Senegal and Togo, and issues CFA francs used as currency in the member nations. There is a similar set-up for the six francophone countries in central Africa.

The official exchange rate had been unchanged against the French franc since 1948 at CFAFr 1 = Ffr .02 (1 Ffr = 50 CFAFr). In January 1994 the CFA franc was devalued by 50 percent against the French franc (and thus other major international currencies) in the 13 francophone African countries. Because the exchange rate was determined by forces affecting the French franc, the CFA franc had been overvalued in recent years, thus hurting the export competitiveness of the CFA African countries. However, the devaluation was a French government decision, strongly supported by the International Monetary Fund. To soften the blow to the CFA countries, the French government offered to cancel the official debt owed to it by ten of them, including Burkina, and halved it in the others. By June 1996 the canceled Burkinabè official debt to France totaled CFA Fr119 billion; in 1996 the Paris Club also canceled two-thirds of Burkina's US$80 million debt.

FRANÇOIS, KURT VON (Curt), 1852–1931. Born in Luxembourg, member of a distinguished Prussian military family, he served in the

German army during the Franco-Prussian war. After that war he went with Wissmann and Grenfell to the Congo. In 1888 the German Foreign Office sent him to explore the hinterland of Togo. He traveled through Salaga, to Yendi, to Gambaga, into Busansi (q.v.) country. He was in Zourma, northeast of Pô (q.v.), on 19 April 1888. At Zoaga, near the modern border between Burkina Faso and Ghana, von François and his party were attacked and forced to retreat southward. In 1889 von François was assigned to German Southwest Africa, where he remained until 1895. He wrote several books on his African experiences.

FROBENIUS, LEO, 1873–1938. German explorer and historian. He was a member of the 1910–1912 German Inner-African Exploration Expedition and recorded Mossi (q.v) history and folktales.

FRONT POPULAIRE (Popular Front). Group which took over the government of Burkina on 15 October 1987 and replaced the *Conseil National de la Révolution* (CNR) (q.v.). It was led by Blaise Compaoré, Jean-Baptiste Lingani and Henri Zongo (qq.v.).

FRONT PROGRESSISTE VOLTAIQUE (FPV) (Progressive Voltaic Front). Following Joseph Ki-Zerbo's (q.v.) unsuccessful bid as *Union Progressiste Voltaïque* (UPV) (q.v.) candidate for president in 1978, an alliance of Ki-Zerbo's Marxists and supporters of Joseph Ouédraogo and Frederic Guirma (qq.v.) reorganized as the FPV in 1979. The FPV was banned in November 1980. Several of its leaders were arrested in March 1983 for plotting a coup against the *Conseil de Salut du Peuple* (q.v.) government.

FULANI (Fulbe, Fula, Peul, Peuhl, Toucouleur, Tukolor). One of the major groups of West Africa. They live in every part of the Sahel. In Burkina Faso (q.v.) most of them live in the north and east, especially in Liptako and Gourma (qq.v.). "Fulani" is the Hausa (q.v.) name for these people. They call themselves Fulbe. Their language, Fulfulde, is a *lingua franca* in much of the Sahel (q.v.).

FULSE (Foulsé). One of the earliest groups in the Aribinda (q.v.) area. The terms Ninisi (q .v.), Nioniossé, Lilse (q.v.), Akurumba, Kurumba are all used for the "indigenous" people in this area. Many of the men are known for their excellent work as blacksmiths, and the women for their pottery. Also see KURUMBA.

-G-

GAN. People who live along the Bougouriba River (q.v.) between Bobo Dioulasso and Gaoua (qq.v.). They are probably Mande (q.v.) in origin, and they may have been in Burkina Faso since the sixteenth century. Their leader, Daya Tokpan, put up a brave resistance to the forces of Samory (q.v.), commanded by Sarantyé Mory (q.v.), in June 1897, but the Gan were almost wiped out as a people.

GANDIAGA. Battle between the French and Gourounsi (q.v.) on one side and the Zerma (q.v.) on the other. Hamaria and Chanoine (qq.v.) were in command of the allied armies and Babatu (q.v.) commanded the Zerma. Babatu was defeated. The battle occurred on 14 March 1897.

GANDRAOGO HILLS. 13°29'N 0°39'W. Hills in the area between Dori and Kaya (qq.v.). The chief village in the area is Damkarko Daga. The hills rise to just over 400 meters.

GANIER, FERDINAND, 1848–1900. French officer. He was a native of the Vosges mountain area which the Germans annexed after the Franco-Prussian war. He was commander of the troops in Gourma (q.v.) in 1897–1898, which included Baud and Vermeersch (qq.v.). Ganier established a military garrison at Kodjar (q.v.) from which the French could guard eastern Gourma.

GANZOURGOU. Province to the east of the Nakanbe (White Volta) (q.v.). Zorgho (q.v.), on the Ouagadougou-Fada road, is the administrative center.

GAOUA. 10°20'N 3°11'W. Headquarters of Poni province (q.v.), formerly Lobi (q.v.) cercle. The name means "Gan Way" for one of the earliest groups in the area. From 1902 Europeans have been interested in the ruins of buildings made of blocks of laterite (q.v.) in the area around Gaoua. There is no agreement on the meaning of these ruins. Caves, artifacts, old gold and copper workings and the hills in the area are all interesting to tourists. The area also produces interesting masks and ornaments for dancing. Gaoua is about 140 km. southeast of Bobo Dioulasso (q.v.) and not far from the borders with Ghana and Côte d'Ivoire. It is an important market for peanuts and shea (qq.v.) nuts.

GARANGO. 11°48'N 0°34'W. A market-town 21 km. west of Tenkodogo (q.v.) in Boulgou province (q.v.). It was headquarters of a cercle from 1970 to 1983.

GARANGO, TIEMOKO MARC, 1927– . A native of Gaoua who was educated in Côte d'Ivoire, Senegal and France. He served with the

French army in Indochina and Algeria. Returning home, he became quartermaster-general of the army by 1965. Garango was the Lamizana (q.v.) government's ambassador to Taiwan and then minister of finance and commerce, 1966–1976. His strict austerity measures were unpopular with the bureaucracy but he balanced the budget in 1967 and 1968. He authored *Le redressement financier de la Haute Volta,* published in 1971. Garango was granted clemency in August 1985.

GARATOU. 10°28′N 4°07′W. Hill just south of the Banfora-Gaoua road. Garatou is about 573 meters high.

GARDES DE CERCLE. Native police during French rule. They served as guards of public property, escorts to officials and general peace officers. They were appointed for five-year renewable terms and were responsible to the Military Bureau at Ouagadougou. Most of the guards were veterans of French military service.

GAZARI, ALFA DAN MAHAMA (Gadyari, Gandiara, Gandiari, Gardiara, Gardiare, Gardiari, Gazaré, Kanzaré, Kazaré). Second Zerma (Zabarima) leader. Gazari was born at Kara in the Zerma (q.v.) area of modern Niger. In the 1860s he joined a group of mercenaries under a leader named Alfa Hano (q.v.) who went to Dagomba (modern Ghana) to help the ruler of Dagomba in wars with his enemies. By 1867 the Zerma were busy with raids into Gourounsi (q.v .) country, on the borders of modern Ghana and Burkina Faso. Alfa Hano died about 1870, and Alfa Gazari took his place as leader of the bands of raiders. It was Alfa Gazari who built the Zerma (Zabarima) state, with its capital at Sati (q.v.). Gazari was fatally wounded fighting against the Kipirsi (q.v.) at Goru (Gourou), near Réo (q.v.), in 1883. He was taken back to Sati, where he died. He was replaced by his son, Babatu (q.v.).

GBOUE GBOUE. 12°21′N 3°54′W. Hills between the Voun-Hou and Moun-Hou (q.v.), two branches of the Mouhoun (Black Volta) (q.v.), southwest of Dédougou (q.v.). They are about 457 meters high.

GEAY, LOUIS EUGENE. Administrator of Upper Volta during the absence of Governor (q.v.) Albert Jean Mouragues (q.v.) from March to October in 1950.

GEGMA. The lion clan. The clan of the ruling lineage (Nakomsé [q.v.]) of the Mossi (q.v.).

GNAGNA. Province with Bogandé (q.v.) as its headquarters.

GOARNISSON, FATHER JEAN-MARIE, 1897–d.? . After serving in World War I he received a medical degree and joined the White Fathers (q.v.). He was assigned to Ouagadougou (q.v.) in 1931, where he soon organized a school to train personnel to deal with tropical diseases. He became an authority on trypanosomiasis (sleeping sickness) (q.v.), a disease very common along the banks of the Voltas. Goarnisson also wrote an African Medical Guide. From 1948 to 1960 he served in the Territorial Assembly (q.v.) as a Parti Démocratique Unifié (q.v.) delegate from Ouagadougou.

GOBNANGOU. An elongated plateau from 3–10 kms. wide with a line of cliffs to the north and south of the plateau. The falaises, or cliffs, run some 55 km. between Arly and Diapaga (qq.v.). The cliffs are highest near Yobiri.

GOLD. *see* POURA GOLD MINES

GOMBA (Gombo, gumbo). Okra. A common food in Burkina Faso, it is prized as an ingredient for sauces.

GONDO PLAIN. An inland sea was probably once located in the region southeast of the Bandiagara Scarp (in Mali, northwest of Ouahigouya). The Mouhoun (Black Volta) (q.v.) may have flowed into this sea via the Sourou (q.v.). The Nakomsé (q.v.) reached this area at the end of the fifteenth century, and the Gondo Plain marked their farthest advance north except for an occasional raid. The Songhai (q.v.) clashed with the Mossi (q.v.) in this region on occasion. Part of this area is sometimes called Ghanata.

GOROM-GOROM. 14°26′N 0°14′W. Town which is the headquarters of Oudalan (q.v.) province in northeast Burkina Faso some 56 km. north of Dori (q.v.). Rainfall averages 459 mm. annually.

GOROUAL. River formed by the Béli (q.v.) and Goudébo in the Oudalan (q.v.). When there is rain these intermittent streams may become raging torrents unable to carry off the water fast enough, but for most of the year they are dry beds. The Goroual (q.v.) is a tributary of the Niger.

GOROUBI. Intermittent tributary of the Niger. During the wet season the Goroubi rises in the area about Fada N'Gourma (q.v.) and drains much of Gourma (q.v.). Crossing the Torodé region of Niger, it reaches the Niger River below Say.

GOUIN (Ciranba Goin). Sénufo-related people in the Banfora (q.v.) area. They were active in the fight against Samory (q.v.) in 1897.

GOUIRIKO (Gwiriko). Empire which was an extension of the Kong Ouattara Empire into the Bobo (q.v.) lands. It was founded by Famagan Ouattara (q.v.) in about 1714 and lasted until 1897.

GOURCY. (Gourci) 13°13'N 2°21'W. Holy city and former capital of Yatenga (q.v.). The rulers of Yatenga are installed here. Located north of Yako (q.v.) on the main highway between the two Mossi (q.v.) capitals of Ouagadougou and Ouahigouya (qq.v.), it was headquarters of a cercle, 1970–1983.

GOURMA (Gurma, Gourmantché). The Hausa (q.v.) term for all the right bank of the Niger. The Mossi (q.v.) kingdom of Bingo or Fada (q.v.) probably dates from early in the thirteenth century. Today it is far smaller than it once was, having lost the lands north of the Sirba (q.v.) and the Torodé lands west of Say. At times the French governed the area as part of Niger. The people are called Gourmantché (sing. Gourmanga), but they call themselves "Bimba." Fada N'Gourma is the headquarters of Gourma province.

GOUROUNSI (Sing. is "Gourounga." Variations are Gurunsi, Grunshi, Grussi, Gruinse, Gorise). The meaning of the term is vague and some authorities object to it. Roughly the word is a general name for those people who live in the area between the Mouhoun (Black Volta) on the west and the Nazinon (Red Volta) (qq.v.) on the east, and Koudougou (q.v.) in the north and Wa (Ghana) in the south. The Sissala, Kasséna, Awuna, Nouna, Léla, Isala and Frafra (qq.v.) are usually included in any list of the Gourounsi. Since these peoples were highly individualistic, they never organized any centralized government to protect themselves, so they were often raided by their more powerful neighbors. The area had almost been conquered by the Zerma (Zaberma) (q.v.) when the British and the French arrived there 1886–1890.

GOVERNOR. Between 1919 and 1933 three French administrators served as lieutenant governor of Upper Volta: Frédéric-Charles-Edouard-Alexandre Hesling (q.v.), 1919–1927, Alberic-Auguste Fournier (q.v.), 1928–1932, and Gabriel-Omer Descemet, 1932. A fourth administrator, Henri-Louis-Joseph Chessé, closed out affairs as Upper Volta was divided between the Soudan, Niger and Côte d'Ivoire. With the recreation of the colony in 1947, five more men served as head of the government: Gaston Mourgues, Albert-Jean Mouragues (q.v.), Roland-Joanes-Louis Pré (q.v.), Salvador-Jean

Etcheber (q.v.), and Yvon Bourges (q.v.). Then, as Upper Volta went through the process of becoming independent, Paul-Jean-Marie Masson (q.v.) held the difficult post of high commissioner.

GROUPE DE RECHERCHE ET D'APPUI POUR L'AUTOPROMOTION PAYSANNE (GRAAP). Located in Bobo Dioulasso (q.v.), the GRAAP is a development training non-government organization (q.v.) started by a Catholic missionary order with long experience in Burkina.

GROUPEMENT D'ACTION POPULAIRE (GAP). An Islamic party organized in 1966 as a breakaway from the *Union Démocratique Voltaïque* (UDV). Its leaders were Massa (q.v.) Nouhoun Sigué and Saïdou Ouédraogo. It was banned in February 1974. The GAP was unsuccessful in electing any delegates to the National Assembly in the April 1978 elections.

GROUPEMENT DE SOLIDARITE VOLTAIQUE (GSV). Group founded by members of the *Mouvement Démocratique Voltaïque* (MDV), *Mouvement Populaire de l'Evolution Africaine* (MPA) and *Parti Social d'Education des Masses Africaines* (PSEMA) (qq.v.) to oppose Ouëzzin Coulibaly (q.v.). Joseph Conombo, Gérard Ouédraogo and Nazi Boni (qq.v.) were leaders of the union.

GRUNER, HANS. Member of the German team that tried to annex Gourma (q.v.) in 1895.

GRUNSHI. *see* GOUROUNSI

GUIBA. *see* DJIBA

GUILONGOU. 12°37′N 1°18′W. Religious center of the central Mossi (q.v.). It is the place where Oubri (q.v.) lived and it is the location of his relics.

GUIRMA, FREDERIC FERNAND. Diplomat. Guirma was educated in France and the United States. He was the first ambassador of Upper Volta to the United States, 1960–1963, and representative to the United Nations. He was also the author of two collections of folktales. A critic of the Zerbo (q.v.) government, Guirma was arrested by the Conseil de Salut du Peuple (q.v.) in March 1983 and released in June.

GUISSOU, HENRI, 1910–1979. Political leader. Guissou was a member of the French National Assembly from 1948 to 1960 and a member of the Territorial Assembly (q.v.) from Koudougou (q.v.) from 1948 to 1952, as well as a member of the Senate of the French Community, 1959–1961. One of the leaders of *Union Voltaïque* (UV) and *Parti Démocratique Unifié* (PDU) (q.v.). Guissou was a political ally of Joseph Conombo (q.v.). He served as ambassador to France, 1961–1963 and 1966–1972, and Germany 1963–1966.

GUITTI. Mossi (q.v.) kingdom founded early in the sixteenth century by a son of Oubri (q.v.) named Wumtanago. It was southeast of the Falaise de Bandiagara in the border area between modern Mali and northwest Burkina Faso.

GUR. Term which designates the languages of the Voltaic area.

GURENSI (Gorensi). People in the area of Ziou in the area near where the Nazinon (Red Volta) (q.v.) crosses from Burkina Faso into Ghana. They are related to the Nankanse and Tallensi.

GURMA. *see* GOURMA

GURUNSI. *see* GOUROUNSI

GWIN. *see* GOUIN

GWIRIKO. *see* GOUIRIKO

-H-

HABE (Haabe, singular Kado, Kaado). A Fulani (q.v.) term meaning all non-Fulani people. In Murdock, Habé is used for the Bobo (q.v.), Dogon, Tombo and related groups in the area south of the Cliffs of Bandiagara in Mali and Burkina Faso.

HAMALLI. A Muslim brotherhood.

HAMARIA (Amariya). Gourounsi (q.v.) leader who was born in the Builsa-Sissala (q.v.) area on the Ghana-Burkina Faso border. While very young he joined the Zerma (Zaberma) (q.v.) forces and quickly became a leader of the Zerma under Alfa Gazari and Babatu (qq.v.). In 1894 he joined a revolt against the Zerma and formed an alliance with the French against Babatu in 1896. In March 1897 the French and Hamaria administered a decisive defeat to Babatu at Gandiaga (q.v.) (modern Ghana). The French recognized Hamaria as the "King of the Gourounsi". In April 1915 he was accused of causing trouble, dethroned and sent to prison.

HANO, ALFA DAN TADANO. Zerma (Zaberma) leader. In the 1860s he came to Dagomba (modern Ghana) from Zerma (modern Niger) with a group of mercenaries to serve the ruler of Dagomba. Tradition has it that Hano was a deeply religious Muslim, who had studied at a Koranic school in Salaga, and who may have made the pilgrimage to Mecca. Soon after he arrived in Dagomba, Hano began to go on raids into the pagan Gourounsi (q.v.) country between the Red and Black Voltas. The trade in captives was so profitable that Hano and his men soon moved to the Gourounsi area and began to establish control over the area. He died about three years after this move. His successor as Zerma (q.v.) chief was Alfa Gazari (q.v.). All dates for Hano are disputed. He may have died about 1870.

HARMATTAN. *see* DRY SEASON

HAUSA (Haoussa). The Hausa are a large and diverse West African group of people, most of whom live in northern Nigeria and southern Niger. Hausa traders, particularly of kola nuts from the forest areas, may have come to modern Burkina Faso as early as the fourteenth century. A trade route across Gourma developed.

The Hausa language is the main commercial *lingua franca* of West Africa.

HAUT-SENEGAL-NIGER. The name for the French Soudan from 1904 to 1920. The upper Volta basin was under this jurisdiction before March 1919.

HEALTH. In 1991 the infant mortality rate was put at 135 per 1,000, one of the highest in the world. Average life expectancy was estimated by the World Bank in 1990 at 48 years. Malnutrition and related diseases are common in Burkina. Trypanosomiasis (sleeping sickness), malaria and bilharzia are endemic. Most health care is still located in the cities. Reflecting the massive number of water projects constructed in the 1980s, a UNICEF report stated that 78 percent of the population (q.v.) had access to safe water by the early 1990s — the third-highest proportion in sub-Saharan Africa. Beneath that statistic, more people in urban than in rural areas presumably have access to safe water.

The government's most spectacular success was the massive "Vaccination Commando" in November 1984 in which more than 2.5 million children were vaccinated against measles, meningitis and yellow fever. Onchocerciasis (river blindness) (q.v.) has been endemic in many river valleys; a UN-assisted control program (1974–1986) has brought it under control.

HENDERSON, FRANCIS B., 1859–1934. British naval officer. In November 1896 Lt. Henderson was sent into the territory north of the Gold Coast to salvage as much of the area as he could from the French or Germans. He failed in an attempt to rescue the people of Dokita (q.v.) from Sarantyé Mory (q.v.) in March 1897, and after Wa fell to the forces of Samory (q.v.) a few weeks later, Henderson was captured and carried to Samory's camp. After a conference with Samory, Henderson was released and allowed to return to the Gold Coast. He was commissioner of the Gold Coast 1896–1902 and of Asante 1902–1904. He was invalided home to Britain in 1904, but returned to active duty during World War I and retired as a commander in the British navy.

HENRIC, FRANÇOIS, 1871–1955. French medical officer who was attached to the Voulet-Chanoine (qq.v.) mission that conquered the Mossi (q.v.) in 1896–1897.

HESLING, FREDERIC-CHARLES-EDOUARD-ALEXANDRE, 1869–. First lieutenant governor (q.v.) of Upper Volta after it was established in 1919. Edouard Hesling has been criticized for working the people of Upper Volta too hard; the judgment may be just, but he didn't work the people any harder than he worked himself. He believed in economic development, and he accomplished much for Upper Volta. He started a campaign to improve the lot of women. He established a postal system and a network of telephones and telegraph. By the end of his administration Upper Volta had the best system of roads (q.v.) in West Africa. Hesling began a system of vocational training in the country, and hundreds of Africans were employed in government service. Modern Ouagadougou (q.v.) was started during his term. His greatest concern was agriculture. He established experimental stations and worked hard to increase production of cotton (q.v.), rubber, tobacco, peanuts (q.v.), or any other crop which might have a chance to grow in the parched soil of Upper Volta. Finally, Hesling asked the traditional chiefs for their advice and persuaded them to give support to his programs for economic development. After he left his position in Ouagadougou, he continued his campaign for making West Africa economically self-supporting. On the eve of the world depression in 1929, he was director of the Colonial Cotton Association in Afrique Occidentale Française.

HIPPOPOTAMES, MARE AUX. 11°34′N 4°10′W. Forest reserve and lake to the northeast of Bobo Dioulasso (q.v.). The lake drains into the Mouhoun (Black Volta) (q.v.).

HOUET. Province of which Bobo Dioulasso (q.v.) is the headquarters. In 1985 this was the most heavily populated province in Burkina.

HOUNDE. 11°30'N 3°31'W. Town located about 100 km. northeast of Bobo Dioulasso (q.v.) on the main road to Boromo and Ouagadougou (qq.v.), and headquarters of a cercle, 1970–1983. It was the scene of bitter fighting in the insurrections against the French in 1915 and 1916.

HUGOT, CAPTAIN. French officer under Destenave (q.v.) who took part in the conquest of the Volta area. He was defeated in an attempt to take the Bwa village of Massala, east of Dédougou (q.v.), in 1897. A short time later he defeated Babatu (q.v.) at Douce (modern Ghana), and he died soon after, 27 July 1897, at Funsi, between Wa and Navrongo.

-I-

ID AL FITR. The Muslim holiday (Breaking of Fast) which comes on the first night after the end of the fasting month of Ramadan (q.v.).

ID AL KABIR. *see* TABASKI

ILBOUDO, PIERRE, 1936– . Diplomat. Born in Kombissiri (q.v.), educated at Dakar and in France, Ilboudo was in the Voltaic delegation to the United Nations, 1961–1963. He came home in 1963 to become secretary-general to the ministry of foreign affairs. In January 1966 he was made secretary of state for foreign affairs in the Lamizana (q.v.) government. He was then named ambassador to West Germany, and later was ambassador to the European Economic Community.

IMAM. Leader of a mosque.

IMPORTS. In recent years Burkina Faso imported large amounts of machinery, iron and steel products, vehicles and tires, foodstuffs, petroleum products, pharmaceuticals, and other intermediate goods to be processed locally. France and Côte d'Ivoire are the main sources of Burkina's imports.

INDEPENDANTS D'OUTRE-MER (IOM). Political bloc founded by Léopold Sédar Senghor of Senegal in the French National Assembly in 1948. It was replaced by the *Convention Africaine* (CAF) in 1957. In Upper Volta the IOM was supported by the Union Voltaïque. Nazi Boni, Joseph Conombo, Henri Guissou and Mamadou Ouédraogo (qq.v.) were leaders in Upper Volta. Their common denominator was opposition to Houphouët-Boigny and the Rassemblement Démocratique Africaine (RDA) (q.v.).

INDIGENAT. The Indigénat decree of 30 September 1887 gave French colonial administrators disciplinary powers over territories ruled by them. Sixteen offenses were made punishable by not more than 15 days in jail or a 100 franc fine. This power did not extend to persons who were French citizens, and it was abolished in 1946.

INFORMAL SECTOR. The informal sector is made up of small businesspeople, traders, artisans, and peddlers. Such small-scale and labor-intensive production activities often survive and thrive outside the formal economy by avoiding government regulations and taxes. Burkina's informal sector has long played a significant role in agriculture and the service sectors. In addition, however, the World Bank notes that Burkina's informal sector produces more than 40 percent of the value-added in manufacturing.

   While informal-sector activities are frequently equated with smuggling, they still often play an essential role in employment creation and development of the country's industrial activity. And in the absence of a dynamic large-scale industrial sector, those seeking a livelihood may have little option. According to correspondent and consultant to non-governmental agencies Robin Sharp, informal sector trade between Sahelian countries—avoiding border formalities—is estimated to often exceed official trade by two or three times. In the case of gold smuggling informal sector trade may exceed official trade by ten times.

INTERCROPPING. Two or more complementary crops grown in the same field. Intercropping works best when crops of different heights, root depths and maturity periods are combined. Common examples include cowpeas intercropped with millet (q.v.), or groundnuts and sorghum (q.v.). The amount of nitrogen that can be "fixed" improves significantly with intercropping, and yields are substantially higher than when crops are grown singly. Writer and development consultant to international agencies Paul Harrison estimates that 80 percent of the farmlands of West Africa were so cultivated in the mid–1980s. Alley cropping is a promising adaptation which has already proved effective in the humid tropics, but the results are less clear in semi-arid areas.

L'INTRUS. Independent newspaper launched in Ouagadougou (q.v.) in mid–1986.

ISALA. One of the Gourounsi (q.v.) peoples who live along the Burkina Faso-Ghana border to the east of Léo. They were especially hard hit by the Zerma (q.v.) raids for slaves. Isala (Sissala, Sisala) is a Voltaic language spoken to the south of Léo.

ISLAM. Muslims began to enter the Voltaic area before 1400. Hausa, Dioula, Yarsé, Fulani and Songhai (qq.v.) merchants and nomads infiltrated the area peacefully at times. At other times they tried to impose their religion (q.v.) on the local residents by force. Doulougou (q.v.), the 24th Moro Naba, who began his reign about 1795, openly affiliated with Islam, and the first mosque was built in Ouagadougou (q.v.) during his reign. Moro Naba Koutou (q.v.) became a Muslim in 1960. Despite the Mossi (q.v.) history as the most important people of the West African savanna (q.v.) to have resisted Islam, it is a major force in Burkina Faso today. Perhaps 40 percent of the population (q.v.) is Muslim (roughly, half the Mande [q.v.], one quarter of the Mossi, and most of the Fulani).

Most Burkinabè Muslims are not interested in theology, but many of the more devout affiliate with one of several Muslim sects. The Qadiriyya (q.v.) is the oldest and largest Muslim sect. The Tijaniyya (q.v.) are a much smaller and more devout group who tend to be very rigid in their beliefs and practices. There are a few members of the Hamallist movement, a reformist group, and of the Ahamdiyya, a modernist sect.

IZARD, MICHEL. Researcher in Burkina 1957–1971, mostly in Yatenga (q.v.). He was chief of research of the *Centre national de la recherche scientifique* (CNRS) and headed the *Centre voltaïque de la recherche scientifique* (CVRS), 1968–1969.

-J-

JAMAA. Newspaper started by Blaise Compaoré's Popular Front (q.v.) in December 1988.

JAMAHIRIYA (Jamaa community). In Libyan socialism a society ruled by community groups. In Burkina, the 7,300 Comités de Défense de la Révolution (CDRs) (q.v.) of the Sankara (q.v.) period were modeled after these.

JELGOBE. Fulbe (Fulani) (q.v.).

JEUNE AFRIQUE. French-language weekly published in Tunis and Paris since 1947.

JEYAABE (singular jeyaado). Fulani (q.v.) slaves.

JUULA. *see* DIOULA

-K-

KABORE, ABDUL SALAM. Major. Minister of public health and national chairman of the Comités de Défense de la Révolution (CDRs) (q.v.), 1983–1984.

KABORE, ALBERT LEONARD, 1944– . Government administrator, Ministry of Posts and Telecommunications, 1967– .

KABORE, ALFRED. A civilian appointed minister of foreign affairs to replace Saye Zerbo in the Lamizana (qq.v.) government in February, 1976. He served in the post less than a year.

KABORE, BOUKARY. Army officer. Sankara (q.v.) loyalist who led opposition to Blaise Compaoré (q.v.) following the October 1987 coup in which Sankara was killed. Known as the "Lion of Bulkiemdé", Kaboré led the failed revolt at Koudougou (q.v.) air base, then escaped to exile in Ghana.

KABORE, CHARLES BILA. Secretary-general in President Lamizana's (q.v.) office in 1974.

KABORE, CYRILLE, 1947– . Geologist. He was educated at ORSTOM (q.v.) and served as a geological engineer and head of operations of the Bureau of Geology and Mines, Ouagadougou.

KABORE, DOMINIQUE, 1919–1972. Born near Ouagadougou, Kaboré studied at William Ponty and at the French School for Overseas Administrators. In 1958 he joined the French civil service and was assigned to Bobo Dioulasso (q.v.) in 1959. In 1960–1962 he was assigned to President Yaméogo's Economic and Social Council, and he was commissioner at Fada N'Gourma (q.v.), 1962–1966. Kaboré held several cabinet posts under Lamizana (q.v.).

KABORE, FRANÇOIS DE SALLES. Secretary general of the Organisation Voltaïque des Syndicats Libres (OVSL) (q.v.) at the time it was founded in 1960. It was Upper Volta's third labor union in size at the time. He was released from prison in 1983.

KABORE, GASTON JEAN-MARIE, 1951– . Film director. Educated at Bobo Dioulasso, Ouagadougou, and Paris, Kaboré served as the director of cinema (q.v.), Ouagadougou, 1977– . "Wend Kuni" is one of his better-known films, and "Zan Boko" was a prize-winner at the 11th FESPACO (q.v.) in 1989.

KABORE, JOHN BOUREIMA, 1932– . Burkinabè diplomat. He was ambassador to the United States and jointly to the United Nations from 1963 to 1966. After 1966 he was attached to UNESCO in Paris.

KABORE, PHILIPPE ZINDA, 1919–1947. Born in the cercle of Koudougou (now Boulkiemdé province [q.v.]), he attended William Ponty from 1937 to 1939, and the School of African Medicine and Pharmacy from 1939 to 1942, becoming a pharmacist. In 1946, while western Upper Volta was still part of Côte d'Ivoire, he was elected to the French National Assembly. At the time he was the youngest member of that body. He had the support of Houphouët-Boigny's party. In Paris he played an important role in the recreation of Upper Volta as a separate territory. He died suddenly in May 1947, a few days after having denounced the Moro Naba (q.v.) in Ouagadougou (q.v.). The most prestigious secondary school in Ouagadougou was named for him.

KABORE, ROCH MARC CHRISTIAN, 1954– . Politician. Educated in law at Dijon University. Kaboré joined the Front Populaire (q.v.) in 1987, and became a power in the *Organisation pour la Démocratie Populaire/Mouvement du Travail* (ODP/MT) (q.v.). He was the head of the International Bank of Burkina (BIB), 1984–1989; minister of transport and communication, 1989–1990; and minister of state without portfolio, 1990–1992. Kaboré remained in government, becoming the minister of planning and finance, 1992–1993; minister of state in charge of relations with institutions, 1993–1994; and prime minister as of March 1994.

KABORE, VICTOR. Diplomat. He served as Burkina's ambassador to Ghana, France, the United Kingdom and Italy.

KADIOGO. Province that includes Ouagadougou (q.v.). It is Burkina's smallest province in geographic area.

KADO. Earliest known people in the Yatenga (q.v.) area. As the Mossi (q.v.) moved into Yatenga, the Kado and Dogon were forced northward into modern Mali.

KALENZAGA, ANDRE-DESIRE, 1942– . Economist, civil servant. Educated in Kaya (q.v.), Ouagadougou, France, Kalenzaga became the director of internal commerce, 1972–1974 and director of the

Office of the Minister of Public Works, 1974–1975, and ultimately the director-general of Air Volta in 1975.

KALENZAGA, CHRISTOPHE. Representative of Kaya (q.v.) in the Territorial Assembly (q.v.) from 1947 to 1959, and president of the Assembly in 1949. Kalenzaga, a member of *Union Voltaïque* (UV) and *Rassemblement Démocratique Africaine* (RDA) (q.v.) sat in the Council of the French Republic, 1948–1960 and also the Senate of the French Community. He served briefly as minister of justice in Yaméogo's government in 1959, but was dropped. He later became ambassador to West Germany.

KAMPTI. 10°08′N 3°27′W. Village 40 km. southwest of Gaoua (q.v.) and near the border of Côte d'Ivoire in Poni (q.v.) province. It is surrounded by a number of hills. It is a market for peanuts (q.v.), shea nuts and sesame. The area was often raided from Kong in the nineteenth century, and it was on Sarantyé Mory's (q.v.) route in 1897.

KAMSAOGHO NABA. One of the ministers of the Moro Naba (q.v.), he was a eunuch without heirs and was entrusted with the rule of some of the most wealthy of the districts under Ouagadougou (q.v.).

KANGO. The 26th Yatenga Naba, 1757–1787. Son of Naba Nabasere, he came to power in 1754, but was overthrown before the year was out and forced to live in exile for three years, first in Kong, and then in Ségou, while Wobgho (q.v.) ruled in his stead. Finally, with the aid of Dioula (q.v.) of Kong and Bamhara of Ségou, Kango returned to Yatenga (q.v.) and regained his position in 1757. The foreign mercenaries that restored Kango were called the Kambwêse. They were probably the first men to use guns in Yatenga, and they caused much trouble for Naba Kango before they were finished. Kango is known as a great Naba. He moved the capital from Gourcy to Ouahigouya (q.v.). Most of his reign was occupied with military exploits. He crushed the old nobility and took away their powers. He sacked and burned Yako (q.v.). He warred against his former benefactors of Ségou, and he pushed the borders of Yatenga to the east at the expense of Djibo (q.v.). It is said that all Yatenga was forested, and that there were elephants and lions before Kango. He burned the forests to expand the available agricultural lands. The results were disastrous. The soil dried and began to blow away. Water disappeared from the beds of streams. And the wild life moved south in search of better forage. When Kango died in 1787 he left no sons.

KANTCHARI. 12°29′N 1°31′E. Headquarters of a subdivision of Tapoa province (q.v.) on the road from Fada N'Gourma (q.v.) to Niamey, only 20 km. from the Niger border.

KAPOK. The *Bombax costatum* is also known as the silk cotton tree and may grow to 45 meters. The silky material around the seeds is used as a fiber, and oil, similar to cottonseed oil, is extracted from the seeds. The tree is often seen in the western part of Burkina Faso.

KARABORO. People who live along the border with Côte d'Ivoire in the area where the Komoé (q.v.) enters Côte d'Ivoire. Binger (q.v.) crossed through their lands, which he called Karaborola. These people were astride the route Samory (q.v.) took north in 1897.

KARAMA, YOYE. Fetish priest who was one of the leaders in the resistance to the French in the Banfora (q.v.) area in 1915–1916.

KARAMADJI. Leader of the Tuareg (q.v.) insurgents against the French in the area north of Dori and Aribinda (qq.v.) in 1916.

KARAMOKO. A local teacher in a Koranic school.

KARAMOKO BA. *see* SANOGO, MAMADOU

KARANKASSO. 10°45′ N 3°50′ W. Site of a proposed irrigation dam on the Bougouriba (q.v.)

KARANTAO, AL HADJ MAMADOU. A Marka (q.v.) Muslim whose father, Sidi Mamadou Karantao, came from Mali to the Volta area about 1790. Mamadou was born at Douroula, studied at Safané (qq.v.), and after a pilgrimage to Mecca, returned to his homeland to organize a jihad against his pagan neighbors. He established a small state at Ouahabou, near Boromo (qq.v.), about 1850. Mamadou died about 1878.

KARANTAO, KARAMOKO MOKTAR. Son of Al Hadj Mamadou (q.v.). He consolidated the position of his family in Ouahabou (q.v.) and formed an alliance with the Muslim Zerma (Zaberma) (q.v.) forces against the pagans between the Black and Red Voltas. Binger (q.v.) visited Ouahabou 20-26 May 1888. In his report, he says that Karamoko was a nephew of Mamadou, and guesses that Karamoko was 55-60 years of age. Karamoko waged war with the Bobo, Dyan and Dagari (qq.v.) with varying success, but his dreams of conquest were ended by the arrival of the French. In 1897 he was forced to accept French suzerainty.

KARANTAO, M'PA. Chief of Ouahabou (q.v.) at the start of World War I. In 1915 the French arrested M'Pa and sent him to prison for complicity in the insurrection that swept across the whole area west of the Black Volta. He served time in prison, but was eventually pardoned. By 1920 he was receiving a salary as chef du canton of Ouahabou, a position he continued to hold through the 1920s.

KARFIGUELA FALLS. 10°42'N 4°49'W. Waterfalls on the Komoé (q.v.) northwest of Banfora (q.v.). Above the falls the Komoé is called the Koba.

KARGOUGOU, MOUSSA. Member of *Union Nationale des Indépendants* (UNI) who became minister of foreign affairs in Lamizana's (q.v.) 1977 government, until 1980.

KARITE. *see* SHEA TREE

KASENA (Kasséna, Kasene, Kasuna). One of the Gourounsi (q.v.) groups. They live in the area between Pô (q.v.) and Navrongo (Ghana). They were one of the peoples that the Zerma (q.v.) hit the hardest.

KAYA. 13°05'N 1°05'W. Town 98 km. northeast of Ouagadougou on the road to Dori (qq.v.). The headquarters of Sanmatenga (q.v.) province, it is a market of some importance in the area, and bauxite deposits are in the hills nearby. There are several places by this name in Burkina Faso.

KAYAO. 12°01'N 1°51'W. Kayao is a small village near the Nazinon (Red Volta) (q.v.) and to the southwest of Ouagadougou (q.v.). At one time it was a small Mossi (q.v.) state bordered by Gourounsi and Kipirsi (qq.v.) lands. The Zerma (q.v.) overran them a few years before the French arrived.

KAZARE. *see* GAZARI

KEEMSE. The ancestors.

KENEDOUGOU (Kenedugu). Sénufo kingdom whose chief city was Sikasso in modern Mali. At one time much of the southwestern corner of Burkina Faso was part of this kingdom, and the rulers of Kénédougou frequently raided the area, trying to reestablish their authority. The kingdom fell to the French in May 1898. Kenedougou and Leraba are the western-most provinces in Burkina. Orodara (q.v.) is the headquarters of Kenedougou province.

KIBARE. Newspaper published in the 1970s during the Lamizana (q.v.) period.

KIBGA. Ancient people of Yatenga (q.v.) who no longer exist.

KIBSI (Kibissi). People who lived in the Yako (q.v.) area before the Mossi (q.v.) arrived. Some were displaced northward toward Bandiagara with the Dogon, others retreated southward and became the Kipirsi (q.v.).

KIPIRSI. (Singular is Kipirga). One of the many groups who were in Burkina Faso (q.v.) before the Mossi (q.v.). They lived in the hills between the Nazinon (Red Volta) and Mouhoun (Black Volta) (qq.v.), which are sometimes called the Kipirsi Mountains, northeast of Ouagadougou (q.v.). Most of their villages were constructed with defense in mind. They were often attacked, by the Mossi, by the Zerma (q.v.), by others, and they tenaciously fought back. Many of their number were captured and taken into slavery (q.v.). They made submission to the French in May of 1897. Tauxier (q.v.) said they were Gourounsi (q.v.). George Peter Murdock did not list them at all.

KITI. Term adopted by the *Conseil National de la Révolution* (CNR) (q.v.) in August 1985 for a presidential decree.

KI-ZERBO, JOSEPH, 1922– . Historian. Born at Toma (q.v.), a Somogo town on the road between Tougan and Koudougou (qq.v), he was educated in mission schools at Ouagadougou, Bamako and Bobo Dioulasso. He became a teacher in 1943 and three years later went to Dakar to write for *Afrique Nouvelle.* Receiving a scholarship, he next went to Paris to study history. His thesis was on the "French Penetration of the Countries of the Upper Volta." He received his degree in 1956. Now a Marxist, Ki-Zerbo taught in France for two years before he returned to West Africa in 1958 to campaign against de Gaulle's referendum. He married a daughter of Lazare Coulibaly, a Malian trade unionist, and for a year they taught in Sekou Touré's independent Guinea. Then they returned to Ouagadougou (q.v.), to teach at the Lycée.

By 1965 Ki-Zerbo had been made director of education and was busy plotting the overthrow of the government. After the January 1966 coup he was director of education and sports under Lamizana (q.v.) until 1968. In 1969 he was a leader of the *Mouvement de Libération Nationale* (MLN) (q.v.). In 1972 he published *Histoire de l'Afrique Noire.* While a professor of history at the University of Ouagadougou, he served in the National Assembly, 1970–1974. In

1974 Ki-Zerbo became Voltaic representative to UNESCO. He was the *Union Progressiste Voltaïque* (UPV) (q.v.) candidate for president in 1978, but came in last (Lamizana was elected). In 1979 the UPV reorganized as the *Front Progressiste Voltaïque* (FPV) (q.v.), an alliance of Ki-Zerbo Marxists and Joseph Ouédraogo's (q.v.) supporters. The FPV was banned in November 1980. Ki-Zerbo was placed under house arrest in October 1983 by the Sankara (q.v.) regime, but he moved to Côte d'Ivoire in December.

In March 1984 the National Union of African Teachers of Upper Volta (SNEAHV) (q.v.) leadership, associated with Ki-Zerbo's banned FPV, called a teachers' strike. The Conseil National de la Révolution (CNR) (q.v.) dismissed 1,500 teachers the next day. In July 1985 Ki-Zerbo and his wife, in self-imposed exile since October 1983, were sentenced by a Ouagadougou court for tax evasion and illicit enrichment. In 1991, after eight years in exile, Joseph Ki-Zerbo returned to Burkina to attend the conference of the National Convention of Progressive Patriots/Social Democratic Party (CNPP/PSD). In 1993 following a CNPP-PSD split, six of its parliamentary members joined Joseph Ki-Zerbo's new *Parti pour la démocratie et le progrès*. He was editor of the UNESCO *General History of Africa*, Vol. I.

KI-ZERBO, JOSEPHINE. Wife of Joseph Ki-Zerbo (q.v.). In 1966 she, as principal of the Ecole Normale des Filles, sent her students to join anti-government demonstrations. She was also a leader of the Mouvement de Libération Nationale (MLN) (q.v.). Also see KI-ZERBO, JOSEPH.

KO. The language of the Kipirsi (q.v.), although they are sometimes known by that name.

KO (Koo, Kona, Koko). A Gourounsi (q.v.) group who live near Boromo (q.v.).

KOALA. Small Gourmantché state in western Liptako (q.v.) which was destroyed during the Fulani (q.v.) jihad about 1807.

KOBGHA. The 41st Yatenga Naba. The oldest son of Naba Wobgho (q.v.), he served as chief of the Yatenga (q.v.) Mossi (q.v.) from 1902 to 1914. He belonged to the Tougouri (q.v.) faction in Yatenga, and he had the support of the French. He died on 2 September 1914 and was buried at Somniaga (q.v.). His successor was the Chief of Bogoya, who became Yatenga Naba Tougouri. The famine (q.v.) which started in 1914, the year Kobgha died, is called the Kobgha Famine.

KODJAR. 11°50′N 1°55′E. Center of French activity 1894–1897 in the colonizing race between the French, English and Germans.

KOLA (Cola) NUTS. The trade in kola nuts from the forest areas of modern Ghana and Côte d'Ivoire probably started in the fourteenth century. Dioula-Mande (q.v.) merchants dominated the trade across the Black Volta area, and Hausa (q.v.) traders followed the route across Gourma (q.v.).

KOLOKO. 11°05′N 5°19′W. Village on the route from Bobo Dioulasso (q.v.) to Sikasso (Mali), about 8 km. from the border. It is 662 meters above sea level. The Plandi (q.v.), westernmost tributary of the Mouhoun (Black Volta) (q.v.), begins nearby.

KOM. Boussouma Naba, 1890 to 1907. He resisted the French when they first came to his area, but made submission to them in 1897. He used the fact that his legs were paralyzed as an excuse to avoid the French as long as he could. He was a staunch Muslim who could speak Arabic. He tried to force his people to accept Islam (q.v.), and when Pissila (q.v.) rejected a Muslim he had appointed as chief of that town, he had the place destroyed in 1907. The French forced him to leave Boussouma (q.v.) for this action and he later died in exile in Ouagadougou (q.v.).

KOM I. The 22nd Moro Naba (q.v.). Son of Naba Zombre (q.v.) and Habo, a Yarsé (q.v.). Since his mother was Muslim, she had him circumcised. Kom later required that all his court be circumcised, and it became a Mossi (q.v.) custom to have males and females circumcised after this time. The tomb of Habo in Ouagadougou (q.v.) is highly honored today. While Kom did not become a Muslim, Muslims were highly respected during his reign. Kom ruled in the latter part of the eighteenth century.

KOM II, 1890–1942. The 32nd Moro Naba, he ruled from 1905 to 1942. He was 16 when he followed his father, Naba Sigiri I (q.v.), as Moro Naba. He was Djiba (q.v.) Naba during the reign of his father. His name was Saidou Congo. The Mossi (q.v.) electoral college opposed him because of his youth, but the French forced his election. Soon after he came to power, the French began to reorganize the kingdom. This caused a revolt in 1910, but the French easily restored order. Kom II was in power when Upper Volta was created in 1919, and he supported Hesling's (q.v.) campaign to improve the economy of the new colony. He supported the French in two world wars. In dismay he witnessed the dismemberment of Upper Volta at the end of 1932 because of the depression. Again and again he protested the use of Mossi labor outside the colony. In 1938 Kom II went to Abidjan to defend Mossi interests and was successful in getting an administrator assigned to Ouagadougou (q.v.). In 1939 he received the Legion of Honor from the French. He lived to see the French humiliated in 1940, but he took no pride in their defeat. He died in March 1942, at a low point in both French and Voltaic history.

KOMBERE. A Mossi (q.v.) nobleman regional chief.

KOMBISSIRI (Kombisiri, Kornbissiguiri). 12°04′N 1°20′W. Headquarters of Bazéga (q.v.) province located 40 km. southeast of Ouagadougou (q.v.), on the main road south to Ghana. Moro Naba Sawadogho built the mosque here, and it is an important Muslim center. In December and January 1896–1897 Moro Naba Wobgho (q.v.) tried in vain to rally his people against the French. Wobgho returned here a last time in June 1898, accompanied by a British officer, Northcott (q.v.), who was ready to support the cause of the deposed Moro Naba against the French. The matter had already been settled in far-away Paris, so Northcott and Wobgho retreated down the road to the south. There is a Forestry Service research nursery at Nagbangre, just out of Kombissiri.

KOMOE. The Komoé (Comoé) rises in the hills of Sindou (q.v.) and on the Sikasso Plateau behind the Cliffs of Banfora (q.v.). Near Banfora the river has several falls which have some potential for hydraulic energy. The Komoé (Koba above Karifiguela Falls), and its tributary, the Léraba (q.v.), form the border between Côte d'Ivoire and Burkina Faso for some distance. The Komoé is one of the major rivers of Côte d'Ivoire, reaching the ocean near Grand Bassam.

KOMOE, CHUTES DE LA. Waterfalls north of Banfora (q.v.) where the Komoé (q.v.) comes down the *Falaise de Banfora* (q.v.). It is just off the Orodara (q.v.) road.

KOMONO. Area in Burkina Faso just north of the border with Côte d'Ivoire, and east of the Komoé (q.v.). Binger (q.v.) stayed at the main Komono village, Niambouanbo from 17-25 March 1888. In May, June and July 1897 they fought bravely against the *sofa* (q.v.) of Samory (q.v.).

KOMPIENGA. Site of hydroelectric dam project which was begun in 1985 and completed in 1988 and was designed to meet approximately one-quarter of Burkina's power needs. It is located on the southern border with Togo southeast of Tenkodogo (q.v.) in Gourma province (q.v.).

KONE, BEGNON DAMIEN. Political leader from Banfora (q.v.). He was a supporter of Ouëzzin Coulibaly and Maurice Yaméogo (qq.v.) in the *Rassemblement Démocratique Africaine* (RDA) and *Parti Démocratique Unifié* (PDU) (qq.v.). He was a member of the Territorial Assembly (q.v.) from 1952 and its president from 1959–1965 as well as a member of the Grand Council of Afrique Occidentale Française (AOF) 1953–1957 and the Council of the French Republic 1958–1959. After the coup of January 1966 which brought Lamizana (q.v.) to power, Koné was arrested and sentenced to hard labor for misappropriation of public funds. He was released in August, 1970.

KONE, LEANCE. Son of the former president of Territorial Assembly (q.v.), Begnon Koné (q.v.). He was sentenced in 1968 for attempting to overthrow the Lamizana (q.v.) military government and restore Yaméogo (q.v.).

KONE, RENE LOMPOLO, 1921–1974. Playwright, editor, politician. Born in Tingrela (where his grandfather had been king) near Banfora (q.v.) and a graduate of the Lycée William Ponty, he was editor of *Trait d'Union,* 1954–1957. Koné was a cultural leader in Ouagadougou (q.v.) during the Yaméogo (q.v.) years. In January 1961 he was appointed Yaméogo's foreign minister. He was director of the National School of Administration under the Lamizana (q.v.) regime. He wrote several plays, among them *Soumaloue, La légende de Teli Soma Oulé* and *La jeunesse rurale de Banfora.*

KONGOUSSI. 13°19'N 1°32'W. Headquarters of Bam province in the Boussouma hills near the southern end of Lake Bam (qq.v.).

KONKISTENGA. *see* DIMA

KONKOLI. 12°33'N 3°02'W. Hill east of Dédougou (q.v.) and on the left bank of the Mouhoun (Black Volta) (Bafing [qq. v.]). It is over 550 meters above sea level.

KONKOLOKO (Komkouliko, Konkouliko). 11°58'N 3°20'W. Sometimes called the peak of Konkoloko. It is the highest of the Kipirsi (q.v.) hills at 630 meters above sea level. It is southwest of Safané (q.v.) and just north of the modern railroad (q.v.).

KONKOMBA. Very early people in the Gourma (q.v.) area of eastern Burkina Faso.

KONSEIGA, GEORGES. Member of the *Union Voltaïque* (UV) who was a delegate from Ouagadougou (q.v.) in the first Territorial

Assembly (q.v.). In 1948 he became the Territorial Assembly's first president.

KORSIMORO. 12°49'N 1°04'W. Town northeast of Ouagadougou (q.v.) on the road to Kaya (q.v.). An earth and rock dam is located here.

KOSSI. Province in western Burkina Faso with headquarters at Nouna (q.v.). Also the name of a tributary of the Mouhoun (Black Volta) (q.v.).

KOTOU, MONT. 10°17'N 3°03'W. Hill between Gaoua (q.v.) and the Mouhoun (Black Volta) (q.v.) and near Mont Koya (q.v.). These hills are about 600 meters above sea level and they are sacred to the people of the area.

KOU (Baoulé [q.v.]). Tributary of the Mouhoun (Black Volta) (q.v.) which rises just north of the Falaise of Banfora (q.v.), and a very short distance from where the Komoé (q.v.) begins. The Kou flows northward for many kilometers, crossing the Bobo Dioulasso-Sikasso highway near Koumi (q.v.) and gradually turning northeast until it joins the Voun Hou and the Sourou (q.v.) north of Dédougou (q.v.). Between Koumi and Dinderesso (q.v.), west of Bobo Dioulasso (q.v.), an experimental rice (q.v.) project was undertaken by the Taiwanese.

KOUDA (Kuda). The 7th Moro Naba (q.v.). He was the son of Koudoumie and Pabré (qq.v.). He reigned in the sixteenth century, and spent most of his time at Saponé (q.v.). He drowned in a stream nearby. Two of his sons followed him as Moro Naba.

KOUDOU FALLS. 11°41'N 2°19'E. Waterfall on the Mékrou River in the extreme southeastern end of the country. It is on the Benin border and in the *Parc National du W* (q.v.).

KOUDOUGOU. 12°16'N 2°22'W. Third city of Burkina Faso and headquarters of Boulkiemdé (q.v.) province, it is located on the railroad (q.v.) and on the road from Ouagadougou to Dédougou. It is about 96 kms. from Ouagadougou by highway, and about 112 kms. from Dédougou (qq.v.). A purported grave of Naba Oubri (q.v.) is located here and is a place of sacrifices (Also see GUILONGOU). It was the site of troubles in World War I, and was under the government of Côte d'Ivoire from 1933 to 1947. It is the headquarters of the Sukomse religious sect. It was also the hometown of President Yaméogo (q.v.), and he is said to have built a home there valued at more than

US$800,000. Sofitex (q.v.) (formerly Voltex), a modern textile factory which began operation in 1971, operates at Koudougou, and leather goods, shea products and cotton (q.v.) are important products marketed there. Chromium and manganese (q.v.) have been found in the neighborhood in small amounts. The city is located at about equal distance between the Mouhoun and Nazinon (qq.v.), and sleeping sickness is a major health problem in the area.

KOUDOUMIE (Kumdumye, Kundumie). The 6th Moro Naba (q.v.), he was a son of Naba Nyingnemdo (q.v.). Tradition says that he bribed the electors to elect him while his cousin, Yadéga, was away at war. Yadéga, with the aid of his sister, Pabré (q.v.), broke away and formed the independent kingdom of Yatenga (q.v.), with a capital at Gourcy. The split between the Mossi Nakomsé (q.v.) allowed a number of semi-autonomous principalities to develop. Koudoumie ruled probably in the middle of the sixteenth century, but some authorities would place the start of his reign as early as 1337. During Koudoumie's rule large numbers of Muslim Yarsé (q.v.) began to move into the area between the Red and White Voltas. Koudoumie frequently raided into Gourounsi (q.v.) territory and he died in an attack on Boromo (q.v.), perhaps the only time a Moro Naba marched with an army across the Black Volta. Koudoumie is buried at Zawara.

KOUGRI (The Rock), 1932–1982. Oldest son of Moro Naba Sagha II (q.v.), he became the 34th Moro Naba in 1957. At birth he was named Moussa Congo, and in time he became Guiba Naba. He studied in France from 1946 to 1950. In pursuit of his desire to be a constitutional monarch, Kougri tried to take over the government of Upper Volta on 17 October 1958, but was checked by the army. Little more than a month later he shocked traditionalists by marrying a young girl, Ouedraogo Diarra, in a civil ceremony. He opposed membership in the Mali Federation (q.v.), and was very unpopular with Yaméogo (q.v.) supporters. In August 1968 Lamizana (q.v.) made him commander of the Voltaic national order, a purely ceremonial position. In 1960 he became a Muslim. He died in December 1982.

KOULANGO. People who live along the west bank of the Mouhoun (Black Volta) (q.v.) around Bouna (q.v.).

KOULIDIATI, JEAN-LUC NOUNDICA. Military captain. Appointed minister for information in 1976, and killed in a helicopter crash four months later. Also killed were national gendarmerie commander Boude Bagnamou and director of information services Bernard Koueobo.

KOUMBARA. 12°54'N 3°24'W. The main Marka (q.v.) military base during the Boussé (q.v.) crusade against the Samo (q.v.) at the end of the nineteenth century. It is located near the Sourou river (q.v.) and about 40 km. from Boussé.

KOUMI. 11°08'N 4°26'W. Village located about 13 kms. west of the Orodara-Sikasso road near the Kou River (q.v.) bridge. The area is famous for prehistoric sites, basket making, masks, dancing and the Grand Seminary of the White Fathers (q.v.), *Saint-Grégoire le Grand*.

KOUNDA. 12°07'N 1°29'W. The chief holy place of the Mossi (q.v.), located about 25 km. south of Ouagadougou (q.v.). Moro Naba Wobgho (q.v.) spent the first week here after Voulet (q.v.) took the Mossi capital in September 1896. In January 1897 negotiations between Voulet and Wobgho's brother, Mazi (q.v.), probably occurred here.

KOUPELA. 12°11'N 0°21'W. A town 105 km. east of Ouagadougou (q.v.) on the road to Fada N'Gourma (q.v.), and 46 km. north of Tenkodogo (q.v.). Located between three of the Mossi (q.v.) capitals, it played an important role in Mossi history. Voulet (q.v.) passed through the town several times in 1897. The White Fathers (q.v.) established their first Voltaic mission here in 1900, and it became a Catholic (q.v.) diocese in 1956. It is the headquarters of Kouritenga (q.v.) province. There are several other places in Burkina Faso called Koupéla.

KOURI (Koury). 12°45'N 3°30'W. Headquarters of a cercle from 1899–1910. It is located on the Nouna-Tougan road near where the Mouhoun (Black Volta) and the Sourou (qq.v.) join. There are several smaller places in Burkina Faso by the same name.

KOURITA (Kurita). Son of a dead Moro Naba who represents his dead father among the living. He is exiled from the capital and may never come into the presence of the new Moro Naba.

KOURITENGA. Province located between Ouagadougou and Fada N'-Gourma and north of Tenkodogo, of which Koupéla (qq.v.) is the headquarters.

KOURORI. 13°32'N 0°08'E. Location of megaliths as discovered by Paul Delmond. They are very similar to the stones of the Druids in France. The place is some 60 km. southeast of Dori (q.v.).

KOUTOU (Kutu, Halillou). The 28th Moro Naba. He reigned from about 1850 to 1871. He was the son of Naba Sawadogho and his wife, Bilkabore. He was educated at the Koranic school at Sarabatenga and could read and write Arabic. He was a loyal Muslim, and built a mosque near the gate of his palace in Ouagadougou (q.v.). Most of his children except Alhassan, the future Moro Naba Sanem (q.v.), were sent to Koranic schools. The normal religious functions of the traditional ruler were left to Koutou's officers to perform. Koutou had to contend with several revolts during his reign. Perhaps the most serious was that of a Fulani (q.v.) marabout (q.v.) named Wali or Modibo Mamadou in the Boulsa (q.v.) area. Three of his sons later served as Moro Naba: Sanem, Wobgho and Sigiri (qq.v.).

KOYA, MONT. 10°14′N 3°03′W. Peak southeast of Gaoua (q.v.) and west of the Mouhoun (Black Volta) (q.v.) in Lobi (q.v.) country. This hill is just south of Mont Kotou. Both are sacred to the people in the area.

KRAUSE, GOTTLOB ADOLF, 1850–1938. Krause was born in Ockrilla, Germany, and made his first visit to Africa in 1869, when he made a trip to North Africa. He became a friend of Nachtigal, the famous German explorer. The following year he served in the German army in the Franco-Prussian war. Then from 1873 to 1876 he studied natural science and geography at Leipzig. From 1879 to 1881 he explored the Sahara and North Africa, and 1884 found him in Lagos.

Krause tried to get financial support for an expedition to explore the interior of Togo without success. On 12 May 1886 he left Accra for Salaga, which he reached 18 June. On 7 July he left Salaga with a caravan which had kola nuts (q.v.) for Timbuktu. Following the left bank of the Nakanbe (White Volta) (q.v.) northward, they passed through Dagomba and to Walewale, crossed the White Volta, passed through Pô (q.v.), crossed the Red Volta, and reached Béré, 70 km. south of Ouagadougou, in August. The caravan rested there several weeks before going on, through Kombissiri (q.v.), to the capital, which they reached on 24 September 1886. Krause was received by Naba Sanem (q.v.), and he remained until 26 October. Then the caravan headed north again. Krause visited Téma (q.v.), Ouahigouya, Koumbri and Bani, and then entered into Macina territory. At Douentza, at the northeast end of the Bandiagara Scarp (in present-day Mali), the caravan left him.

On 7 December he got word that Sanem wished him to return to Ouagadougou. Krause completed the long trip back in a month, and remained in Ouagadougou until 22 January 1887. Going south, he crossed Gourounsi (q.v.) country, by Bouganiéna and Kasougou to

Sati (q.v.), where he remained three weeks. This enforced stay was caused by an attack of Zerma (q.v.) forces under Babatu (q.v.). Then by Wa, Bole and Kintampo, he returned to Salaga in April 1887. In later years Krause became a merchant in Togo and a critic of German administration. He finally returned to Germany as a result of World War I, and then died in Zurich in 1938. Krause was the first recorded European to visit Ouagadougou and Ouahigouya (qq.v.).

KUBO. Small Ouattara (q.v.) state in Diébougou (q.v.) area which was the scene of many struggles in the latter part of the nineteenth century.

KURUMBA (Kouroumba; singulars Kurumdo or Kouroumdo). The Kurumba are among the earliest people in Burkina Faso (q.v.). The Mossi (q.v.) call them the Foulse or Fulse (q.v.), and the Dogon call them the Tellem. They call themselves the Kurumba or Kouroumba. They are also classified with the Ninisi (q.v.). They once had a kingdom known as Loroum (q.v.). They called their leader the Ayo, and he lived at Mengao (q.v.). Today they live in the Aribinda, Liptako, Djilgodji and Yatenga (qq.v.) area. Megalithic stone stelae, stone circles, and stone slabs in Kurumba territory have caused much speculation.

KUSASI. Murdock lists the Kusasi with the Mole-speaking Gurensi (q.v.). They live along the Nakanbe (White Volta) (q.v.), near the Ghana border north of Gambaga and below the Busansi (q.v.).

KUTU. *see* KOUTOU

-L-

LA. 12°53′N 2°27′W. The capital of the Mossi (q.v.) under Oubri's son, Nasbire (q.v.), and also the capital of Yatenga (q.v.) in the beginning. The first two Yatenga nabas (q.v.) were crowned here.

Lâ. 12°04′N 3°30′W. Marka (q.v.) village south of Dédougou (q.v.). The village was attacked and destroyed by French forces under Colonel Molard on 20-22 February 1916. On 16 May 1916 the French executed 16 hostages here after a French soldier's grave was found desecrated.

LABBO (sing.), LAWBE (pl.). Woodworker among the Fulani (q.v.).

LABOURET, HENRI, 1878–1959. Labouret first came to Africa as a soldier, and he took part in the conquest of the northern area of Côte d'Ivoire. He first came to Upper Volta in 1912. During the insurrections of World War I he was assigned to duty in the Marka and Bobo (qq.v.) area in the bend of the Black Volta. Labouret was wounded and twice cited for outstanding conduct during this period. After the war he resigned from the army and became an administrator. He was stationed at both Diébougou and Gaoua (qq.v.), and became an expert on the peoples of this area. Lt. Governor Hesling (q.v.) praised him officially several times for his abilities in the pacification of the region. Labouret became proficient in several local languages, and he was an inveterate collector of local folklore and traditions. In 1924 he returned to France and began a new career as teacher and writer on African themes. Two of his most important works were about Lobi (q.v.) country. He was one of the founders of the French *Société des Africanistes*.

LAGO. 13°20′N 2°30′W. Logo is one of the more important towns in the history of Yatenga (q.v.). Southwest of Ouahigouya and northwest of Gourcy (qq.v.), it was in the heartland of Yadéga's empire.

LALLE. 12°26′N 0°52′W. A town which is northwest of Ouagadougou (q.v.). It was one of the more troublesome provinces in the kingdom of Ouagadougou. A civil war in this area plagued both Sanem and Wobgho (qq.v.) in the last years of the nineteenth century.

LAMBERT, COMMANDANT G. E. French commander at Ouagadougou (q.v.), 1905–1907. He tried to close Catholic mission schools and replace them with state-supported schools. In 1908 he wrote an excellent history of the Mossi (q.v.).

LAMBWEGHA. The 11th Yatenga Naba. He ruled in the middle of the seventeenth century. He brought Zandoma and many of the Kurumba (qq.v.) villages under the control of Yatenga (q.v.).

LAMIZANA, ABOUBAKAR SANGOULE, 1916– . Second president of Upper Volta. Lamizana was born at Dianra (q.v.) near Tougan (q.v.), a member of the Samo (q.v.) ethnic group and a Muslim. He married Mouilo Kékélé Bintou. In January 1936 Lamizana joined the French army and was stationed in Morocco and Algeria 1943–1947. After returning home for two years as chief adjutant, in 1949 he was transferred to the Center for African and Asian Studies in Paris as instructor of Bambara. Between 1950–1961 he had tours of duty in Indochina and Algeria. After Upper Volta independence, Lamizana returned to become chief of the general staff of the army in 1962. When it was obvious that President Yaméogo (q.v.) had lost control of affairs in Upper Volta, Lt. Colonel Lamizana assumed control on 3 January 1966 and became acting head of state.

As president, Lamizana tried to maintain stability while contending with the problems which plagued his people. He saw himself as a soldier doing his duty, and made it clear that he would be happy to relinquish power as soon as he was convinced that civilian rule would not destroy stability. Following the December 1970 elections, a new government was formed under Gérard Kango Ouédraogo (q.v.), but by December 1973, the world energy crisis, drought, and inflation and recession combined to undermine confidence in Ouédraogo. Military government was reimposed in February 1974. In 1976 Lamizana announced another attempt to restore civilian rule.

In the May 1978 elections Lamizana ran as the *Union Démocratique Voltaïque* (UDV-RDA) (q.v.) candidate and won the runoff election over Macaire Ouedraogo of *Union Nationale de Defense de Démocratie* (UNDD) (q.v.) and was sworn in as president of the Third Republic in June 1978. In February 1979 the major labor unions launched a campaign against the Lamizana government, and an October 1980 strike of school teachers became a general strike. After surviving a National Assembly no confidence vote, the Lamizana government ordered an end to all marches and demonstrations and agreed to salary demands by striking teachers. However, Lamizana was deposed by a "colonel's coup" (q.v.) led by Col. Saye Zerbo (q.v.) on 25 November 1980, the Constitution (q.v.) of 1977 was suspended, and an attempted counter coup by riot police failed. Lamizana was imprisoned 1980–1982 and transferred to house arrest in late 1982. In November 1982 21 pro-Lamizana senior army officers were pensioned off. In January 1984 under the Sankara (q.v.) government, leaders of the Zerbo and Lamizana regimes were tried; former President Lamizana was acquitted on charges of embezzlement. He was chairman of the *Union Nationale des Anciens Burkinabès* (UNAB) (National Union of Burkinabè Elders) in 1986 and 1987.

LAMIZANA, MAURICE. Samogo. Employed in French service between the World Wars. Adviser to Nana Kom II (q.v.).

LANFIERA (Lanferia). 12°59′N 3°25′W. A town in northwest Burkina Faso, just east of the Sourou River (q.v.), and near the Mali border. It is about 31 km. from Tougan (q.v.). Fariku Sanogo of Tissé established Islam (q.v.) here in the early nineteenth century, and Fariku's son, Mamadu Sanogo (q.v.), better known as Karamoko Ba, made Lanfiéra the leading Islamic center in northern Dafina (q.v.). Crozat (q.v.) visited Lanfiéra from 2-5 September in 1890. Monteil (q.v.) was there almost two weeks in April 1891. Destenave (q.v.) visited there in June 1895, and Voulet (q.v.) arrived in November 1896. Voulet heard and believed stories that Karamoko Ba was plotting against the French, and so the great Muslim leader was executed on 24 November 1896.

LARALLE NABA. One of three chief lieutenants of the Moro Naba. He makes sacrifices to the royal ancestors, is keeper of the royal tombs, and is one of the four electors who select a new Moro Naba when the old one dies.

LATERITE (latérite). Ferrous reddish soil which covers much of Africa.

LELE (Léla, Lyéla, Lyéle). People who live in the former cercle of Ténado (Sanguie province [q.v.]), west of Koudougou (q.v.), in Kipirsi (q.v.) country between the Mouhoun (Black Volta) and Nazinon (Red Volta) (qq.v.). There are other groups in Africa with this name.

LEO. 11°06'N 2°06'W. Headquarters of Sissili province (q.v.), this town is located just north of the border with Ghana. In the last two decades of the nineteenth century it was one of the more important Zerma (Zaberma) (q.v.) headquarters in the center of Gourounsi (q.v.) country. Babatu (q.v.) was defeated here in March 1897, just a short time after his defeat at Gandiaga (q.v.) (Ghana). Henderson (q.v.) tried to station men loyal to the British at Léo at this time, and the town was headquarters for Chanoine (q.v.) during March, April and May 1897 while he was campaigning against the Zerma and staking out French claims against the British.

LEPROSY. A disease of the skin and nerves leading to disfigurement and deformity. Burkina has one of the highest rates in Africa.

LERABA. Tributary of the Komoé (q.v.). It has several branches which rise in the hills of Sindou (q.v.). For a short distance it forms the border between Burkina Faso and Mali. For a much longer distance, it is the border with Côte d'Ivoire.

LIGIDI. The 40th Yatenga Naba. He ruled from 1899–1902, but actually had only ceremonial power. Before taking the name of Ligidi he was called Koudougou. He was a younger brother of Naba Boulli (q.v.), a member of the Tougouri (q.v.) faction in the Yatenga (q.v.) dynastic squabbles.

LIGUE PATRIOTIQUE POUR LE DEVELOPPEMEMT (LIPAD). When Thomas Sankara (q.v.) came to power in August 1983 LIPAD was one of the two main civilian political groupings that, with the radical officers led by Sankara, Compaoré, Zongo and Lingani (qq.v.), made up the *Conseil National de la Révolution* (CNR) (q.v.) coalition. The other was the *Union des Luttes Communistes* (ULC) (q.v.). LIPAD, founded in 1973 and led by Hamidou Coulibaly, has been characterized as a "pro-Soviet" party. A year after the CNR came to power LIPAD was removed from the CNR and its ministers from the government.

LILSE (Lyela). A group of people who live south of the Samo (q.v.), east of the Dafing (q.v.) and west of the Mossi (q.v.) in the area between the Mouhoun (Black Volta) and Nazinon (Red Volta) (qq.v.). They are identified with the Fulse, Kurumba, Kibsi (qq.v.) and other very early peoples of northwest Burkina Faso.

LINEAGE SOCIETIES (sociétés lignagères). A stateless society or community organized on the basis of descent from a common ancestor, as in the case of the Gourounsi (q.v.) of western Burkina.

LINGANI, JEAN-BAPTISTE BOUKARY, 1945–1989. Military officer. He was promoted from major to major general in 1984. He had his military training in France. Lingani was one of the leaders of the November 1982 coup in which the Conseil de Salut du Peuple (CSP) (q.v.) overthrew the Saye Zerbo (q.v.) regime. He became secretary-general of the CSP, but was imprisoned by the CSP Ouédraogo government along with Thomas Sankara (q.v.) in early 1983. Together with Sankara, Henri Zongo and Blaise Compaoré (qq.v.), Lingani was one of the leaders of the August 1983 coup and he became Minister of National Defense in the Conseil National de la Révolution (CNR) (q.v.). In August 1986 he was appointed coordinator of Burkina Faso and mandated to act for President Sankara, along with Compaoré and Zongo. In October 1987 Sankara and 13 associates were killed in a coup led by Compaoré, Lingani and Zongo. In June 1989 when Compaoré was elected president of Popular Front (q.v.) executive committee, Lingani was named first deputy chairman and Zongo second deputy chairman. In September 1989 Lingani and Zongo were accused of plotting against Compaoré and executed.

LIPTAKO (Libtako). The northeastern Dori (q.v.) region of Burkina Faso. Barth (q.v.), who was in the area in July of 1853, described it as an immense plain, scarcely broken except for an occasional baobab tree (q.v.). Liptako was once part of the Fulani (q.v.) emirate of Gwandu (Gando), and before that it was part of Gourma (q.v.). The Liptako Emirate was founded by Seydou in 1810. Monteil (q.v.) signed a treaty for France with the leader of Liptako on 23 May 1891, and Destenave (q.v.) reconfirmed the treaty in October 1895. The Liptako Torobé Peul (Fulani) describe themselves as "people who can't be frightened". Liptako is part of the Sahel (q.v.) and was especially hard hit by drought in 1972–1974. Considerable prospecting in the area has occurred since World War II. Manganese (q.v.) was discovered in 1960 and an international mining consortium was organized in 1974. See also TAMBAO.

LOBI. People who live in the Gaoua and Diébougou (qq.v.) region southeast of Bobo Dioulasso (qq.v.). The term is actually a blanket term which includes the Dyan (Dian) (q.v.), Dorosie (q.v.), Gan, Kulango, Lobi-Dagari, Tusyan, Vigye (q.v.) and others. It is believed that most of these people began to move into their present locations after 1790 from the area of modern Ghana. They never organized centralized states, and were often raided from Kong, from Ouahabou (q.v.) and from Bobo Dioulasso. Sarantyé Mory (q.v.), Samory's son, pillaged the area just before the French arrived. The Lobi lands were annexed by the French in 1897, but they were not effectively subdued until 1903. Henri Labouret (q.v.) was administrator of the area from the end of World War I to 1924. The region produces shea products, peanuts, cotton (qq.v.) and other crops, and is thought to have once been the source of considerable quantities of gold.

LOBI RUINS. Ruins first reported to the outside world by Lt. Schwartz. Since 1902 ruins have been reported in a number of places between the Bougouriba and Poni rivers (qq.v.). Their origin is still a mystery. They may have once been buildings used to house slaves that worked the mines of the area.

LOCUST (*parkia biglobosa, Néré*). A winged edible insect which migrates in swarms and may consume vegetation of entire districts. In 1928 a five-year plague of locusts began which caused widespread famine (q.v.) in Burkina Faso.

LOCUST BEAN TREE (*parkia biglobosa*). A tree that grows to 15 meters with a gnarled trunk and dense crown. The fruit is a pod with multiple seeds embedded in a mealy pulp. Both the pulp and seeds are used as food and in drinks. The bark's tannin is used in tanning and dyeing.

LOI CADRE. Act of the French National Assembly in June of 1956 which granted universal suffrage and a single electoral college to the overseas territories of France. The territorial assemblies were granted internal autonomy.

LOLOWULEIN. Journal of the Revolutionary Defense Committees which began publication in early 1985. Its name is Dioula (q.v.) for Red Star.

LOME CONVENTION. The Lomé Convention is a trade and aid agreement signed by the European Community and 69 African, Caribbean and Pacific (ACP) nations. First signed in 1975 and revised in 1979 and 1984, Lomé IV was signed in December 1989, and includes 46 African states. The Convention established the European Development Fund (EDF) which is the main source of multilateral European Union aid to the ACP nations. Other features include the Stabilization of Export Earnings Scheme (Stabex) to cover losses of earnings caused by drops in prices or production of the main ACP agricultural exports, and Sysmin which is a special financing facility for minerals. Lomé IV also provides designated funding to the European Investment Bank which lends on commercial terms.

LOMPO. *see* DIABA LOMPO (Jaba Lompo)

LOMPO, FRANÇOIS. Administrator who held several positions in the government of Upper Volta. In 1956 he was minister of public instruction. In 1966 he was inspector general of finances and administration. In 1971 he was minister of public works, transport and town planning.

LOROPENI. 10°18'N 3°32'W. Village west of Gaoua, between Gaoua and Banfora (qq.v.), in Lobi (q.v.) country. It was destroyed by Sarantyé Mory (q.v.) in 1897. There are interesting ruins here.

LOROUM (Louroum, Lurum). Kurumba (q.v.) (Foulse or Tellem) kingdom in the Djilgodji (q.v.) region founded about the beginning of the fifteenth century. The capital, Mengao (q.v.), is southwest of Djibo (q.v.). The king was known as the ayo.

LOTO. Small Dioula (q.v.) state in the Diébougou (q.v.) area founded by Ouattara (q.v.) Dioula from Bobo Dioulasso (q.v.) in the nineteenth century. It was conquered by the French in 1897. Also see OUAT-TARA, BE-BAKARY.

LOUDA PLAIN. 13°01'N 1°06'W. An area south of Kaya (q.v.) where irrigation dams were built between 1950–1956 in an attempt to improve the agricultural potential of the region. In 1967 Taiwan conducted a rice (q.v.) growing project here.

LOUMBILA (Lombila). 12°31'N 1°23'W. Village about halfway between Ouagadougou and Ziniaré (qq.v.) where metal statuettes of the Moro Naba are kept. There is also a dam here on the Massila to furnish water to Ouagadougou.

LOUTA. 13°30'N 3°10'W. Town in northwest Dafina (q.v.) near the Mali frontier. In the 1860s it was the center of a Fulani (q.v.) state.

LOUVEAU, EDMOND JEAN, 1895–d.? . French administrator. Born at Mamers, France, he served in World War I and afterwards joined the French colonial service. From 1930 to 1934 he was chef de cabinet to Lt. Governor Maurice Beurnier of Senegal. In 1937 he became the chief administrator of that part of Upper Volta which at the time was attached to Côte d'Ivoire. In June 1940, after the fall of France, Louveau was the only senior administrator in West Africa to declare for de Gaulle. He encouraged officials in Upper Volta to cross into the Gold Coast in order to continue the battle against the Germans. In August 1940 he was arrested and sent to France for trial. There, in October 1941, Louveau was sentenced to life at hard labor for treason. He escaped in December 1943 and joined the Free French in Algiers. From 1946 to 1952 he served as Governor of Soudan. In 1947 he published a book on his war-time experiences called *Au bagne. Entre les griffes de Vichy et de la milice* (In Prison: Between the Claws of Vichy and the Militia).

LURUM. *see* LOROUM

-M-

MAABUUBE (sing. maabo). Bards in Fulani (q.v.) areas who play the lute, sing and recite genealogies, and beg.

MACCUDO (sing.), MACCUBE (pl.). Captives. People of servile condition in Djilgodi.

MADIDOU. Aulliminden Tuareg (q.v.) leader who often conducted raids across the Oudalan, Aribinda, Liptako and Yagha (qq.v.) in the 1890s. The French finally contained the raids by the end of the decade.

MAGUET, EDOUARD. French administrator at Dédougou (q.v.) during the revolts (q.v.) which started in 1915 who played an active role in trying to contain the revolts and punish the insurgents.

MAIZE. The third most important food grain of Burkina Faso. It is planted in late March or early April. In case of need, some is harvested green in July, but most is harvested in August. Late maize is sown in August and harvested in December or January, but yields for the late crop are poor.

MAKUMA. Ouattara (q.v.) state located to the north of the Mouhoun (Black Volta) (q.v.) between Bobo Dioulasso (q.v.) and San, mostly in present-day Mali.

MALI FEDERATION. Proposed union of several West African states promoted by Léopold Senghor of Senegal and Modibo Keita of Soudan. Dahomey and Upper Volta were in line to join in 1958, but Houphouët-Boigny of Côte d'Ivoire persuaded Maurice Yaméogo (q.v.) to back out of the Mali Federation and instead join the *Conseil de l'Entente* (q.v.) (Benin, Côte d'Ivoire, Niger, Togo and Burkina Faso) in 1959. The Bobo (q.v.) section of Upper Volta was very unhappy with this turn of events.

MAMPRUSI (Mamphusi). The senior Mossi (q.v.) state, it is located in modern Ghana. There are many traditions about the founding of the Mossi states with different names and facts, but all the traditions do agree that a daughter of the ruler of Mamprusi ran off from her father, had a son by a Mande (Busansi ?) (q.v.) hunter, and that this son was the founder of the Nakomsé (q.v.) line of Mossi nobility.

MANDE (Manding, Mandingo, Mandinka, Malinké, Wangara). The largest group in the northern bend of the Niger. The Busansi, Dafing, Dioula, Marka, Samo, Samogho and Sia (qq.v.) in Burkina Faso (q.v.) are Mande groups. The suffix "-dougou" or "-so" show the strong Mande influence on the names in Burkina Faso.

MANE. 12°59'N 1°21'W. Town northeast of Ouagadougou (q.v.) near the Nakanbe (White Volta) (q.v.). It is one of the ancient Mossi (q.v.) principalities, having been founded by Nyaseme, son of Moro Naba Koudoumie (q.v.), in the middle of the sixteenth century.

MANGA. 11°40'N 1°4'W. Headquarters of Zoundweogo province (q.v.), located SSE of Ouagadougou and north of Pô (qq.v.).

MANGANESE. Burkina Faso has one of the world's largest supplies of manganese, some 13 million metric tons, but it is located in the isolated northeastern section of the country and it was long regarded as uneconomic to transport to markets. The manganese is at Tambao (q.v.), 70 km. from the Niger River, and 20 km. from the Mali border. The shortest route to the ocean requires a rail connection to Ouagadougou (q.v.). In 1974 the Tambao Mining Company (Interstar Mining of Canada, 15 percent, and the government, 85 percent) was organized to exploit the Tambao deposits. Exports (q.v.) from the Tambao manganese mine began in May 1993. Production was forecast at 70,000 tons in the first year, with capacity of 140,000 tons which was scheduled to rise to 250,000 tons in 1995.

MARABOUT. A devout Koranic teacher and cleric.

MARANSE (Maransé). Early in the eighteenth century groups of Songhai (q.v.) merchants began to settle in the villages to the east of the Nakanbe (White Volta) (q.v.). Their descendants are the Maransé.

MARC, LUCIEN FRANÇOIS, 1877–1914. French administrator. He was born at Rouen and graduated from Saint Cyr. He joined the colonial army when he was 21, and was stationed in Madagascar before coming to Upper Volta. He held positions in Mossi (q.v.) and Gourounsi (qq.v.) towns and was then transferred to Timbuktu. Returning to France, he earned a doctorate from the University of Paris with a dissertation on "Le pays Mossi" in 1909. He was killed early in World War I.

MARIGOT. A marsh, swamp, or tributary.

MARKA (Marica). The Marka are a Mande-Soninké group who came to the Dafina (q.v.) area soon after the fall of the Songhai (q.v.) empire in the beginning of the seventeenth century. Tradition says there were two leaders of the migration. Konata founded a settlement at Gnemeredougou, and Soare founded Douroula (q.v.).

MARKOYE. 14°39′N 0°02′E. Market village in the extreme northeastern corner of Burkina Faso and near the manganese (q.v.) deposits at Tambao (q.v.). Markoye is about 70 km. north of Dori and is famous for its weekly camel and cattle market.

MASSA. A religious cult founded about 1951 in southwest Burkina Faso among the Bobo and Senufo (qq.v.). Members believe in good deeds and obedience to authorities.

MASSON, PAUL. Chef de cabinet to Governor (q.v.) Albert Jean Mouragues (q.v.) in 1948. His appointment as high commissioner to the new Republic in 1958 was very unpopular in Upper Volta.

MATIAKOUALI (Matiacoali). 12°22′N 1°92′E. Town on the road from Fada N'Gourma (q.v.) to Niamey, Niger.

MAUBERT, ADMINISTRATOR. He served in Fada N'Gourma (q.v.) as commandant early in the period of French rule, and his reports on the Gourma (q.v.) were published in 1909. He was commandant at Bobo Dioulasso (q.v.) when the insurrections in Bobo (q.v.) country began. His personal aggressive leadership of the French forces against the insurgents played an important role in bringing the revolt to an end.

MAZI (Massy). Seventh son of Moro Naba Koutou (q.v.) and brother to Sanem, Wobgho and Sigiri (qq.v.). He was chief of Doulougou (q.v.) and as such was called Naba Kuliga. The French tried to get Mazi to accept the throne of his brother, Moro Naba Wobgho, in 1897. There are different accounts of what happened. One account says he accepted and died before the French could endow him with a new title. Another story says Mazi committed suicide rather than betray his brother. The Mossi (q.v.) believed Mazi was destroyed by spirits. The French believed he was poisoned.

MEKROU. Stream which rises in Benin and forms part of the border between Burkina Faso and Benin before flowing on into the Niger through the *Parc National du W* (q.v.).

MENGAO. One of the capitals of the Kurumba (q.v.) kingdom of Loroum (q.v.). Two cult sites are located near here. These sites date back to the sixteenth century and are probably Dogon. They were reported by Kouradin Ferrari d'Occhieppo in 1962.

METIS. Half-caste, mulatto.

MIGRATORY LABOR. During the colonial period Burkina was seen by the French administration as a reservoir of labor for their plantations, construction sites and other enterprises in Côte d'Ivoire. A system of forced labor was even introduced for a time.

Even when not forced, migrant workers from Upper Volta have been the largest of any West African country. In the early 1970s one-ninth of the population of Côte d'Ivoire was made up of Voltaic nationals. That presence has continued, and has generally been in the interest of both the Ivoirien and Burkina governments. It is estimated that some 750,000 Burkinabè were working abroad in 1990.

From the Burkina side a major cost of having four of every ten adult males working abroad is that the women at home must carry extra responsibilities and burdens. At the same time, the worker remittances have been a way to cope with drought and has slowed the abandonment of some villages in northern Burkina. Employment abroad has also lessened the pressure of migration on Burkina's cities. Also see EXPORTS.

MILITARY REGIONS. The six military region command posts in 1985 were at Dori, Ouahigouya, Dédougou, Bobo Dioulasso, Kombissiri, and Fada N'Gourma (qq.v.).

MILLET. Millet and grain sorghum (q.v.) are the two most important food crops for local consumption in Burkina Faso. Millet is a small seeded cereal, planted in April and not harvested until November or December. Bulrush millet requires less growing time than sorghum (guinea corn) and its harvest takes place in August, about the same time as the early maize (q.v.) harvest. The French term "sorgho" sometimes refers to both sorghum and millet.

MINIANKO. Mande (q.v.) ethnic group in the Senufo (q.v.) group of western Burkina and of Mali.

MINING. *see* POURA GOLD MINES, MANGANESE, and TAMBOA. In addition, zinc production was scheduled to begin in 1994 at Perkoa. Antimony and marble have been mined on a small scale for some years.

MINVIELLE, CAPTAIN. French resident at Dori (q.v.) in 1898. His ability to speak Arabic was a great help in dealing with the local Muslims. He was able to check the Tuareg (q.v.) raids on the area.

MISE EN VALEUR. *Mise en valeur* was a policy of economic development in colonies to profit both the mother country and the colonies. The policy is associated with Albert Sarraut, colonial minister of France from 1920 to 1924. Edouard Hesling (q.v.) tried to carry out the policy in Upper Volta.

MOATIBA. The 19th Moro Naba. He was Moro Naba from about 1729 to 1737. Tradition is not clear as to whether he was a son or adviser to Moro Naba Oubi. Most sources say that he was a Fulani (q.v.) adviser to Naba Oubi, and that he seized the *nam* (power) as an usurper. He died under mysterious conditions, perhaps poisoned.

MOGHO (Mooga, p. Moose). Land of the Mossi (q.v.).

MOGHO NABA. *see* MORO NABA

MOLARD, COLONEL. After the French defeat at Yankasso (q.v.) on 23 December 1915, Colonel Molard was given command of the French forces fighting the insurgent Marka and Bwa in the bend of the Black Volta and in time brought an end to the revolt.

MOLEX, JULES. One of the French officers who was active in the hinterland of Dahomey after 1894. He was second in command to Baud (q.v.) at Fada N'Gourma (q.v.) in February, 1897 and later was resident at Fada. He wrote a valuable report on the Gourma (q.v.) published in 1898.

MONTEIL, PARFAIT LOUIS, 1855–1925. French officer and explorer. He was a graduate of Saint Cyr and he spent much of his career in West Africa. In 1885 he explored the upper Senegal area, but his greatest expedition took him from Saint Louis to Tripoli and is described in *De Saint-Louis à Tripoli par le lac Tchad: voyage au travers du Soudan et du Sahara, accompli pendant les années 1890–91–92.* Pages 65–190 concern Monteil's trip from Sikasso to Say. This is the first known journey of a European across Upper Volta from west to east. Monteil signed treaties at Bobo Dioulasso (q.v.) on 20 March 1891 and at Lanfiéra (q.v.) on 3 April. He went by La and Yako and reached Ouagadougou (qq.v.) on 28 April. He was not allowed entry into the Mossi (q.v.) capital, so he continued by way of Boussouma and Kaya to Dori (qq.v.), which he reached on 22 May. The next day he signed a treaty there. From Dori Monteil followed Barth's (q.v.) path to Say and signed a treaty at Say on 24 August 1891.

MOODIBBO (moodibaabe; pl. Moodibbe). A Fulani (q.v.) clerk.

MORE. Moré is the language of the Mossi (q.v.). It belongs to the Voltaic or Gur (q.v.) subfamily of the Nigritic or Niger-Congo family of languages. It is sometimes called Molé or Moshi.

MORO NABA (plural is Moro Nanamsé) (Mogho Naba, Moogo Naaba). The ruler of the Mossi (q.v.) kingdom of Ouagadougou (q.v.). "Mogho" means "the world". Literally the Moro Naba is the "ruler of the world", or "the sun on the earth". But the world is actually the ancestral land of the Mossi, the land between the Red and White Voltas.

MOSSI (Molé, Moshi). The singular is Moaga. Murdock classified the Mossi as a Voltaic people belonging to the Molé cluster and related to the Birifor (q.v.), Dagomba, Gurensi (q.v.), Mamprusi (q.v.) and Wala (q.v.). There are probably nearly 5 million Mossi in West Africa, nearly all of whom live or have their family homes in Burkina Faso (q.v.). Some one-half million Mossi from Burkina work in Côte d'Ivoire, Ghana and other neighboring countries. Although the Mossi empire had a strong tradition of resisting Islam (q.v.), probably one-third of the Mossi are now Muslim.

MOSSI KINGDOMS. The Southern Kingdoms. These are the kingdoms said to have been founded by the sons of Nédéga (q.v.). Mamprusi (q.v.) or Mamphusi was the first kingdom of the Nakomsé (Nakomce) (q.v.) line. Its chief place was Gambaga. Nédéga was ruler here, and he was followed by Tusugu. Dagomba was founded by Sitobu. A smaller kingdom was Nanumba (Nanune), said to have been founded by Nmantambu. These Southern Kingdoms are all located in modern Ghana.

The Northern Kingdoms founded by the Nakomsé, or descendants of Nédéga through his daughter Yennega (q.v.) and her husband Rialle (q.v.) were located in the area of modern Burkina Faso (q.v.). Tenkodogo (q.v.) was founded by Ouédraogo (q.v.), grandson of Nédéga. Zandoma (q.v.) was founded by Rawa (q.v.), great-grandson of Nédéga. Gourma (q.v.) was founded by Diaba Lompo (q.v.). Ouagadougou (q.v.) was founded by Oubri (q.v.). Yatenga (q.v.) was founded by Yadega (q.v.) or Yedega.

MOSSI SEPTENTRIONAUX. The Northern Mossi (q.v.). Some authorities believe that we should distinguish two separate groups of Mossi. The Northerners, after crossing the Niger between modern Niamey and Say, moved north and west via modern Dori and Aribinda (qq.v.) between the thirteenth and fifteenth centuries. These are the Mossi who most likely came into contact with Mali and Songhai (q.v.). The Southern Mossi, on the other hand, are the Mamprusi (q.v.) or Nakomsé Mossi (q.v.). Their ancestors crossed Gourma (q.v.) to the area of modern Gambaga (Ghana) before spreading northward between the Red and White Voltas. The Northern and the Southern Mossi reunited in the Djilgodji and Yatenga (qq.v.) areas.

MOTTO. On 4 August 1984 the Sankara (q.v.) government adopted a new national motto "La patrie ou la mort; nous vaincrons" (The homeland or death: we will triumph).

MOUHOUN. Former Black Volta river, renamed by the Sankara (q.v.) government in August 1986. Also province located in the bend of the Mouhoun (Black Volta) of which Dédougou (q.v.) is the headquarters.

MOUN-HOU. Local name for the Mouhoun (Black Volta) (q.v.) north of Bobo Dioulasso (q.v.) after the Kou (Baoulé) (q.v.) joins it.

MOURAGUES, ALBERT JEAN. Governor (q.v.) of Upper Volta, 1948–1952; of the Soudan in 1953; and of Mauritania, 1954–1955 and 1956–1958. He was accused of interference in the local elections of Upper Volta in June 1948 in favor of the *Union Voltaïque* (UV) candidates.

MOUSSA AMINOU. Dori (q.v.) marabout (q.v.) who was killed when he attempted to begin a jihad in 1949.

MOUSSA OF SATI (Musa). Muslim ruler of the area between the Sissala and the Awuna (qq.v.) at the end of the nineteenth century. He formed an alliance with the Zerma (q.v.) under Alfa Gazari, but under Babatu (qq.v.) the Zerma turned on Moussa and Moussa was killed when the Zerma took Sati (q.v.) in 1883.

MOUVEMENT DE LIBERATION NATIONALE (MLN). A radical Marxist movement first created in Dakar in August 1958 by Joseph Ki-Zerbo (q.v.) to support a "no" vote in the 28 September referendum on the Constitution of the Fifth French Republic. When Guinea was the only territory to vote "no" Ki-Zerbo moved to Guinea for awhile. In January 1960, however, he returned to Upper Volta, and was soon active in the underground movement against Yaméogo (q.v.). In 1970 Ki-Zerbo organized a new MLN which won 10 percent of the vote and six seats in the 1970 elections, but it was banned in 1974.

MOUVEMENT DEMOCRATIQUE VOLTAIQUE (MDV). Political party organized in the late 1940s in the Yatenga (q.v.) area. At first it was called the *Indépendants de l'Union Française*. It was Gaullist and opposed to the leadership of the Moro Naba (q.v.) and chiefs. The leaders were Gérard Kango Ouédraogo (q.v.), a cousin of the Yatenga Naba, and Michel Dorange (q.v.), a European merchant and former army officer. This group won 27 seats in the Territorial Assembly (q.v.) elected in 1957.

MOUVEMENT DES INDEPENDANTS DU PARTI DU REGROUPE-MENT AFRICAIN. A small faction of the Parti du Regroupement Africain (PRA) (q.v.) led by Babiri Seiba. It supported Lamizana (q.v.) in the 1978 presidential elections.

MOUVEMENT DU REGROUPEMENT VOLTAIQUE (MRV). Voltaic branch of Senghor's *Parti du Regroupement Africain*. Organized in August 1958 with Gérard Kango Ouédraogo (q.v.) the first secretary general. Blaise Bassoleth (q.v.) became the leader of the MRV in October 1959.

MOUVEMENT NATIONAL DES PIONNIERS (MNP) (National Movement of Pioneers). Established by the *Conseil National de la Révolution* (CNR) (q.v.) in 1985 for children too young to be involved in *Comités de Défense de la Révolution* (q.v.).

MOUVEMENT NATIONAL POUR LE RENOUVEAU (MNR). On 30 May 1974 President Lamizana (q.v.) abolished all political parties in Upper Volta and announced that the Movement for Renewal would be the only authorized political, social and cultural organization for the nation. In 1975 the name became the Mouvement National pour le Renouveau.

MOUVEMENT POPULAIRE DE L'EVOLUTION AFRICAINE (MPEA and MPA). Western non-Mossi party organized in 1955 under the leadership of Nazi Boni (q.v.) and associated with the *Convention Africaine* of Léopold Sédar Senghor of Senegal. In the Territorial Assembly (q.v.) election in March 1957 this party won five seats, all from Dédougou (q.v.).

MOUVEMENT PROGRESSISTE DE LA VOLTA (MPV). Western party founded at Bobo Dioulasso (q.v.) on 1 September 1946. Its first president was Sanny Sanon and its secretary general was Bakary Traoré.

MWEMBA. Muslims who control the office of imam (q.v.) in Ouagadougou (q.v.). They serve as advisors to the Moro Naba (q.v.) and have great prestige.

-N-

NAAM or GROUPEMENTS NAAM. *see* SIX-S

NABA (Naaba, pl. nanamse). The Mossi (q.v.) chief, mayor, official or ruler. Holder of the *nam* (q.v.) or authority. The Moro Naba (q.v.) and the Yatenga Naba rule kingdoms. Under Governor (q.v.) Edouard Hesling (q.v.) they were honored and paid a salary. The Moro Naba was paid 20,000 francs, while the Yatenga Naba got only 4,000 francs. Ministers such as the baloum naba or ouidi naba (qq.v.) were paid 2,000 francs by the French. The larhalle naba got 1,800 francs. Chiefs of towns or small villages were also called naba.

NAHOURI. Province located south of Ouagadougou (q.v.) on the Ghana border, of which Pô (q.v.) is the headquarters.

NAKANBE. Former White Volta river, renamed by the Sankara (q.v.) government in August 1986.

NAKOMSE. (There are several variants such as Nakombse, singular nakombga; and Nakomcé with nabiga as singular.) The Mossi (q.v.) nobility. The descendants of Nédéga (q.v.) of Mamprusi (q.v.) through his daughter Yennega (Nyennega, Yenenga) (q.v.) and her mate, Rialle (q.v.). Their son was Ouédraogo (q.v.). Before the French arrived, the Nakomsé could be put to death only for adultery with a wife of the Moro Naba (q.v.).

NAKOUROU. *see* TENA KOUROU

NAM. The political authority which one person exercises over another in Mossi (q.v.) territory.

NAMENTENGA. Province located northeast of Ouagadougou and east of Kaya (qq.v.), of which Boulsa (q.v.) is the headquarters.

NAMOUNOU, HILLS OF. Watershed between the Tapoa (q.v.) and Niger Rivers on the east and the Arly and Pendjari (qq.v.) on the southwest in the southeastern part of Gourma (q.v.).

NANA VO. A 1934 resistance movement among the Bobo (q.v.) to oppose the requisitioning of food and animals by the chiefs. Force was used to suppress the revolt. Nana is Bobo for taking without payment, and Vo means end.

NANERGE (Nanergue, Nanèrègè). People in the Mali-Burkina Faso border area northwest of Bobo Dioulasso (q.v.) near the Ngorolaka River (q.v.). They belong to the Senufo-Minianka group.

NAOURI HILL. 11°04′N 1°05′W. Hill to the east of the highway between Pô (q.v.) and the border of Ghana. It is 450 meters high. It is part of a low ridge of hills. There are also two villages and a forest reserve by that name.

NA-POKO. Oldest daughter of the Moro Naba (q.v.). She rules during the interregnum after her father's death. It might also be the oldest daughter of any chief.

NASBIRE (Na Siri, Nassebere, Sibiri). The 4th Moro Naba (q.v.). He was the son of Naba Oubri (q.v.) and his wife, Narimtoré. He was brother of Soarba, Naskyemde and Nyingnemdo (qq.v.). He reigned in the first half of the sixteenth century, lived much of his life at La, and died at Sourgoukienga, near Koudougou (q.v.). He was the father of Yadega (q.v.), the founder of Yatenga (q.v.). It was probably during the reign of Nasbire that the Yarsé (q.v.) began to enter the area between the Red and White Voltas.

NASKYEMDE (Naskiemdé). The 3rd Moro Naba (q.v.). He was the son of Naba Oubri (q.v.) and his wife, Pougsada. Naskyemde was chief of Louda at the time his brother, Naba Soarba (q.v.) died. His reign was early in the sixteenth century. He fought hard to bring the area of Kaya (q.v.) under his rule, and he died in that war.

NASSERE (Nassodoba). Nasséré was the Yatenga Naba (q.v.) when Sonni Ali of Songhai (q.v.) defeated the Mossi (q.v.) in 1483 in the battle of Kobi.

NATENGA. A term meaning the chief's land. It is also used to mean the land of the Mossi (q.v.) of Ouagadougou (q.v.).

NATIONAL ANTHEM. The anthem was adopted on 11 December 1959. It was written by the Abbé Robert Ouédraogo, who attended the Seminary at Pabré (q.v.) at the time Yaméogo (q.v.) was there. The first verse and refrain are:

> Proud Volta of my ancestors
> Your fiery and glorious sunshine
> Shrouds you with golden light,
> Oh, Queen clothed with fairness.

Refrain
> We will make you stronger and more beautiful.
> To your spirit we will always be true,
> And our hearts beat with pride,
> Praising your beauty.

On 4 August 1984 the Sankara (q.v.) government adopted a new anthem, "L'hymne de la victoire" or "Ditanyè". The first verse and refrain appear below (see *Carrefour africain,* No. 844, August 17th, 1984).

> Against the humiliating bondage of a thousand years
> The enslavement of a century
> Against shameful degradation
> Of the neocolonialists and their local traitors
> Many succumbed but some resisted
> But the setbacks, successes, sweat and blood
> Have only strengthened our courageous people
> and enriched their heroic struggle.

Refrain
> And one night stirred the history of one people

And on one night began their triumphal march
One night has pointed us toward our goal
Our people with all the people of the world
In the victory of liberty and progress
We will have our homeland or death.

NATIONAL UNION FOR THE DEFENSE OF DEMOCRACY. *see* UNION NATIONALE DE DEFENSE DE DEMOCRATIE (UNDD).

NAZINON. Former Red Volta river, renamed by the Sankara (q.v.) government in August 1986.

NEBIE, BAMINA GEORGES. Member of the Territorial Assembly (q.v.) from 1957–1959 from Léo (q.v.) as a member of the *Parti Démocratique Unifié* (PDU) (q.v.). He represented Upper Volta as Ambassador to the U.S.S.R. for several years. He served for a time as secretary-general of the *Union Démocratique Voltaïque* (UDV), and as minister of public works.

NEDEGA. (Bawa, Gbewa, Toese) First of the Nakomsé (q.v.). The Mossi (q.v.) kingdoms all trace their royal lines back to Nédéga. He lived at Gambaga (modern Ghana) and founded the Mamprusi kingdom (q.v.), probably in the thirteenth century. His grandfather was said to have been Tohajiye (q.v.). His father was Kpogonumbo, and his mother, Soyini or Solyini, was a Gourma (q.v.) princess, according to tradition. Nédéga is said to have had eight sons, several of whom later ruled the Mossi kingdoms in what is now Ghana, and one daughter, Yennega (q.v.), who mated with a Busansi (q.v.) hunter, Rialle (q.v.). Their son, Ouédraogo (q.v.), founded the first of the Mossi kingdoms in what is now Burkina Faso (q.v.).

NESOMBA. The four highest dignitaries at a Mossi (q.v.) court.

N'GOLO. Native of Diawalla in the Sénufo country of southwest Burkina Faso. He was commander of the left flank of Samory's (q.v.) army during the invasion of 1897. He followed a route through Ouangolodougou, Timpereba, Niangoloko (q.v.), Tiéfora (q.v.) and joined Samory at Sidéradougou (q.v.).

NGOROLAKA. Stream which forms the border between Burkina Faso and Mali for some distance. It rises in the area northwest of Bobo Dioulasso (q.v.) and flows into Mali as a tributary to the Bani.

NIANGOLOKO. 10°17'N 4°55'W. Town 23 km. northeast of the border with Côte d'Ivoire on the main road from Ferkessédougou (Côte d'Ivoire) to Banfora (q.v.).

NIEBE. Niébé, or cowpeas, are widely grown in Burkina.

NIENIGE (Niéniégue, Niniga, Nienigue). Habé (q.v.) people who live in the bend of the Mouhoun (Black Volta) (q.v.) between Satiri, Ouarkoyé and Boromo (qq.v.).

NIKIEMA, NORBERT, 1947– . Linguist. He was educated in Ouagadougou, and became a researcher and lecturer at the University of Ouagadougou (q.v.) 1976–.

NIKIEMA, ROGER, 1935– . Head of the Information Service of Radio Upper Volta in 1970. At that time he moved to Dakar to work at the University of Dakar. He authored three volumes of poetry: *Dessein contraire, L'adorable rivale,* and *Mes flèches blanches.*

NINISI (Nioniossé, Nyonyosé). The indigenous or aboriginal peoples of Burkina Faso: "Children of the earth." They are also called Tinguimbissi, Nioniossé or Nyonyosé. Robert Pageard uses the term "Nyonyosé" for early Voltaïques and "Ninisi" for early Mande (q.v.). Fulse (Foulse), Lilse, Kibsi, Kipirsi, Kurumba, Kado (qq.v.) are names of some of the early peoples. The Tengsoba, the earth priest, plays an important role in Burkina Faso, and the priests are selected from these people.

NOBERE. 11°33'N 1°12'W. Town south of Ouagadougou (q.v.) on the main highway to Ghana between Kombissiri and Pô (qq.v.) in Zoundweogo province (q.v.). It is the chief village of a district of about five hundred square kilometers along the east bank of the Nazinon (Red Volta) (q.v.). Tradition says that the Ninisi (q.v.) of the area were conquered by Biligo, son of Moro Naba Oubri (q.v.), and that Biligo founded Nobéré. Wobgho (q.v.) tried to organize resistance to the French in this area at the end of 1896.

NOIRE, CAPTAIN. Last military resident of Yatenga (q.v.). He assumed command at Ouahigouya (q.v.) on 15 September 1902 and was replaced by Administrator Bernard 22 April 1904. Noire conducted searches for minerals, conducted a census, established a school and set up native courts. He also began to construct a system of highways for Yatenga. He wrote the first monograph on Yatenga in 1904, *Monographie du Cercle de Ouahigouya.*

NON-GOVERNMENTAL ORGANIZATIONS (NGOs). In response to the 1970s drought, NGOs have taken a front-line role in working with farmers and others in rural villages. As foreign governments have become more aware of the limitations of government-to-government aid, they have channelled an increasing share through NGOs. By the mid–1980s there were more than 70 different foreign NGOs working in Burkina. One estimate is that aid from all NGOs in 1986 amounted to some 18 percent of Burkina's national budget.

An important strength of the best NGOs is that they have been able to think in terms of small-scale projects, and to start by defining projects in consultation with the people themselves. While some indigenous NGOs emerged only from the need of foreign agencies for local partners, or as former government officials or persons educated abroad climbed on the aid bandwagon, some of the best Burkina NGOs are exceptions. Catholic missionary orders with long experience in-country have given rise to two Burkina-based development training organizations: *Centre d'Etudes Economiques et Sociales d'Afrique Occidentale* (CESAO) and *Groupe de Recherche et d'Appui pour l'Autopromotion Paysanne* (GRAAP) (qq.v.), both based in Bobo Dioulasso (q.v.). And the autonomous national federation of the *Groupements Naam* has some 200,000 peasants linked to it.

NORTHCOTT, HENRY P. –1899. British officer. Lt. Colonel Northcott was appointed first British commissioner and commandant of the Northern Territories of the Gold Coast in 1897. One of his duties was to occupy as much territory as possible ahead of the French. Establishing his headquarters at Gambaga in June 1898, he led a column of troops, accompanied by Moro Naba Wobgho (q.v.), across Busansi (q.v.) territory to Kombissiri (q.v.). Here his force was stopped by the French with news that the territory had been conceded by the British to France. During the rest of 1898 and early 1899 Northcott organized local government in the Northern Territories and worked on a plan to provide transportation to the area. Later in 1899 Northcott joined General Paul Methuen's forces in South Africa and he was killed fighting the Boers, on 28 November, in the battle of Modder River.

NOTES ET DOCUMENTS VOLTAIQUES. A series of publications on Voltaic topics published by *Centre National de la Recherche Scientifique* (CNRS) in Paris and the *Centre Voltaïque de la Recherche Scientifique* (CVRS) (q.v.) in Ouagadougou beginning in October 1967.

NOUHAO (Nahau). Intermittent stream which rises in Busansi (q.v.) country around Tenkodogo (q.v.) and joins the Nakanbe (White Volta) (q.v.) at the border of Ghana. For a short distance below Bittou (q.v.) it forms the border between Ghana and Burkina Faso. The Ouare, Koukouga and Marsa are tributaries of the Nouhao. This area was plagued by river blindness (q.v.).

NOUMBIEL. 9°32′N 2°44′W. Proposed location of a hydroelectric and irrigation dam on the Mouhoun River (q.v.) on the border with Ghana (to the east of Gaoua). With expected generating output equal to Kompienga and Bagré (qq.v.) combined, such a project would make Burkina virtually self-sufficient in energy, provided that water supply from rainfall does not decline.

NOUMOUDARA. 10°59′N 4°24′W. The center of Tiéfo (q.v.) country, 25 km. southwest of Bobo Dioulasso (q.v.) and just above the Falaise of Banfora (q.v.). The village was attacked by the *sofa* (q.v.) of Samory (q.v.) in July 1897. The chief of Tiéfo, Amoro, conducted a desperate defense before he committed suicide rather than surrender. Samory destroyed the village and put most of the people to death. Soon after his victory Samory began to retreat from Upper Volta to avoid capture by the French. Today Noumoudara is on the main road from Banfora to Bobo Dioulasso (qq.v.) and the railroad (q.v.) passes nearby.

NOUNA. 12°44′N 3°52′W. Town in extreme northwestern Burkina Faso near the Mali border and some 56 km. northwest of Dédougou (q.v.). It was the scene of conflict during the rebellion of June and July in 1916. The town was a district headquarters for Tougan (q.v.) when the area was part of Soudan, and is headquarters of Kossi province (q.v.).

NOUNOUMA (Nouna, Nourouma, Nunuma, Nanoumba, Nibulu). One of the Gourounsi (q.v.) groups. Their chief town is Tchériba (q.v.), on the road between Dédougou and Koudougou (qq.v.), but some are found south of this road in the Boromo and Léo (qq.v.) areas between the Mouhoun (Black Volta) and the Nazinon (Red Volta) (qq.v.).

NUMBADO. Paramount chief of the Gourmantché.

NUNGU (Noungou). Local Gourma (q.v.) name for Fada N'Gourma (q.v.).

NYADFO (Niandfo). The 10th Moro Naba (q.v.). He was the son of Naba Zwetembusma and his wife, Nakoum. All sources agree that he had a long reign, probably in the first half or middle of the seventeenth century. He was the first Moro Naba to live at Ouagadougou, and his tomb is located there. Ouagadougou (q.v.), however, did not become the capital until a century later under Naba Zombre (q.v.).

NYENNEGA. *see* YENNEGA

NYESGA. Area between Yatenga and Yako (qq.v.).

NYINGNEMDO (Gningnemdo). The 5th Moro Naba (q.v.). Son of Naba Oubri (q.v.) and brother of nabas Soarba, Naskyemde and Nasbire (qq.v.), he was father of Naba Koudoumie (q.v.). He reigned in the middle of the sixteenth century from La (q.v.), but he spent much of his reign fighting in the south, and his tomb is at Komtoega in Busansi (q.v.) country near Tenkodogo (q .v .).

NYONYOSE. *see* NINISI

-O-

L'OBSERVATEUR. Ouagadougou (q.v.) newspaper founded in 1973 by Martial and Edouard Ouédraogo. Its offices were burned in 1984. It reappeared in early 1989.

OFFICE DE LA RECHERCHE SCIENTIFIQUE ET TECHNIQUE OUTRE-MER (ORSTOM). Founded as the *Office de la Recherche Scientifique d'Outre-Mer* (ORSOM) in 1943 by the Ministry for Overseas France to do basic research in the French colonies. Began publication in 1963 of *Cahiers ORSTOM*.

OFFICE OF SAHELIAN RELIEF OPERATIONS (OSRO). United Nations drought relief operation which bought and distributed grain in Upper Volta and other Sahelian areas during the 1970s.

ONCHOCERCIASIS. *see* RIVER BLINDNESS

ORGANISATION DE COORDINATION ET COOPERATION POUR LA LUTTE CONTRE LES GRANDES ENDEMIES (OC-CGE). Research center for tropical diseases located in Bobo Dioulasso (q.v.) organized in 1968 by eight African states and France.

ORGANISATION POUR LA DEMOCRATIE POPULAIRE/MOUVE-MENT DU TRAVAIL (ODP/MT). Political group formed in April 1989. At an ODP/MT congress in March 1991, it adopted Blaise Compaoré (q.v.) as its official candidate in the presidential election of

1991. It also replaced its Marxist-Leninist ideology with a commitment to free enterprise policies.

ORGANISATION VOLTAIQUE DES SYNDICATS LIBRE (OVSL) (Voltaic Organization of Free Unions). Labor union founded in 1960. In 1979 two of its leaders were arrested, resulting in week-long strikes in Ouagadougou (q.v.) which forced their release. In 1983 the secretary-general was Boniface Kaboré.

ORGANISME REGIONAL DE DEVELOPPEMENT (ORD). Regional development organizations to promote rural development (q.v.). The country was divided into 11 regions in 1965. The ORDs were still active in the latter 1980s.

ORODARA. 10°59'N 4°55'W. Headquarters of Kénédougou (q.v.) province. Town on the road from Sikasso to Bobo Dioulasso (q.v.), about 76 km. southwest of Bobo Dioulasso. The town is some 720 meters above sea level and on the watershed between the tributaries of the Mouhoun (Black Volta) and the Komoé (qq.v.). The Falaise of Banfora (q.v.) is only a few kilometers to the east of Orodara. In 1984 Thomas Sankara (q.v.) named the Orodara airport after Kwame Nkrumah.

OUAGADOUGOU (Wagadugu). 12°22'N 1°31'W. The capital of Burkina Faso and of Kadiogo (q.v.) province. The major Nakomsé (q.v.) capital. Home of the Moro Naba (q.v.). Ouagadougou was probably founded in the twelfth century. The 10th Moro Naba, Nyâdfo, who lived in the middle of the seventeenth century, was the first Moro Naba to live at Ouagadougou, but it did not become the permanent capital until the reign of the 21st Moro Naba, Zombre (q.v.), a century later. The 24th Moro Naba, Doulougou (q.v.), built the first mosque in Ouagadougou early in the nineteenth century. Gottlob Adolf Krause (q.v.) became the first known European to visit Ouagadougou when he arrived on 24 September 1886. The French captured the city a decade later, and in 1919 Lt. Governor (q.v.) Edouard Hesling (q.v.) began the building program which was to create the modern city, which the French sometimes called "Bancoville" (q.v.).

The two decades between 1934 and 1954 saw Bobo Dioulasso (q.v.) outstrip Ouagadougou as the chief town in modern Burkina Faso, but in December 1954 the railroad (q.v.) from Abidjan was opened to Ouagadougou and a new period of rapid growth began. By the 1990s Ouagadougou was the most populous city and primary administrative and commercial center in Burkina. Ouagadougou is located close to the center of the country, at about equal distance between the Nazinon (Red Volta) and Nakanbe (White Volta) (qq.v.). Ouagadougou's is the primary international airport in Burkina Faso. The city is 297 meters above sea level. March and April are the warmest and August the coolest month. From November to April there is little rain, and the most in July and August. It averages 854 mm. annually. Its population was 60,000 in 1960, 442,000 in 1985 and 500,000 in 1990. Estimates in the mid–1990s range from 600,000 to one million, with some projections of growth to 1.5 million by the year 2010.

OUAHABOU (Wahabu). 11°41′N 3°06′W. Town located a short distance west of Boromo (q.v.) on the Bobo Dioulasso-to-Ouagadougou highway. Al Hadj Mamadou Karantao (q.v.) founded a small Muslim state with Ouahabou as its capital about 1850. Under Mamadou's son, Karamoko Moktar, the power of Ouahabou expanded. Binger (q.v.) visited Ouahabou from 20–26 May 1888 and it was occupied by French troops under Captain G. M. Cazemajou (q.v.) in April 1897.

OUAHIGOUYA (Ouayougui). 13°35′N 2°25′W. Capital of Yatenga (q.v.). The first settlement in the area dates back to the twelfth century, and there are interesting early iron furnaces in the area. Yatenga Naba Kango (q.v.) moved the Yatenga capital here about 1757. Krause (q.v.) visited the place in November 1886, the first recorded visit by a European. French troops under Destenave (q.v.) arrived in May 1895. In 1897 the French built a military base at Ouahigouya. The Yatenga capital is about 178 km. northwest of Ouagadougou (q.v.) and is on the main highway to Mopti and the Mali lake area of the Niger. It is 324 meters above sea level. It is the headquarters of Yatenga province, and an important market for livestock.

OUARAGA (Warga, Waraga). The 20th Moro Naba (q.v.). He was the oldest son of Naba Oubi and his wife, Tenkienga. His rule was delayed for several years either by the usurpation or regency of Moatiba (q.v.). Michel Izard (q.v.) gives 1737–1744 as the dates for the reign of Ouaraga, and Skinner (q.v.) dates the period as about 1660–1680. Ouaraga reorganized Mossi (q.v.) government at all levels, and he instituted the ceremony of the pretended departure of the emperor and most of the other ceremony that surrounds the Moro Naba to the present time. Ouaraga fought with Yako, Mané, Rissiam and the Kipirsi (qq.v.). It is said that he introduced the punishment of castration. Most authorities list Ouaraga as one of the great Moro nabas.

OUARGAYE (Wargaye). 11°32′N 0°01′E. Old Mossi (q.v.) province southeast of Tenkodogo (q.v.).

OUARKOYE. 12°05′N 3°40′W. Bwa town to the east of the Mouhoun (Black Volta) (q.v.) on the road from Bobo Dioulasso to Dédougou (qq.v.). Crozat (q.v.) visited the town on 25–28 August 1890, Monteil was there in March 1891, and Destenave (q.v.) was there in 1895. The town was destroyed by the French on 2 June 1897 when people from there tried to disrupt French supply lines. It was a center of opposition to the French in 1915–1916, and the French destroyed the town again early in 1916.

OUATTARA (Watara, Wattara). Dioula (q.v.) family which established itself at Kong and in western Burkina Faso in the bend of the Mouhoun (Black Volta) (q.v.). In the eighteenth century they conquered much of southwest Burkina Faso except for the Lobi (q.v.) lands.

OUATTARA, AMORO. Chief of Tiéfo (q.v.). He played an important role in the war against Tiéba Traoré (q.v.) of Sikasso (Kénédougou [q.v.]) in 1893. Samory (q.v.) attacked Amoro's capital of Noumoudara (q.v.) in July 1897. Amoro held out against superior forces for over a week before finally committing suicide to avoid capture.

OUATTARA, BAKARY. Ruler of Kong who died on a raid into the Dyan (q.v.) area of Burkina Faso early in the nineteenth century.

OUATTARA, BAKO MOROU. A brother of Diori Ouattara (q.v.). Bako Morou was ruler of Gouiriko (q.v.), Dioula (q.v.) kingdom in the bend of the Black Volta (Mouhoun [q.v.]), from 1839–1851.

OUATTARA, BE-BAKARY. Dioula (q.v.) leader from Bobo Dioulasso (q.v.) who established the state of Lorhosso in the southwestern part of Lobi (q.v.) country at the beginning of the nineteenth century. He later moved his headquarters to Loto, near Diébougou (qq.v.). He was poisoned while fighting the Sissala (q.v.).

OUATTARA, DABILA. Ruler of Kong who raided Lobi (q.v.) country, especially the lands of the Wilé and Dagari (qq.v.), in the 1880s. He was killed on one of these raids.

OUATTARA, DIORI. Ruler of Gouiriko (q.v.), 1809–1839. He died in the battle of Matroukou, in the Tiéfo (q.v.) country, fighting against the armies of Kénédougou (q.v.).

OUATTARA, FAMAGAN (Famara). Brother of Shehu Umar Ouattara, founder of the Dioula (q.v.) state at Kong. Famagon (Fa Maghan) conquered Tiéfo and Bobo (qq.v.) country about 1714 and founded the kingdom of Gouiriko (q.v.) (Gwiriko). Famagan ruled to 1729 and was followed by Famagan denn Tieba, 1729–1742, and Kere-Massa, 1742–1749. The kingdom of Gouiriko lasted until the 1890s.

OUATTARA, GUIMBE. Daughter of Diori Ouattara (q.v.). She was born at Sia (Sya) (q.v.) about 1836. She was active in the campaigns against Kénédougou (q.v.), and was hostess to Binger, Crozat and Monteil (qq.v.) when these Frenchmen visited Bobo Dioulasso (q.v.). Angry at the Tiéfo (q.v.) for their rebellion against the Gouiriko (q.v.) state, she got revenge by calling in the forces of Samory (q.v.), and she was with Samory when he destroyed Noumoudara (q.v.). Guimbe was the most influential Dioula (q.v.) in Bobo Dioulasso for many years. She died in 1919.

OUATTARA, HENRI. Diplomat. He served as ambassador of Upper Volta to Côte d'Ivoire, Mali, Nigeria and Senegal after Independence.

OUATTARA, KARAKARA. Ruler of Kong who attacked the Dyan, Gan and Dagari (qq.v.) in the area north of Gaoua (q.v.) in the 1850s.

OUATTARA, KARAMOKO. He held the title of ruler of Gouiriko (q.v.) from 1909 to 1915; by that time the state no longer existed.

OUATTARA, KONGONDINN. Chief of the Dioula (q.v.) of Bobo Dioulasso (q.v.) at the time Binger (q.v.) was there in 1888. Kongondinn refused to see Binger because he was afraid that he might die if he saw a white person.

OUATTARA, MAGAN-OULE. Ruler of the Dioula Gouiriko (q.v.) state from 1749 to 1809.

OUATTARA, PINTIEBA. Ruler of the Dioula (q.v.) Gouiriko (q.v.) state from 1897 to 1909. He actually had very little power or influence. He made a deal with Commandant Caudrelier (q.v.) at Diébougou (q.v.) in 1897 that he would help the French take Bobo (q.v.) country if they would recognize him as king.

OUATTARA, TIEBA NIANDANE. Ruler of Gouiriko (q.v.) from 1892–1897. Tiéba Niandané ruled at a time that the Dioula (q.v.) state was being attacked on all sides. The French replaced him with a distant relative who was willing to collaborate with them, Pintiéba Ouattara (q.v.). Tiéba died in 1904.

OUBRI (Wubri). The founder of Oubritenga (q.v.), which in time became the Mossi (q.v.) kingdom of Ouagadougou (q.v.). Oubri was the son of Naba Zoungrana (Zungrana) (q.v.) of Tenkodogo (q.v.) and a Ninisi (q.v.) woman, Pougtoenga. Oubri established a new kingdom northwest of his father's lands, and is the first Moro Naba (q.v.). Yamba Tiendrébéogo (q.v.) says that Oubri ruled for 62 years, from 1182–1244, but the most recent authorities date the start of Oubritenga about 1495. The distinctive scars (*cicatrices*) of the Mossi, two series of three lines cut across the cheek, date from Oubri's time. The Tensé festival also dates from this period. At the end of his reign Oubri died fighting the Kipirsi (q.v.). He was buried near Koudougou (q.v.). He was followed as ruler of Oubritenga by four sons in turn, Soarba, Naskyemde, Nasbire and Nyingnemdo (qq.v.).

OUBRITENGA. The land of Oubri (q.v.), founder of the Mossi (q.v.) kingdom of Ouagadougou (q.v.). The date for the formation of Oubritenga is not certain, but it was probably in the latter years of the fifteenth century. Guilongou (q.v.), 12°37′N 1°18′W, near modern Ziniaré (q.v.) and northeast of Ouagadougou, was Oubri's chief place. Oubritenga is also a province with headquarters at Ziniaré.

OUDALAN (Udalan). The area between Dori (q.v.) and the Béli River border area (q.v.) with Mali in northeast Burkina Faso. This area has been a source of controversy between Mali and Burkina because of discrepancies in maps of 1919, 1932, and 1947. The Tuareg (q.v.) of the area are called the Oudalan Tuareg. Also the northernmost province with Gorom-Gorom (q.v.) as its headquarters.

OUEDRANGE NABA. The second-in-command of the Mossi (q.v.) cavalry and head groom of the Moro Naba's stables.

OUEDRAOGO (Ouidiraogo, Wedraogo, Widiraogo, Weddaogo). Traditions differ widely as to Ouédraogo. In some stories Ouédraogo is a woman, in others an Amazon, in still others a man. In some stories Ouédraogo is Mossi (q.v.), in others a Busansi (q.v.). It seems that Ouédraogo was the grandson of Nédéga (q.v.), ruler of Gambaga, and son of Yennega (q.v.) and her mate, Rialle (q.v.). Yennega was Mossi and Rialle was Busansi. The name Ouédraogo means "Stallion". Ouédraogo probably was born in the neighborhood of modern Bittou (q.v.). He is the progenitor of the Nakomsé Mossi (q.v.). He founded a state around Tenkodogo (q.v.). Ouédraogo married Pouriketa (q.v.), a Busansi woman. Their sons, Rawa, Diaba Lompo and Zoungourana (qq.v.), founded the other Mossi states. Oubri (q.v.) was his grandson. Ouédraogo died at Sabatenga.

OUEDRAOGO, ARZOUNA. Military officer. He served as minister of interior and minister of defense in the Lamizana (q.v.) government.

OUEDRAOGO, BERNARD LEDEA. Former teacher and grassroots organizer. Bernard Lédéa Ouédraogo founded the Six "S" Association (*Se Servir de la Saison Sèche en Savanne et au Sahel*) (q.v.) in 1976. Six-S (q.v.) provides technical and financial help for the grassroots self-reliance *Naam* movement which started in 1967 and was modeled on earlier Mossi (q.v.) self-help groups. By 1985 there were more than 1,350 *Naam* groups in Burkina Faso, with similar organizations in other West African countries. Ouédraogo was named co-winner of the 1989 "Africa Prize for Leadership for the Sustainable End of Hunger".

OUEDRAOGO, BERNARD TIBO. He represented Ouagadougou (q.v.) in the Territorial Assembly (q.v.), 1948–52 as a member of the *Union Voltaïque* (UV). He served a term as president of the Territorial Assembly (q.v.), 1951–1952.

OUEDRAOGO, BOUGOURAOUA. Member of the *Union Voltaïque* (UV) who represented Ouahigouya (q.v.) in the Territorial Assembly (q.v.) from 1947 to 1952. He was a member of the Grand Council of Afrique Occidentale Française (AOF), 1948–1952. From 1948 to 1953 he served in the Assembly of the French Union (q.v.), and then he became a member of the Senate of the French Community.

OUEDRAOGO, CLEMENT OUMAROU. Labor leader and politician. The *Union de Communistes Burkinabès* (UCB) (q.v.) was begun in 1985 by Blaise Compaoré (q.v.) and other army officers active in the October 1987 coup which brought the Popular Front (q.v.) to power. The first two years of the Popular Front government saw a steady gain in the political influence of the UCB and Ouédraogo, its secretary-general. In April 1989 the ODP/MT (q.v.) was created as an offspring of the UCB. However, Compaoré maneuvered to oust Clément Oumarou Ouédraogo from the ODP/MT and the Popular Front in April 1990. In December 1991 Ouédraogo, by then head of *Parti du travail du Burkina* (PTB), was assassinated. He was an important leader in the 20-party Confederation of Democratic Forces (CFD) that organized the boycott of the presidential election earlier in the month.

OUEDRAOGO EDOUARD, 1919– . He joined the French army in 1937, and was a prisoner of the Germans from June 1940 until he escaped in August 1942. He was secretary to the minister of public health after independence, and after the coup in January 1966 he became minister of public works, posts and telecommunications. In 1973, Edouard

Ouédraogo became the editor of *L'Observateur* (q.v.), a newspaper owned by his older brother, Martial, a wealthy Voltaic businessman.

OUEDRAOGO, GERARD KANGO, 1925– . Gérard Kango Ouédraogo was born in Ouahigouya (q.v.), a member of the Yatenga (q.v.) royal family, and uncle of the Yatenga Naba (q.v.). He was educated at Ouahigouya and at Bamako (Mali). He then joined the French administrative service and in 1947, when Upper Volta was reconstituted, he became chief of the secretariat of Governor (q.v.) Gaston Mourgues. Then he was transferred to Dakar to work in the office of the High Commissioner of French West Africa.

Returning to Ouahigouya in 1952, he joined Michel Dorange (q.v.) in organizing the Voltaic section of the Gaullist RPF, which they called the *Indépendants de l'Union Française, liste Évolution Voltaïque or Progressiste Voltaïque*. By 1956 this had become the *Mouvement Démocratique Voltaïque* (MDV) (q.v.). During this period Gérard Kango Ouédraogo was a member of the Territorial Assembly (q.v.), 1952–1959, the French National Assembly, 1956–1960, the Grand Council of *Afrique Occidentale Française*, 1953–1959, and in December 1958 he joined the cabinet of Maurice Yaméogo (q.v.) as minister of finance. From 1961 to 1966 he was ambassador to the United Kingdom. After the coup of January 1966 Ouédraogo served as adviser to the Ministry of Foreign Affairs of the military government. In 1970, when it was announced that civilian rule would be restored, Gérard Kango became chairman of the *Union Démocratique Voltaïque* (UDV-RDA) (q.v.), and his party won control of the new National Assembly in the 20 December 1970 elections. On 13 February 1971 he became premier and minister of veterans' affairs. However, harsh drought conditions and debt problems soon undermined Ouédraogo's position, and in December 1973 the National Assembly, now under control of Joseph Ouédraogo and Joseph Conombo (qq.v.), censured the premier. He tried to fight back, refusing to resign, but in February 1974 Lamizana (q.v.) dismissed him and the army resumed control of the government.

He was elected speaker of the National Assembly by a one-vote margin and served 1978–1980. Under house arrest 1980–1984, he was sentenced in 1984 to ten years' imprisonment for embezzlement and tax evasion. Granted partial amnesty in 1985, he was released from prison in 1986. Ouédraogo was the presidential candidate of the *Rassemblement Démocratique Africaine* (RDA) in 1991. However, the decision by the five opposition candidates to boycott the presidential election unless Blaise Compaoré (q.v.) called a national conference led to Compaoré's election.

OUEDRAOGO, GUILLAUME. Member of the Union Voltaïque (UV) and representative from Ouagadougou (q.v.) in the Territorial Assembly (q.v.), 1946–1952. He was president of the Territorial Assembly in 1950 and 1951.

OUEDRAOGO, IDRISSA, 1954– . Award-winning filmmaker. Born in Banfora (q.v.). His 1990 film "Tilai" won the main prize at the 1991 FESPACO (q.v.), and "Yaaba" (The Grandmother) received a special prize at the 1989 Cannes Film Festival.

OUEDRAOGO, JEAN BAPTISTE PHILIPPE, 1942– . Army surgeon major. Born in Kaya (q.v.) and educated in France. Following the 7 November 1982 coup led by Col. Gabriel Yoryan Somé (q.v.) which deposed Saye Zerbo (q.v.), Ouédraogo was appointed head of state. The group formed the *Conseil de Salut du Peuple* (CSP) (q.v.). The CSP government was overthrown in August 1983 when Sankara (q.v.) and the *Conseil National de la Révolution* (CNR) (q.v.) came to power. Ouédraogo was granted clemency in August 1985.

OUEDRAOGO, JOSEPH. Political leader. Educated in Catholic schools, Joseph Ouédraogo became active in the Catholic labor movement and was a member of the *Union pour la Défense des Interêts de la Haute Volta* (UV) in the period after World War II. He was a member of the Territorial Assembly (q.v.) from 1952 to 1959, and the president of that body in 1952–1953. In 1956 he joined the *Parti Démocratique Unifié* (PDU) (q.v.) as a supporter of Ouëzzin Coulibaly (q.v.) and as a member of PDU was selected a member of the Senate of the French Community, was elected mayor of Ouagadougou (q.v.), and served in the government as minister of finance, 1957–1958 and minister of interior, 1958–1959. Joseph Ouédraogo and Yaméogo (q.v.) became political enemies in 1959. Yaméogo had Ouédraogo removed from his position as mayor of Ouagadougou for malfeasance in office 29 August 1959, and Ouédraogo organized the *RDA-Orthodoxe* to oppose Yaméogo. Joseph Ouédraogo was interned for some time after Yaméogo became president and he was one of the leaders in the coup against Yaméogo in January 1966.

In 1970 Ouédraogo became secretary-general of the *Union Démocratique Voltaïque* (UDV-RDA) (q.v.), and he was elected to the new National Assembly in the December elections of that year. The Assembly then elected him as its president. In late 1973 he played a key role in the attempt to get rid of Premier Gérard Kango Ouédraogo, a move which caused the military to close the National Assembly and restore military rule in February 1974. Joseph Ouédraogo finished third of the four major candidates in the 1978 presidential election in which Lamizana (q.v.) was elected. He was then defeated by a single vote by Gérard Kango Ouédraogo who became National Assembly Speaker in 1978.

In 1979 an alliance of Ki-Zerbo's (q.v.) *Union Progressiste Voltaïque* (UPV) and Joseph Ouédraogo's supporters reorganized as the *Front Progressiste Voltaïque* (FPV) (q.v.). The FPV was banned in November 1980.

OUEDRAOGO, JOSEPHINE. Minister for family affairs and national solidarity in the Conseil National de la Révolution (CNR) (q.v.) government beginning in 1985. She was active in campaigns to improve the position of women, and against female circumcision. She was an important influence on Sankara (q.v.).

OUEDRAOGO, MACAIRE, 1935– . Economist and politician. Educated in Ouagadougou and France, he became director-general of the National Development Bank (BND) 1974–1978. He was the *Union Nationale de Defense de Démocratie* (UNDD) (q.v.) candidate for president in 1978. In the run-off voting against Lamizana (q.v.), he received nearly 44 percent of the vote.

OUEDRAOGO, MAMADOU. One of the early leaders of the *Union Voltaïque* (UV) who represented Ouahigouya (q.v.) in the Territorial Assembly (q.v.), 1946–1952 and was a member of the French National Assembly, 1948–1956. He did not stand for reelection in 1956. He directed construction of an earth and rock dam near Korsimoro (q.v.).

OUEDRAOGO, MATHIEU. He was elected mayor of Ouagadougou (q.v.) in the December 1965 elections as Yaméogo's *Union Démocratique Voltaïque* (UDV-RDA) (q.v.) candidate. A coup toppled Yaméogo (q.v.) and his followers from office a few days later.

OUEDRAOGO, MAXIME. Minister of labor who was arrested in 1963 for misuse of public funds.

OUEDRAOGO, NIANDE. Military captain. One of the major streets in Ouagadougou (q.v.) is named for him.

OUEDRAOGO, NONGMA ERNEST. Secretary of state for interior and security in the Thomas Sankara (q.v.) government, 1983. He later became the *Bloc socialist burkinabè* leader, and was imprisoned in August 1995 for allegedly insulting the head of state.

OUEDRAOGO, OUAMDREGRE, 1925–1966. Playwright whose best-known play is *L'Avare Moaga* (The Miserly Moaga).

OUEDRAOGO, PIERRE. Soldier, captain. National chairman of the *Comités de Défense de la Révolution* (CDRs) (q.v.) 1984–1987. A key figure in the *Union de Communistes Burkinabès* (UCB) (q.v.) and the October 1987 coup which brought the Popular Front (q.v.) to power.

OUEDRAOGO, SIDIYETE. *see* SIDIYETE

OUEDRAOGO, TENGA. The baloum naba (q.v.), chief steward of the royal household, under Moro Naba Kom II (q.v.). He was appointed member of the first municipal commission of Ouagadougou (q.v.) in 1927. In 1931 he visited France and the Colonial Exposition at Vincennes, and he returned to Ouagadougou as an enthusiastic advocate of Western culture. He was a candidate for the Constituent Assembly in the elections of 1945, while Ouagadougou was still part of Côte d'Ivoire, and he lost by a narrow margin to Houphouët-Boigny.

OUEDRAOGO, VICTOR. *Parti Démocratique Unifié* (PDU) (q.v.) representative from Kaya (q.v.) in the Territorial Assembly (q.v.), 1957–1959 who became minister of public service and labor in the 1971 government.

OUEDRAOGO, YALAGDO, –1957. He was elected to the Territorial Assembly (q.v.) as a member of the *Mouvement Démocratique Voltaïque* (MDV) (q.v.) from Ouahigouya East in March 1957. In May he was elected President of the Territorial Assembly, but he was killed in an automobile accident in July.

OUEMTANANGO (Wumtanâgo). Son of Oubri (q.v.) who drove the Kado (q.v.) from Yatenga (q.v.) into the Bandiagara area and lived for a time at Guitti (q.v.), a few kilometers northeast of Gourcy.

OUESSA (Wessa). 11°03'N 2°47'W. Frontier post just north of the border with Ghana and east of the Mouhoun (Black Volta) (q.v.), on the highway between Diébougou and Léo (qq.v.).

OUIDI DIOBO. *see* SIDIBE, OUIDI

OUIDI NABA (Widi Naba). One of the four chief officers of the Moro Naba. He was commander of the Mossi (q.v.) Cavalry in war. He also served as prime minister to the Moro Naba (q.v.) and as governor of his own area to the north of Ouagadougou (q.v.).

OURSI. 14°41'N 0°27'W. Village northwest of Gorom-Gorom (q.v.) in the far northeastern part of Burkina Faso. Just to the west of the village is the *Mare d'Oursi,* which is a marsh or dry lake in the dry season (q.v.).

OXFAM. Oxford Committee for Famine Relief, a non-profit organization that aided drought areas of Sahelian countries.

-P-

PABRE. The sister of Yadega (q.v.), the first Yatenga Naba (q.v.). She helped Yadega establish the new Mossi (q.v.) kingdom which at first was centered at Gourcy. She took the royal amulets of Rialle (q.v.) from Moro Naba Koudoumie (q.v.) and carried them to Gourcy for her brother.

Two places in Burkina Faso are called Pabré. There is a Catholic (q.v.) Seminary at the Pabré 19 km. north of Ouagadougou (q.v.). A brick factory and agricultural station are also located there.

PADORO. Group who came from the Ghana area into Burkina around 1600. They are related to the Gan, Dorosié and Komono (qq.v.).

PALM, JEAN-MARC. Burkina's foreign minister under Compaoré (q.v.). Secretary-general of the Union of Communist Struggle. Brother of Jean-Pierre Palm (q.v.), key adviser to Compaoré.

PALM, JEAN-PIERRE. Police chief in 1987. Key adviser to Compaoré (q.v.) and brother of Jean Marc Palm (q.v.).

PAMA (Pamma). 11°15′N 0°42′E. Gourma (q.v.) village 40 km. west of the border with Benin and about the same distance north of the Togo border. Chief town of the Gourma during the seventeenth century. It is on the edge of the *Réserve de Faune de Pama.* A vast swampy area north of Pama long made the whole region unhealthy and river blindness (q.v.) has been a major problem. Commander Destenave and Administrator Molex (qq.v.) met here on 5 March 1898 to discuss the border between Mossiland and Dahomey. A year before that meeting, Germans under Von Carnap (q.v.) signed a treaty with the chief of Pama on 14 January 1895. The French under Decoeur (q.v.) arrived in the village a few hours later.

PANA. Small group in the Tougan (q.v.) area along the border of Mali and Burkina Faso.

PARC NATIONAL DE PO. A park of 155,000 hectares, located to the north and west of Pô (q.v.). Elephant, buffalo, antelope, hartebeest, duiker, reedbuck, and warthog have been found there.

PARTI AFRICAIN DE L'INDEPENDANCE (PAI). A political party organized in Senegal on 18 September 1957. A Marxist-Leninist party, it was introduced into Upper Volta by students returning from the University of Dakar and was soon banned. Connected to Ligue Patriotique pour le Développement (LIPAD) (q.v.).

PARTI D'ACTION PAYSANNE (PAP). A small party formed in March 1960 by Gabriel Ouédraogo. It did not last long.

PARTI DE LA FEDERATION AFRICAINE (PFA). Party founded in 1958 which supported the Mali Federation (q.v.) in 1959–1960, in opposition to Houphouët-Boigny and Yaméogo (q.v.) and the *Rassemblement Démocratique Africaine* (q.v.). In Upper Volta its branch was called the *Parti National Voltaïque* (PNV). Nazi Boni and Laurent Bandaogo (qq.v.) were the leaders. It was outlawed in October 1959. With the PNV outlawed, Boni organized the *Parti Républicain de la Liberté* (PRL) (q.v.), but it was also banned.

PARTI DEMOCRATIQUE UNIFIE (PDU). The party was organized in 1956 by Henri Guissou, Djibril Vinama, Joseph Conombo, Christophe Kalenzaga, Joseph Ouédraogo and Ouëzzin Coulibaly (qq.v.). It became the territorial section of the *Rassemblement Démocratique Africaine* (RDA) (q.v.) in 1957 and Maurice Yaméogo (q.v.) became its leader after the death of Coulibaly in 1958. The PDU was created as a union of the *Parti Démocratique Voltaïque* (PDV) and *Parti Social d'Education des Masses Africaines* (PSEMA) (q.v.). The PDU won the elections of 1957 but victory caused the merger to dissolve. In 1959 the PDU became the Union Démocratique Voltaïque (UDV-RDA) (q.v.).

PARTI DEMOCRATIQUE VOLTAIQUE (PDV-RDA). Political party formed in 1948 by Djibril Vinama and Dr. Ali Barraud (qq.v.) with the support of Daniel Ouëzzin Coulibaly (q.v.) as the Voltaic branch of Houphouët-Boigny's *Rassemblement Démocratique Africaine* (RDA). It was made up of young, educated, anti-chief people, mostly from the western areas. In 1956 it merged with the *Parti Social d'Education des Masses Africaines* (PSEMA) to become the *Parti Démocratique Unifié* (PDU) (qq.v.).

PARTI DU REGROUPEMENT AFRICAIN (PRA). Founded in March 1958 by Léopold Sédar Senghor of Senegal and Nazi Boni (q.v.) and others as an opposition group to the *Rassemblement Démocratique Africaine* (RDA) (q.v.). It was a moderate party with its main support about Bobo Dioulasso (q.v.). The *Mouvement Démocratique Voltaïque* (MDV) and the *Parti Social d'Education des Masses*

Africaines (PSEMA) were affiliated with the PRA. In 1959 PRA supporters in Upper Volta organized the *Parti National Voltaïque* (PNV-PFA), but this was quickly banned. Nazi Boni was the PRA leader in Upper Volta before his death in May 1969. In 1970 Diongolo Traoré (q.v.) became the PRA leader. The party won 12 seats in the legislative elections that year—second to the *Union Démocratique Voltaïque* (UDV-RDA)—and gained two ministerial posts in the government. The PRA was banned in 1974 by the military government. In 1978, as the *Parti du Rassemblement Africain* under Dr. Paley Welte and Laoussene Ouédraogo, the PRA endorsed Lamizana (q.v.) for president, and won six seats in the National Assembly. The party was abolished in 1979 and most of its members joined the UDV.

PARTI DU REGROUPEMENT NATIONAL (PRN). Small political party organized in 1970 and banned four years later. Its secretary-general was Emmanuel Batiebo.

PARTI NATIONAL VOLTAIQUE (PNV-PFA). Political group formed by Nazi Boni and Laurent Bandaogo (qq.v.) in October 1959 to support the *Parti de la Fédération Africaine* (PFA) (q.v.) and federation with Mali and Senegal. The party was banned in a few days because of its opposition to Yaméogo (q.v.) and the *Rassemblement Démocratique Africaine* (q.v.). Boni then organized the *Parti Républicain de la Liberté* (PRL) (q.v.), which was also banned in January of 1960. Boni was soon forced to leave the country and many of his associates were arrested.

PARTI REPUBLICAIN DE LA LIBERTE (PRL). Political party organized by Nazi Boni (q.v.) and others in October 1959 to replace the banned *Parti National Voltaïque* (PNV-PFA) and to support the *Parti du Regroupement Africain* (PRA) (q.v.) and the Mali federation (q.v.). It was opposed to Yaméogo (q.v.) and was banned in its turn two months later.

PARTI SOCIAL D'EDUCATION DES MASSES AFRICAINES (PSEMA). Party started by Henri Guissou and Dr. Joseph Conombo (qq.v.) in 1954 from the *Union Voltaïque* (UV). It was the party of the Mossi (q.v.) chiefs. In 1956 PSEMA merged with the *Parti Démocratique Voltaïque* (PDV) to become the *Parti Démocratique Unifié* (PDU) (q.v.), but the union lasted only a year. By 1957 the PSEMA was in opposition to Yaméogo (q.v.).

PARTI TRAVAILLISTE VOLTAIQUE (PTV). Labor party organized by François de Salles Kaboré (q.v.) and other labor leaders in 1970. It was banned in 1974 when all political activity was halted by the military government.

PASSORE. Province between Yatenga and Oubritenga (qq.v.) with its headquarters at Yako (q.v.).

LE PATRIOTE (The Patriot). *Ligue Patriotique pour le Développement* (LIPAD) (q.v.) newspaper.

PEANUTS (*arachide,* groundnuts). An important cash crop grown in Burkina Faso. Most of the crop is grown in the western part of the country. Groundnut production has consistently fallen since the 1970s, mainly because of low producer prices.

PEAS AND BEANS. Interplanted with other crops. Peas, including chick-peas (*pois de terre*), and beans are important for domestic consumption.

PENDJARI. Tributary of the Oti and Volta rivers which rises in Benin's Atakora mountains, flows northeast to the Burkina Faso border, turns sharply to the west and then southwest, separating the Pendjari Park from Arly Reserve (q.v.). In this region the Pendjari is the border between Benin and Burkina Faso. The Pendjari becomes the Oti in Togo.

PENDJO. Intermittent stream which rises east of Yobiri in the Gobnan Gou of southeastern Burkina Faso. It joins the Pendjari (q.v.) at the border with Benin.

PENI. 10°57'N 4°29'W. Village southwest of Bobo Dioulasso (q.v.) on the main road to Banfora (q.v.) and just behind the Cliffs of Banfora. Tiéba Traoré (q.v.) destroyed the village in 1893.

PEOPLE'S REVOLUTIONARY TRIBUNALS. *see* TRIBUNAUX POPULAIRES DE LA REVOLUTION

PETEGA (Petaga). 14°18'N 1°41'W. Jelgobe (Fulani), Songhai and Ku-rumba (qq.v.) village 20 km. north of Djibo (q.v.). Related to chief-ship of Baraboullé (q.v.). Some Dogon live in the area.

PEUL (Peuhl, Fulbe). *see* FULANI

PILIMPIKOU (Plimpikou). 12°43'N 2°16'W. Hill of 549 meters near Nanoro, south of Yako (q.v.), and northwest of Ouagadougou (q.v.). Another hill, Tanmiougou, is nearby, in the Kipirsi (q.v.) hills. Pilimpikou is a sacred mountain to the Mossi (q.v.).

PISSILA (Pissala). 13°10'N 0°49'W. Located 30 km. northeast of Kaya (q.v.) on the road to Dori, Pissila was headquarters of a cercle until

1983. It is on the watershed between the Nakanbe (White Volta) and the Sirba (qq.v.).

PLANDI (Pendia). The most western tributary of the Mouhoun (Black Volta) (q.v.). It rises north of Koloko (q.v.) and just east of the border with Mali. It is joined by the Dienkoa at 11°19′N 4°49′W. Together the two streams become the Mouhoun (Black Volta).

PO. 11°10′N 1°09′W. A Kasena (q.v.) village about 20 km. north of the border with Ghana on the main road from Navrongo (Ghana) to Ouagadougou (q.v.), it is headquarters of Nahouri province (q.v.). It is said to have been the point from which Rawa (q.v.), son of Ouédraogo (q.v.), began his campaign into the north, which led to the formation of Rawatenga (q.v.) or Zandoma (q.v.), one of the early Mossi (q.v.) states. There is a small national forest and animal reserve/game ranch, Nazinga, near Pô.

The national training center for commandos is headquartered at Pô. A commando unit under Compaoré's (q.v.) command established Sankara (q.v.), former Pô commander, in power in August 1983.

POA. A Mossi (q.v.) province.

PONI. Poni is a southern province in Burkina Faso, with headquarters at Gaoua (q.v.).

The Poni is a tributary of the Mouhoun (Black Volta) (q.v.) which rises in the hills of Lobi (q.v.) between Lokosso and Kampti (q.v.) and passes by the edge of Gaoua.

POPULAR FRONT. *see* FRONT POPULAIRE

POPULATION. Burkina Faso's population was estimated to be 9.74 million in mid–1993 (10.6 million in 1996) and growing at 2.6 percent per year. Overall, the population density is 35.5 inhabitants per square km., which is high for Africa, but the northern and eastern areas are sparsely populated. The 1991 population was 86 percent rural. While 70 percent of the urban population lived in Kadiogo and Houet (qq.v.) provinces—including the cities of Ouagadougou and Bobo Dioulasso (qq.v.) respectively, 17 of the 30 in 1995 provinces were without any major urban area. Burkina's major cities have thus far been spared such severity of in-migration to cities as have Lagos or Kinshasa because many rural Burkinabè have gone to Côte d'Ivoire or Ghana in search of employment. However, some estimates are that Ouagadougou's 1990 population of 500,000 will grow to 1.5 million in only 20 years.

The 1991 Demographic Survey showed a total population of 9.19 million, with ethnic group percentages as listed below.

Bissa	4.4%	Marka	0.1%
Bobo	3.7	Minianka	0.0
Bwa (Bwamu)	3.0	Mossi	48.6
Dafing	3.9	Nounouma	1.5
Dagara	2.1	Peul	6.8
Dioula	0.7	Samo	2.1
Djerma	0.1	Sembla	0.0
Dogon	0.2	Sénufo	1.5
Gouin	0.8	Siamou	0.2
Gourmantché	7.0	Sissala	0.1
Hausa	0.3	Silanse	0.0
Kassena	1.8	Touareg (Bella)	1.1
Ko	0.2	Other Burkinabè	5.0
Koussasse	0.2	Other Nationals	0.5
Léla	2.2		
Lobi	2.2		

POUA (Poa). 12°13′N 2°06′W. A village located a short distance east of Koudougou (q.v.) on the road to Ouagadougou (q.v.). Here the Gourounsi (q.v.) began their rebellion against the Zerma (Zaberma) (q.v.) under Babatu (q.v.) in 1893.

POUGOULI (Puguli, Pwa). Group in Lobi (q.v.) country near the Bougouriba River (q.v.) east of Bobo Dioulasso (q.v.). They are closely related to the Dyan and use a language similar to the Dagari (qq.v.). It is said that they crossed the Mouhoun (Black Volta) (q.v.) to their present location about 1740.

POUNDOU. 12°12′N 3°35′W. A Bobo (q.v.) village near Ouarkoyé (q.v.) where a French road guard named Allamasson was killed late in 1915. This was one of the first events in the Bobo insurrection of 1915–1916. The French destroyed the village on 14–15 February 1916.

POURA GOLD MINES. 11°35′N 2°46′W. The gold mines are in the hills on the left bank of the Mouhoun (Black Volta) (q.v.) about 23 km. southeast of Boromo (q.v.). It is believed that gold has been extracted here since ancient times and the mines were exploited until 1966. An attempt to reopen them in 1981 was not successful. The mines re-opened in 1984. Together with subsequent mining (q.v.) activity in the north and Sebba (q.v.) regions, 1987 marketed gold production of 2.6 tons yielded US$38 million in export revenues. However, smuggled gold was estimated at 4 tons annually. Official production rose to 3.7 tons in 1988 to make gold Burkina's largest export, but fell to 2.2 tons in 1989. While it was back up to 2.9 tons in 1991, it was only 1.8 tons in 1992. (Gold exploration began in the Sebba region in 1988 but has since closed down, as has the *Société des mines de Guiro*, 1985–1993. Agreements were signed in 1996 for exploration in southeastern Burkina Faso.)

POURIKETA. Wife of Ouédraogo (q.v.) whom some traditions say was the mother of Rawa (q.v.), founder of Zandoma (q.v.), Diaba Lompo (q.v.), founder of Fada N'Gourma (q.v.), and Zoungourana (q.v.), Naba of Tenkodogo (q.v.). She was Busansi (q.v.).

PRE, ROLAND-JOANES-LOUIS, 1907– . French administrator who was governor of Gabon, 1946–1947; of French Guinea, 1948–1950; of Upper Volta, 1952–1953; of French Somaliland, 1954; and high commissioner of Cameroun, 1954–1956. From 1937–1939 Pré was secretary-general of the Federation of Building and Public Works, and from 1940–1942 the director of the Federation of Building and Public Works in France. He was active in the Resistance during the Vichy period, and was one of de Gaulle's men after 1944.

PRESENCE AFRICAINE. Présence africaine; revue culturelle du monde noir began publication in 1947 in Paris. Bi-monthly, in both French and English.

PROGRAMME POPULAIRE DE DEVELOPPEMENT (PPD) (People's Development Program). Launched in October 1984 by the *Conseil National de la Révolution* (CNR) (q.v.) to mobilize the local population through *Comités de Défense de la Révolution* (CDRs) (q.v.) for modest-size rural construction projects such as roads (q.v.), dams, sports facilities and health (q.v.) clinics. The program lasted 15 months.

PROTESTANTS. Most of the Protestants in Burkina Faso belong to evangelical denominations. The oldest missionary group, the American Assemblies of God, has worked in Burkina Faso since 1926. Other mission groups that have established churches include the WEC mission, Sudan Interior Mission, Christian and Missionary Alliance, Southern Baptists, and a small Mennonite mission. The *Eglise Apostolique* (q.v.) broke away from the Assemblies of God in 1957–1958. Most church leadership is now in Burkinabè hands.

PROVINCES. A country-wide territorial division of 30 provinces, under high commissioners, and 250 departments, under prefects, with local government divided into districts and villages, came into effect on 15 September 1983 to replace the 1970 system of eight departments and 44 cercles. Fifteen more were created in 1996.

PUGHSIURE. Mossi (q.v.) system by which subjects gave chiefs their daughters who were given as wives to subjects who in turn were pledged to give their first daughter. In 1934 the custom caused a clash between the Catholic church (q.v.) and traditional Mossi leaders.

-Q-

QADIRIYYA BROTHERHOOD. The main Muslim sect, which is a brotherhood of Sufism, in Burkina Faso. The Tijaniyya (q.v.) are a smaller and more devout group.

QUELEA BIRDS. A genus of African weaver birds which, because of their large numbers, pose a major threat to cereal crops and thus to the subsistence farmers of Burkina Faso.

-R-

RABO. Term adopted by the *Conseil National de la Révolution* (CNR) (q.v.) in August 1985 for an order issued by ministers, high commissioners and prefects of the Burkina government.

RAFNAMAN (Hamman, Hamnian, Ras Haman). 14°59′N 0°37′W. An intermittent lake in the extreme north of Burkina Faso on the Béli River (q.v.) near the border with Mali.

RAILROAD. The Abidjan-Niger railroad or *Régie du Chemin de Fer Abidjan-Niamey* (RAN), planned from 1893, was started inland from Abidjan in 1904. Plans were for it to be eventually built all the way to the Niger River across from Niamey. It had reached Bouaké (Côte d'Ivoire) by 1912 and Bobo Dioulasso (q.v.) by 1934, where it was stopped by the depression. Construction resumed later in the 1930s, and the earthworks were completed to Ouagadougou (q.v.) when World War II began in 1939. After the war work resumed, and the rails reached the capital in 1954. Conversion to diesel power began in 1947. The 1,175 km. railroad from Abidjan to Ouagadougou is Burkina Faso's main transport axis linking Banfora, Bobo Dioulasso, Koudougou, Ouagadougou (qq.v.) to each other and to the Ivoirien port.

The Burkinabè-Ivoirien company was divided in 1987 with Burkina Faso's 517 km. managed by the *Société des chemins de fer du Burkina* (SCFB). However, external donors have not been enthusiastic to finance an Ouagadougou-Niamey link, the line has never operated efficiently, and overall traffic has steadily decreased. Most international lenders and aid donors have also opposed construction of the 320-km. Ouagadougou-Tambao-Tin Hrassan railway to allow exploitation of manganese (q.v.) and other minerals at Tambao (q.v.) in the far northeast. However, the Sankara (q.v.) regime strongly supported it in 1985, and the first 35 km. were completed with voluntary labor. With donor assistance 105 km. was completed to Kaya (q.v.) by the end of 1988. Although Compaoré (q.v.) renewed Sankara's commitment to continue the railway to Tambao, there are no short-term plans to continue beyond Kaya. In 1995 Sitarail (French, Belgian, Ivoirien and Burkinabè consortium) began operating the Abidjan-Ouagadougou-Kaya railway line.

RAINY SEASON. Most of the rain falls in Burkina Faso between June and October. Rainfall is greatest in the southwest and smallest in the northeast, and ranges from approximately 500 mm. to 1,145 mm. annually.

RAMADAN. The ninth month of the Muslim year, observed as a sacred fast month by many people in Burkina Faso.

RANDAU, ROBERT. *see* ARNAUD, ROBERT

RASSEMBLEMENT DEMOCRATIQUE AFRICAIN (RDA). An interterritorial party for French colonies in Africa organized in Bamako in October 1946. Felix Houphouët-Boigny of Côte d'Ivoire was its leader. The *Parti Démocratique Voltaïque* (PDV), *Parti Démocratique Unifié* (q.v.) and then the *Union Démocratique Voltaïque* (UDV-RDA) were its affiliates in Upper Volta. Ouëzzin Coulibaly and his wife (qq.v.) were the early organizers in Upper Volta. Maurice Yaméogo (q.v.) was successor to Coulibaly.

RATENGA. Mossi (q.v.) principality located in the northeast area of what later became Yatenga (q.v.). Boulzanga and Zimtanga were two of its important villages. Rissiam (q.v.) and Lake Bam (q.v.) were on the southern borders, and Boussouma (q.v.) was on the eastern side. Djilgodji (q.v.) was to the north of Ratenga.

RAWA. One of the great Nakomsé (q.v.) founding fathers. Son of Ouédraogo (q.v.), he had both Mossi (q.v.) and Busansi (qq.v.) antecedents. He was born in the Tenkodogo (q.v.) area. Authorities differ on the date he began his career. Some say as early as 1175, others as late as 1480. The latter date is probably more nearly correct. His first headquarters was at Pô (q.v.) in Kasena (q.v.) country. Later he moved far to the north, living in Doubaré, Sanga and Zandoma (q.v.) and founding Rawatenga (q.v.) or Zandoma, which later became Yatenga (q.v.).

RAWATENGA. The kingdom or land ruled by Rawa (q.v.). It included most of the land between the Nazinon (Red Volta) and Nakanbe (White Volta) (qq.v.) from Pô (q.v.) in the south to the Plains of Gondo (q.v.) and the Cliffs of Bandiagara in the north. In time the area came to be called Zandoma (q.v.) and then Yatenga (q.v.) was the name used for the northern part of the area.

RECHERCHES VOLTAIQUES. Published by the *Centre National de la Recherche Scientifique* (CNRS) in Paris and the *Centre Voltaïque de la Recherche Scientifique* (CVRS) (q.v.) in Ouagadougou beginning in 1965, when it replaced *Etudes voltaïques* (q.v.).

RECTIFICATION MOVEMENT. Policy changes introduced after the overthrow of Sankara in 1987 by Blaise Compaoré (q.v.) and the Popular Front to *Conseil National de la Révolution* (CNR) (q.v.) program.

RED VOLTA (NAZINON). *see* VOLTA RIVER

REGROUPEMENT DES OFFICIERS COMMUNISTES (ROC). The Association of Communist Officers was founded in 1983 with Thomas Sankara (q.v.) as its leader.

RELIGION. According to Burkina's 1991 Demographic Survey, the religious affiliation of the population was 52 percent Muslim, 26 percent traditional (animist), 21 percent Christian, and 1 percent "without religion". Both Islam (62 percent) and Christianity (34 percent) (qq.v.) are much more products of the cities than is animism (3 percent). The particular surprise from this survey is that traditional religions are reported at less than a plurality. The extent of Islamization may seem surprising because the Mossi (q.v.) are often noted as the most important West African savanna (q.v.) people to have resisted Muslim invaders. However, their conversion has come through contacts that began about 1684 with Mande (q.v.) traders who settled among them.

RELIGION, TRADITIONAL. *see* WEND' POUS NEBA

REO. 12°19′N 2°28′W. Headquarters of Sanguie province (q.v.) located 13 km. northwest of Koudougou (q.v.) on the road to Toma and Tougan (qq.v.) in the Kipirsi (q.v.) lands between the Mouhoun (Black Volta) and Nazinon (Red Volta) (qq.v.).

REPUBLICS. The First Republic of Upper Volta was from 1960–1966, the Second 1971–1974, and the Third 1978–1980. The Fourth Republic (Burkina Faso) began in 1991.

REVOLTS OF WORLD WAR I. The revolts were caused by resentment at abuses by black collaborators with the French, by requisitions of men to serve the French as laborers and soldiers, and by religious antagonism of the Muslims toward the French. They were mostly limited to the Bobo and Marka (qq.v.) areas at first. By 1916 they had spread to the Gourounsi (q.v.). The Tuareg (q.v.) around Dori (q.v.) also revolted in 1916. In 1917 there was trouble in Lobi (q.v.) country.

RIALLE (Rialé, Riaré). A Mande or Busansi (qq.v.) hunter who mated with Yennega (q.v.), daughter of Nédéga (q.v.), ruler of Gambaga. Their son was Ouédraogo (q.v.). Some authorities argue that Rialle, Yennega and Ouédraogo are all mythical characters.

RICE. An important food for all the peoples of West Africa. In Burkina Faso *oryza glaberrima* is derived from a native wild species called *oryza barthii*. An Asiatic type, *oryza sativa,* is being grown today. Rice is both a food and cash crop in Burkina.

RIM. 13°43'N 2°31'W. Historic archeological site southwest of Ouahigouya (q.v.). Rim I predates 3000 B.C.; Rim II dates between 1700 and 900 B.C.; and Rim III dates to the first millennium. Stone tools and pottery were discovered in the first two, with iron and urn burials in the third.

RIMAIBE. Fulani (q.v.) in the area of Djibo (q.v.).

RISSIAM (Risiam, Riziam, Risyam). 13°18'N 1°35'W. Village near the Lake of Bam (q.v.) which was once the chief place of one of the autonomous Mossi (q.v.) kingdoms. It was the traditional enemy of Mané (q.v.). After 1850 Rissiam came under the control of Yatenga (q.v.).

RISSIAM, MASSIF DE. Nakanbe (White Volta) (q.v.) highlands between Gourcy and Kaya (qq.v.) that are often called the Boussouma Mountains.

RIVER BLINDNESS (Onchocerciasis). A disease carried by the *Simulium Damnosum* fly which breeds in flowing water. River blindness has been a major health (q.v.) problem in the Volta rivers and their tributaries. In 1975 the World Bank and World Health Organization established a fund for a 20-year control program (Onchocerciasis Control Program, OCP) in seven West African countries to destroy the larvae of the simulium (blackfly) by aerial spraying. In late 1986 it was announced that river blindness had been brought effectively under control in Burkina.

ROADS. The length of the road network in Burkina Faso increased from approximately 8,700 km. in 1983 to some 13,200 km. in the early 1990s. However, only about 14 percent was tarred.

ROUAMBA, TENSORE PAUL. Diplomat. He received his university education in France. He became ambassador to the United States, Canada and the United Nations, 1966–1972, and ambassador to Nigeria and to Ghana, 1972. In 1984 he was sentenced to life in prison for his role in a plot to overthrow the *Conseil National de la Révolution* (CNR) (q.v.).

RURAL DEVELOPMENT. Burkina Faso (q.v.) is still a country of 7,000 villages, with more than 80 percent of the population (q.v.) dependent on subsistence agriculture. About one-third of the total land area is cultivated, with harvests dependent on rainfall levels. Burkina's is a harsh climate (q.v.). By an unjust twist of meteorology, rainfall variability becomes greater as the average rainfall in an area decreases. After 20 years of recurrent drought (in the 1970s agricultural output fell by 13 percent), the pressure of a relatively high population density (see POPULATION) on land and agricultural resources, and the uncertain impact of global warming still to come, one might well ask what is the outlook for revival or survival.

At the same time, the people of Burkina are the country's greatest resource — hard-working, resourceful, adaptable. And there is a considerable resource in those farmers with traditional farming experience and wisdom in rural land, crop, tree, and livestock management. They have for years confronted the tension of whether to stake their livelihood on the production of food crops or cash crops. The elimination of river blindness (q.v.) opens some less-arid areas to settlement. This may partially compensate for shortened fallow periods as population pressures increase on the usable land and as lessened rainfall in the northern areas forces some farmers to move further south.

The government in the mid–1980s strongly encouraged community discussion of collective actions, which built on the importance that self-help organizations have traditionally had in village life in Burkina. In 18 months in 1983–1984, 1,000 wells and boreholes were dug. Popular development efforts in 1984–1985 resulted in the construction of more than 250 community water storage tanks. From 1983–1986 available water supplies increased from 9 million to 300 million tons. A UNICEF report stated that 78 percent of the population had access to safe water sources by the early 1990s—making Burkina the third-highest ranking country in sub-Saharan Africa.

The survival of a number of villages and many people is due in part to self-reliance efforts that range from land reclamation contour ridging to well-digging to tree-planting. Survival is due to remittances from emigrants working abroad in countries like Côte d'Ivoire and Ghana, and to emergency food aid by international governmental and non-government organizations. Survival is due to support by the Burkina government of these among many measures, and its recognition of the seriousness of the problems that confront the country.

As writer and development consultant to international agencies Paul Harrison suggests, Africa's green revolution must initially use lowest-cost technologies that depend as little as possible on imports, that entail the least risk to farmers, that are built on a foundation of conservation of soil, water, and trees.

-S-

SABOU. 12°04′N 2°14′W. Village located on the main road from Bobo Dioulasso to Ouagadougou just below Koudougou (qq.v.). It is 88 km. west of the capital. Sabou is known to tourists for its pool of tame crocodiles who eat live chickens.

SADI, ABDERRAHMAN ES, ca. 1596–1655. Secretary to the government of Timbuktu and historian whose *Tarikh es Sudan* is the chief source for accounts of contacts between the Mossi (q.v.) and the empires of Mali and Songhai (q.v.).

SAFANE. 12°08′N 3°13′W. Town in the bend of the Mouhoun (Black Volta) (q.v.) on the old Dioula (q.v.) trade route from Djenne to the Gonja country of modern Ghana. It is an important Muslim center of learning for the Dafing (q.v.) area. A coalition of Bobo and Kipirsi (qq.v.) defeated Zerma (q.v.) forces here in 1885. It was the center of much activity during the 1915–1916 insurrection against the French.

SAGHA I. The 23d Moro Naba (q.v.), he ruled at the end of the eighteenth century. He was the son of Naba Kom I (q.v.) and his wife, Tiga. At the start of his reign two of his uncles started a rebellion, but the revolt was put down and many rebellious chiefs were executed. Sagha (q.v.) means "rain" and is something the Mossi (q.v.) always need.

SAGHA II. The 33d Moro Naba, he was the son of Naba Kom II (q.v.), and he ruled from 1942 to 1957. Before becoming Moro Naba (q.v.) he was known as Issoufou Congo. He was a lieutenant in the French Colonial Army, stationed in Côte d'Ivoire at the time of his election. After assuming the *nam* (q.v.) he pledged allegiance to the Vichy government of Petain, but after the invasion of North Africa he supported the new order of de Gaulle. At the end of the war he played a role in the organization of the *Union pour la Defénse des Intérêts de la Haute Volta* (also known as the *Union Voltaïque*) and had a hand in convincing the French to reconstitute Upper Volta. In 1953 he was instrumental in organizing the Syndicate of Traditional Chiefs. He died 12 November 1957, not many months after Ouëzzin Coulibaly (q.v.) organized Upper Volta's first African government. There was a rumor that he had been poisoned, but the autopsy did not confirm this.

SAGHA. The 27th Yatenga Naba (q.v.), he was the son of Naba Piga I. Sagha ruled Yatenga (q.v.) from 1787 to 1803. Most of his reign was spent at Ziga (q.v.). It is said that he had 133 sons. Several of his sons ruled in turn as Yatenga Naba after his death, and the scramble for power between his sons caused a civil war between 1825 and 1834. In fact, his descendants fought between themselves for the rest of the century.

SAHEL. The zone that borders the southern edge of the Sahara. In general the Sahel is above 14° north latitude, or the area of Burkina Faso north of Djibo and Dori (qq.v.). The Sahel is a region with less than 500 millimeters of rain a year. Famines (q.v.) are not uncommon. The population is nomadic, mostly Fulani, Tuareg or Songhai (qq.v.). There are many buttes and hills. In the wet season there are lakes and marshes and good waterholes, but in the dry season (q.v.) water is hard to find.

SAMAMBILI. Place where the electoral college of Ouagadougou (q.v.) met to select a new Moro Naba (q.v.). In 1889 Boukary Koutou surrounded the village with his supporters and forced the electors to select him as their ruler. He became Moro Naba Wobgho (q.v.).

SAMBLA. One of the Mande (q.v.) groups of western Burkina, north of Bobo Dioulasso (q.v.). They are similar to the Samo and especially the Samogho and Bolon (qq.v.).

SAMO. Mande (q.v.) group who moved into northern Dafina (q.v.) along the Sourou (q.v.) probably in the fifteenth century. One tradition says they came from the Busansi (q.v.) country, but it is much more likely that they came from Mali. Many of the Samo are Muslim. They were often attacked by the Fulani (q.v.) and the Yatenga Mossi (q.v.).

SAMOGHO (Sambla, Samoro, Somogo, Don). Mande (q.v.) group much like the Samo. They live in the area between Bobo Dioulasso (q.v.) and Sikasso.

SAMORY TOURE (Samori), ca. 1830–1900. Dioula (q.v.) and Malinké who was born in the area of modern Guinea, where by 1880 he had established a state centered on Bissandugu. He was the *almami,* the civil and religious head of government, with power resting on his army, the *sofa* (q.v.). By 1893 the French had forced Samory to move the center of his power to Dabakala, in Côte d'Ivoire southeast of Kong. In 1896 his army threatened the region of Upper Volta, and between May and July 1897 the *sofa* occupied most of the Lobi (q.v.) and Sénufo area south of Bobo Dioulasso (q.v.) and between the Léraba (q.v.) and Black Volta rivers. Samory came to within a short distance of Bobo Dioulasso before his army encamped at Darsalami (q.v.). At the end of July he laid siege to Noumoudara (q.v.), chief village of the Tiéfo (q.v.), and destroyed the village early in August. By this time French forces were nearby, so Samory began a retreat. In September 1898 he was captured in Côte d'Ivoire and sent into exile, where he died in 1900.

SANAN. *see* SAMO

SANEM (Sanom, Sanum). The 29th Moro Naba (q.v.). He was the oldest of Naba Koutou's 13 sons, and three of his brothers followed him to the throne. Known as Alhassan (Alassane) in his youth, his right to the throne was contested by his brother, Boukary Koutou, when Naba Koutou (q.v.) died. It took several months for the electoral college to resolve the dispute. With the selection of Alhassan, Boukary Koutou was sent into exile. Wars with Boussouma and Boulsa (qq.v.) and a rebellion of Lallé (q.v.) occupied all of the reign of Sanem. The first Europeans reached Ouagadougou (q.v.) at the time of Sanem. The German, Krause (q.v.), came in September 1886, and the Frenchman, Binger (qq.v.), in June 1888. Sanem gave Binger a cow and a little girl and ordered him out of the kingdom. Naba Sanem's reign was from 1871 to 1889; he died without male children, leaving one daughter, Aminata.

SANEM. The 35th Yatenga Naba (q.v.), he ruled from 1877 to 1879.

SANGUIE. Province located to the west of Koudougou with Réo (qq.v.) as its headquarters.

SANKARA, MARIAM. Wife of former head of state Thomas Sankara (q.v.). Following her husband's death in the 15 October 1987 coup led by his former associates, she and their two young sons moved to Libreville, Gabon in June 1988.

SANKARA, THOMAS, 1949–1987. Army captain and head of state. Born at Yako (q.v.) on 21 December 1949, his father was a gendarme officer. Ethnically, Sankara was half Mossi, half Peul. He received military training in Madagascar, France and Morocco. He later became president of the *Conseil National de la Révolution* (CNR) (National Council of the Revolution) (q.v.) and head of state 1983–1987. He was prime minister January–May 1983 in Jean-Baptiste Ouédraogo's (q.v.) *Conseil de Salut du Peuple* (CSP) (q.v.) government and minister of information 1981–1982 in the Saye Zerbo (q.v.) *Comité Militaire de Redressement pour le Progrès National* (CMRPN) (q.v.) government. Sankara was killed 15 October 1987 in Ouagadougou in a coup led by his former associates. He was buried in Dagnoen cemetery on the edge of Ouagadougou in a grave marked only by a whitewashed cement slab. Nostalgia for Sankara both in and outside Burkina has not been lessened by the fact that there was never a judicial inquiry into his death, and this was the first coup in Burkina's history in which the head of state was killed.

Sankara was a forceful, charismatic and articulate president who was well-known for his forthright approach to politics—some said a lack of political finesse—and his strong commitment to participatory democracy. He was pro-Libya and anti-France, and had hopes for a Burkina-Ghana union, shared with his friend the Ghanian head of state Jerry Rawlings. Sankara met Fidel Castro, Samora Machel and Maurice Bishop at the New Delhi Non-Aligned Nations Conference in 1983. He traveled widely in Africa, visited Cuba, China, North Korea and Eastern Europe. He addressed the 1986 Eighth Summit of Nonaligned Nations in Zimbabwe.

In the 1974–1975 Upper Volta-Mali war Sankara distinguished himself, and in 1976 he was posted to Pô (q.v.) as leader of the parachute commandos (CNEC). Sankara and Compaoré (qq.v.) met at parachute school in Rabat, Morocco in early 1978. He was one leader of the November 1982 coup against Zerbo that brought the CSP to power. Named prime minister in January 1983, he was dismissed as too radical in May 1983. Sankara, Jean-Baptiste Lingani and Henri Zongo (qq.v.) were confined to prison or house arrest until the 4 August 1983 coup organized by Blaise Compaoré who led the paracommandos of Pô. Following that coup, Sankara became chairman of the CNR and head of state.

Spartan in his personal lifestyle, he had a strong vision of increased pride and self-reliance for Burkina, including agricultural self-sufficiency, and to improve the health (q.v.) and status of women. Part of that vision led to the 1984 change of the country name to Burkina Faso—"Land of upright people." He characterized the CNR "August Revolution" as "democratic" and "anti-imperialist," necessary "to take power out of the hands of our national bourgeoisie and their imperialist allies and put it in the hands of the people". It would be hard to overstate how much Sankara inspired young people throughout Africa with his vision of an independent and proud Africa.

Sankara promoted the *Comités de Défense de la Révolution* (CDRs) (q.v.) and encouraged community discussion of collective actions. This approach was particularly useful to combat the danger posed by the major drought in 1985. Popular development efforts in 1984–1985 resulted in the construction of more than 250 community water storage tanks. The CNR launched a mass vaccination campaign that immunized 2.5 million children, a major literacy drive, and an internationally acclaimed tree-planting exercise.

Political tensions rose as a result of Sankara's strong commitment to the rural areas, which alienated a number of his trade union (q.v.) and urban supporters. He was killed in Ouagadougou in the 15 October 1987 coup led by his former associates. It was alleged that Sankara was about to order the arrest of Compaoré and others who disagreed with him.

Plans to include Sankara in a shared "national heroes" memorial with Daniel Ouëzzin Coulibaly, Philippe Zinda Kaboré, and Nazi Boni (qq.v.) were announced by the Compaoré government in May 1991.

SANKOIRE, MONT. 10°59'N 0°36'E. Hill on the border of Burkina Faso and Togo.

SANMATENGA. Province in the center of Burkina Faso with its headquarters at Kaya (q.v.).

SANOGO, MAMADOU. Mamadou Sanogo was better known as Karamoko Ba. His father was Imam (q.v.) Fariku Sanogo, founder of Islam (q.v.) in Lanfiéra (q.v.). The son followed in the father's footsteps as leader of the Muslim community in northern Dafina (q.v.). Together they made Lanfiéra a leading center for Islamic studies. Karamoko was host to Crozat in 1890 and Monteil (qq.v.) in 1891 when they passed through Lanfiéra. In 1896 Ouidi Sidibé (q.v.) of Barani (q.v.) accused Karamoko Ba of conspiracy against the French and Voulet (q.v.) had Karamoko Ba executed on 24 November 1896.

SAPONE. 12°03'N 1°36'W. Saponé is a village located about 36 km. south of Ouagadougou (q.v.). It was headquarters of a cercle

1970–1983. In the early years the nominations for Moro Naba (q.v.) took place here. Moro Naba Kouda (q.v.) made it his home in the second half of the sixteenth century. In the latter part of the nineteenth century it was captured several times by the Zerma (Zaberma) (q.v.) and many of its people were taken into slavery (q.v.).

SARA. 11°43'N 3°50'W. Bwa village northeast of Bobo Dioulasso (q.v.) which was destroyed after a battle of two days during the revolts (q.v.) of 1916. Several men in French service were killed there in November 1915. The French first captured the town in March 1899.

SARANTYE MORY TOURE (Sarankeni Mory, Sarankènyi Mori, Sarantie Mori, Sarangye Mori). Samory Toure's (q.v.) son, heir (proclaimed in 1890) and chief lieutenant. From 1896 until the capture of Samory in September 1898 Sarantyé Mory commanded the right wing of Samory's army operating in Côte d'Ivoire, the northern area of the Gold Coast and in Upper Volta. Sarantyé Mory's army in 1897 numbered about 7–8,000 men.

SARYA (Saria). 12°16'N 2°09'W. Town on the railroad (q.v.) east of Koudougou (q.v.) where a cotton (q.v.) experimental station was organized by Lt. Governor Hesling (q.v.) on 1 February 1924. Millet, rice, peanuts, shea nuts and sorghum (qq.v.) have all been grown here experimentally. There is also an agricultural training school located at Sarya.

SATI. 11°13'N 2°17'W. One of the Gourounsi (q.v.) capitals. It is located near Léo (q.v.) and the border with Ghana. Binger (q.v.) called it Sansanné Gandiari, the camp of Gandiari, because Alfa Gazari (q.v.) (Gandiari), the second Zerma (q.v.) leader, was at Sati in 1888. Voulet (q.v.) signed a treaty of protection with Hamaria (q.v.) on 19 September 1896 at Sati.

SAVANNA. Lands between the Sahel (q.v.) and the forest in West Africa.

SAWADOGO. A son of Naba Doulougou (q.v.), he was the 25th Moro Naba (q.v.). Sawadogho sent his son, the future Moro Naba Koutou (q.v.) to study the Koran under Yarsé (q.v.) teachers. Sawadogho developed Kombissiri (q.v.) as a Muslim center and had a mosque built there. He was in poor health during the last years of his reign. Izard (q.v.) says that he ruled from about 1825 to about 1842.

SAWADOGO, JEAN-MARIE, 1940– . Administrator. He was the managing director of the administrative council of the social security fund and later head of the labor and social affairs division, *Organisation Commune Africaine et Malgache,* 1985–1987.

SAWADOGO, MOUSSA, 1927– . Politician and administrator. Born in Kaya (q.v.) and educated in Côte d'Ivoire and William Ponty, Sawadogo authored several plays. *L'oracle,* set at the court of Boussouma (q.v.) at the end of the nineteenth century, and *La fille du Volta,* a play about Yennega (q.v.), premiered in Ouagadougou (q.v.) in 1961. *Kango* (q.v.) is a play about one of the greater Yatenga (q.v.) nabas; these three are his best known works. He has also written *Le Moro Naba Wogbo et la pénétration française au Mossi.*

SAWADOGO, RAM CHRISTOPHE, 1947– . Sociologist. Sawadogo was a researcher at CVRS (q.v.) and acting director of the public service commission. He later became a sociologist for the World Health Organization Onchocerciasis (q.v.) Program, Ouagadougou.

SCAL, CAPTAIN. French officer who replaced Voulet (q.v.) as resident at Ouagadougou (q.v.) 20 February 1897. He was briefly involved in the campaign against the Zerma (q.v.) in Gourounsi (q.v.) territory and the northern part of the Gold Coast. He signed a temporary agreement with the British on boundaries. His health was poor during the last months of his tour of duty in the Mossi (q.v.) lands, and he was replaced as resident in June 1898 by Capt. Arminon.

SEBBA. 13°26'N 0°32'E. Capital of the Yagha (q.v.) area. When Barth (q.v.) visited the village on 6 July 1853 he found the ruler of the area seated before the mosque reading the Koran to his people. Barth reported that the village had about 200 huts, and he felt the milk the people gave him was very good. Sebba is not far from the Niger border.

SEDGHO, LAURENT. Military officer. He held the important post of minister of peasant cooperative action in the Popular Front (q.v.) government of Blaise Compaoré (q.v.) 1988–1990.

SEGUENEGA. 13°27'N 1°58'W. Headquarters of a cercle prior to 1983, and located on the northern route between Ouagadougou and Ouahigouya (qq.v.).

SEMBLA (Semu). A Mande (q.v.) group who live east of Bobo Dioulasso (q.v.).

SENEGALAIS. Referred to troops in French service from any part of West Africa.

SENO. Province in the northeast of Burkina Faso with its headquarters at Dori (q.v.).

Also, another name for the Gondo Plain (q.v.) area in Mali between the cliffs of Bandiagara and the border with Burkina Faso.

SENUFO (Sénoufo, Senufu). People who live in Côte d'Ivoire, Mali and Burkina Faso. The Gouin (q.v.), Karaboro (q.v.), Minianka, Nafana, Nanerge (q.v.), Turka, Tyefo and Wara (q.v.) are related groups who are called Sénufo. In Burkina Faso they live in the southwest around Bobo Dioulasso, Orodara, Banfora and Sindou (qq.v.), and their language is used there.

SERE. A son of Zoungourana (q.v.), ruler of Tenkodogo (q.v.).

SERIBA, CHARLES TRAORE. Long-time outspoken President of the Supreme Court of Upper Volta. He was fired by Lamizana (q.v.) in 1980.

SHAYKH (or Seeku in Fulfulde or Shehu in Hausa [q.v.]). A religious leader with a reputation for learning and piety.

SHEA TREE (*Karité; Tâaga* in Moré). The *butyrospermum parkii* is the most valuable tree in Burkina Faso. It flourishes near villages where it can escape grass fires so common in the open bush. Its fruits are dropped in May. The fruit resembles a yellow plum and contains nuts in a sweet pulp which is edible when ripe. Shea butter is obtained from oil in the kernels of the nuts. It is sold in markets as yellowish loaves, which look like oily cheese. It is used for cooking, as an illuminant, as an ointment and as a hair-dressing. *Karité* has long been an important cash crop and export of Burkina Faso.

SIA (Sya). Mande (q.v.) group now much mixed with the Bobo (q.v.) around Bobo Dioulasso (q.v.). They are mostly Muslims.

SIAN, LAKE OF. 13°06′N 1°13′W. Lake located a few kilometers west of Kaya (q.v.).

SIDERADOUGOU (Sidéradugu). 10°40′N 4°15′W. Town located about 36 km. southeast of the Falaises of Banfora (q.v.) in the region where the Bougouriba River (q.v.) rises. The Karaboro (q.v.) and Tyefo live in the area. Binger (q.v.) was coolly received when he visited in Sidéradougou in April 1888. Samory (q.v.) camped there in July 1897 before going on to destroy Noumoudara (q.v.), and returned for August and September.

SIDIBE, DIAN. Son of Malik Sidibé, a Fulani (q.v.) who established a state around Ouankoro in modern Mali. Dian moved south about 1862 and established his own government at Barani (q.v.), some 90 km. northwest of Dédougou (q.v.). Dian was overthrown by his brother, Ouidi, in about 1875, and went into exile at Dokuy, some 80 km. south of Barani, where he died in 1878.

SIDIBE, IDRISSA. Son of Ouidi Sidibé (q.v.). He succeeded his father as chief of the Fulani (q.v.) state of Barani (q.v.) in 1901 and continued to rule as an ally of the French into the 1920s.

SIDIBE, OUIDI (Ouidi Diobo, Widi). Son of Malik, brother of Dian, and father of Idrissa. He took the rule of Barani (q.v.) from his brother and in time extended his powers to govern most of the Red or Oulé Bobo and the Samo (q.v.). He ruled from about 1862 to 1901. He allied himself with the French from 1894 and the French left him in control of Dafina (q.v.) after the battle of Boussé (q.v.). The Samo often revolted against Ouidi, necessitating frequent support from French forces. In November 1896 Voulet (q.v.) helped Ouidi take Lanfiéra (q.v.).

SIDIYETE OUEDRAOGO. Hero of Yatenga (q.v.) resistance to the French. He was born in Sissamba (q.v.) and became the leader of the Sagha (q.v.) (Sissamba or Yemdé) forces in the civil war against the Tougouri (q.v.) faction. He was commander of the troops of Naba Baogho (q.v.) at the battle of Thiou (q.v.) in which Baogho was fatally wounded. After Bagaré of the Tougouri faction became Yatenga Naba Boulli (q.v.) in June 1894, Sidiyété led the Sissamba forces in a continuous guerilla campaign against Naba Boulli. Boulli called in the French to help him. Sidiyété was defeated by Voulet (q.v.) at Sim (q.v.) in August 1896, but he escaped to fight on. Frequently he forced Naba Boulli to flee from Ouahigouya (q.v.), but the French always returned to support their ally. By March 1898 the fire-power of the French had decimated the Sissamba forces. Sidiyété escaped into Gourounsi (q.v.) country for a time, but he was finally captured in January 1902 and condemned to death, a sentence the French commuted at first to life at hard labor. He spent two years in prison, but in 1904 was exiled to the Soudan. In 1916 the French gave Sidiyété a job in Dafina (q.v.), and he finally returned home to Sissamba in the 1920s.

SIDWAYA. "The Truth". The government French-language daily newspaper of Burkina Faso founded in April 1984.

SIGIRI (Sighiri, Siguiri, Sigry). He was the 13th and youngest son of Naba Koutou (q.v.). During his younger days while his father and brothers ruled he was known as Mamadou. The French installed him as the 31st Moro Naba 28 January 1897 and he lived until February 1905. The Mossi (q.v.) rulers of Tenkodogo and Ouahigouya (qq.v.) took part in the ceremonies when Sigiri was installed in recognition of the French policy that Ouagadougou (q.v.) should have priority over the other two Mossi kingdoms. The Lallé Naba, who was hostile to the supremacy of Ouagadougou, was captured and executed by the French.

SIGUE, NOUHOUM. Veterinarian associated with the *Union Voltaïque* (UV) and the *Rassemblement Démocratique Africaine* (RDA) (qq.v.). He was a member of the Council of the French Republic, 1948–1958. He was also active in the *Groupe d'Action Paysanne* (GAP) for a time.

SIKASSO PLATEAU. The area west of Bobo Dioulasso and Banfora and the *Falaises de Banfora* (qq.v.). It is the highest part of Burkina Faso. The Léraba, Komoé and Mouhoun (Black Volta) (qq.v.) all rise in the area. The Sénufo are the chief inhabitants of the region.

SILK COTTON TREE. *see* KAPOK

SILMI-MOSSI. People who claim descent from Fulani (q.v.) nomads and Mossi (q.v.) women.

SIM. 13°48'N 2°35'W. A village a short distance from Thiou (q.v.) in Yatenga (q.v.). A battle was fought here on 10 August 1896 between the French under Paul Voulet (q.v.) and Sissamba (q.v.) forces under Sidiyété Ouedraogo (q.v.), who opposed Bagaré (Boulli [q.v.]), the French-supported ruler of Yatenga.

SINDOU. 10°40'N 5°10'W. Village west of Banfora (q.v.). The hills of Sindou (*Aiguille de Sindou*) between Sindou and Banfora are famous for their lace-like rock formations. Many archeological discoveries have been made in the area. Sindou is only a short distance from the border with Mali and with Côte d'Ivoire, in Sénufo territory.

SINGOU. A tributary of the Pendjari River (q.v.) which drains the Singou Forest Reserve. There is a village by that name between Pama (q.v.) and Arli at 11°18'N 1°02'E.

SIRBA. A tributary which joins the Niger River above Niamey, Niger. It rises in the area of Boulsa and Koupéla (qq.v.) and flows northeastward toward the Niger during the rainy season. The Faga (q.v.) is the main tributary of the Sirba. For a short distance the Sirba forms the border of Burkina Faso and Niger. Barth (q.v.) crossed the Sirba on 2 July 1853 in the rainy season on a bundle of reeds. He said that the banks were about 6 meters high, the river was about 65 meters wide, and that it was 3 meters deep in the middle of the channel.

SISSALA. One of the group called the Gourounsi (q.v.). They live in the area along the border of Burkina Faso and Ghana near Léo (q.v.). They suffered much at the hands of the Zerma (q.v.) at the end of the nineteenth century. Also see ISALA.

SISSAMBA. 13°30'N 2°28'W. Village in Yatenga (q.v.) near Ouahigouya (q.v.) which was the former capital of Yatenga and the center of opposition to Naba Boulli (q.v.) from 1894. The Sissamba faction was the group who supported the Sagha (q.v.) or Yemdé claims to rule in Yatenga. Sidiyété Ouedraogo (q.v.) was the leader of the Sissamba faction.

SISSILI. Province south of Ouagadougou (q.v.) on the border with Ghana with its headquarters at Léo (q.v.).

SIX-S. The Six "S" Association (*Se Servir de la Saison Sèche en Savanne et au Sahel*) was founded in 1976 by Bernard Lédéa Ouedraogo (q.v.). Six-S provides technical and financial help for the grassroots self-reliance *Naam* movement started in 1967 in Burkina Faso. The *Naam* movement is derived from traditional Mossi (q.v.) village self-help cooperatives in which a grouping of young men and women form each rainy season to help with planting and harvesting. Six-S employs ultra-low-cost technologies that can be taught and spread quickly, local materials, and labor that is underutilized during the dry season (q.v.). By 1985 there were more than 1,350 *Naam* groups in Burkina Faso, with similar organizations in Senegal, Mauritania, Mali, Niger and Togo.

SKINNER, ELLIOTT PERCIVAL, 1924– . Professor and diplomat. American anthropologist who served as the United States ambassador to Upper Volta from 1966 to 1969. He was born in Trinidad-Tobago. He did research in the Nobéré and Manga (qq.v.) area 1955–1957. Skinner was professor at New York University 1959–1963, and then in Columbia University's Anthropology Department 1963– . He served as Board chairman of the African-American Scholars Council. Skinner is the most prolific writer on Upper Volta/Burkina Faso in the English language.

SLAVERY. Gustave Binger (q.v.) reported that in 1888 slavery formed the basis of all commercial dealings in Mossiland. An adult slave was worth from 50,000 to 65,000 cowries, and horses were worth from two to four slaves.

SLEEPING SICKNESS (trypanosomiasis). *see* HEALTH

SOARBA (Sorba). The son of Oubri (q.v.) and Pougbiendiga and brother of three rulers of the Ouagadougou Nakomsé (q.v.) kingdom, he was the second Moro Naba (q.v.). He ruled early in the sixteenth century, from about 1518–1540. He lived at Lougsi and may have been assassinated by orders of his brother Nasbire (q.v.).

SOBATANGA. 14°03′N 2°13′W. Mesa northeast of Ouahigouya (q.v.) and near the border of Mali. The most northern tributary of the Nakanbe (White Volta) (q.v.) rises in this area. The elevation is about 364 meters.

SOFA. Any African infantrymen. A Mande (q.v.) term for soldiers of West African chiefs in the nineteenth century. From 1894 to 1898 the *sofa* with firearms in the regular army of Samory Touré (q.v.) operated close to or within the borders of what is now southwestern Burkina Faso (q.v.).

SOFITEX. The *Société burkinabè des fibres textiles* carries out processing and marketing of cotton (q.v.). The *Compagnie française pour le développement des fibres textiles* owns 34 percent of the equity in SOFITEX while the Burkina government and parastatals own 65 percent and local banks 1 percent.

SOHONDYI. Warrior caste of the Ouattara (q.v.) army of Kong and Bobo Dioulasso (q.v.) in the eighteenth century. Most were Sénufo. They established several small states, some of which lasted well into the nineteenth century.

SOLIDARITE VOLTAIQUE. In December 1957 the *Mouvement Démocratique Voltaïque* (MDV), *Mouvement Populaire de l'Evolution Africaine* (MPEA), and *Parti Social d'Education des Masses Africaines* (PSEMA) (qq.v.), all opponents of the *Rassemblement Démocratique Africaine* (RDA) (q.v.), combined to make Nazi Boni (q.v.) president of the Assembly. He lost this position in April 1958.

SOME, GABRIEL YORYAN, 1930–1983. Politician and former chief of staff and minister of defense. During the Mali federation (q.v.) of Senegal, Mali and Upper Volta, he was a *Parti Démocratique Unifié* (PDU) (q.v.) member from Diébougou (q.v.) of the Third Territorial

Assembly (q.v.) 1957–1959. Somé was one of the leaders of the 1966 coup that deposed President Maurice Yaméogo (q.v.) and established Lt. Colonel Sangoulé Lamizana (q.v.) as head of state. He was minister of the interior and security from February 1971 to 1973, and again 1976–1978. Col. Somé was one of the leaders of the officers' coup in November 1982 that deposed Saye Zerbo (q.v.). He continued as Army chief of staff under the government until appointed secretary-general of national defense in May 1983, and was one of the most powerful figures in the Jean Baptiste Ouédraogo *Conseil de Salut du Peuple* (q.v.) government. He was killed on 8 August 1983 following the coup that brought Thomas Sankara (q.v.) to power.

SOME, VALERE. Valère Somé was active in the Union of Communist Struggles—Reconstructed, and was minister of higher education in the *Conseil National de la Révolution* (CNR) (q.v.) regime. He was the author of Sankara's October 1983 Political Orientation Speech delivered in Tenkodogo (q.v.). He fled the country after the Compaoré (q.v.) October 1987 coup.

SOMNIAGA. Village about eight kilometers from Ouahigouya (q.v.) where the royal mausoleum of Yatenga (q.v.) is located. Yatenga Naba (q.v.) Vateberegum made the village his home in the middle of the seventeenth century, and he was the first Yatenga ruler buried there. Traditionally the Yatenga Naba's favorite wife and his jester were buried alive with him; today it is a live cat and a cockerel.

SOMOGO. *see* SAMOGHO

SONABEL. In 1983 the *Société Nationale Burkinabè d'Electricité* replaced VOLTELEC which had been established in 1977 as a state corporation to produce, distribute and sell electricity.

SONGHAI (Songhay). Group who at one time had a great West African empire, with a capital at Gao beginning about 1009 A.D. Their greatest power was reached in 1465–1492 under Sonni Ali and 1493–1528 under Askia Muhammad. Between 1465 and 1528 Songhai forces often raided territory which is now in Burkina Faso (q.v.) in wars with the Mossi (q.v.). They were defeated by forces from Morocco in 1591 and their power declined rapidly after that. The Zerma (q.v.) were a branch of the Songhai. There are many Songhai in northeastern Burkina Faso.

SONO. 12°50′N 3°29′W. North of Louri and southwest of Lanféria. French Commandant Caudrelier (q.v.) established a base here in May

1897. It was headquarters of a cercle from then until 1899, when the headquarters were moved to Kouri (q.v.).

SORGHO, DAOGO MATHIAS. He represented Tenkodogo (q.v.) in the Territorial Assembly (q.v.) 1952–1959. He was a member of the *Union Voltaïque* (UV) and later of the PDU-RDA. He was president of the Territorial Assembly (q.v.) 1954–1957 and after that was appointed minister of public health by Ouëzzin Coulibaly (q.v.).

SORGHUM. Grain sorghum and millet (q.v.) are the two most important cereal food crops grown in Burkina Faso. Sorghum is also called guinea corn or durra or giant millet. Sorghum production is about twice that of millet. It is almost impervious to disease or insects. It is planted with the earliest rains and harvested in August.

SOULA HILLS. 13°22'N 0°15'W. Hills southwest of Dori (q.v.) that rise to about 429 meters.

SOUM. Province in the north of Burkina Faso which borders Mali with its headquarters at Djibo (q.v.).

SOUM, MARE DE. 14°47'N 1°05'W. Marsh lake and waterhole northeast of Djibo (q.v.), near the Mali border north of Aribinda (q.v.). It is often dry in times of drought.

SOUROU. Province to the west and north of Ouagadougou (q.v.) and southwest of Yatenga (q.v.) province on the border with Mali; its headquarters is at Tougan (q.v.).

SOUROU DAM. 12°45'N 3°27'W. Dam for irrigation and to control water flow between the Sourou and Mouhoun (qq.v.).

SOUROU RIVER (Bagué [q.v.]). The most northern and a major tributary of the Mouhoun (Black Volta) (q.v.). It rises in Mali near Koro southeast of the *Falaise de Bandiagara* (an intermittent stream that rises west of Ouahigouya also joins the Sourou in Mali) and joins the Mouhoun north of Dédougou (q.v.) at the apex of the bend of the Mouhoun. It is alternately a tributary and distributary of the Mouhoun (Black Volta). During the floods between August and November the current of the Mouhoun may run 160 kilometers up the Sourou. It is believed that at one time the Mouhoun flowed through the Sourou to an inland sea where the Gondo Plain (q.v.) now is.

STEWART, DONALD WILLIAM, 1860–1905. British officer and graduate of Sandhurst. In October 1896, he was ordered to go to

Ouagadougou (q.v.). He had reached Gambaga when he learned that the French under Voulet (q.v.) had taken the Mossi (q.v.) capital. Stewart and Voulet met at Tenkodogo (q.v.) on 9 February 1897, and Stewart agreed to withdraw. From 1897 to 1904 Stewart was stationed at Kumasi, first as resident and then as commissioner to Ashanti. He was appointed commissioner to British East Africa, 1904–1905.

SWEET POTATOES. *Ipomoea batatas,* on ridges, are grown in areas too dry for yams (q.v.) and even in the dry season (q.v.).

SY, GENERAL BABA. He was appointed defense minister in the Lamizana (q.v.) military government in 1974.

SYEMOU. Small group who live in Orodara (q.v.).

SYNDICAT NATIONAL DES ENSEIGNANTS AFRICAINS DE HAUTE VOLTA (SNEAHV) (National Union of African Teachers of Upper Volta). Union of elementary school teachers whose leaders in 1984 were associated with Ki-Zerbo's *Front Progressiste Voltaïque* (FPV) (q.v.).

-T-

TABASKI. The Id al Kabir Muslim holiday in Burkina Faso which celebrates Ibrahim's (Abraham's) willingness to sacrifice his son Ishmael (Isaac) to God.

TAGBALADOUGOU FALLS. 10°47'N 4°42'W. A tributary of the Komoé (Comoé) (q.v.) goes 150 meters over the *Falaise de Banfora* NNE of Banfora (qq.v.) town. The peak flow is June-September.

TAGOUARA, PLATEAU OF. Another name for the Sikasso Plateau (q.v.).

TAGWA (Tagba). Ethnic group in Senufo (q.v.) group.

TAMARIND. The *tamarindus indica* attains heights of 21-24 meters. A valuable tree which grows in Burkina Faso. The fruit or pod of this tree contains an acid pulp used as food and as a laxative. It is used for flavoring drinks and as an antidote for fever. The leaves furnish red or yellow dye, and the Fulani (q.v.) use ashes from the wood and pulp for tanning and dyeing goatskins. The tree is host for nests of wild silkworms whose silk is spun into thread used to make cloth.

TAMASSARI. 10°39'N 5°20'W. A place west of Sindou (q.v.) and near the Mali border where interesting ruins are located.

TAMBAO. Location of limestone and manganese (q.v.) deposits in the extreme northeastern corner of Burkina Faso. Manganese was discovered in 1960. An international consortium was organized in 1974 to develop these deposits. Work on the 353 km. railroad (q.v.) extension from Ouagadougou (q.v.) began in October 1981. In February 1985 the "Battle for the Railroad" was launched to lay the rails on the 105 km. Ouagadougou-Kaya roadbed with voluntary labor, and that line was opened by the end of 1988. There are plans for a dam at nearby Tin Akof (q.v.), and a cement works at Tin Hrassan (q.v.).

TANKAMBA. Early inhabitants of the Gobnangou (q.v.) area of southeastern Burkina, southern Gourma (q.v.). The group is related to the Somba who live in modern Benin and Togo.

TANMIOUGOU. 12°46'N 2°17'W. One of the high points in the Kipirsi (q.v.) hills below Yako (q.v.). It is 549 meters.

TANSOBA. Mossi (q.v.) field commander in time of war. He is one of the four electors with a voice in the selection of a new Moro Naba (q.v.).

TAPOA. The extreme eastern province of Burkina Faso, with its headquarters at Diapaga (q.v.).
    Also an intermittent stream which rises in Gourma (q.v.) and flows across the northern border of the National Park of W into the Niger. For a short distance the Tapoa forms the border with Niger.

TARIQAS. Brotherhoods or Muslim communities in West Africa. The major sects are the Qadiriyya, Tijaniyya and Ahmadiyya (qq.v.).

TATENGA. *see* RISSIAM

TAUXIER, LOUIS, 1871–1942. French administrator who was first sent to Ouagadougou (q.v.) in 1908 and served in Yatenga (q.v.) from September 1913 to July 1916. He is a recognized authority on the Voltaic peoples and wrote many articles and books on the peoples of French West Africa.

TCHERIBA. 12°16'N 3°05'W. Tchériba is a village on the highway between Dédougou and Koudougou (qq.v.) just a short distance west of the Mouhoun (Black Volta) (q.v.). It was the chief village of the

Nounouma (q.v.), a Gourounsi (q.v.) group. The village was destroyed by the French on 20 April 1916 during that year's revolts (q.v.).

TEGESSIE (Téguessié, Tégé, Tégésye, Tésé, Loron-Lobi, Lorhon, Touna, Tuni). Lobi (q.v.) group who live around Kampti (q.v.) near the border of Côte d'Ivoire. They speak a Kulango dialect. It is believed that they once lived near Lawra (Ghana), but crossed the Mouhoun (Black Volta) (q.v.) to their present location about 1770.

TEMA. 13°03′N 1°46′W. Téma is a village north of Ouagadougou and west of Mané (qq.v.) that was once the chief place of one of the ancient Mossi (q .v.) principalities.

TENA KOUROU. 10°45′N 5°25′W. Téna Kourou is the highest point in Burkina Faso. The mountain peak is located in the far southwest corner of the country, west of Banfora (q.v.) and adjacent to the Mali border, and stands 749 meters.

TENADO. 12°12′N 2°36′W. Headquarters of a cercle prior to 1983, and located on the main road from Koudougou to Dédougou (qq.v.) just east of the Mouhoun (Black Volta) (q.v.).

TENGA (pl. Tense). The earth-goddess of Mossiland.

TENGABISSI (Tinguimbissi). The Children of the Earth. The indigenous population who were ruled by the nakomsé (q.v.) or Mossi (q.v.) nobility. This is the vast majority of the population (q.v.) east of the Nazinon (Red Volta) (q.v.). The term Ninisi (q.v.) or Nioniossé means much the same thing.

TENGASOBA (Tengdana among the southern Mossi). A land priest who is in charge of earth shrines. A female tengasoba is thought to be more powerful than a male tengasoba. These priests have charge of farming and bushlands, make sacrifices for rain and fertility and officiate at ceremonial occasions. They may also preside at funerals.

TENKODOGO (Tenkudugu, Tinkoudogo, Tânkudgo). 11°47′N 0°22′W. Headquarters of Boulgou province (q.v.). It was once called Tankourou. Tradition says that Ouédraogo (q.v.) founded his kingdom with Tenkodogo as its chief place, but Tenkodogo was probably founded much later. The Busansi (q.v.) live in this area, and Ouédraogo's father, Rialle (q.v.), was supposed to be Busansi. Tenkodogo has always been overshadowed by Ouagadougou and Ouahigouya (qq.v.). Voulet and Stewart (qq.v.) met here on 9 February 1897 and Yaméogo (q.v.) and Nkrumah on 31 July 1962.

On 2 October 1983 Thomas Sankara (q.v.) delivered his famous Political Orientation Speech here, the manifesto of his movement.

TENSE (Tinsé). Mossi (q.v.) ceremony opening the agricultural season to ward off supernatural disasters. It is said to have been started during the reign of Oubri (q.v.).

TERRITORIAL ASSEMBLY. *see* ASSEMBLEE TERRITORIALE DE LA HAUTE VOLTA

THEVENOUD, JOANNY, 1878–1949. The Apostolic Vicar of Ouagadougou (q.v.). From 1903 to 1949 Father Thévenoud was the leading Catholic (q.v.) missionary in Upper Volta. A member of the order of White Fathers (q.v.), he was Bishop of Ouagadougou from 1921 until his death in 1949.

THIERRY, OBERLEUTNANT. German officer who was active, along with Julius von Zech, in the attempt to establish German claims to Gourma (q.v.) ahead of the British or French. In May 1897 French forces under Baud (q.v.) and German forces under Thierry met at Pama (q.v.) and almost came to blows.

THIOU. 13°48′N 2°40′W. In 1894 a battle was fought here between the Sagha (Yemdé) (q.v.) faction and the Tougouri (q.v.) faction in the Yatenga (q.v.) civil war. Yatenga Naba Baogho (q.v.) was mortally wounded and the Sagha (q.v.) faction never recovered from this loss. Bagaré, the Tougouri candidate, soon became Yatenga Naba Boulli (q.v.), but he held Ouahigouya (q.v.) only with French support. Thiou is 36 km. northwest of Ouahigouya and just 30 km. to the border of Mali. Destenave (q.v.) passed here on 7 May 1895.

TIEFO (Tyéfo). People who live south of Bobo Dioulasso (q.v.) and whose chief place is Noumoudara (q.v.). The town was destroyed by Samory (q.v.) in August 1897 and most of the people were killed. The Tiéfo have never recovered.

TIEFORA. 10°38′N 4°33′W. Village about 26 km. east of Banfora (q.v.). Near here the Karaboro (q.v.) defeated part of Samory's (q.v.) forces in August 1897 as they were retreating from Burkina Faso. A dam is located near here on a branch of the Komoé (q.v.).

TIENDREBEOGO, DIDIER NOBILA. One-time mayor of Ouagadougou who was executed on 12 June 1984 as leader of a plot to overthrow Sankara (q.v.) and the *Conseil National de la Révolution* (CNR) (q.v.).

TIENDREBEOGO, YAMBA, 1907– . Lahallé-Naba (second minister of Ouagadougou, he is responsible for sacrifices to the royal ancestors) of Ouagadougou (q.v.) beginning in 1928, he served as vice president of the traditional chief's syndicate from 1947 to 1960. He collected traditions, sayings, stories and proverbs of the Voltaic people. At one time he conducted a popular radio program called "Chez le Larhalle," in which he told about the folklore of the Mossi (q.v.). Several of his collections have been published.

TIENTARBOUM, FELIX. Army major. Tientarboum was minister of youth and sports 1971–1975, and one of the leaders in the November 1980 coup. He became minister of foreign affairs in the *Comité Militaire de Redressement pour le Progrès National* (CMRPN) (q.v.) under Saye Zerbo (q.v.), but was dismissed in October 1982 shortly before Zerbo was deposed in November. He favored the release of Lamizana (q.v.) and his officers.

TIENU. The Gourmantché God.

TIJANIYYA. One of the three major Muslim sects in West Africa. It spread across West Africa in the first half of the nineteenth century.

TIN AKOF, SEA OF. 14°58′N 0°10′W. Waterhole or lake on the upper reaches of the Goroual (q.v.) just south of the Mali border in the extreme northeastern part of Burkina Faso. A dam is scheduled to be built here to furnish water for the Tambao (q.v.) manganese (q.v.) project.

TINGUIMBISSI. *see* TENGABISSI

TIN HRASSAN. Site of limestone deposits near Tambao and Tin Akof (qq.v.).

TINIE (Tingué). 14°20′N 1°28′W. Village situated on the summit of a small hill northeast of Djibo (q.v.). Barth (q.v.) was held up here 30 July–1 August 1853 by heavy rains. He said that the lowlands about the village were a vast uninterrupted sheet of water. The town was a Songhai (q.v.) town, but there were many Fulani (q.v.) in the area. Barth said the head man of the village when he was there was named Abu Bakr.

TIOU (Tou). 13°56′N 2°46′W. Frontier post on the Mali border 54 km. northwest of Ouahigouya (q.v.). Tiou is on the main road to Mopti and the Niger lake country in Mali.

TIRAILLEURS. African troops used by the French during the colonial period. The first unit was recruited in Senegal in 1857.

TITAO. 13°46′N 2°04′W. Village 43 km. northeast of Ouahigouya on the Djibo (qq.v.) road. It was headquarters of a cercle until 1983. It is located in the area where the Nakanbe (White Volta) (q.v.) rises.

TOBY, JEAN-FRANÇOIS, 1900–1964. Toby was a French administrator stationed in Ouagadougou (q.v.) in 1941–1942. He became governor of Niger, 1942–1954, and of French Polynesia, 1954–1958.

TOHAJIYE ("The Red Hunter"). Legendary ancestor of the Mossi (q.v.). Tohajiye lived in the area of modern Niger. His son, Kpogonumbo, crossed the Niger into Gourma (q.v.). The son of Kpogonumbo was named Gbewa, Bawa or Nédéga (q.v.). Nédéga moved to the Mamprusi (q.v.) country and settled at Gambaga.

TOMA. 12°46′N 2°53′W. Headquarters of a cercle prior to 1983, it is 44 km. southeast of Tougan (q.v.).

TOMBO. Group of people listed by Murdock in the Habé (q.v.) cluster with the Dogon, Kado (q.v.) and Toro who were displaced by the Mossi (q.v.) when they conquered Yatenga (q.v.).

TONGOMAYEL. 14°04′ N 1°29′ W. Located southeast of Djibo (q.v.), Tongomayèl chiefdom is a branch of the Fulani (q.v.) Djibo chiefdom, from which it split in 1898.

TOOROODO TOROBE. Fulani (q.v.) clan.

TOTEBALBO. The 33d Yatenga Naba (q.v.). Before he became the ruler of Yatenga (q.v.) he was chief of Ouro. His father was Naba Sagha (q.v.), and several of his brothers served as rulers of Yatenga. Naba Totebalbo ruled from 1834 to 1850. During this time Yatenga fought with Macina in Djilgodji and Rissiam (qq.v.). A son became Naba Piga II, 1884–1885.

TOUAREG. *see* TUAREG

TOUBAB. Name francophone West Africans use for Europeans.

TOUGAN. 13°04′N 3°04′W. Tougan is the headquarters of Sourou province (q.v.) in Samo-Marka country between Dédougou and Ouahigouya (qq.v.) and just 30 km. from the Mali border. It is an important crossroads market.

TOUGOURI. A town in Namentenga (q.v.) province.

TOUGOURI (Tuguri). Oldest son of Naba Sagha (q.v.). He was chief of Bogoya before becoming 29th Yatenga Naba (q.v.). He conducted two campaigns against Yako (q.v.) and installed his own candidate as Yako Naba, but Ouagadougou came to the aid of Yako (qq.v.) and forced Tougouri to give up his ambition to annex Yako. Later descendants of Tougouri contested the *nam* (q.v.) with their cousins, taking Tougouri's name as the name of their faction. Tougouri ruled from about 1806 to 1822.

TOURE, ADAMA. Active member of *Ligue Patriotique pour le Développement* (LIPAD) (q.v.). Adama Toure became minister of information in the *Conseil National de la Révolution* (CNR) (q.v.) under Sankara (q.v.) in August 1983. He was fired and placed under house arrest in August 1984, and released in 1985.

TOURE, SAMORY. *see* SAMORY

TOURE, SARANTYE MORI. *see* SARANTYE MORI

TOURE, SOUMANE. Union leader. He was leader of the Voltaic Federation of Commercial and Industrial Unions until he became leader of the *Conféderation Syndicale Voltaïque* (CSV) (q.v.) in 1978. He was the most influential and radical union leader in Upper Volta, and often in prison. Soumane Toure was arrested by the *Conseil de Salut du Peuple* (CSP) (q.v.) in the purge of May 1983. He was also prominent in the *Ligue Patriotique pour le Développement* (LIPAD) (q.v.). He was placed in detention by the *Conseil National de la Révolution* (CNR) (q.v.), and accused of embezzlement in January 1985. He was involved in the *Front Populaire* (q.v.) coup of October 1987.

TOURKA (Turka, Turuka). A Sénufo group in southwest Burkina Faso between Banfora and Orodara (qq.v.).

TOURNY, FALLS OF. 10°46′N 5°09′W. Waterfalls on the Leraba Orientale north of Sindou (q.v.).

TOUSSIAN (Tousia, Tusyan). A Lobi (q.v.) group who live west of Orodara (q.v.).

TRADE UNIONS. The trade union movement in most of Africa has little independence and influence. But individual unions thrive and are an important element in Burkina Faso's urban political life. However, the working masses they claim to represent are almost entirely a minority—salaried urban workers.

TRAORE, DAOUDA. Military officer. Member of the *Union Démocratique Voltaïque* (UDV-RDA) (q.v.) at one time. He was appointed minister of interior in Lamizana's (q.v.) government, 1968–1970. From 1971 to 1974 he was minister of defense in Premier Gérard Ouédraogo's (q.v.) cabinet and then minister of interior and security, 1978–1980.

TRAORE, DIONGOLO. Politician. He replaced Nazi Boni (q.v.) as leader of the *Parti de Regroupment Africain* (PRA) (q.v.) in July 1970. Many of the party wanted to ally with the *Mouvement de Libération Nationale* (MLN) (q.v.) of Joseph Ki-Zerbo (q.v.).

TRAORE, TIEBA. Faama of Sikassa (Kénédougou [q.v.]), 1866–1893. Son of Daoula Traoré. Tiéba was captured after the battle of Bléni (q.v.) and held for ransom by the Bobo and Dioula (qq.v.) near Satiri. After he became ruler of Sikasso he waged unrelenting war against the Sénufo lands of modern Burkina Faso (q.v.), which he claimed as part of Kénédougou. Samory (q.v.) failed in an attempt to take Sikasso in 1887–1888. In 1888, 1891 and 1892 Tiéba campaigned in Samogho, Turka and Karaboro (q.v.) territory. On 18 January 1893 he was poisoned at Bama (q.v.), 31 km. northwest of Bobo Dioulasso (q.v.). His brother, Babèmba Traoré was his successor as Faama of Sikasso. He continued the raids against territories in modern Burkina Faso.

TRAORE, TIEGOUE, 1948– . Economist. He was the head of research and surveys of agricultural and industrial projects for the *Organisation Commune Africaine et Malgache,* 1977–1983.

TRAORE, ZOUMANA. Secretary-general of the *Union Syndicale des Travailleurs Voltaïque* (USTV) (q.v.) and an inspector of primary education. He played an active role in the overthrow of Maurice Yaméogo (q.v.) in the coup of January 1966 and in the labor pressure on Lamizana (q.v.) in December 1975. Lamizana appointed him minister of public service and labor in February 1976. At that point Traoré was one of the most powerful men in Upper Volta.

TRENTINIAN, LOUIS-EDGARD DE, 1851–1942. French officer. Born in Brest, son of a French officer, Trentinian fought in the Franco-Prussian war and then attended Saint Cyr. He was Lt. Governor of the Soudan from 1895 to 1898 and, after a brief break, from 1898 to 1899. While he was in charge of the French administration of the Soudan, the territory of modern Burkina Faso (q.v.) was under his general supervision. Trentinian played an active role in establishing policy for French rule over Upper Volta. He was interested in bringing the Voltaic peoples into a money economy, and so encouraged the cultivation of rubber, cotton (q.v.), corn and vegetables. In September 1899 he was appointed a member of a commission to reorganize French West Africa.

TRIBUNAUX POPULAIRES DE LA REVOLUTION (TPRs) (People's Revolutionary Tribunals). Established by Sankara (q.v.) and the *Conseil National de la Révolution* (CNR) (q.v.) in October 1983 to deal primarily with anti-government activity and major cases of corruption. The TPRs were made up of magistrates, soldiers and members of the *Comités de Défense de la Révolution* (CDRs) (q.v.). They were based on similar Ghanian people's courts.

TUAREG (Touareg). Descendants of the Berbers who moved into the Sahel (q.v.) area in the eleventh century. They held political dominance on the middle Niger from 1780 until the French arrived about 1893. Some Aulliminden Tuareg and their Bella (q.v.) serfs live in the Oudalan (q.v.) area north of Dori and Aribinda (qq.v.). In 1916 the Tuareg were active against the French and the Fulani (q.v.). They conducted almost continuous raids in the seventeenth and eighteenth centuries.

TUI (Grand Balé). Tributary of the Mouhoun (Black Volta) (q.v.). It rises in Bobo (q.v.) country between Sara and Ouarkoyé (qq.v.) and flows east and slightly south, joining the Mouhoun (Black Volta) (q.v.) southeast of Boromo (q.v.). There is a Tui forest reserve.

TYEFO. *see* TIEFO

-U-

UDUALAN. *see* OUDALAN

UNION DE COMMUNISTES BURKINABES (UCB) (Union of Burkinabè Communists). A communist party begun in 1985 by Compaoré (q.v.) and other army officers who were active in the October 1987 coup.

UNION DEMOCRATIQUE DE LA JEUNESSE VOLTAIQUE (UDJV). Small political group formed in 1957. It did not last very long.

UNION DEMOCRATIQUE VOLTAIQUE (UDV-RDA). Government party founded by Maurice Yaméogo (q.v.) as the Voltaic branch of the *Rassemblement Démocratique Africaine* (RDA). This followed the death of Ouëzzin Coulibaly (q.v.) and the break-up of the *Parti Démocratique Unifié* (PDU) (q.v.) in 1959. It was banned in 1966, reformed in 1970 by Gérard Kango Ouédraogo (q.v.), and won the elections in 1970. It was banned again in 1974. As a UDV-RDA leader Dr. Joseph Issoufou Conombo (q.v.) was elected premier by the National Assembly in 1978 and served until the Lamizana (q.v.) government was overthrown in November 1980.

UNION DES FEMMES DU BURKINA (UFB) (Women's Union of Burkina). Mass organization launched in 1986 by the *Conseil National de la Révolution* (CNR) (q.v.).

UNION DES INDEPENDANTS DU PAYS LOBI (UIPL). Lobi (q.v.) ethnic group led by Dabiré Ditté. Ditté Pierre Dabiré was listed as a member of the Territorial Assembly (q.v.) from Gaoua, 1947–1957. The UIPL joined Nazi Boni's (q.v.) *Mouvement Populaire de l'Evolution Africaine* (MPEA) (q.v.) in 1954.

UNION DES LUTTES COMMUNISTES (ULC). Small Marxist group founded early in 1983 during the rule of Jean-Baptiste Ouédraogo (q.v.). The ULC played a role in bringing Sankara (q.v.) to power (also see *Ligue Patriotique pour le Développement,* LIPAD). Its leaders were Basile Guissou and Eugene Dondasse.

UNION GENERALE DES ETUDIANTS VOLTAIQUES (UGEV). A students' group which on occasion published *Jeune Volta.*

UNION MONETAIRE OUEST-AFRICAINE (UMOA) (West African Monetary Union). Organization of francophone West African nations (Benin, Burkina Faso, Côte d'Ivoire, Mali, Niger, Senegal and Togo) which centralizes foreign currency reserves and issues CFA francs (q.v.) used as currency in the member nations through its regional central bank, *Banque centrale des états de l'Afrique de l'ouest* (BCEAO) based in Dakar. In January 1994 its name was changed to the *Union économique et monétaire ouest-africaine* (UEMOA). Also see FRANC ZONE.

UNION NATIONALE DE DEFENSE DE DEMOCRATIE (UNDD) (National Union for the Defense of Democracy). Party of followers of former President Maurice Yaméogo (q.v.), headed by his son Hermann Yaméogo (q.v.). Won 13 National Assembly seats in 1978, and was one of three legal parties in 1979. It was banned in November 1980.

UNION NATIONALE DES INDEPENDANTS (UNI). Political splinter group of the *Rassemblement Démocratique Africaine* (q.v.) formed in 1973 with Moussa Kargougou (q.v.) as leader. It was banned the following year when Lamizana (q.v.) ordered an end to all political parties save his *Mouvement pour le Renouveau*. Kargougou was its only member elected to the National Assembly in the 1978 elections. He was foreign minister in the Lamizana government, 1977–1980.

UNION NATIONALE DES PAYSANS DU BURKINA (UNPB) (National Union of Peasants of Burkina). Launched in April 1987 to deal especially with implementation of the August 1984 land reform.

UNION POUR LA DEFENSE DES INTERETS DE LA HAUTE VOLTA (UDIHV). Also called *Union Voltaïque* (UV). Political group formed soon after World War II. It was an alliance of young Catholic-trained Voltaics and traditional chiefs who opposed domination by Côte d'Ivoire, Felix Houphouët-Boigny and the *Rassemblement Démocratique Africaine* (RDA) (q.v.). Moro Naba Sagha (q.v.) was one of its founders. Joseph Conombo, Henri Guissou, Laurent Bandaogo, Christophe Kalenzaga, Joseph Ouédraogo and Maurice Yaméogo (qq.v.) all belonged to the UV in the beginning. It divided into the *Parti Social d'Education des Masses Africaines* (PSEMA) and *Mouvement Populaire de l'Evolution Africaine* (MPEA) (qq.v.) in 1954.

UNION POUR LA NOUVELLE REPUBLIQUE VOLTAIQUE (UNRV). A split-off from the federalist *Parti de Regroupment Africain* (PRA) (q.v.). It was founded in 1970 and banned in 1974. Blaise Bassoleth (q.v.) was president and Gansondré Bakary Traoré was secretary-general.

UNION PROGRESSISTE VOLTAIQUE (UPV). Party formed by dissidents from several parties in 1977, including intellectuals, unionists, and non-Mossi. Joseph Ki-Zerbo (q.v.) was the socialist UPV candidate for president in 1978, but came in last (Lamizana [q.v.] was elected) although the UPV won 9 seats in the National Assembly. In 1979 the UPV reorganized as the *Front Progressiste Voltaïque* (FPV) (q.v.) when Ki-Zerbo and Joseph Ouédraogo (qq.v.) joined hands. The FPV was banned in November 1980.

UNION SYNDICALE DES TRAVAILLEURS VOLTAIQUE (USTV). One of the most powerful labor groups in Upper Volta, founded in

1958. It helped overthrow Yaméogo (q.v.) in January 1966, and exerted great pressure on the military government of Lamizana (q.v.) in 1975. Zoumana Traoré (q.v.) was the USTV's leader.

UNION VOLTAIQUE (UV). *see* UNION POUR LA DEFENSE DES INTERETS DE LA HAUTE VOLTA (UDIHV)

UNIVERSITE D'OUAGADOUGOU. Founded in 1969 as the *Centre d'Enseignement Supérieur*, it became a university in 1974. The academic year runs from October-June. The Polytechnical University in Bobo Dioulasso (q.v.) was opened in 1995.

UPPER IVORY COAST. In September 1932 Upper Volta was abolished and most of the southwest of former Upper Volta became part of Ivory Coast; from 1937 it was known as Upper Ivory Coast. In 1947 Upper Volta was reconstituted.

-V-

VAGALA. Small group along the border with Ghana usually classified with the Gourounsi (q.v.). They live in the same area as the Tamprussi.

VERMEERSCH, L. French officer who was second in command to Joseph Baud (q.v.) in 1895, 1896 and 1897. He took part in the French campaigns in Gourma (q.v.).

VIGYE (Vigués). Lobi (q.v.) group who are closely associated with the Tusyan. In June 1897, Samory's (q.v.) *sofa* (q.v.) destroyed their chief village, Karangasso. Soma Ouattara was their leader at this time.

VILLAGES DE LIBERTE. Settlements of freed slaves often used by the French as porters.

VINAMA, DJIBRIL. Political associate of Dr. Ali Barraud, Ouëzzin Coulibaly and Nazi Boni (qq.v.). He was one at the organizers of the *Parti Démocratique Voltaïque* (PDV) and played an active role in the formation of the *Parti Démocratique Unifié* (PDU) (q.v.) in 1956. He was an ardent supporter of the Mali Federation (q.v.) and attended the Bamako conference which adopted the constitution for the Mali Federation. He was once mayor of Bobo Dioulasso (q.v.).

VOLTA RIVER. The Volta got its name from the Portuguese in the fifteenth century because of its winding course to the sea. All the branches flow slowly because of the relatively flat terrain through which they meander. After flowing separately in Burkina Faso (q.v.), all branches of the Volta eventually join in Ghana. In August 1986 the government of Burkina changed the names of the White Volta to Nakanbe, Red Volta to Nazinon, and Black Volta to Mouhoun (qq.v.). The names remain unchanged in Ghana. Only the Mouhoun (Black Volta) and the Pendjari (q.v.) have a constant flow. The lowest water level on all the branches is in January and the highest is in August and September. Historically, the valleys of all the branches were unhealthy and very few people lived close to the rivers.

The Mouhoun (Black Volta) is the most important part of the Voltaic system. It begins as two streams not far from Bobo Dioulasso (q.v.). The most western stream begins near Koloko (q.v.) and is called the Plandi (q.v.). The other stream is the Dienkoa and it starts just south of Orodara (q.v.). These two streams join just west of Bobo Dioulasso. Another stream starts south of Koumi (q.v.) and flows west and north of Bobo Dioulasso. It is called the Kou or the Baoulé (qq.v.). All these streams join west of Satiri as the Mouhoun (Black Volta), called the Moun Hou (q.v.) in that region. Still further north the Voun Hou and the Sourou (q.v.) join the Mouhoun (Black Volta) on the left bank near Kouri (q.v.). Then the Mouhoun (Black Volta) turns sharply to the south. It is sometimes called the Bafing (q.v.) in this area. The Tui and the Bougouriba (qq.v.) are the largest tributaries before the river reaches the border with Ghana near Ouessa (q.v.). By this time the river has traveled 512 km. from its sources. From this point the Mouhoun (Black Volta) forms the border of Ghana and Burkina Faso.

The Nazinon (Red Volta) rises some 51 km. northwest of Ouagadougou near Boussé (qq.v.). It flows in a southeasterly direction and enters Ghana just to the east of Ziou.

The Nakanbe (White Volta) rises in the northern part of Yatenga (q.v.) above Titao (q.v.). Below Kongoussi (q.v.) it cuts through the Boussouma Hills (q.v.) and flows east of Ouagadougou about 50 km. It enters Ghana some 40 km. to the east of the Nazinon (Red Volta). They combine near Gambaga.

The Pendjari is also part of the Volta system. It begins in the Atakora mountains of Benin (former Dahomey) and flows northward to the Burkina Faso border. Then it bends south and west to form the border between Benin and Burkina Faso for about 170 km. It becomes the Oti after entering Togo and eventually reaches the Volta in Ghana.

VOLTA VALLEY AUTHORITY. *see* AUTORITE DES AMENAGEMENTS DES VALLEES DES VOLTAS (AVV)

VOULET, PAUL GUSTAVE LUCIEN, 1866–1899. French officer. He commanded the forces that restored Yatenga Naba Boulli (q.v.) to power in Ouahigouya and conquered Ouagadougou (qq.v.) in 1896. He signed a treaty with the Gourounsi (q.v.) at Sati (q.v.) and secured Ouidi Sidibé (q.v.) at Lanfiéra (q.v.) before the year was out. In 1897 he helped pacify Gourma (q.v.), halted the English at Tenkodogo (q.v.) and placed Sigiri (q.v.) on the throne of Ouagadougou. He was killed in the Zinder campaign in 1899.

-W-

W, PARC NATIONAL DU. Park maintained jointly by Benin, Niger and Burkina Faso. The name comes from the double bend of the Niger River in the northeastern part of the park. The Burkina Faso headquarters for the park is located at Diapaga (q.v.).

WAGADUGU. *see* OUAGADOUGOU

WAHABOU. *see* OUAHABOU

WAHIGUYA. *see* OUAHIGOUYA

WALA (Wilé). Voltaic group related to the Mossi (q.v.) who at one time may have lived in the Wa area of Ghana but now live in the area of Diébougou and Gaoua (qq.v.).

WANGARA. One name for the Dioula Mande (q.v.) merchants who traded north-south along the Mouhoun (Black Volta) (q.v.) between Djenne and the Akan areas in what is today Ghana.

WARA (Ouara). Small group usually classified with the Sénufo who occupy five villages in the hills of southwestern Burkina Faso. They call themselves the Saama.

WARAGA. *see* OUARAGA

WARGAYE (Ouargaye, Warge). A dependency of Tenkodogo (q.v.).

WATARA. *see* OUATTARA

WAYLUBE. Blacksmiths, a hereditary profession, in Fulani (q.v.) area.

WENDOU. Chief place and oldest Fulani (q.v.) village of Liptako (q.v.) before Dori (q.v.).

WEND' POUS NEBA. Traditional religion (q.v.) does not have a formal structure or theology, and its practices are extremely flexible. Though often dismissed or misunderstood by Europeans, animist beliefs reflect the spirituality of people who live in harmony with their natural environment and who understand the essential unity of the visible and invisible worlds. People now living are a continuation of the life stream of the first beings; the ancestors are each person's intermediaries with the creator of the universe.

In Moré (q.v.) the traditional religion is called Wend' Pous Neba. Winnam (q.v.) is the traditional deity of the Mossi (q.v.) and Tenga (q.v.) is the chief female deity. Land priests and priestesses are concerned with the relation of the living with spirits and all nature. They make animal sacrifices and offer gifts at earth shrines for rain, fertility and protection against hostile forces. They also officiate on ceremonial occasions and funerals.

WEST AFRICAN ECONOMIC COMMUNITY. see COMMUNAUTE ECONOMIQUE DE L'AFRIQUE DE L'OUEST (CEAO)

WHITE FATHERS. Catholic (q.v.) missionary group which has been active in Burkina Faso since founding missions in Koupéla (q.v.) in 1900 and in Ouagadougou (q.v.) in 1901. The White Sisters arrived in 1911.

WHITE VOLTA (NAKANBE). see VOLTA RIVER

WIDRAOGO. see OUEDRAOGO

WILE. see WALA

WINNAM (Winde or Naba Zid' winde or Zid Ouende). The traditional deity of the Mossi (q.v.). The "Sun God". Usually associated with the female deity, called Tenga (q.v.).

WOBA. Ancient inhabitants of Gourma (q.v.).

WOBGHO (Wobogo), ca.1848–1904. The 30th Moro Naba. Before he became the ruler of Ouagadougou (q.v.) he was called Boukary Koutou (Boukari, Bakari). He was the second son of Naba Koutou (q.v.) and Queen Hawa, and he was an unsuccessful candidate for the throne against his older brother in 1871, and was forced by Naba Sanem (q.v.) to stay away from Ouagadougou as long as Sanem was alive. During those years Boukary Koutou supported himself by raids into Gourounsi and Kipirsi (qq.v.) lands. In 1888 he was host to

Binger (q.v.) at Banéma, a village near the Red Volta (Nazinon) (q.v.). He made a great impression on Binger.

When Naba Sanem died in 1889, Boukary Koutou forced the electors to select him as the new Moro Naba (q.v.). He took the name Wobgho, which means "elephant". From the beginning of his reign he struggled with a civil war in Lallé (q.v.), which had started several years before under Sanem. Wobgho called upon the Zerma (q.v.) for aid and their intervention was disastrous. The Zerma crossed the Red Volta and ravaged the countryside without regard to friend or foe. Finally the Zerma were forced back across the river. Crozat (q.v.) visited Wobgho in September 1890, but the emperor refused to allow Monteil (q.v.) to enter Ouagadougou in April 1891. In July 1894 Wobgho signed an alliance with an English agent, Ferguson (q.v.). After that he refused to receive any other Frenchmen. The French occupied Ouagadougou in September 1896.

Wobgho did his best to organize resistance and appealed to the British for support. His forces attempted several attacks on the French, and Wobgho spent part of the winter of 1896–1897 at Nobéré (q.v.). On 21 January 1897 the French proclaimed the deposition of Wobgho, and a week later Wobgho's youngest brother, Mamadou, was declared by the French to be his successor, as Moro Naba Sigiri (q.v.). Manga and part of Busansi (qq.v.) country remained loyal to Wobgho, and he continued to search for support until he was surprised and defeated by the French south of Tenkodogo (q.v.) in June. He escaped across the Gold Coast border, and the next year he was able to persuade Col. Northcott (q.v.), British commander in the Northern Territories of the Gold Coast, to help him retake Ouagadougou. Crossing into Busansi country by Zabré (q.v.), they reached Kombissiri (q.v.), just 40 km. south of the capital before they were met by the French, who told Northcott that an agreement had been signed between France and Britain giving the Mossi (q.v.) lands to France. Northcott and Wobgho returned to the Gold Coast, ending the dreams of Wobgho, who retired to Zangoiri, near Gambaga (Gold Coast), where he died in 1904.

WOGODOGO. *see* OUAGADOUGOU

WUBRI. *see* OUBRI

WUBRITENGA. *see* OUBRITENGA

-Y-

YAAYRE. Waterhole just northwest of Dori (q.v.) where the Fulani and Gourmantché (qq.v.) fought in 1809.

YACOM-BATO. Former king of Gourma (q.v.) who was defeated by the French and Bantchandé (q.v.) on 19 February 1897. He committed suicide by poison soon afterwards.

YADEGA. Son of the 4th Moro Naba, Nasbire (q.v.), and grandson of Oubri (q.v.). After his cousin, Koudoumie (q.v.), took the throne of Oubri, Yadega founded his own kingdom at Lago and Gourcy (qq.v.). His sister, Pabré (q.v.), stole the amulets and regalia of Oubri from Koudoumie to give legitimacy to her brother's new kingdom. These events may have taken place in 1540, but Delafosse (q.v.) says they happened in the eleventh century and Marc and Tauxier (qq.v.) say the thirteenth century. Yadega's kingdom became Yatenga (q.v.).

YAGHA (Yaga). Emirate of Yaga. Fulani (q.v.) area southeast of Dori (q.v.). The capital of Yagha was Sebba (q.v.). Barth (q.v.) visited the area in the rainy season in July 1853, and Destenave (q.v.) visited in May 1897. Barth reported huts made of matting, pits for dyeing, blacksmiths, tamarind trees, buffalo and elephants. He commented on the mosque at Sebba.

YAGUIBOU, TELESPHORE, 1935– . Judge, diplomat, and a Gourounsi (q.v.) from Pô (q.v.). He was educated at the University of Dakar and got his law degree from the University of Paris. He was a judge in Bobo Dioulasso (q.v.) from 1965 to 1967. From 1967 to 1972 he was secretary-general to the military cabinet in Ouagadougou (q.v.). He was permanent representative to the United Nations, 1972–1977, and was ambassador to the United States.

YAKO (Yaako). 12°58′N 2°16′W. Town on the southern route from Ouagadougou to Ouahigouya (qq.v.), and headquarters of Passoré province (q.v.). It is about 104 km. northwest of Ouagadougou, and 73 km. south of Ouahigouya. Its location between the two most powerful Mossi (q.v.) kingdoms made it a frequent field of conflict. The town was taken by the French in August 1896. It is the birthplace of Thomas Sankara (q.v.).

YALGADO OUEDRAOGO HOSPITAL. The hospital of Ouagadougou (q.v.). It has the best medical facility in Burkina Faso.

YAM. One of the important items in the Burkinabè diet. There are two main varieties, the white and the yellow. They are planted in mounds late in November or December. When harvested some may weigh up to 50 pounds. They are eaten like potatoes.

YAMEOGO, ANTOINE WIOUGOU, 1928– . Politician and economist. He was born at Koudougou (q.v.) and educated at University of Dakar, Bordeaux and Paris. Yaméogo became the inspector of financial administration 1956–1960. He was director of the treasury and minister of national economy 1959–1962. Later he became a senior economist and director of the International Monetary Fund, 1963–1976.

YAMEOGO, DENIS. Half-brother of President Maurice Yaméogo (q.v.). He became minister of social affairs in 1957 then minister of justice and in 1965 was minister of interior and security. When President Yaméogo was forced out of office in the January 1966 coup, Denis Yaméogo was removed from office and arrested by the army. His high-handed actions against opponents was part of the reason for the coup.

YAMEOGO, EDOUARD. Businessman, politician, editor. He graduated from the National Institute of Agriculture in Paris. He became minister of national development, 1962–1966, and minister of planning, industry and mines, 1971–1973. He was a member of the *Union Démocratique Voltaïque* (UDV-RDA) (q.v.).

YAMEOGO, HERMANN. Hermann Yaméogo, eldest son of former President Maurice Yaméogo (q.v.), was sentenced to seven years' imprisonment in 1968 for plotting to overthrow the government and restore his father; he was reprieved in 1969. He subsequently headed the *Union Nationale de Defense de Démocratie* (UNDD) (q.v.), a party of followers of his father, which came in second with 13 National Assembly seats in 1978; it was banned in November 1980. In 1987 he and others founded the Movement of Progressive Democrats (MPD).

In March 1990 Yaméogo, a political "moderate", was appointed to the executive committee of the Popular Front (q.v.). However, in July Yaméogo's MPD was suspended from Popular Front due to an alleged internal MPD crisis. In March 1991 Hermann Yaméogo, now president of the Alliance for Democracy and Federation (ADF), announced his intention to run for president. In mid-August 1991 he and two other ADF members resigned from the transitional government only weeks after being appointed. The December 1991 presidential election was boycotted by opposition parties and Blaise Compaoré (q.v.) was elected president. Fewer than one quarter of the registered voters participated. In early 1992 Compaoré constituted the third transitional government in 8 months; Hermann Yaméogo and some other opposition members rejoined it.

YAMEOGO, MAURICE, 1921–1993. First president of Upper Volta. He was born at Koudougou (q.v.) and attended the Catholic mission secondary school at Pabré (q.v.). He became a civil servant in the French colonial government and for several years he was active in the *Confédération Française des Travailleurs Chrétiens* (CFTC) (q.v.). In December 1946 he was elected to represent Koudougou in the Territorial Assembly (q.v.) as a member of the *Union Voltaïque* (UV) party. From 1948 to 1952 he was also a delegate to the Grand Council of French West Africa. In March 1957 he was elected to the Third Territorial Assembly as a member of the *Mouvement Démocratique Voltaïque* (MDV) (q.v.), and Ouëzzin Coulibaly (q.v.) asked him to join the cabinet as minister of agriculture. In January 1958 Yaméogo joined Coulibaly's *Parti Démocratique Unifié* (PDU) (q.v.) to protect Coulibaly's narrow majority. Yaméogo was promoted to minister of the interior in February as part of an RDA-controlled cabinet. In September 1958 Coulibaly died and in October the Assembly elected Yaméogo president of the Council of Ministers. In December Yaméogo became premier. A year later, on 11 December 1959, he became president of the Republic of Upper Volta. The following August Upper Volta gained its full independence with Yaméogo as the first president. In October 1965 he was reelected by 99.98 percent of the vote.

Yaméogo had been in power for seven years. In that time he had almost eliminated his opposition, he had come close to bankrupting the nation with his presidential perquisites, and he had cut himself off from reality by surrounding himself with sycophants who told him only what he wanted to hear. Shortly after his reelection he married a beauty queen half his age in a wedding reputed to have cost $40,000. The couple went to Paris and Brazil on a honeymoon rumored to have cost twice that much. Returning in November, the nation's first family received a cool reception in Ouagadougou (q.v.). An austerity budget was announced in December with higher taxes and lower pay for civil servants. That was the end. On 3 January 1966 the unions went on general strike and mobs took to the streets in the capital. By the end of the day Yaméogo had resigned and the military had established its rule. In December 1966 Yaméogo failed in a suicide attempt. In April 1969 the former president was tried for embezzlement and in May sentenced to five years hard labor and a fine of over US$100,000.

In August 1970, the tenth anniversary of independence, he was released from prison. After a visit to Houphouët-Boigny in Côte d'Ivoire he retired to Koudougou to write his memoirs. He was placed under house arrest by the *Conseil National de la Révolution* (CNR) (q.v.) from October 1983 to August 1984. In 1986 he was made deputy chairman of the *Union National des Anciens Burkinabès* (UNAB). In 1991 he was politically rehabilitated by the Compaoré (q.v.) government; he died on 15 September 1993 while traveling from Côte d'Ivoire back to Ouagadougou.

YAMEOGO, MRS. MAURICE (Nathalie Félicité Monaco Adama, "Miss Côte d'Ivoire"). She married President Yaméogo in October 1965. The cost of the marriage celebrations and honeymoon caused outraged reactions among the young educated people in the capital. She was arrested with her husband at the time of the 1966 coup. She was tried in May 1968 for plotting against the government the previous September. Convicted on 5 June 1968, the sentence of imprisonment was suspended.

YANGA. The southern part of Gourma (q.v.).

YANKASSO. 12°13'N 3°12'W. Village just north of Safané and 46 km. southeast of Dédougou (qq.v.). Here on 23 December 1915 a French force under Commandant Simonin and the Lt. Governor of Haut-Senegal-Niger (q.v.) attacked the Marka insurgents in the village and was repulsed. The French returned on 2 March 1916 and destroyed the village.

YANSE (sing. Yanna). The Yansé live in Yanga, in the area below Tenkodogo (q.v.). Their language is Yanna.

YAO, MARC OUBKIRI, 1943– . Diplomat. Born at Boromo (q.v.), he attended the University of Paris and International Institute of Public Administration, 1963–1967. He served in the Ministry of Foreign Affairs, 1968–1973. Yao then was a counsellor in Upper Volta's UN delegation, and later was appointed ambassador to the U. S. S. R.

YARSE (Yarcé, sing. Yarga). People of Mande (q.v.) origin who have intermixed with the Mossi (q.v.). Most of them are Muslim merchants. It is said that the Yarsé began to settle in Mossi territory during the time of Moro Naba Nasbire or Moro Naba Koudoumie (qq.v.).

YATENGA (Yaadtinga). The northern Mossi (q.v.) kingdom founded by Yadéga about 1540. Much of the area was once part of Zandoma (q.v.). Gourcy was once the chief place of the kingdom, but Yatenga Naba Kango (q.v.) moved the capital to Ouahigouya (q.v.) about 1757. It became a French protectorate in 1895. From 1933 to 1947 Yatenga was separated from the rest of Upper Volta and made a part of the French Soudan.

It is now also a province with headquarters at Ouahigouya. In 1985 it was the second most-populous province, following Houet (q.v.).

YATENGA NABA. *see* NABA

YE, ARSENE BONGNESSAN. *see* BONGNESSAN, ARSENE YE

YEMDE. The 34th Yatenga Naba (q.v.). The last of the sons of Naba Sagha (q.v.) to rule, Yemde was also the last great Yatenga (q.v.) ruler. He headed Yatenga from 1850 to 1877. During this time the boundaries of his country were expanded at the expense of Rissiam (q.v.), and there were frequent raids into Dogon and Samo (q.v.) territories. There were several clashes with troops of Macina in the Djilgodji (q.v.) area. Yemde is buried at Somniaga (q.v.).

YENDABILI. King of Gourma (q.v.), 1709–1736. The greatest ruler of Gourma, he decisively defeated the Tomba of modern Benin, and regained the Pamma region for the Gourmantché. He established the capital at Nungu or Fada N'Gourma (qq.v.).

YENKOARI. Chief of Gourma (Nungu) (q.v.), 1883–1892. At his death a civil war began in Gourma (q.v.).

YENNEGA (Nyennega, Yennenga, Poko). Only daughter of Nédéga (q.v.), chief of Gambaga. She was the wife of Rialle, mother of Ouédraogo (qq.v.), and progenitrix of the Nakomsé Mossi (q.v.)

YERIANGA, SEA OF. The Sea of Yérianga and the Sea of Gouaroudou are marsh-lakes in the Pama (q.v.) Forest Reserve north of the border with Benin. This is the lowest area in Burkina Faso.

YISSOU (Yssou). Chief of the Kamélé in Bouna (Bona) (q.v.). He was a famous fetish priest who was one of the leaders of the revolt against the French in Dafina (q.v.) in 1915. The Marka thought that Yissou could not be harmed by the white man, but Yissou was killed in the battle of Bouna (q.v.).

YOMBOLI. 14°39′N 0°18′W. Battle of 2 June 1916 here ended Tuareg (q.v.) resistance to the French.

YOUGBARE, DIEUDONNE. He was made the Catholic (q.v.) bishop of Koupéla (q.v.) in 1956, the first indigenous West African to receive episcopal consecration.

-Z-

ZABERMA. *see* ZERMA

ZABRA SOBA. Head war chief of the Ninsi when the Mossi (q.v.) arrived in the area of Ouagadougou (q.v.).

ZABRE (Zabéré). 11°10′N 0°38′W. Village located between the Nazinon (Red Volta) and Nakanbe (White Volta) (qq.v.) just north of the border with Ghana in Boulgou province (q.v.).

ZAGRE, BILA JEAN, 1925– . Military officer. He was born in Ouagadougou and attended the military school at Bingerville in Côte d'Ivoire. He served in the French army from 1943 to 1960. In 1960 he became aide-de-camp to President Yaméogo (q.v.), a post he held through 1961. Zagré then was chief of the lst bureau in the general staff, 1962–1965. He served in the Lamizana (q.v.) military government 1966–1976 as secretary of state for interior and security and minister of information. After serving as Army chief of staff he was placed under house arrest, 1980–1983.

ZANDOMA (Zondema). The Mossi (q.v.) kingdom founded by Rawa, son of Ouédraogo (qq.v.). It is also called Rawatenga (q.v.). The state, which was formed in the area between the Red and White Voltas, later became part of Yatenga (q.v.). Rawa pushed the Kado (q.v.) or Dogon northward into the area of modern Mali. Rawa's tomb is at a place called Zandoma.

ZANNA (Sana). The 16th Moro Naba (q.v.), Zanna was the son of Naba Nakyê and his wife, Tontvelobo. Skinner (q.v.) says that Ouagadougou (q.v.) became the permanent capital during the reign of Naba Zanna (also see ZOMBRE). Izard (q.v.) places his reign at the end of the seventeenth century. A great famine (q.v.) occurred during his reign. His tomb is in Ouagadougou.

ZAOSE. A small group, sometimes called Gmara, who live around Jabo and Tibga in Gourma (q.v.) southeast of Koupéla (q.v.).

ZATU. Term adopted by *Conseil National de la Révolution* (CNR) (q.v.) in August 1985 for a law proclaimed by the President.

ZEKKAT. A tax on the cattle of nomads.

ZERBO, SAYE, 1932– . Head of state, military officer. Zerbo, a Samo (q.v.) and cousin of Lamizana (q.v.), was educated in Mali and Senegal. He gained paratrooper experience in Indo-China and Algeria. He graduated from the French *Ecole supérieure de guerre* in 1973 and became minister of foreign affairs 1973–1976. In November 1980 Col. Zerbo led a coup against Lamizana, after which the Constitution (q.v.) of 1977 was suspended. The 31-member *Comité Militaire de Redressement pour le Progrès National* (CMRPN) (q.v.) was established with backing from the customary chiefs. Zerbo was overthrown by the November 1982 officers' coup led by Col. Gabriel Yoryan Somé (q.v.) which formed the *Conseil de Salut du Peuple* (CSP) (q.v.) government. In 1984 Zerbo was sentenced to 15 years' imprisonment for embezzlement and fraud by the Popular Tribunal of the Revolution. The sentence was commuted to house arrest at the end of 1985.

ZERMA (Djerma, Zaberma, Zarma, Zabermabé). Warriors who came from the area of modern Niger as mercenaries to Dagomba in the 1860s. Their first leader was Alfa Dan Tadano Hano (q.v.). Soon after they arrived in Dagomba they began to make raids into Gourounsi (q.v.) country. About 1870 Alfa Hano died and Alfa Gazari (q.v.) became the second leader of the Zerma. In time Gazari established a Zerma state with Sati (q.v.) as its chief place. Gazari was killed in 1883, and Babatu (q.v.) became the third and last of the Zerma leaders. At Gandiaga (Ghana) (q.v.) 14 March 1897 the French and the Gourounsi defeated the Zerma. The Zerma retreated into Dagomba and gradually disbanded. The name Zerma is also used for the people who came from the Dosso area of modern Niger and settled in the area around Dori (q.v.). All the Zerma are related to the Songhai (q.v.).

ZID WINNAM. *see* WINNAM

ZIGA. 13°25'N 2°19'W. Several kings of Yatenga (q.v.) lived here in the nineteenth century. There are several towns by this name in Burkina Faso, and also a forest reserve. This Ziga was a center of opposition to the French in the years just after the French came to Yatenga. The people of Ziga supported the Sagha (q.v.) party against the French-supported Tougouri (q.v.) faction in the Yatenga civil war.

ZINA, IKIE. Warrior from a village named Dafina (q.v.). He conquered many of the villages of the Marka and gave the name of his village to the area where the Marka lived. The people of the area are called the Dafing (q.v.).

ZINIARE. 12°35'N 1°18'W. Town some 34 km. northeast of Ouagadougou on the Kaya (q.v.) road. It was once the center of Oubri's kingdom, Oubritenga (q.v.). Ziniaré is headquarters of Oubritenga province (q.v.), and the birthplace of President Blaise Compaoré (q.v.).

ZITENGA. Mossi (q.v.) principality whose chief place was Tikaré. Rissiam (q.v.) was to the east and north, Yatenga (q.v.) to the west, Téma to the south, and Mané (q.v.) to the southeast. It was annexed to Yatenga.

ZOAGA. Small ethnic group related to the Mossi (q.v.).

ZOMBRE. The 21st Moro Naba (q.v.). The son of Naba Warga, he reigned from about 1744 to 1784. It was probably during his reign, rather than that of Moro Naba Zanna (q.v.), that Ouagadougou (q.v.) became the permanent capital. After a long rule, Zombre was deposed by his oldest son. After three years of retirement, Zombre regained his throne for the remainder of his life. The son was made chief of Djiba (Guiba), establishing the tradition that the heir to the throne would hold the chiefdom of Djiba (q.v.). The tomb of Zombre is at Ouagadougou.

ZONGO, FRANÇOIS-XAVIER. Minister of justice in the Lamizana (q.v.) military government 1976–1978.

ZONGO, HENRI. Military officer, captain. When Jean-Baptiste Lingani and Thomas Sankara (qq.v.) were imprisoned by the *Conseil de Salut du Peuple* (CSP) Ouédraogo (q.v.) government in early 1983, Zongo and Blaise Compaoré evaded arrest. Together with Sankara, Compaoré, and Lingani (qq.v.), Zongo was one of the leaders of the August 1983 coup. He became minister of state enterprises in the *Conseil National de la Révolution* (CNR) (q.v.), and of economic promotion in 1985. In August 1986 he was appointed coordinator of Burkina Faso and mandated to act for President Sankara, along with Compaoré and Lingani. In October 1987 Sankara was killed in a coup led by Compaoré, Lingani and Zongo. In June 1989 when Compaoré was elected president of the Popular Front (q.v.) executive committee, Lingani was named first deputy chairman and Zongo second deputy chairman. In September 1989 Zongo and Lingani were accused of a plot against Compaoré and executed.

ZORGHO. 12°15′N 0°36′W. Headquarters of Ganzourgou province (q.v.), located on the highway between Ouagadougou and Fada N'-Gourma (qq.v.). It is about half-way between the two Mossi (q.v.) capitals. There are several small places in Burkina Faso by this name.

ZOROME, MALICK. Member of the *Union Démocratique Voltaïque* (UDV-RDA) (q.v.). He was one of the first graduates of the *Ecole Nationale d'Administration* (ENA) in France. He served as Lamizana's (q.v.) minister of foreign affairs, 1967–1970, and minister of justice, 1971–1974.

ZOUGBA, ALAIN. Secretary-general of the Burkinabè Communist Group.

ZOUNDWEOGO. Province north of Pô (q.v.) of which Manga (q.v.) is the headquarters.

ZOUNGOURANA (Zungrana). Son of Ouédraogo and Pouriketa (qq.v.) and legendary member of the Nakomsé (q.v.) line. He was probably the grandson of Yennega and Rialle, the son of Ouédraogo and the father of Oubri (qq.v.), the first Moro Naba (q.v.). He married a Ninisi (q.v.) woman, Poughtoenga. Tiendrébéogo (q.v.) says he ruled from 1132 to 1182. Michel Izard (q.v.) says he died about 1495. He probably was the first or second Nakomsé ruler of Tenkodogo (q.v.). His tomb is supposed to be in the village of Zomtoega, not far from Tenkodogo.

ZOUNGRANA, PAUL. Roman Catholic (q.v.) archbishop of Ouagadougou and cardinal. Born in Ouagadougou, the son of a Mossi (q.v.) mechanic, he was educated at the seminary at Koumi (q.v.) and ordained a priest in October 1942. He completed a novitiate with the White Fathers (q.v.) in Algiers, took a doctorate in canon law in Rome, and a degree in social sciences in Paris. He then returned home to teach canon law at Koumi. Zoungrana was made archbishop of Ouagadougou in 1960 and a cardinal in 1965. He was West Africa's first cardinal.

ZWETEMBUSMA. The 9th Moro Naba (q.v.). He was the son of Moro Naba Kouda (q.v.), brother of Naba Dawema (q.v.) and father of Naba Nyâdfo. He reigned at the beginning of the seventeenth century or end of the sixteenth century. The place of his residence is uncertain, either Saponé, Loumbila (qq.v.) or Gourpila. He was active in expanding Nakomsé (q.v.) power toward the east.

Bibliography

A Note on the Bibliography

Twenty years ago it could be said that "there is very little material on Upper Volta written in English". That is much less true in 1997, although the majority of the material is still published in French. While this bibliography is intended first as a resource for English-language readers, one cannot restrict coverage of a francophone country to English-language materials. This edition contains some 1,300 entries arranged by subject category, even though dissertations are not included. This compares to around 600 entries in the 1978 edition. More than one-third of the titles are English-language, compared with just over one-quarter in the 1978 edition. In part that reflects an increased ease in searching obscure sources through computerized catalog and periodicals data bases. But it also reflects increased attention to Burkina Faso by English-speaking scholars, governments, international agencies, journalists, and nongovernmental organizations. For example, the majority of entries concerning the Sahelian drought, agricultural research, and river blindness eradication included here is in English. There is increased coverage of the cinema as FESPACO has become more widely known. In general, this edition's intent has been to add on to the McFarland 1978 bibliography by incorporating omitted items and titles published since it went to press. Many items from that edition are also included for easier reference.

To an earlier list of writers in English that included Elliott P. Skinner's prolific writing on the Mossi, Peter B. Hammond on technology in Yatenga, Allan Carpenter and Janice E. Baker, Myron Joel Echenberg, Victor Du Bois on current events, and explorers Barth, Ferguson and Frobenius, the following additions come to mind. Joel W. Gregory has written on labor migration, and Della McMillan on public health and planned settlements following river blindness control. Christopher Roy has written on the fine arts in Burkina Faso, and Mahir Saul on economic changes and merchant behavior. Although most well-known for his writing in French, historian Joseph Ki-Zerbo has played a major role in the first volume of UNESCO's General History of Africa. And while his study of urban consumption spending determinants and Burkina's sugar industry are in French, T. Thiombiano has done an article in English on state agricultural policies. ORSTOM's *Cahiers des Sciences Humaines* normally includes both an English and French summary for each article, and sometimes also German or Spanish.

In French, new names since the mid-1970s include Filiga Michel Sawadogo writing on the law, Suzanne Lallemand on anthropology, and Larhallé-Naba Yamba Tiendrébéogo passing on folktales and proverbs and Mossi history. Junzo Kawada also captures Mossi oral history. Geographer Jean-Yves Marchal's writing is part of that important scholarship published by ORSTOM. Henri Barral and Michel Benoit have both studied nomadic and pastoral peoples. Linguistics and sociology have been subjects of Anne Retel-Laurentin's work.

The publications of the Centre National de la Recherche Scientifique et Technologique (CNRST) in Ouagadougou and ORSTOM contain important research specific to Burkina Faso. CNRST is publisher of *Science et Technique: (Série: Sciences Sociales et Humaines)* and *Science et Technique: (Série: Science Naturelles)*. ORSTOM has published many books and monographs as well as *Cahiers des Sciences Humaines* (formerly *Cahiers ORSTOM*). Both CESAO and GRAAP have published development training materials. Local scholarly journals include *CEDRES Etudes* published by the University of Ouagadougou Faculty of Economic Science and Management; University of Ouagadougou *Annales (Sciences Humaines et Sociales)*, *Annales du Collège Littéraire Universitaire,* and *Cahier du CERLESHS* (humanities and social science). *Cahiers du Luto* deals with oral literature, *Ecrans d'Afrique* with film, *Journal du Syndicat Autonome des Magistrats Voltaïques* with law, and *Revue des Retraites* with social science. The Burkina Faso Chamber of Commerce produces a number of semi-official publications, such as *Bulletin économique et fiscal du Burkina Faso* and *Le Courrier consulaire du Burkina Faso.*

For current news on Burkina Faso in English, the Political, Social, Cultural Series of *Africa Research Bulletin* published by Basil Blackwell is important and has been a very useful source during work on this book. Colin Legum's *Africa Contemporary Record* annual is extremely useful, but has been on a delayed publication schedule. Under the editorship of Marion E. Doro, volume 22 (1989–90) has appeared with a 1995 copyright date, and a double volume is planned for 1990–92. The annual *Africa South of the Sahara* published in London by Europa has been very helpful as well. Another important resource is *Keesing's Contemporary Archives.*

Samuel Decalo's bibliography on Burkina Faso (Clio Press, 1994) contains more than 400 annotated entries, and probably includes that many more references sprinkled throughout the text. Scholars of Africa are greatly indebted to Hans Zell Publishers for increased awareness of African publications, particularly the quarterly *African Book Publishing Record*. Historians of francophone Africa will take note of Gloria Westfall's *French Colonial Africa: A Guide to Official Sources*.

This survey of the press is particularly prone to errors of incompleteness, and does not attempt to include many of the political party publications. Most of the following items were published in Ouagadougou. The weekly *Carrefour Africain* was started in 1959. *Kibare* was a newspaper published during the latter 1960s and last half of the 1970s. *Sentiers Voltaïques* was a religion periodical, *L'Eclair* was published by the MLN in the 1970s, *Le Patriote* was the newspaper of LIPAD. *Sidwaya,* the government daily French-language newspaper, was started in 1984. *L'Intrus,* an independent paper, was launched in mid-1986. *Lolowulein* (Red Star), journal of the Revolutionary Defense Committees, began publication in early 1985. *Jamaa* was started by the Popular Front in 1988. The oldest independent newspaper, *L'Observateur,* was founded in 1973 by Martial and Edouard Ouedraogo. Although its offices were burned in 1984, it reappeared in early 1989. Internationally, the best-known French-language weekly is *Jeune Afrique*. In English, *West Africa* magazine has considerably expanded its francophone coverage in the past decade.

The following list of subjects and authors from the 1978 edition may also help readers use the bibliography.

French Administration: Robert Arnaud (Robert Randau); André de Beauminy; Henri D'Arboussier; Maurice Delafosse; Robert Delavignette; Maurice Deschamps; Georges Hardy; Henri Labouret; Stephen H. Roberts.

Busansi (Bisa, Bissa): Gabriel Gosselin; Odette P. Pegard (Soeur Jean Bernard); André Prost.

Explorers: Heinrich Barth; Louis Binger; François Crozat; George Ekem Ferguson; Kurt von François; Gottlob Krause; Parfait Louis Monteil.

Fulani, Songhai, Tuareg: Paul Delmond; R. de Gaalon; Joseph Paul Irwin; R. L. Moreau; Paul Riesman; Jean Rouch.

Gourma: Michael Cartry; A. Chantoux; P. Davy; J. T. Maubert; M. Sidibé.

Gourounsi: Gérald L. Ponton; Robert S. Rattray; Louis Tauxier.

Kurumba (Kouroumba): Anne-Marie Schweeger-Hefel; Wilhelm Staude.

Language: Pierre G. Alexandre; Gaston Canu; A. Chantoux; Jean Cremer; Félix Dubois; Fernand Froger; Charles Lamothe; M. de Lavergne de Tressan; André Prost.

Lobi: Jack Goody; Jean-Camille Haumant; Henri Labouret; Charles Lamothe; Georges Savonnet.

Mande (Bobo, Marka, Samo, etc.): Jean Capron; Georges Chéron; Myron Joel Echenberg; Françoise Héritier-Izard.

Mossi: Salfo Albert Balima; Georges Chéron; A. A. Dim Delobsom; Michel Izard; Jean Marie Kohler; Guy Le Moal; Eugène Mangin; Lucien Marc; Robert Pageard; Gérard Rémy; Elliott P. Skinner; Louis Tauxier; Dominique Zahan.

The Southwest-Sénufo: Jean Hébert; Bohumil Holas; Georges Savonnet.

Yatenga: Peter B. Hammond; Michel Izard; Françoise Héritier-Izard; Louis Tauxier.

Contents of Bibliography

SOCIETY
Anthropology, Ethnology, and Traditional Societies
Education
Religion
Sociology and Urbanization

SCIENCE
Geography: Demography
Geography: Atlases
Geography and Geology
Public Health and Medicine
Vegetation and Flora

SELECT LIST OF BURKINA FASO (GOVERNMENT) PUBLICATIONS

General Reference

Reference

Africa Research Bulletin. Oxford UK: Blackwell. 1964– . Monthly. Particularly the Political, Social, Cultural Series.

Afrique Contemporaine. [Contemporary Africa]. Paris: La Documentation Française. 1962– . Quarterly.

"Burkina Faso." In *Africa South of the Sahara.* London: Europa Publications. 1971– . Annual.

"Burkina Faso." In *Africa Contemporary Record,* edited by Colin Legum. New York: Africana Publishing, 1966–1990. Annual. Under the editorship of Marion E. Doro, volume 22 (1989–90) appeared with a 1995 copyright date, and a double volume is planned for 1990–92.

"République de Haute-Volta." [Republic of Upper Volta]. in *Africa Administration: Directory of Public Life, Administration and Justice for the African States,* vol. 1, edited by Walter Z. Duic, pp. 489–550. New York: K. G. Saur, 1978.

Sociétés et fournisseurs d'Afrique Noire. [Business Firms and Suppliers of Black Africa]. Paris: Ediafric. 1964– . Annual. (This trade directory ceased publication in the late 1980s. The section on Burkina normally averaged about 17 pages.).

Bibliography

African Bibliographic Center (Washington, DC). *French-Speaking West Africa: Upper Volta Today, 1960–1967, A Selected and Introductory Bibliographical Guide.* Westport, Connecticut: Negro Universities Press, 1968. 37 p.

African Book World and Press: A Directoire Repertoire du Livre et de la Presse en Afrique. 4th ed. Oxford UK: Hans Zell Publishers, 1989. 340 p.

Baratte-Eno Belinga, Thérèse, et al. *Bibliographie des auteurs africains de langue française.* 4th ed. Paris: Fernand Nathan, 1979. 245 p.

Beudot, Françoise. *Eléments de bibliographie sur les pays du Sahel.* [Elements for a Bibliography of the Sahelian Countries]. Paris: OECD, 1986. 175 p.

Burkina Faso. *Bibliographie nationale agricole burkinabè.* [National Burkinabè Agricultural Bibliography]. Ouagadougou: Ministère de l'Agriculture et de l'Elevage, 1984. 44 p.

Blackhurst, Hector. *African Bibliography.* Edinburgh: Edinburgh University Press. 1984– . Annual.

Brasseur, Paule. *Bibliographie générale du Mali. (Ancien Soudan français et Haut-Senegal-Niger).* Dakar: IFAN, 1964. 461 p.

Brasseur, Paule and Maurel, Jean-François. *Les sources bibliographiques de l'Afrique de l'Ouest et de l'Afrique équatoriale d'expression française.* Dakar: Bibliothèque de l'Université, 1971.

Capron, Jean. "Bibliographie générale des Bwa."*Etudes Voltaïques,* 5, (1964). pp. 201–205. (Sixty-eight titles.)

Carson, Patricia. *Materials for West African History in French Archives.* London: Athlone Press, University of London, 1968. 170 p.

Cartry, Michel. "Bibliographie des Gourmantché" *Notes et Documents Voltaïques,* Ouagadougou, 1, 3 (Apr.–Jun. 1968). pp. 28–42. (181 titles on Gourma).

Cartry, Michel and Charles, Bernard. *L'Afrique au sud du Sahara: guide des recherches.* Paris: Centre d'Etude des Relations Internationales, Fondation Nationale des Sciences Politiques, 1962.

Conover, Helen F. *Official Publications of French West Africa, 1946–1958: A Guide.* Washington, D.C.: Library of Congress, 1960.

Coulibaly, Dramane, and Martinet, Daniel. *Inventaire des études, recherches et enquêtes menées sur le marché céréalier au Burkina Faso entre 1977 et 1988.* [Inventory of Studies, Research and Inquiries into the Cereal Market in Burkina Faso between 1977 and 1988]. Paris: OECD, 1989. 103 p.

Darch, Colin, ed. *Africa Index to Continental Periodical Literature, no. 4–5 (1979–1980),* Munich; New York; London; Paris: Hans Zell, 1983. 375 p.

Darch, Colin and Mascarenhas, O. C. *Africa Index to Continental Literature, no. 3 (1978),* Munich; New York; London; Paris: Hans Zell, 1980. 191 p.

Dauphin, Joanne Coyle; Agnès Rosset and Brigitta Rupp. "Inventaire des ressources documentaires africanistes à Paris." *Récherche, Enseignement, Documentation Africanistes Francophones: Bulletin d'Information et Liaison*, 1, 1 (1969). Paris: Centre d'Analyse et de Recherches Documentaires pour l'Afrique Noire.

Decalo, Samuel. *Burkina Faso* (World Bibliographical Series, vol. 169). Oxford, UK; Santa Barbara CA: Clio Press, 1994. 132 p.

Dinstel, M., compiler. *List of French Doctoral Dissertations on Africa*, 1884–1961, Boston: G. K. Hall, 1966.

Doute, Gilbert. "La République de Haute-Volta." *Notes et études documentaires*, Paris, Septembre 1971. 75 p.

Duignan, Peter and Gann, Lewis Henry. *Colonialism in Africa, 1870–1960*. vol. 5, *A Bibliographical Guide to Colonialism in Sub-Saharan Africa*. New York: Cambridge University Press, 1973. 552 p.

Gagner, Lorraine and Cook, Kenneth, compilers. *Upper Volta: A Selected and Partially Annotated Bibliography*. New York: U.N. Institute for Training and Research, 1972. 13 p.

Gervais, Raymond R. "Archival Documents on Upper Volta: Here, There, and Everywhere." *History in Africa*, Los Angeles, 20 (1993). pp. 379–384.

―――. "Saving Francophone Africa's Statistical Past." *History in Africa*, Los Angeles, 20 (1993). pp. 385–390.

Gosselin, Gabriel. "Bibliographie générale des Bisa." *Etudes voltaïques*, Ouagadougou, 5, 1964 (1966). pp. 199–200. (39 titles from 1887.)

Guissou, B. L. "Quelques obstacles à la recherche en Haute Volta." *Notes et documents voltaïques*, Ouagadougou, 13 (Jul.–Sep. 1982). pp. 29–54.

Hall, David, ed. *International African Bibliography*. London: Mansell. Quarterly from 1971.

Halstead, John P. and Porcari, Serafino. *Modern European Imperialism: A Bibliography of Books and Articles, 1815–1972*. Vol. 2: French and Other Empires. Boston: G. K. Hall, 1973. pp. 1–169.

"Haute-Volta." [Upper Volta]. In *Répertoire des centres de documentation et bibliothèques*, pp. 169–201. [Catalogue of Documentation Centres and Libraries]. Abidjan: Conseil d'Entente, Service de Documentation, 1980.

Hess, Robert L. and Coger, Dalvan M. *Semper ex Africa: A Bibliography of Primary Sources for Nineteenth-Century Tropical Africa as Recorded by Explorers, Missionaries, Traders, Travelers, Administrators, Military Men, Adventurers, and Others*. Stanford, Calif.: Stanford University Hoover Institution Bibliographical Series, no. 47, 1972. 800 p.

Izard, Françoise and Huart, Michèle d'. *Bibliographie générale de la Haute-Volta, 1926–1955*. Paris and Ouagadougou: CNRS and CVRS, 1967. 246 p.

Izard, Françoise; Michele d'Huart and Phillipe Bonnefond. *Bibliographie générale de la Haute-Volta 1956–1965*. Paris and Ouagadougou: CNRS and CVRS, 1967. 300 p. (Recherches voltaïque, no. 7.)

Izard, Michel. "Bibliographie générale des Mossi." *Etudes voltaïques,* Ouagadougou, Memoire no. 3 (1962). pp. 103–111. (214 titles.)

Janvier, Geneviève. *Bibliographie de la Côte d'Ivoire.* 3 vols. Abidjan: L'université d'Abidjan, 1972–1975.

Johnson, G. Wesley. "The Archival System of Former French West Africa." *African Studies Bulletin,* London, 8, 1 (April 1965). pp. 48–58.

Joucla, Edmond A. *Bibliographie de l'afrique occidentale française.* Paris: Société d'Editions Géographiques, Maritimes et Coloniales, 1937. 704 p.

Konate, I. Aminata. *Catalogue des publications de la Communauté Economique de l'Afrique de l'Ouest de 1974 à 1982.* Ouagadougou: CEAO, 1982. 21 p.

Low, Victor N. ed. *African History and Societies to 1914: A Critical Survey of Relevant Books with Special Reference to West Africa. Vol. 2: West Africa, Region by Region.* London: Frank Cass, 1984.

Martineau, Alfred, et al. *Bibliographie d'histoire coloniale (1900–1930).* Paris: Société de l'histoire des colonies française, 1932. 667 p.

Mérand, Patrick, and Séwanou, Dabla. *Guide de la litterature africaine (de langue française).* Paris: Harmattan, 1979. 219 p.

Rémy, Gérard. *Les migrations de travail et les mouvements de colonisation mossi. Recueil bibliographique.* Paris: ORSTOM, 1973. 128 p. (Trav.-Docum. ORSTOM, no. 21.)

Scheven, Yvette. *Bibliographies for African Studies 1970–1986.* London: Hans Zell, 1988. 637 p. (Cumulative listing of 4,500 bibliographies published between 1970 and 1986.)

Somda, Nurukyor Claude. "Bibliographie générale du Dagara." *Notes et documents voltaïques,* Ouagadougou, 14 (Jan.–Mar. 1983). pp. 73–80.

Some, D. and Yonli, E. E. " Index des tomes 1 à 11: 1967 à 1978 des *Notes et documents voltaïques." Notes et documents voltaïques,* Ouagadougou, 12, 1–4 (Oct. 1978–Oct. 1979). pp. 174–194.

U. S. Imprints on Sub-Saharan Africa: A Guide to Publications Catalogued at the Library of Congress. Washington DC: Library of Congress African Section, 1986.

Upper Volta. Ministère du Plan. *Inventaire des études et des rapports de mission.* Ouagadougou, 1978. 392 p.

Urvoy, Yves. "Essai de bibliographie des populations du Soudan central." *BCEHS,* Paris, 19 (1936). pp. 243–333.

Westfall, Gloria. *French Colonial Africa: A Guide to Official Sources.* London and New York: Hans Zell Publishers, 1992. 226 p.

Wieschhoff, H. A. *Anthropological Bibliography of Negro Africa.* New York: Kraus Reprint, 1970. 461 p. (American Oriental Series, vol. 23.)

Witherell, Julian W. *French-speaking West Africa: A Guide to Official Publications.* Washington DC: Library of Congress, 1967. 201 p.

Witherell, Julian W., comp. *The United States and Sub-Saharan Africa:*

Guide to U. S. Official Documents and Government-Sponsored Publications, 1976–1980. Washington DC: Library of Congress, 1984. (Burkina Faso, pp. 577–590)

Yaranga, Zofia. *Bibliographie des travaux en langue française sur l'Afrique au Sud du Sahara.* [Bibliography of French-Language Works on Sub-Saharan Africa]. Paris: Centre d'Etudes Africaines. 1984– . Bi-annual.

Zell, Hans M. *African Books in Print/Livres Africains Disponibles.* 3d ed. 2 vols. London and New York: Mansell Publishing, 1984.

Zell, Hans and Jay, Mary (eds). *The African Book Publishing Record.* London and Munich and New York: Hans Zell Publishers. (Quarterly list since 1975 of new/forthcoming items in English, French and some African languages.)

The Country and People

"Afrique Occidentale Française." *Encyclopédie de l'Afrique Française,* vol. 2. Paris: Editions de l'Union Française, 1952–1953. 820 p.

"Haute-Volta." *Afrique,* Paris, April 1966. 56 p.

"La Haute-Volta." *Magazine A. O. F.,* 17, ser. 11, 2 (Nov. 1955). p. 9.

"Le redressement voltaïque." *Europe-France-Outremer,* Paris, 467 (Dec. 1968). pp. 8–40. (Special Issue on Upper Volta.)

Adloff, Richard. *West Africa: The French-Speaking Nations Yesterday and Today.* New York: Holt, Rinehart, Winston, 1965. 361 p.

Annuaire des Etats d'Afrique Noire: Gouvernements et Cabinets Ministeriels, Partis Politiques. 2d ed. Paris: EDIAFRIC, 1962. 443 p.

Asamani, J. O. *Index Africanus.* Stanford: Hoover Institution Press, 1975. pp. 176–178 for material on Upper Volta.

Bulletin de L'Afrique Noire. *Personnalités Publiques de l'Afrique, 1969.* Paris: EDIAFRIC, 1968. 450 p. (Special issue.)

Burkina Faso: Statistical Annex. Washington DC: International Monetary Fund, 1994. 40 p.

"Burkina Faso." In *Africa South of the Sahara,* pp. 191–208, London: Europa Publications, 1995. (annual)

Carpenter, Allan and Baker, Janice E. *Enchantment of Africa: Upper Volta.* Chicago: Children's Press, 1974. 96 p.

Catchpole, Brian and Akinjogbin, I. A. *A History of West Africa in Maps and Diagrams,* London: Collins Educational, 1985.

Church, R. J. Harrison. *West Africa.* 8th ed. London: Longman, 1979.

Ciré Ba, Birahim. "Esquisse historique sur les Bobo et Bobo Dioula." *Bulletin de l'Enseignement de l'A. O. F.,* Goré, 19, 7 (1929). pp. 3–9. (also found in *Education Africaine,* 24 [1954]. pp. 45–52.)

———. "Les Bobos—la famille les coutumes." *L'Education Africaine,* N.S. 23 (1954). pp. 61–75.

Cornevin, Robert, ed. *Hommes et destins: dictionnaire biographique d'outre mer,* Paris: Académie des sciences d'outre mer, 1975–1981. 4 vols. 668, 789, 543, 734 pp.

Delafosse, Maurice. *Haut-Sénégal-Niger. Le pays, les peuples, les langues, l'histoire, les civilisations.* Paris: E. Larose, 1912. (Reprint of 1912 edition by G.-P. Maissonneuve and Larose, 1972. 3 vols. 428 p., 426 p., 316 p.)

Froelich, Jean Claude; Pierre Alexander and Robert Cornevin. *Les Populations de Nord Togo.* Paris: Presses Universitaires de France, 1963. 199 p. (Monographies ethnologiques africaines.)

Gilfond, Henry. *Countries of the Sahara: Chad, Mali, Mauritania, Niger, Upper Volta, and Western Sahara.* New York: F. Watts, 1981. 64 p.

Guernier, Eugène, director. *Encyclopedie de l'empire français: l'encyclopedie coloniale et maritime: Afrique occidentale française.* 2 vols. Paris: Encyclopedie Coloniale et Maritime, 1949. 394 p., 410 p.

Jakande, L. K., ed. *West African Annual,* 1970. New York: International Publications Service; London: James Clarke, 1970.

Jeune Afrique. *Atlas de la Haute-Volta,* Paris: Editions Jeune Afrique, 1975. p. 48.

Lajus, Miches. "La République voltaïque." *La Revue Française,* Paris, Nov. 1959.

Les élites africaines, 1970–71. Paris: EDIAFRIC, 1970. 298 p. (Special issue, *Bulletin de l'Afrique Noire,* Paris.)

Le Moal, Guy. "Peuple Mossi." *Encyclopédie Mensuelle d'Outre-Mer,* Paris, 3, 41 (Feb. 1954). pp. 17–21.

Lear, Aaron. *Burkina Faso.* Edgemont, Pennsylvania: Chelsea House, 1986. p. 95.

Lippens, Philippe. *La république de haute-volta.* Paris: Berger-Levrault, 1972. 62 p. (Published by the International Institute of Public Administration, Paris.)

Moroney, Sean. "Burkina Faso." In *Africa,* pp. 45–58. New York: Facts on File, 1989, Vol. 1.

Murdock, George Peter. *Africa: Its Peoples and Their Culture History.* New York: McGraw-Hill, 1959. 456 p. (Chapter 11 on the Nuclear Mande; 12 on the Voltaic people; 17 on Blacks of the Soudan fringe; 53 on the Tuareg; and 55 on the Fulani.)

Murray, Jocelyn. *Cultural Atlas of Africa.* Oxford UK: Phaidon Press, 1981. 240 p.

Newland, H. Osman. *West Africa. A Handbook of Practical Information.* London: D. O'Connor, 1922. 441 p.

Ponton, Gérald L. "Les Gourounsi du groupe voltaïque." *Outre-Mer,* Paris, 5 (April–Sept. 1933). pp. 97–117.

Richard-Molard, Jacques. *Afrique Occidentale Française.* 3e éd. Paris: Berger-Levrault, 1956. 239 p.

————. *Cartes ethno-démographiques de l'Afrique Occidentale* (Feuilles no. 1). Dakar: IFAN, 1956.

Rubon, R. and Sacx, M. *Mon pays: la Haute-Volta.* Paris: ISTRA, 1964. 88 p.

Seck, Assane and Mondjannagni, Alfred. *L'Afrique occidentale.* Paris: Presses Universitaires, 1967. 290 p.

Sidibé, M. "Le Fada N'Gourma." *Bulletin de l'enseignement de l'Afrique occidentale française,* Dakar, 6, 39 (July 1918). pp 111–130.

Taylor, Sidney, ed. "Upper Volta." In *The New Africans,* pp. 472–483. New York: Putnam, 1967.

Thompson, Virginia and Adloff, Richard. *French West Africa.* Stanford, Calif.: Stanford University Press, 1957. 626 p. (Reprint by Greenwood Press, New York, 1969.)

Tiendrébéogo, Gérard. *Langues et groupes ethniques de Haute-Volta.* Paris: ACCT; Abidjan: ILA, 1983. 63 p.

United States Department of Commerce. *Basic Data on the Economy of Upper Volta.* Washington DC: GPO, 1965. 6 p.

United States Department of State. *The Newly Independent Nations: Upper Volta.* Washington DC: GPO, 1962. 9 p.

————. *Upper Volta. Background Notes.* Washington DC: GPO, 1973. 4 p.

————. *Upper Volta, a Country Profile,* Washington DC: Office of U.S. Foreign Disaster Assistance, 1978. 53 p.

Uwechue, Ralph, et al. "Burkina Faso." In *Know Africa: Africa Today,* pp. 587–615. London: Africa Books, 1991.

Vieyra, J. *Conseil de l'Entente. Ivory Coast, Dahomey, Upper Volta, Niger, Togo: Five Countries Still to be Discovered.* Paris: Presse Africaine Associée, 1969. 40 p.

Weekes, Richard V., ed. *Muslim Peoples: A World Ethnographic Survey,* 2d ed., (Includes multi-page sections each on the Bambara, Dyula, Fulani, Mossi, Senufo, Songhay, Soninké), Westport, Conn.: Greenwood Press, 1984. 953 p., 2 vol.

Zech, Comte von. "Pays et populations de la frontière Nord-Ouest du Togo." *Etudes dahoméennes,* 2 (1949). pp. 9–36.

Guides and Travel

"Burkina Faso." In *Africa on a Shoestring,* edited by Geoff Crowther, pp. 130–140. Hawthorn, Australia; Berkeley, California: Lonely Planet, 1989.

"Burkina Faso." In *West Africa: A Survival Kit,* edited by Alex Newton, pp. 112–130. Berkeley, California: Lonely Planet, 1988.

"Eating Habits (Burkina Faso)." *The Economist,* London, 326, 7797

(Feb. 6, 1993). p. 72. Highlights Ouagadougou restaurant 'L'eau vive'.

"La Haute Volta." In *Beautés du monde: l'Afrique Occidentale*, pp. 1–10. [Beauties of the World: West Africa]. Paris: Librairie Larousse, 1980.

"Regards sur la Haute-Volta." Paris: Union des comités pour le développement des peuples; Poitiers: Collectif Tiers-monde, 1981. 116 p. (A guide book)

Allen, Philip M. and Segal, Aaron. *The Traveler's Africa: A Guide. to the Entire Continent.* New York: Hopkinson and Blake, 1973. (See pp. 671–682.)

Bennett, Nicholas. *Zigzag to Timbuktu.* New York: Transatlantic, 1967; London: John Murray, 1963. 136 p. Impressions of trip Ghana-Upper Volta-Mali.

Bienvenue en Haute Volta. [Welcome to Upper Volta]. Boulogne, France: Editions Delroisse, 1972. 128 p.

Blumenthal, Susan. *Bright Continent: A Shoestring Guide to Sub-Saharan Africa.* New York: Anchor Books 1974. (Upper Volta section, pp. 261–274.)

Brydon, David. *Africa Overland.* 2nd ed. Brentford, England: Roger Lascelles, 1991. (See pp. 238–242.)

French West Africa, Agence Economique. *Guide du tourisme en Afrique occidentale française*, 3d ed. Paris, 1935. 158 p.

Guide Ouest-africain. Paris: Diloutremer, 1965. (Pages 305–360.)

Hudges, Jim, and Trillo, Richard. "Burkina Faso." In *West Africa: The Rough Guide*, pp. 241–297. London: Harrap-Columbus, 1990.

Klotchkoff, Jean-Claude. *Le Burkina Faso aujourd'hui.* Paris: Jaguar, 1993. 239 p. (Tourist guide book, including photos and maps)

Rochon, Marie Claude. *Deux ans en Haute-Volta.* Paris: La Pensée Universelle, 1976. 189 p.

Taussig, Louis. *Sub-Saharan African Travel Resource Guide: East and West Africa* (Travel Resource Guide no. 1). Oxford UK: Hans Zell, 1992. 288 p.

Theau, Remi Gatard, et al. *Réflexions à la suite d'un sejour dans deux petits villages de Haute-Volta.* Poitiers: Collectif Tiers monde, 1979. 72 p. (Serious guidebook to people and issues of Third World countries)

Turbanisch, Gerhard. *Guide gastronomique de Ouagadougou.* [Gastronomic Guide to Ouagadougou]. Ouagadougou: G. Turbanisch, 1988. 55 p.

History

History

"L'itinéraire de Binger en Haute-Volta et la carte provisoire de l'A.O.F." *Notes africaines,* 54 (Apr. 1952). pp. 52–53.

"La Mission Decoeur et la Haut-Dahomey." *BCAF,* Paris, 1 (April 1895). 103 ff.

Afrique Occidentale Française. *Bulletin du Comité d'Etudes Historique et Scientifiques, AOF.* Paris: Larose, almost annually from 1917.

Alexandre, Pierre. "A West African Islamic Movement: Hamallism in French West Africa." *In Protest and Power in Black Africa,* edited by Robert I. Rotberg and Ali A. Mazrui, pp. 497–512. New York: Oxford University Press, 1970.

Andah, Bassey W. "Prehistoric Reconnaissance of Parts of North Central Upper Volta: Its Bearing on Agricultural Beginnings." *Bulletin de l'IFAN, sér B,* Dakar, 42, 2 (April 1980). pp. 219–250.

Arnaud, Robert. "Le dernier épisode de la conquête du Soudan français. L'affaire de Tabi." *Renseignements coloniaux et documents publiés par le Comité l'Afrique Française et le Comité du Maroc,* Paris, (August 1922). pp. 201–239.

Balesi, Charles John. *From Adversaries to Comrades-in-Arms: West Africans and the French Military, 1885–1918.* Los Angeles: Crossroads Press, 1979. 196 p.

———. "West African Influence on the French Army of World War I." In *Double Impact: France and Africa in the Age of Imperialism,* edited by G. Wesley Johnson, pp. 93–104. Westport, Conn.: Greenwood Press, 1985.

Balima, Salfo Albert. *Notes sur l'organisation de l'empire mossi.* Paris: Institut des Hautes Etudes d'Outre-Mer, 1959. 52 p.

———. "Les quatre épreuves du long règne (1905–1942) de Naba Koom II." *Afrique histoire,* 6 (1982). pp. 61–65.

Bamouni, Paulin B. "Le royaume mossi de Haute-Volta." *Afrique Littérature Artistique,* 37 (1975). pp. 63–66.

Barth, Heinrich. *Travels and Discoveries in North and Central Africa, 1849–1855.* Centenary Edition, vol. 3. London: Frank Cass, 1965. Material on northeastern Upper Volta is found on pp. 190–218.

Bassolet, François Djoby. *L'Evolution de la Haute Volta de 1898 au 3 janvier 1966.* Ouagadougou: Imprimerie Nationale de la Haute-Volta, 1968. 135 p.

Bayili, Emmanuel. "Les rivalités franco-britanniques et la zone frontière Haute Volta-Ghana, 1896–1914." *Cahiers du Centre de Recherches Africaines Historiques,* 1 (1980). pp. 73–104.

Bazie, Jean Hubert. *Chronique du Burkina.* Ouagadougou: La presse écrite, 1985. 127 p.

Biwante. *Biwante: recit autobiographique d'un Lobi du Burkina Faso* (recorded by Michele Fieloux), Paris: Karthala, 1993. 246 p.

Boni, Nazi. *Crépuscule des temps anciens; Chronique du Bwamu.* [Twilight of Former Times. The story of life in a Bwa village in the bend of the Black Volta and the revolt of 1916]. Paris: Présence africaine, 1962 (reprinted 1994). 257 p.

————. *L 'Histoire synthetique de l'Afrique résistante*. Paris: Présence africaine, 1971. 310 p.

Bourgi, Robert. *Le general de Gaulle et l'Afrique noire, 1940–1969*, Paris: Librairie general de droit et de jurisprudence; Dakar: Nouvelles editions Africaines, 1980. 515 p.

Bretout, Françoise. *Mogho Naba Wobgho: la résistance du royaume mossi de Ouagadougou*. [Mogho Naba Wobgho: The Resistance of the Mossi Kingdom of Ouagadougou]. Paris: Afrique Biblio Club, 1976. 92 p.

Chailley, Marcel. *Les Grandes missions françaises en Afrique occidentale*. Dakar: IFAN, 1953. 145 p. (*Initiations africaines,* no. 10.)

Chanoine, J. "Mission au Gourounsi." *Bulletin de la Société de Géographie Commerciale,* Paris, 19 (1897). pp. 752–760.

————. "Mission Voulet-Chanoine." *Bulletin de la Société de Géographie Commerciale,* Paris, 20 (1898). pp. 220–279.

Chantoux, Alphonse. *Histoire du pays gourma; Traditions orales*. Fada N'Gourma: Editions Ti Dogu, 1966. 61 p.

Chéron, E. Georges. "La pénétration française en pays Mossi—première partie." *Notes et documents voltaïques,* Ouagadougou, 5, 2 (Jan.–Mar. 1972). pp. 4–58.

Cohen, William B. *Rulers of Empire: The French Colonial Service in Africa*. Stanford CA: Hoover Institution Press, 1971. 279 p.

Conombo, Joseph I. *M'ba Tinga: traditions des Mosse dans l'Empire du Mogho-Naba*. [M'ba Tinga: Traditions of the Mossi in the Empire of Mogho Naba]. Paris: Harmattan, 1989. p. 185.

Cooke, James J. *New French Imperialism, 1880–1910: The Third Republic and Colonial Expansion*. Hamden, Conn.: Archon Books, 1973. 223 p.

Cross, Nigel and Barker, Rhiannon. *At the Desert Edge: Oral Histories from the Sahel,* London: Panos Institute, 1991?. 248 p. (Burkina section, pp. 97–125).

Crowder, Michael. *West Africa Under Colonial Rule*. Evanston, Ill.: Northwestern University Press, 1968. 530 p.

Crozat, François. "Rapport du Docteur Crozat sur sa mission au Mossi." *Journal Officiel de la République Française,* Paris, 5–10 October 1891.

D'Arboussier, Henri. "La Conquête du Togoland: L'Action des partisans Mossi." *Bulletin du Comité de l'Afrique française: Renseignements Coloniaux et documents,* 25 (1915). pp. 49–55.

Davies, Oliver. *West Africa Before the Europeans,* London: Methuen (distributed in USA by Barnes & Noble), 1967. 364 p.

Davis, Shelby Cullom. *Reservoirs of Men: A History of the Black Troops of French West Africa,* Reprint. Westport, Conn.: Negro Universities Press, 1970. 205 p.

Davy, P. *Histoire du pays gourmantché*. Paris: CHEAM, 1964.

De Lusignan, Guy. *French-Speaking Africa Since Independence.* New York: Frederick A. Praeger, 1969. 416 p. (Chap. 4 on Entente States.)

De Tessieres, Yves. "Un épisode du partage de l'Afrique: la mission Monteil de 1890–1892." *Revue française d'histoire d'outre-mer,* France, 59, 3 (1972). pp. 345–410.

Delafosse, Maurice. "Afrique occidentale française." In *Histoire des colonies françaises et de l'expansion de la France dans le monde,* edited by Gabriel Hanotaux and Alfred Martineau, pp. 1–356. Paris: Librairie Plon, 1931.

Delavignette, Robert Louis. *Les paysans noirs.* Paris: Stock, 1931. 224 p. From author's life at Banfora. 1932 Grand Prize for Colonial Literature.

————. *Les vrais chefs de l'Empire Français.* Paris: Gallimard, 1939. 262 p. (English translation, Freedom and Authority in French West Africa. London: Thomas Nelson, 1950. Frank Cass, 1968. 152 p.)

Diallo, L. "Collecte, parmi les autochtones, de traditions orales concernant l'époque de Naaba Wubri" [Collection, Among the Natives, of Oral Traditions of the Naaba Wubri area]. *Journal of Asian and African Studies,* Tokyo, 35 (1988). pp. 113–156.

Diallo, Liliane. "Aux origines du Wubri-tenga de Guilongou après une tradition orale recueillié dans ces villages." [On the Origins of the Wubri-tenga of Guilongou According to an Oral Tradition Collected in these Villages]. *Genève-Afrique,* Switzerland, 23, 2 (1985). pp. 7–36.

Domergue, Danielle. "L'échec d'une conquête: le pays lobi (1900–1926)." [The Failure of a Conquest: Lobi Country]. *BIFAN,* Dakar, sér. B, 39, 3 (July 1977). pp. 532–553.

Dory, Daniel. "Entre la découverte et la domination: les Lobi." [Between Discovery and Domination: The Lobi]. *Bulletin de l'Association de Géographie,* Paris, 61, 505/506 (1984). pp. 373–382.

Doti-Sanou, Bruno. *L'émancipation des femmes Madare: l'impact du projet administratif et missionaire sur une société africaine, 1900–1950,* Leiden; New York: E. J. Brill, 1994. 254 p.

Du Bois, Victor D. "The Struggle for Stability in the Upper Volta." Part 1, "The Period Before Independence." Part 2, "The Early Years of Trial, 1960–1965." Part 3, "The Fall of Maurice Yaméogo." Part 4, "Foreign Reaction to the Overthrow of President Maurice Yaméogo." Part 5, "The Military Regime of President Sangoulé Lamizana." *American University Field Staff Reports, West Africa Series,* Hanover, New Hampshire, 12, 1–5 (Mar.–Aug. 1969).

————. "UAM at the Crossroads." *Africa Report,* Washington DC, April, 1963. pp. 3–5. (First annual meeting, UAM, Ouagadougou, 10–14 March 1963.)

Duperray, Anne-Marie. *Les Gourounsi de Haute-Volta: conquête et colonisation, 1896–1933,* [The Gurunsi of Upper Volta: Conquest and Colonization]. Stuttgart: F. Steiner, 1984. 280 p.

———. "Les Yarsé du Royaume de Ouagadougou: l'écrit et l'oral." [The Yarsé of the Wagadugu Kingdom: Written and Oral Sources]. *Cahiers d'études Africaines,* Paris, 25, 2 (1985). pp 179–212.

Echenberg, Myron Joel. "Jihad and State-Building in Late Nineteenth Century Upper Volta: The Rise and Fall of the Marka State of Al-Kari of Boussé." *Canadian Journal of African Studies,* Montreal, 3, 3 (1969). pp. 531–561. Also in *Notes et Documents Voltaïques,* Ouagadougou, 3, 3 (1970).

———. "Late Nineteenth-Century Military Technology in Upper Volta." *Journal of African History,* Cambridge UK, 12, 2 (1971). pp. 241–254.

———. "Les migrations militaires au Afrique occidentale française, 1900–1945." *Journal of African Studies,* Montreal, 14, 3 (1980). pp. 429–450.

———. "Paying the Blood Tax: Military Conscription in French West Africa, 1914–1929." *Journal of African Studies,* Montreal, 9, 2 (1975). pp. 171–192.

Fage, John Donelly. "Reflections on the Early History of the Mossi-Dagomba Group of States." In *The Historian in Tropical Africa,* edited by Jan Vansina, Raymond Mauny and L. V. Thomas, pp. 177–192. London: Oxford University Press, 1964.

Ferguson, George Ekem. *Papers of George Ekem Ferguson 1890–1897.* Edited by Kwame Arhin. Leiden: Afrika Studiecentrum, 1974. 180 p.

Foltz, William Jay. *From French West Africa to the Mali Federation.* New Haven: Yale University Press, 1965. 235 p.

François, Kurt von. "Voyage à Salaga et au Mossi." *Revue de Géographie,* Paris, 1888.

Frobenius, Leo. *Histoire et contes des Mossi.* [History and Folktales of the Mossi]. Stuttgart: F. Steiner, 1986. 93 p.

Fuglestad, Finn. *A History of Niger, 1850–1960,* New York and London: Cambridge University Press, 1983. 272 p. (Burkina Faso was part of Haut-Senegal-Niger prior to 1919; when Upper Volta was dissolved in 1932 some of the country became part of Niger)

Gervais, Raymond. "La politique cotonnière de la France dans le Mossi colonial (Haute-Volta) (1919–1940)." [French Cotton Policy in Colonial Mossi (Upper Volta), 1919–40]. *Revue française d'histoire d'outre-mer,* France, 81, 1 (1994). pp. 27–54.

Goody, John R. (Jack). "The Mande and the Akan Hinterland." In *The Historian in Tropical Africa,* edited by Jan Vansina, Raymond Mauny and L. V. Thomas, pp. 193–218. London: Oxford University Press for the International African Institute, 1964.

Guilhem, Marcel. *Histoire de la Haute-Volta, l'Afrique et le Monde.* 2d ed. Paris: Ligel, 1976. 387 p.

Guyot, J. L. *Le droit coutumier mossi avant la pénétration française,* Paris: Institut des Hautes Etudes d'Outre-mer, 1957.

Hama, Boubou. *Enquête sur les fondements et la genèse de l'unité africaine.* Paris: Présence Africaine, 1966. (Interesting information on the early Mossi of the three Diamarés is found on pp. 210–212.)

Hardy, Georges. *La Politique coloniale et le partage de la terre aux XIXe et XXe siècles.* Paris: Albion Michel, 1937. 499 p.

Hargreaves, John D. *West Africa: The Former French States.* Englewood Cliffs, NJ: Prentice-Hall, 1967. 183 p.

Hébert, Jean. *Esquisse d'une monographie historique du pays dagara.* Diébougou, Burkina Faso: Diocèse de Diébougou, 1976. 263 p.

———. "Les Gwi et les Turka." *Notes et documents voltaïques,* Ouagadougou, 3, 1 (Oct.–Dec. 1969). pp. 12–51.

———. "Révoltes en Haute-Volta de 1914 à 1918." [Revolts in Upper Volta from 1914 to 1918]. *Notes et documents voltaïques,* Ouagadougou, 3, 4 (July–Sept. 1970). pp. 3–55.

———. "Samory en Haute-Volta." *Etudes voltaïques,* Ouagadougou, 2, 1961 (1963). pp. 5–55.

———. "Une page d'histoire voltaïque: Amoro, chef des Tiefo." BIFAN, Dakar, ser. B, 20, 3–4 (July–Oct. 1958). pp. 377–405.

Héritier-Izard, Françoise. "Des cauris et des hommes: production d'esclaves et accumulation de cauris chez les Samo (Haute-Volta)." In *L'esclavage en Afrique précoloniale,* pp. 477–507. Paris: Maspéro, 1975.

Hertslet, Sir. Edward. *The Map of Africa by Treaty.* 3d ed. London: Frank Cass, 1967. 3 vols. 1404 p.

Hilton, T. E. "Note on the History of Kusasi." *Transactions of the Historical Society of Ghana,* 6 (1962). pp. 83–84.

Hodgkin, Thomas L. and Schachter, Ruth. *French-Speaking West Africa in Transition.* New York: Carnegie, 1960. pp. 375–436.

Iliasu, A. A. "The origins of the Mossi-Dagomba states." *Research Review, Institute of African Studies,* Legon, Ghana, 7, 2 (1971). pp. 95–113.

Irwin, Joseph Paul. *Liptako Speaks: History from Oral Tradition in Africa.* Princeton NJ: Princeton University Press, 1981. 221 p.

———. "Chronique du Liptako Précolonial." *Notes et documents voltaïques,* 9 (1975–1976). pp. 3–47.

Izard, Françoise. "Recherches sur l'histoire du peuplement en Haute Volta." *Notes et documents voltaïques,* Ouagadougou, 1, 1 (Oct.–Dec. 1967). pp. 9–13.

Izard, Michel. *Gens de pouvoir, gens de terre: les institutions politiques de l'ancien royaume du Yatenga.* [People of Power, People of the Earth: The Political Institutions of the Ancient Kingdom of Yatenga]. Cambridge UK: Cambridge University Press; Paris: Editions de la Maison des sciences de l'homme, 1985. 594 p.

————. *Introduction à l'histoire des royaumes Mossi*, 2 vols. Paris and Ouagadougou: CNRS and CVRS, 1970. 432 p. (Recherches voltaïques, nos. 12 and 13.) (Paris: Laboratoire d'anthropologie sociale, Collège de France. 1970.)

————. *The Mossi Kingdom of Yatenga, 1896–1960*. Ouagadougou: Catholic Press, 1967.

————. *L'Odyssée du pouvoir; un royaume africain: état, société, destin individuel*. Paris: Editions de l'école des hautes études en sciences sociales, 1992. 154 p.

————. *Traditions historiques des villages du Yatenga. 1-Cercle de Gourcy*. Paris and Ouagadougou: CNRS and CVRS, 1965. 226 p.

————. *Le Yatenga précolonial: un ancien royaume du Burkina*. [Precolonial Yatenga: a former kingdom of Burkina]. Paris: Karthala, 1985. 164 p.

————. "Les Archives orales d'un royaume africain: recherches sur la formation du Yatenga." Paris: Laboratoire d'Anthropologie Sociale, Collège de France, 1980.

————. "Les captifs royaux dans l'ancien Yatenga." In *L'esclavage en Afrique précoloniale*, pp. 281–296. Paris: Maspéro, 1975.

————. "Changements d'identité lignagère dans le Yatenga." *Journal des Africanistes*, Paris, 46, 1–2 (1976). pp. 69–81.

————. "La formation de Ouahigouya." [The Formation of Ouahigouya]. *Journal de la Société des Africanistes*, Paris, 41, 2 (1971). pp. 151–187.

————. "Histoire d'un empire: les Mossi du Yatenga." *Balafon*, Abidjan, Air Afrique, 38 (Jan. 1978). pp. 34–41.

————. "Mission chez les Mossi du Yatenga." *L'homme*, Paris, 6, 1 (Jan.–Mar. 1966). pp. 118–120.

————. "Naaba Kângo, souverain du Yatenga." *Notes et documents voltaïques*, 2, 3 (Apr.–Jun. 1969). pp. 3–26.

————. "Note sur la situation de la recherche historique en Haute-Volta." *Notes et documents voltaïques*, 2, 1 (Oct.–Dec. 1968). pp. 22–34.

————. "Paysans partisans. A propos de la guerre dans les sociétés burkinabé." [Partisan Peasants: On War in Burkina Faso Societies]. *Cahiers des Sciences Humaines*, (Trente ans). Paris: ORSTOM, 1993. pp. 61–64.

————. "The Peoples and Kingdoms of the Niger Bend and the Volta Basin from the 12th to the 16th Century." In *General History of Africa*, Vol. 4, edited by D. T. Niane, pp. 211–237. Berkeley and Los Angeles: University of California Press, 1984.

————. "La politique extérieure d'un royaume africain: le Yatenga au 19e siècle." *Cahiers d'études africaines*, Paris, 22, 3–4 (1982). pp. 87–88, 363–385.

————. "Le royaume du Yatenga." In *Eléments d'ethnologie,* edited by Robert Cresswell, pp. 216–248. Paris: Armand Colin, 1975.

————. "Le royaume du Yatenga et ses forgerons: une recherche d'histoire du peuplement." [The Yatenga Kingdom and its metal-workers: Historical Research of a People]. In *Métallurgies africaines: nouvelles contributions,* edited by N. Echard, pp. 256–279. Paris: Société des Africanistes, 1983.

————. "The Yarsé and Pre-Colonial Trade in Yatenga." In *The Development of Indigenous Trade and Markets in West Africa,* edited by C. Meillassoux, pp. 214–227. Oxford UK: Oxford University Press for International African Institute, 1971.

Johnson, G. Wesley, ed. *Double Impact: France and Africa in the Age of Imperialism,* Westport, Conn.: Greenwood Press, 1985. 407 p.

Kaboré, Gomkoudougou Victor. *L'organisation politique traditionnelle et évolution politique des Mossi de Ouagadougou.* [Traditional Political Organization and Political Evolution of the Mossi of Ouagadougou]. Paris and Ouagadougou: CNRS and CVRS, 1966. 224 p. (Recherches voltaïques, no. 5.)

Kambou-Ferrand, Jeanne-Marie. *Peuples voltaïques et conquête coloniale, 1885–1914: Burkina Faso.* Paris: Harmattan, 1993. 480 p.

Kawada, Junzo. *Genèse et évolution du système politique des Mosi méridionaux (Haute Volta).* [The origin and evolution of the political system of the central Mosi]. Tokyo: Institute for the Study of Languages and Cultures of Asia and Africa, 1979. 330 p.

————. *Technologie voltaïque: rapport de mission, 1973–1975.* Ouagadougou: Musée national, 1975. 49 p.

————. *Textes historiques oraux des Mosi méridionaux.* [Oral History Texts of the Central Mossi]. Tokyo: Institute for Research on Languages and Cultures of Asia and Africa, 1985. p. 307.

————. *Le Zitenga: Rapport de mission dans le cercle de Ziniaré.* Paris and Ouagadougou: CNRS and CVRS, 1967. 90 p.

————. "Chronologie des Busuma Naaba." *Notes et documents voltaïque,* Ouagadougou, 2, 2 (Jan.–Mar. 1969). pp. 42–53.

————. "Histoire orale et imaginaire du passé." [Oral and Imaginary History of the Past]. *Revue de l'Institut de Sociologie,* Brussels, 3/4 (1988). pp. 127–136.

————. "Histoire orale et imaginaire du passé: le cas d'un discours 'historique' africain." [Oral history and imagining the past: the case of an African historical discourse (the Mossi royal genealogy)]. *Annales: Economies, Socits, Civilisations,* France, 48, 4 (1993). pp. 1087–1105.

————. "L'Introduction à l'histoire des Royaumes Mossi de Michel Izard." *Notes et documents voltaïque,* Ouagadougou, 6, 2 (Jan.–Mar. 1973) pp. 12–17.

Ki-Zerbo, Joseph. *Alfred Diban, premier chrétien de Haute-Volta.* [Alfred Diban, the First Christian of Upper Volta]. Paris: Editions du CERF, 1983. 148 p.

———. *Histoire de l'Afrique noire d'hier à demain.* Paris: Librairie A. Hatier, 1972. 708 p. 2d ed. 1978. 731 p.

———. *Methodology and African Prehistory,* Vol. 1, The UNESCO General History of Africa. Berkeley: University of California Press, 1980. 450 p.

———. *Le monde africain noir: historie et civilization.* Paris: A. Hatier, 1972. 96 p.

———. "Women and the Energy Crisis in the Sahel." *Unasylva,* 33, 131 (1981). pp. 24–29.

Kiba, Simon. "La Haute Volta après quelques mois de liberté." *Afrique Nouvelle,* 16, 994–995 (Aug. 31 and Sep. 14, 1966).

Kiethega, Jean-Baptiste. *L'or de la Volta Noire: Archéologie et histoire de l'exploitation traditionelle.* [The gold of the Black Volta: archaeology and history of traditional exploitation (Poura region)]. Paris: Karthala, 1983. 247 p.

Kittler, Glen D. *The White Fathers.* New York: William Allen, 1958. 318 p.

Kohler, Jean Marie. *Notes historiques et éthnographiques sur quelques commandements régionaux de l'ouest Mossi (Haute-Volta): document de travail.* Paris: ORSTOM, 1967. 80 p.

Koulibaly, Fabegna. "Histoire des Marka de Haute-Volta." *Notes et documents voltaïques,* Ouagadougou, 3, 3 (Apr.–June 1970). pp. 43–52.

Krause, Gottlob Adolf. "Brief aus Afrika: The Position of Salaga." *Proceedings of the Royal Geographical Society,* London, 1893. S.74.

———. "Krause's Reise." *Petermann's Mitteilungen,* Berlin, 1887. pp. 57, 92, 152, 217; 1888. p. 88.

———. "Voyage en Afrique." *Société de Géographie, Comptes rendus des séances,* Paris, 1888. p. 117.

Labouret, Henri. *Monteil, explorateur et soldat.* Paris: Berger-Levrault, 1937. 304 p.

———. "Les bandes de Samori dans la Haute Côte d'Ivoire, la Côte de l'Or et le pays Lobi. L'expansion anglaise sur la Volta Noire de 1894 à 1897." *Renseignements Coloniaux et Documents Comité l'Afrique française et le Comité du Maroc,* Paris, 8 (Aug. 1925). pp. 341–355.

———. "Le chemin de Fer du Mossi." *Renseignements Coloniaux, BCAF,* Paris, 1938. pp. 253–260.

Lavroff, D. G. "L'évolution constitutionnelle de la République de Haute-Volta: la constitution du 27 novembre 1977." *Année africaine 1977.* pp. 170–208.

Le Moal, Guy. "Enquête sur l'histoire du peuplement du pays bobo." *Notes et documents voltaïques,* Ouagadougou, 1, 2 (Jan.–Mar. 1968). pp. 6–9.

————. "Le peuplement du pays Bobo; bilan d'une enquête." *Cahiers ORSTOM* (Sciences humaines), Paris, 13, 2 (1976). pp. 137–142.

————. "Vestiges préhistoriques en pays Bobo (Haute Volta)." *Cahiers ORSTOM* (Sciences humaines), Paris: ORSTOM, 18, 2 (1981–1982). pp. 255–259.

Le Vine, Victor T. "The Coups in Upper Volta, Dahomey, and the Central African Republic." In *Protest and Power in Black Africa,* edited by Robert I. Rotberg and Ali A. Mazrui, pp. 1035–1071. New York: Oxford University Press, 1970.

Legassick, Martin. "Firearms, Horses and Samorian Army Organization." *Journal of African History,* Cambridge UK, 7, 1 (1966). pp. 95–115.

Levtzion, Nehemia. *Muslims and Chiefs in West Africa: A Study of Islam in the Middle Volta Basin in the Pre-Colonial Period.* Oxford: Clarendon Press, 1968. 228 p. (Oxford Studies in African Affairs.)

Lusignan, Guy de. *French-Speaking Africa Since Independence.* New York: Praeger, 1969. 416 p. (Lusignan was a correspondent for *Le Monde.*)

Madiéga, Y. Georges. *Contribution à l'histoire précoloniale du Gulma (Haute Volta).* [Contribution to the Precolonial History of Gulma]. Wiesbaden, Germany: Franz Steiner, 1982. 260 p.

————. "Esquisse de la conquête et de la formation territoriale de la colonie de Haute-Volta." [Survey of the Conquest and Territorial Shaping of the Colony of Upper Volta]. *BIFAN,* Dakar, 43, 3/4 (1981). pp. 218–277. Item with same title appears in *Les cahiers du LUTO,* 2 (Dec. 1981). pp. 5–74.

————. "Jaba Lompo et Naba Wedraogo: les Bemba et les Nakomsé sont-ils apparentés?" *Les cahiers du LUTO,* 2 (Jun. 1981). pp. 5–33.

Mallam Abu. *The Zabarma Conquest of North-west Ghana and Upper Volta: A Hausa Narrative 'Histories of Samory and Babatu and Others',* edited and translated by Stanislaw Pilaszewicz—commentary in English, Warsaw: Polish Scientific Publishers, 1992. 207 p.

Marchal, Jean-Yves. *Chronique d'un cercle de l'A.O.F.: recueil l'archives du poste de Ouahigouya (Haute-Volta) 1908–1941.* [Chronicle of a Cercle in French West Africa: Compilation of the Archives of the Post of Ouahigouya, Upper Volta, 1908–1941]. Paris: ORSTOM, 1980. 215 p. (Trav.-Docum. ORSTOM, no. 125.)

————. "Premisses d'un état moderne? Les projets coloniaux dans le bassin des Volta, 1897–1960." [Premises for a Modern State? Colonial Projects in the (Black and White) Volta Basins]. *Cahiers d'Etudes Africaines,* Paris, 26, 3 (1986). pp. 402–420.

Marie-André du Sacré-Coeur, Sister. *La femme noire en Afrique occidentale.* Paris: Payot, 1939. 278 p.

Markov, P. and Sebald, J. "Gottlob Adolf Krause." *Journal of the Historical Society of Nigeria,* Ibadan, 2, 4 (Dec. 1963). pp. 536–544.

Mauny, Raymond. "Etat actuel de nos connaissances sur la prehistoire et l'archeologie de la Haute-Volta." *A.O.F. Magazine*, 12, 17 (1956). p. 38. (Also in *Notes africaines,* Dakar, 73 (Jan. 1957). pp. 1625.

McFarland, Daniel M. *Historical Dictionary of Upper Volta.* Metuchen, NJ and London: Scarecrow Press, 1978. 217 p.

Meniaud, Jacques. *Sikasso, ou l'histoire dramatique d'un royaume noir du XIXème siècle.* Paris: Bouchy, 1935. 208 p.

Michel, Marc. *L'appel à l'Afrique: contributions et reactions à l'effort de guerre en A.O.F., 1914–1919.* Paris: Publications de la Sorbonne (for l'Institut d'Histoire des relations internationales contemporaines—Afrique, no. 6), 1982. 533 p.

Millogo, Kalo Antoine. *Kokona. Essai d'histoire structurale* [Kokona: Essay on Structural History]. Stuttgart, Germany: F. Steiner, 1990. 231 p.

Monnier, Marcel. *Mission Binger: France Noire, Côte d'Ivoire et Soudan.* Paris: E. Plon, 1894. 298 p.

Monteil Charles. *Les empires du Mali: Etude d'histoire et de sociologie soudanaises.* Paris: Reprint by Maisonneuve et Larose, 1968. 160 p. (Also in *BCEHS,* Paris, 12 [1929]. pp. 291–447.)

Mortimer, Edward. *France and the Africans, 1944–1960: A Political History.* New York: Walker and Company, 1969. 390 p.

Neres, Philip. *French-Speaking West Africa; from Colonial Status to Independence.* London/New York: Oxford University Press, 1962. 101 p.

Pacéré, Titinga Frédéric. *Ainsi on a assassiné tous les Mossé; essai-témoignage.* [Thus All of the Mossi Were Killed]. Sherbrooke, Québec: Editions Naaman, 1979. 174 p.

Pageard, Robert. "Approach pour une étude de la succession Mossi." *Droit Culturale,* 1 (1981). pp. 91–107.

———. "Contribution critique à la chronologie historique de l'Ouest africain, suivie d'une traduction des tables chronologiques de Barth." *Journal de la Société des Africanistes,* Paris, 32, 1 (1962). pp. 91–177.

———. "Une enquête historique en pays mossi." [A Historical Enquiry in Mossi Country]. *Journal de la Société des Africanistes,* Paris, 35, 1 (1965). pp. 11–66.

Pageard, Robert., ed. "Histoire traditionnelle des Mossi de Ouagadougou, par Yamba Tiendrébéogo (dit Naba Abgha)." *Journal de la Société des Africanistes,* Paris, 33, 1 (1963). pp. 7–46.

Perinbaum, B. Marie. "The Political Organization of Traditional Gold Mining: The Western Lobby, c.1850 to c.1910." *Journal of African History,* Cambridge UK, 29, 3 (1988). pp. 437–462.

Péron, Yves. "Samori and Resistance to the French." In *Protest and Power in Black Africa,* edited by Robert I. Rotberg and Ali A. Mazrui, pp. 80–112. New York: Oxford University Press, 1970.

Randau, Robert S. (Robert Arnaud). "Au pays mossi." *Bulletin de la Société de Géographie d'Alger et d'Afrique du Nord,* Algiers, 39 (1934). pp. 427–445.

————. (Robert Arnaud). *Le voyage d'un bon jeune homme aux savanes de trois Volta.* Paris: A. Michel, 1930.

Regelsperger, Gustave. "La Haute Volta. Nouvelle colonie de l'Afrique Occidentale Française." *Revue des Sciences Politiques,* Paris, 34 (1919). pp. 128–138.

Rey, Pierre-Philippe. "Le système politique mossi et les migrations: à propos de trois textes de J. Capron et J. M. Kohler." *Journal des Africanistes,* Paris, 47, 1 (1977). pp. 115–124.

Robert, André P. *L'évolution des coutumes de l'ouest africain et la législation française.* Paris: Editions de Encyclopédie d'Outre-mer, 1955. 255 p. (For Bibliothèque Juridique de l'Union Française)

Roberts, Richard L. *Warriors, Merchants, and Slaves: The State and the Economy in the Middle Niger Valley, 1700–1914.* Stanford CA: Stanford University Press, 1987. 293 p.

Roberts, Stephen H. *The History of French Colonial Policy (1870–1925).* London: Frank Cass, 1963. 741 p.

Savonnet, Georges. "La colonisation du pays Koulango par les Lobi de Haute Volta." *Les Cahiers d'Outre-Mer,* Bordeaux, 15, (Jan.–Mar. 1962). pp. 25–46. English translation also published as "Colonization of the Kulango Area in Upper Ivory Coast by the Lobi of Upper Volta." Washington DC: Joint Publications Research Service, 1962. pp. 6–55.

Semi-Bi, Zan. "L'histoire africaine écrite par des Africains: réflexions à propos du livre de Joseph Ki-Zerbo." *Revue française d'études politiques africaines,* 92 (Aug. 1973). pp. 77–85.

Skalnik, Peter. "The Dynamics of Early State Development in the Voltaic Area." In *Political Anthropology,* edited by S. L. Seaton and H. J. M. Claessen, pp. 469–494. Chicago: Aldine Press, 1979.

————. "Monarchies Within Republics: Early Voltaic States in the Twentieth Century." *Asian and African Studies,* 11 (1975). pp. 177–193.

Skinner, Elliott Percival. *The Mossi of the Upper Volta: The Political Development of a Sudanese People.* Stanford, Calif.: Stanford University Press, 1964. 236 p. [Reprinted as *The Mossi of Burkina Faso,* Prospect Heights, Illinois: Waveland Press, 1989].

————. "The Mossi and Traditional Sudanese History." *The Journal of Negro History,* 43, 2 (April 1958). pp. 121–131.

————. "Traditional and Modern Patterns of Succession to Political Office among the Mossi of the Voltaic Republic." *Journal of Human Relations,* London, 8, 3–4 (1960). pp. 395–406.

Somda, N. C. "Les cauris du Lobi." *Notes et documents voltaïques,* Ouagadougou, (1976–77).

Somda, Nurukyor Claude. "La pénétration coloniale en pays Dagara, 1897–1914." Paris: Audir-Hachette/Bibliothèque Nationale, 1975. 99 p. (Microfiche)

Some, Bozi Bernard. "Quelques sources d'information pour une recherche historique." *Notes et documents voltaïques,* Ouagadougou, 2, 1 (Oct.–Dec. 1968). pp. 35–45.

Suret-Canale, Jean. *The Colonial Era in French West and Central Africa, 1900–1945.* London: C. Hurst, 1970. 550 p.

————. *French Colonialism in Tropical Africa, 1900–1945.* New York: Pica Press, 1971. 521 p.

Tarrab, G. and Coenne, C. *Femmes et pouvoirs au Burkina Faso.* [Women and power in Burkina Faso]. Paris: Harmattan, 1989. 125p.

Thiam, Lindou. *La politique agricole coloniale en Haute-Volta (1891–1960).* Ouagadougou: CEDRES, 1989. 59 p.

Tiendrébéogo, Yamba (Naba Agba)(Larhallé-Naba). *Histoire et coutumes royales des Mossi de Ouagadougou.* [History and Royal Customs of the Mossi of Ouagadougou]. Edited by Robert Pageard. Ouagadougou: chez le Larhallé Naba, Presses Africaines, 1964. 205 p.

————. "Histoire traditionnelle des Mossi de Ouagadougou." [Traditional History of the Mossi of Ouagadougou]. Edited by Robert Pageard. *Journal de la Société des Africanistes,* Paris, 33, 1 (1963). pp. 746.

Trimingham, John Spencer. *A History of Islam in West Africa.* London: Oxford University Press for Glasgow University Publications, 1962. 262 p.

Urvoy, Yves. *Histoire des populations du Soudan central.* Paris: Larose, 1936. 350 p.

Vermeersch, Capt. "Au pays des Bariba." *Bulletin de la Société de géographie commerciale,* Paris, 20 (1898). pp. 147–153.

Voulet, Paul. *Mission au Mossi et au Gourounsi.* Paris: Chapelot, 1898. 320 p.

Voulet, Paul and Chanoine, Julien. "Dans la boucle du Niger, au Mossi et au Gourounsi. La jonction du Soudan au Dahomey." *Bulletin de la Société de Géographie de Lille,* Lille, 29 (1898). pp. 109–41.

White, Dorothy Shipley. *Black Africa and De Gaulle: From the French Empire to Independence.* University Park, Pennsylvania: Pennsylvania State University Press, 1979. 384 p.

Wilks, Ivor. "The Mossi and Akan States." In *History of West Africa,* 3d ed., edited by J. F. A. Ajayi and Michael Crowder, pp. 465–502. Harlow UK: Longman, 1985.

Zahan, Dominique. "The Mossi Kingdoms." In *West African Kingdoms in the Nineteenth Century,* edited by Daryll Forde and P. M. Kaberry, pp. 152–178. Oxford: Oxford University Press, 1967.

————. "Towards a History of the Yatenga Mossi." In *French*

Perspectives in African Studies, edited by Pierre Alexandre, pp. 96–117. London: Oxford University for the International African Institute, 1973.

History: Explorers

"Les Allemands dans l'Afrique Occidentale: Exploration de C. von François." *Revue Français de l'Etrangère et des Colonies,* 9, 72 (15 June 1889). 733 ff.

Abbatucci, Jacques. *Public Health Service in the French Colonies.* Liège: Thone, 1926. 185 p.

Binger, Louis G. *Du Niger au Golfe de Guinée par le pays de Kong et le Mossi, 1887–1889.* 2 vols. Paris: Hachette, 1892. 513 p., 416 p. (Materials on Upper Volta are found, vol. 1, pp. 335–513, vol. 2, pp. 1–60.) Reprinted as single volume: Paris: Musée de l'Homme, 1980. 785 p.

Destenave, Georges Mathieu. "L'occupation et l'organisation de la boucle du Niger, création de la région est et macina." *Bulletin du Comité de l'Afrique française: Renseignements Coloniaux,* vol. 9 (1898). pp. 213–224.

Frobenius, Leo. *The Voice of Africa, being an account of the travels of the German Inner-African Exploration Expedition in the Years 1910–1912,* vol. 2. New York and London: Benjamin Blom, 1968 (reissue). 682 p.

Hubert, Renée. *Au Pays Bobo.* Paris: Nouvelles Editions Argo, 1932. 186 p.

Noll, Ned. "Le Mossi: La mission du Lieutenant Voulet." *La Tour du Monde,* Paris, 33 (14 Aug. 1897).

Rolland, Jacques-Francis. *Le grand capitaine: Un aventuriér inconnu de l'époque colonial.* Paris: Grasset, 1976. 270 p. (Concerning Voulet)

Sebald, Peter. *Malam Musa-Gottlieb Adolph Krause: 1850–1938.* Berlin: Akademie-Verlag, 1972. 291 p.

Tessieres, Y. de. *Un épisode du partage de l'Afrique: La mission Monteil de 1890–1892.* Paris: Geuthner, 1973. 66 p.

Thévenoud, Joanny. *A travers les pays Mossi, Gourounsi, Bobo et Samo,* Rome: Pères Blancs, 1905. 26 p.

———. *Au pays des Bobos.* Paris: Bulletin des Pères Blancs, 1905/1906. 394 p.

———. *Dans la boucle du Niger.* Namur, France: Editions Grandlacs, 1938. 176 p.

Valbert. G. "Deux missions françaises dans la boucle du Niger." *Revue des deux mondes,* (1 Oct. 1891). pp. 684–695. (Missions of Quiquandon and Crozat.)

———. "La voyage du Capt. Binger dans la boucle du Niger." *Revue des deux mondes,* (1 Feb. 1890). pp. 660–671.

Politics

Politics

"Burkina Faso—Cabinet Reshuffle." *West Africa,* London, 4054 (19–25 June 1995). p. 947.

"Burkina Faso—General Strike." *West Africa,* London, 3994 (18–24 Apr. 1994). p. 696–697.

"Burkina Faso—New Cabinet." *West Africa,* London, 3992 (4–10 Apr. 1994). p. 600.

"Burkina Faso—New Political Grouping." *West Africa,* London, 3983 (31 Jan.–6 Feb. 1994). p. 181.

"Burkina Faso—New Prime Minister." *West Africa,* London, 3991 (28 Mar.–3 Apr. 1994). p. 554.

"Burkina: Compaoré Takes Over." *West Africa,* London, 3663 (26 Oct. 1987). pp. 2104–2108.

"Burkina: Sankara's Situation Report." *West Africa,* London, 3528 (8 Apr. 1985). pp. 665–666.

"Election Boycott in Burkina Faso." *Africa Report,* New York, 37, 1 (Jan–Feb 1992). pp. 6–7.

"Les guerres interétatiques: Burkina Faso/Mali." [Interstate Wars: Burkina Faso/Mali]. *Etudes polmologiques,* France, 39 (1986). pp. 40–42.

"Mali and Burkina Faso: Small War Near Timbuktu." *The Economist,* 298 (Jan. 4, 1986). p. 32.

"Mali/Burkina Border Flare-up." *West Africa,* London, 3566 (6 Jan. 1986). pp. 4–5.

"Mali/Burkina: Two Sides, One Peace." *West Africa,* London, 3569 (27 Jan. 1986). pp. 170–172.

"O Captain, Their Captain . . .". *The Economist,* 305 (Oct. 24, 1987). p. 52.

"Sankara's African Diplomacy." *West Africa,* London, 3492 (23 July 1984). pp. 1486–1487.

"Timetable for a Revolution." *West Africa,* London, 3444 (15 Aug. 1983). pp. 1870–1872.

"Upper Volta: A Trade Union Conundrum." *West Africa,* London, 3465 (16 Jan. 1984). pp. 113–114.

"Upper Volta: After the Rhetoric . . .". *West Africa,* London, 3430 (9 May 1983). pp. 1111–1113.

"Upper Volta: Disunity on the Left." *West Africa,* London, 3461 (12 Dec. 1983). p. 2875.

"Upper Volta: Power Struggle Continues." *West Africa,* London, 3437 (29 June 1983). pp. 1490–1491.

"Upper Volta: Organising for the Revolution—Councils for the Defence of the Revolution." *West Africa,* London, 3454 (22 Oct. 1983). pp. 2445–2447.

"Upper Volta: The Rise of Sankara." *West Africa,* London, 3463 (2 Jan. 1984). p. 13.

"Upper Volta: Towards Integration." *West Africa,* London, 3474 (19 Mar. 1984). p. 609.

"Upper Volta: Trade Unions and Revolution." *West Africa,* London, 3478 (16 Apr. 1984). pp. 813–814.

"Upper Volta: Women on the March." *West Africa,* London, 3456 (7 Nov. 1983). pp. 2558–2560.

"Voltaics Return to Civil Rule." *West Africa,* London, (31 Oct. 1977). pp. 2193–2195.

Abo, Klevor. "Burkina Faso: Reality, Realism and Uprightness." *West Africa,* London, 3960 (16–22 Aug. 1993). pp. 1431–1433.

Allen, Chris, et al, ed. *Benin, the Congo and Burkina Faso: Economics, Politics, Society.* London: Pinter, 1989.

Ammi-Oz, Moshe. "L'installation des militaires voltaïques." *Revue français d'études politique africaines,* Paris, 13 (Aug.–Sep. 1978). pp. 59–79; 13 (Oct. 1978). pp. 85–97.

Anderson, Samantha. See *Thomas Sankara Speaks.*

Andriamirado, Sennen. *Il s'appelait Sankara: Chronique d'une mort violente.* [His Name Was Sankara: Chronicle of a Violent Death]. Paris: Jeune Afrique Livres, 1989. 178 p.

———. *Sankara le Rebelle.* [Sankara the Rebel]. Paris: Jeune Afrique Livres, 1987. 237 p.

Augustin, Jean-Pierre and Drabo, Yaya K. "Au sport, citoyens." *Politique Africaine,* Paris, 33 (1989). pp. 59–65.

Bamouni, Babou Paulin. *Burkina Faso: Processus de la revolution.* Paris: Harmattan, 1986. 189 p.

———. "L'évolution politique de la Haute-Volta." *Peuples noirs-Peuples africains,* 6, 34 (Aug. 1983). pp. 53–74.

Banegas, R. *Insoumissions populaires et révolution au Burkina Faso.* Talence: Bordeaux University CEAN, 1993. 140 p.

Benabdessadok, Christine. "Femmes et révolution, ou comment libérer la moitié de la société." [Women and Revolution, or How to Free Half of Society]. *Politique Africaine,* Paris, 20 (1985). pp. 54–64.

Bentsi-Enchill, Nii K. "Bourkina Fasso: Sankara's Year of Change." *West Africa,* London, 3495 (13 Aug. 1984). p. 1616.

———. "Burkina Faso Notebook—1." *West Africa,* London, 3496 (20 Aug. 1984). pp. 1673–1674.

———. "Burkina Faso Notebook—2: Dealing from a Fresh Pack." *West Africa,* London, 3497 (27 Aug. 1984). p. 1721.

———. "Burkina Faso Notebook—3: Why Talkative Thomas Stays in the News." *West Africa,* London, 3499 (10 Sep. 1984). p. 1834.

———. "Upper Volta: Coup Plot Inquiry." *West Africa,* London, 3486 (11 June 1984). pp. 1206–1207.

————. "Upper Volta: Laboratory of Revolution." *West Africa*, London, 3470 (20 Feb. 1984). pp. 369–371.

————. "A Year After Sankara." *West Africa*, London, 3713 (10–16 Oct. 1988). pp. 1884–1885.

Bienen, Henry S. "Populist Military Regimes in West Africa" (Ghana, Burkina Faso, Liberia). *Armed Forces and Society*, USA, 11 (Spring 1985). pp. 357–377.

Bonnafe, P.; M. Fieloux and J. M. Kambou. "Le conflit armé dans une population sans Etat: Les Lobi de Haute-Volta." [Armed Conflict in a Stateless People: The Lobi of Upper-Volta]. In *Guerres de lignages et guerres d'états en Afrique*, edited by Jean Bazin and E. Terry, pp. 73–141. Paris: Editions des archives contemporaines, 1982.

Cherigny, B. "La Haute Volta on le 'luxe' de la démocratie: les élections législatives et presidentielles d'avril-mai 1978." *Pouvoirs*, 9 (1979). pp. 163–181.

Conombo, Joseph Issoufou. *Mon ideé*, Ouagadougou: by author, 1978. 41 p.

Coulibaly, Daniel Ouezzin. *Combat pour l'Afrique*. [Struggle for Africa]. Abidjan: Les Nouvelles Editions Africaines, 1985. 531 p.

Cowell, Alan. "Africa's 'Upright People': Still No Answers." *The New York Times*, 134, 46,284 (9 January 1985). p. A2.

Cudjoe, Alfred. *Who Killed Sankara?: Some Hidden Facts Behind the Tragic Assassination of Capt. Thomas Sankara as Revealed by the African Press: Comments by an Informed Writer*. Accra(?): Compuprint Services, 1988. 114 p.

Dahs, M. M and Kabore, B. "La condition juridique, politique et sociale de la femme en Haute Volta." *Revue juridique et politique*, 28 (Oct.–Dec 1974). pp. 691–700.

Doucet, Lyse. "Burkina—Reaching Understanding." *West Africa*, London, 3536 (3 June 1985). pp. 1105–1106.

————. "Burkina—Economics and Revolution." *West Africa*, London, 3571 (10 Feb. 1986). pp. 295–296.

————. "Burkina—Death of the Known Soldier." *West Africa*, London, 3663 (26 Oct. 1987). pp. 2133–2134.

————. "Burkina—The Assassination of a President." *West Africa*, London, 3664 (2 Nov. 1987). pp. 2182.

Doyle, Mark. "Upper Volta: Leaders Held as Divisions Broaden." *West Africa*, London, 3433 (30 May. 1983). pp. 1284–1285.

Dubuch, Claude. "Langage du pouvoir, pouvoir du langage." [The Language of Power, the Power of Language]. *Politique Africaine Paris*, 20 (1985), pp. 44–53.

Englebert, Pierre. *La révolution burkinabè*. [The Burkinabè Revolution]. Paris: Harmattan, 1986. 264 p.

Englebert, Pierre. "Burkina Faso in Transition." *CSIS Africa Notes,* Washington DC, 111 (April 30, 1990).

Euphorion, P. H. "Du langage animalier en politique." [On the Use of Animal Language in Politics]. *Genève-Afrique,* Geneva, 26, 2 (1988). pp. 97–105.

Faure, A. "La panthère est l'enfant d'un génie: réflexions sur le traitement d'une crise villageoise pendant la révolution burkinabè." *Politique Africaine,* Paris, 44 (Dec. 1991). pp. 102–109.

Faure, Armelle. "Niaogho versus Beghedo. Un conflit foncier à la veille de la révolution burkinabè." [Niaogho versus Beghedo: A Land Management Conflict on the Eve of the Burkinabè Revolution]. *Cahiers des Sciences Humaines,* Paris: ORSTOM, 29, 1 (1993). pp. 105–119.

Front Populaire. *Assises nationales sur le bilan des 4 années de révolution.* [National Conference to Evaluate 4 Years of Revolution]. Ouagadougou: Front Populaire, 1988. 150 p.

Gakunzi, David, ed. *Thomas Sankara. 'Oser inventer l'avenir'. La parole de Sankara.* ['Daring to Invent the Future'. The Words of Sankara]. Paris: Harmattan, 1991. 290 p.

Garreau, M. *Evolution administrative d'un cercle voltaïque (cercle de Ouagadougou).* Paris: CHEAM, 1956. 27 p.

Geekie, Russell. "Compaoré's Campaign." *Africa Report,* New York, 36, 5 (Sep.–Oct. 1991). pp. 55–58.

Germain, Louis. "Burkina Faso: une revolution en cours?" [Burkina Faso: A Revolution in Progress?]. *Etudes,* France, 365, 5 (Nov. 1986). pp. 439–452.

Golan, Tamar. "Lamizana Completes a Circle." *West Africa,* London, (8 and 15 July 1974). pp. 815 and 862.

———. "The Mali-Upper Volta Border Dispute." *West Africa,* London, no. 3004 (20 Jan. 1975). p. 61; no. 3005 (27 Jan. 1975). pp. 98–99; no. 3006 (3 Feb. 1975). p. 130.

———. "Two Crises in Upper Volta." *West Africa,* London, (21 and 28 January 1974). pp. 61 and 97.

Guion, Jean R. *Blaise Compaoré: réalisme et intégrité: portrait de l'homme de la rectification au Burkina Faso,* Paris: Berger-Levrault, 1991. 122 p.

Guirma, Frederic. *Comment perdre le pouvoir? le cas de Maurice Yaméogo,* Paris: Editions Chaka, 1991. 159 p.

Harrison, Saint-Maurice. "Burkina Faso—The Silent Revolution." *West Africa,* London, 4041 (20–26 Mar. 1995). pp. 429–430.

Harsch, Ernest. "Burkina Special Report: A Revolution Derailed." *Africa Report,* 33, 1 (Jan.–Feb. 1988). pp. 33–39.

———. "How Popular is the Front." *Africa Report,* New York, 34, 1 (Jan.–Feb. 1989). pp. 56–61.

———. "The Politics Behind the October 15 Coup." *West Africa,* London, 3664 (2 Nov. 1987). pp. 2182–2183.

Hutchful, Eboe. "New Elements in Militarism: Ethiopia, Ghana, and Burkina." *International Journal,* Canada, 41, 4 (1986). pp. 802–830.

Jaffre, Bruno. *Les années Sankara: de la révolution à la rectification.* [The Sankara Years: From the Revolution to the Rectification]. Paris: Harmattan, 1989. 332 p.

Jouffrey, Roger. "Thomas Sankara et la révolution voltaïque." *Afrique Contemporaine,* France, (Apr.–June 1984). pp. 44–53.

Jouve, Edmond. "Le Burkina Faso et ses chantiers de l'avenir." [Burkina Faso and its Future Prospects]. *Mondes et Cultures,* Paris, 46, 3 (1986). pp. 607–615.

Kanse, Mathias S. "Le CNR et les femmes: de la difficulté de libérer 'la moitié du ciel'." [The CNR and Women: On the Difficulties of Liberating 'the other half']. *Politique Africaine,* Paris, 33 (1989). pp. 66–72.

Kiemde, P. "Le bicaméralisme en Afrique et au Burkina Faso." *Revue burkinabè de droit,* 21 (1992). pp. 23–50.

Labazée, Pascal. "Discours et contrôle politique: les avatars du sankarisme." [Speeches and Political Control: The Avatars of Sankarism]. *Politique Africaine,* Paris, 33 (1989). pp. 11–26.

————. "Réorganisation économique et résistances sociales: la question des alliances au Burkina." [Economic Reorganization and Social Resistances: The Question of Alliances in Burkina Faso]. *Politique Africaine,* Paris, 20 (1985). pp. 10–28.

Marie, Alain. "Politique urbaine: une révolution au service de l'état." [Urban Policy: A Revolution in the Service of the State]. *Politique Africaine,* Paris, 33 (1989). pp. 27–38.

Markakis, John and Waller, Michael, eds. *Military Marxist Regimes in Africa,* London: Frank Cass, 1986.

Martens, Ludo and Meesters, Milde. *Sankara, Compaoré et la révolution burkinabè.* [Sankara, Compaoré and the Burkinabè Revolution]. Antwerp, Belgium: Epo, 1989. 332 p.

Martin, Guy. "Actualité de Fanon: Convergences dans la pensée politique de Frantz Fanon et de Thomas Sankara." [Fanon's Reality: Convergences in the Political Thought of Frantz Fanon and Thomas Sankara]. *Genève-Afrique,* Switzerland, 25, 2 (1987). pp. 103–122.

————. "Fanon's Continuing Relevance: A Comparative Study of the Political Thought of Frantz Fanon and Thomas Sankara." *Journal of Asian and African Affairs,* 5, 1 (1993). pp. 65–85.

————. "Idéologie et praxis dans la révolution populaire du 4 août 1983 au Burkina Faso." [Ideology and Praxis in the Popular Revolution of 4 August 1983 in Burkina Faso]. *Genève-Afrique,* Switzerland, 24, 1 (1986). pp. 34–62. English version in *Issue: A Journal of Opinion,* USA, 15 (1987). pp. 77–90.

Morgenthau, Ruth Schachter. *Political Parties in French-Speaking West Africa.* New York: Oxford University Press, 1964. 445 p.

Nikiéma, Paul. "L'état voltaïque et les sociétés face au développement." *Revue juridique et politique,* 32, (Jan.–Mar. 1978). pp. 97–122.

Nnaji, B. Obinwa. *Blaise Compaoré: The Architect of Burkina Faso Revolution,* Ibadan, Nigeria: Spectrum Books, 1989. 88 p.

Noaga, Killin. *Haro! Camarade commandant.* Ouagadougou: Imprimerie Presses Africaines, 1977. 110 p. (Collection of essays, lectures, addresses.)

Noricki, Margaret A. "Interview: Captain Thomas Sankara, President of the National Council of the Revolution, Upper Volta." *Africa Report,* 29, (July–Aug. 1984). pp. 91–107.

———. "Transforming the Statistics." *Africa Report,* 31, 3 (May–June 1986). pp. 68–72.

———. "Burkina Faso: A Revolutionary Culture." *Africa Report,* 32, 4 (July–Aug. 1987). pp. 57–60.

Otayek, René. "Burkina Faso: Between Feeble State and Total State, the Swing Continues." In *Contemporary West African States,* edited by Donal B. Cruise O'Brien, John Dunn and Richard Rathbone, pp. 13–30. Cambridge, U.K. and New York: Cambridge University Press, 1989.

———. "Burkina Faso Enters a New Political Phase: the Sequel to the Coup of 15 October 1987." *Journal of Communist Studies,* London, 4, 2 (1988). pp. 213–217.

———. "Burkina Faso: la 'rectification' démocratique." *Studia Africana,* 3 (1992). pp. 11–26. And "The Democratic 'Rectification' in Burkina Faso." *Journal of Communist Studies,* London, 8, 2 (1992). pp. 82–104.

———. "The Revolutionary Process in Burkina Faso: Breaks and Continuities." In *Military Marxist Regimes in Africa,* edited by John Markakis and Michael Waller, pp. 82–100. London: Frank Cass, 1986.

Owona, Joseph. "La constitution de la 3e république voltaïque du 21 octobre 1977: retour au parlementarisme rationalisé et au multipartisme limité." *Penant,* Paris, 89, 765 (July–Sep. 1979). pp. 309–328.

Robinson, Pearl T. "Grassroots Legitimation of Military Governance in Burkina Faso and Niger: The Core Contradictions." In *Governance and Politics in Africa,* edited by Goran Hyden and Michael Bratton, pp. 143–165. Boulder, Colorado: L. Rienner, 1992.

Rothchild, Donald and Gyimah-Boadi, E. "Populism in Ghana and Burkina Faso." *Current History,* 88, 538 (1989). pp. 221–224, 241–244.

Sankara, Thomas. *Women's Liberation and the African Freedom Struggle,* London; New York: Pathfinder, 1990. 36 p.

Savonnet-Guyot, Claudette. *Etat et société au Burkina: essai sur le politique africain.* [State and Society in Burkina Faso: Essay on African Politics]. Paris: Karthala, 1986. 227 p.

————. "Le prince et le Naobe." [The Prince and the Naobe]. *Politique Africaine,* Paris, 20 (Dec. 1985). pp. 29–43.

Sawadogo, Michel F. and Yarga, Larba. "Les tribunaux populaires de la révolution en Haute Volta." [The Popular Tribunals of the Revolution in Upper Volta]. *Penant,* Paris, 94, 785 (July-Sep. 1984). pp. 267–283.

Sawadogo, Yambangba. *Ma première campagne électorale.* Bobo-Dioulasso: Imprimerie de la Savane, 1978. 91 p.

Schissel, Howard. "Six Months into Sankara's Revolution." *Africa Report,* New York, 29 (Mar.–Apr. 1984). pp. 16–19.

Schuster, Alain. "Vers la fin des régimes militaires en Afrique occidentale? La voie suivie au Ghana, en Haute-Volta, au Mali et au Nigéria." *Revue Canadienne Etudes Africain,* 11, 2 (1978). pp. 213–232.

Scofield, John. "Freedom Speaks French in Ouagadougou." *National Geographic Magazine,* Washington, 130, 2 (Aug. 1966). pp. 153–203.

Skinner, Elliott Percival. "Political Conflict and Revolution in an African Town." *American Anthropologist,* Monasha, Wisconsin, 74, 5 (Oct. 1972). pp. 1208–1217. (Study of Ouagadougou 1947–1965).

————. "Sankara and the Burkinabè Revolution: Charisma and Power, Local and External Dimensions." *Journal of Modern African Studies,* Great Britain, 26, 3 (1988). pp. 437–455.

————. "Thomas Sankara: A Retrospective." *TransAfrica Forum: A quarterly Journal of Opinion on Africa and the Carribean,* USA, 5, 3 (1988). pp 81–87.

Some, Catherine. *Haute Volta: bilan de la politique de redressement national amorcée le 25 novembre 1980.* Bordeaux: Centre d'étude d'Afrique noire, 1983. 26 p.

Some, Valere D. *Thomas Sankara: l'espoir assassiné.* [Thomas Sankara: Hope Assassinated]. Paris: Harmattan, 1990. 230 p.

Thomas Sankara Speaks: The Burkina Faso Revolution, 1983–87. (Translated by Samantha Anderson). New York: Pathfinder Press, 1988. 260 p.

Thompson, Virginia. *West Africa's Council of the Entente.* Ithaca, N. Y.: Cornell University Press, 1972. 313 p.

Vengroff, Richard. "Upper Volta: Africa's New Hope for Democracy." *Africa Report,* 23 (July–Aug. 1978). pp. 59–64.

————. "Upper Volta: Soldiers and Civilians in the Third Republic." *Africa Report,* New York, 25, 1 (Jan.–Feb. 1980). pp. 4–8.

Whiteman, Kaye. "The Sankara Affair." *West Africa,* London, 3649 (20 July 1987). pp. 1381–1382.

Wilkins, Michael. "The Death of Thomas Sankara and the Rectification of the People's Revolution in Burkina Faso." *African Affairs,* London, 88, 352 (1989). pp. 375–388.

Yaméogo, Hermann. *La IIIe République.* [The Third Voltaic Republic]. Koudougou, Burkina Faso: Imprimerie des Quatre-Vents, 1990. 253 p.

Yarga, Larba. "La fin de la IIIe République voltaïque." *Le Mois en Afrique,* Paris, 182–183 (Feb.–Mar. 1981). pp. 43–51.

———. "Les pouvoirs exceptionnels du Président de la République dans les institutions voltaïques de 1959 à 1980." [The Extraordinary Presidential Powers in the Voltaic Constitutions from 1958 to 1980]. *Revue juridique et politique,* Paris, 34, 3 (July–Sep. 1980). pp. 730–738.

———. "Les prémices à l'avènement du Conseil National de la Révolution en Haute Volta." [The Beginnings of the National Council for the Revolution in Upper Volta]. *Le Mois en Afrique,* Paris, 213/214 (Oct.–Nov. 1983). pp. 24–41.

———. "Le tripartisme dans le droit public voltaïque." [Tripartism in Voltaic Public Law]. *Le Mois en Afrique,* Paris, 174–175 (June–Jul. 1980). pp. 114–129.

Ziégler, Jean and Rapp, Jean-Philippe. *Thomas Sankara: un nouveau pouvoir africain.* Lausanne: ABC; Paris: Pierre-Marcel Favre, 1986. 176 p.

Politics: Constitution, Legal, Administration

Administration et développement au Burkina Faso. [Administration and Development in Burkina Faso]. Toulouse, France: Presses de l'Institut d'Etudes Politiques de Toulouse, 1987. 324 p.

Badou, Emile Toe and Compaore, Franck Sibila. "Deux cas d'ouvrages clé en main au Burkina." [Two Cases of "TurnKey" Enterprises in Burkina]. *Revue Juridique et Politique,* Paris, 42, 2–3 (1988). pp. 185–196.

Bougma, Jacques. *Connaissance de l'organisation politique, institutionelle et administrative du Burkina Faso.* [Knowledge of the Political, Administrative and Constitutional Organization of Burkina Faso]. Ouagadougou: J. Bougma, 1988. 75 p.

Daloze, A. *Droit financier et bancaire.* [Financial and Banking Law]. Ouagadougou: Université de Ouagadougou, 1989. 102 p.

Delouvroy, Jacques. "Le développement du droit judiciaire au Burkina Faso." [The Development of Judicial Law in Burkina Faso]. *Revue Juridique et Politique,* Paris, 91, 3 (1987). pp. 228–244.

Gaudusson, Jean de Bois. "Révolution voltaïque et réforme de l'administration territoriale." [Voltaic Revolution and Reform of Territorial Administration]. In *Année Africaine 1983,* pp. 112–115, 127–144. Paris: Pedone, 1983.

Gibrila, Deen. "Les droits des étrangers au Burkina Faso." [The Rights of Foreigners in Burkina Faso." *Penant,* Paris, 95, 786/7 (Jan.–June 1985). pp. 37–52.

Marcais, Marcel. "L'Ecole Nationale d'Administration de la République de Haute-Volta." *Penant,* Paris, (July–Sep. 1964).

Marchand, P. "L'organisation judiciaire en Haute-Volta." [The Judicial System in Upper Volta]. *Penant,* Paris, (Jan.–Mar. 1964). pp. 121–129.

Meyer, M. P. "La structure dualiste du droit au Burkina Faso." [The Dualist Structure of Law in Burkina Faso]. *Penant,* Paris, 790–791 (1986). pp. 77–89.

Meyer, Pierre. "Burkina Faso: une nouvelle forme de justice à l'essai." [Burkina Faso: An Experiment in a New Kind of Justice]. *Afrique Contemporaine,* Paris, 156 (1980). pp. 51–56.

Nikiéma, Aimé and Yonaba, Salif. "L'organisation judiciaire au Burkina Faso et le destin de la Chambre Constitutionnel." [The Judicial Organization of Burkina Faso and the Fate of the Constitutional Chamber]. *Penant,* Paris, 791 (July–Oct. 1986). pp. 287–301.

Nuytinck, Hilde. "Les principes du nouveau droit de la famille au Burkina Faso." [The Principles of the New Family Law in Burkina Faso]. *Penant,* Paris, 806 (June–Oct. 1991). pp. 258–275.

Pacéré, Frédéric Titinga. *L'avortement et la loi.* [Abortion and the Law]. Ouagadougou: Imprimerie Nouvelle du Centre, 1983. 69 p.

———. *Les enfants abandonnés: faits, droits et protections.* [Abandoned Children: Facts, Laws and Protection]. Ouagadougou: F. T. Pacéré, 1989. 85 p.

Quéré, Jean Claude. *La fonction du personnel au Burkina Faso.* [Personnel Management in Burkina Faso]. Ouagadougou: Université de Ouagadougou, CEDRES, 1986. 177 p.

Sambo, Diallo Seyni. "Les droits de famille dans la coutume mossi." *Penant,* Paris, 77, 715 (Jan.–Mar. 1967). pp. 13–31; 716 (April–June 1967). pp. 151–165. Reprinted as *Family Rights Among the Mossi of Upper Volta.* Washington DC: Joint Publications Research Service, 1967. 36 p.

———. "L'évolution du droit traditionnel, fondement de la dualité des juridictions en Haute Volta." *Penant,* Paris, (July–Sep. 1977). pp. 321–339.

Savadogo, Boukary. *Contribution à l'étude des styles de management en Afrique: le cas de Burkina Faso.* [Contribution to the Study of Styles of Management in Africa: The Example of Burkina Faso]. Ouagadougou: Université de Ouagadougou, CEDRES, 1986. 183 p.

Sawadogo, Filiga Michel. "Le nouveau code burkinabè de la famille: principes essentiels et perspectives d'application." [The New Burkinabè Family Law: Essential Principles and Guidelines for Application]. *Revue Juridique et Politique,* Paris, 44, 3 (1990). pp. 372–406.

———. "Le nouveau code d'investissements au Burkina: changement ou continuité". [The New Investment Code in Burkina Faso: Change or Continuity]. *Revue Juridique et Politique,* Paris, 90, 1/2 (1986). pp. 63–93.

———. "Le traitement fiscale inégalitaire des entreprises au Burkina

Faso: le cas de l'imposition des bénéfices." [Unequal Fiscal Treatment of Burkina Faso Enterprises: The Case of Taxation of Profits]. *Le Mois en Afrique*, Paris, 21, 239/240 (Jan. 1986). pp. 54–68.

Sawadogo, Filiga Michel and Kienda, P. "La réforme du droit des entreprises publiques voltaïques par les ordonnances du 1 juin 1982." [The Reform of the Code of Voltaic Public Enterprises in the Ordinances of 1 June 1983]. *Revue Voltaïque du Droit*, Ouagadougou, 4 (June 1983). PP. 119–148.

Sawadogo, Filiga Michel and Meyer, Pierre. "Droit, état et société: le cas du Burkina Faso." [Law, State and Society: The Case of Burkina Faso]. *Revue de Droit International et Droit Comparé*, Paris, 64, 3 (1987). pp. 225–242.

Sawadogo, S. "L'entreprise et les droits de l'homme: le protections instituées au Burkina." [Businesses and Human Rights: Protections Established in Burkina Faso]. *Revue Juridique et Politique*, Paris, 43, 3/4 (1989). pp. 361–370.

Yerbanga, Ignace and Zonou, Martin. "L'administration de la preuve devant les tribunaux populaires de la révolution au Burkina." [The Presentation of Proof before the Popular Tribunals of the Revolution in Burkina]. *Revue Juridique et Politique,* Paris, 39, 1/2 (Jan.–Mar. 1985). pp. 62–68.

Politics: Foreign Policy

Codo, Leon C. "L'insertion régionale du régime Sankara: entre pragmatisme et idéologie." [The Regional Entry of the Sankara Régime: Between Pragmatism and Ideology]. In *Année Africaine 1984,* pp. 176–195. Paris: Pedone, 1986.

Faujas, Alain. "La Politique extérieure de la Haute-Volta." [The Foreign Policy of Upper Volta]. *Revue française d'études politiques africaines,* Paris, 83 (Nov. 1972). pp. 59–73.

Faure, Yves-André. "Ouaga et Abidjan: divorce à l'africaine?" [Ouaga and Abidjan: An African Divorce?]. *Politique Africaine,* Paris, 20 (Dec. 1985). pp. 78–86.

French, Howard. "Burkina Faso at the Eye of a West African Storm." *Africa Report,* New York, 31, 1 (Jan.–Feb. 1986). pp. 28–30.

Johnson, Segun. "Burkina-Mali War: Is Nigeria Still a Regional Power?" *India Quarterly,* India, 42, 3 (1986). pp. 294–308.

Kafando, Talata. "Burkina Faso: August 1983—the Beginning of Delinking?" In *Adjustment or Delinking?,* edited by Azzam Mahjoob, pp. 109–130. London: Zed Press, 1990.

———. "Coopération arabo-burkinabè: bilan et perspectives." [Arab-Burkinabè Cooperation: Assessment and Prospects]. *Africa Development,* Dakar, 11, 2/3 (1986). pp. 191–212.

Queneudec, Jean-Pierre. "Le règlement du différend frontalier Burkina Faso/Mali par la Cour Internationale de Justice". [The Settlement of the Boundary Dispute between Burkina Faso and Mali by the International Court of Justice]. *Revue Juridique et Politique,* Paris, 42, 1 (1988). pp. 29–41.

Saffu, E. O. "The Bases of Ghana-Upper Volta Relations During the Nkrumah Regime." *Canadian Journal of African Studies,* Ottawa, 4 (1970). pp. 195–206.

Some, Gilbert. "Un exemple de conflit frontalier: le différand entre la Haute-Volta et le Mali." [An Example of Boundary Dispute: The Disagreement between Burkina and Mali]. In *Année Africaine 1978,* Paris: Pedone (1979). pp. 339–370.

Wood, Michael. "Upper Volta: Another Piece in Qaddafi's Puzzle?" *World Today,* 39 (Oct. 1983). pp. 364–368.

Economy

Agriculture

Atampugre, Nicholas. *Behind the Lines of Stone: The Social Impact of a Soil and Water Conservation Project in the Sahel.* Oxford, UK: Oxfam, 1993. 168 p.

Benoit, Michel. "Mutation agraire dans l'ouest de la Haute Volta: le cas de Daboura (sous-préfecture de Nouna)." Paris, *Cahiers ORSTOM* (Sciences humaines), 14, 2 (1977). pp. 95–111.

Broekhuyse, J. and Allen, Andrea M. "Farming Systems Research on the Northern Mossi Plateau." *Human Organization,* Oklahoma City, 47 (Winter 1988). pp. 330–342.

Burkina Faso: développement des cultures irriguées. Ouagadougou: CILSS/Club du Sahel, 1987. 2 vols.

DeBoer, W. F. and Prins, H. H. T. "Decisions of Cattle Herdsmen in Burkina Faso and Optimal Foraging Models." *Human Ecology,* 173, 4 (1989). pp. 445–464. (A critique by Douglas A. Edwards, Steven C. Josephson and Joan Brenner Coltrain appears as "Burkina Faso Herdsmen and Optimal Foraging Theory: A Reconsideration." *Human Ecology,* 22, 2 [June 1994]. pp. 213–215.)

Delgado, Christopher L. *Livestock Versus Foodgrain Production in Southeast Upper Volta: A Resource Allocation Analysis.* Ann Arbor: University of Michigan Center for Research on Economic Development, 1979. 427 p.

————. *The Southern Fulani Farming System in Upper Volta,* East Lansing, Michigan: African Rural Economy Program, 1979. 185p.

Delgado, Christopher L. and McIntire, John. "Constraints on Oxen

Cultivation in the Sahel" (Mali and Upper Volta). *American Journal of Agricultural Economics,* St. Paul, Minnesota, 64, 2 (May 1982). pp. 188–196.

Dupré, Georges and Guillaud, Dominique. " L'agriculture de l'Aribinda (Burkina Faso) de 1875 à 1983: les dimensions du changement." [Agriculture in Aribinda from 1875 to 1983: Measuring the Change]. *Cahiers des Sciences Humaines,* Paris: ORSTOM, 24, 1 (1988). pp. 51–71.

Eicher, Carl K. et al. *An Analysis of the Eastern O.R.D. Rural Development Project in Upper Volta: Report of the M.S.U. Mission,* East Lansing: Michigan State University, 1976. 103 p.

Gallais, Jean. *Pasteurs et paysans du Gourma: la condition sahelienne.* Paris: CNRS, 1975. 239 p.

Gonzalez, J. P. "Serological Evidence in Sheep Suggesting Phlebovirus Circulation in a Rift-Valley Fever Enzootic Area in Burkina Faso. *Transactions of the Royal Society of Tropical Medicine and Hygiene,* 86, 6 (1992). pp. 680–682.

Groten, S. M. E. "NDVI — Crop Monitoring and Early Yield Assessment of Burkina Faso." *International Journal of Remote Sensing,* Great Britain, 14, 8 (1993). pp. 1495–1515.

Hansen, Art and McMillan, Della E. eds. *Food in Sub-Saharan Africa,* Boulder, Colorado: Lynne Rienner, 1986. 410 p.

Harrison, Paul. *The Greening of Africa: Breaking Through in the Battle for Land and Food.* London: Paladin (for International Institute for Environment and Development), 1987, 380 p. For specific Burkina Faso cases see pages 267–274 (immunization campaign), 279–284 (*Naam* movement), 217–219 (fuel-efficient cook stoves), and 164–170 (water conservation measures).

Jaeger, William K. *Agricultural Mechanization: The Economics of Animal Draft Power in West Africa,* Boulder, Colorado: Westview Press, 1986. 199 p.

Kerkhof, Paul; Gerald Foley and Geoffrey Barnard. *Agroforestry in Africa: A Survey of Project Experience,* London: Panos Institute, 1992. 216 p. (projects in Burkina Faso are discussed in pp. 87–95 and 133–141)

Lecaillon, Jacques and Morrisson, Christian. *Economic Policies and Agricultural Performance: The Case of Burkina Faso,* Paris: Organization for Economic Cooperation and Development, 1985. 158 p.

Marchal, Jean-Yves. "La deroute d'un système vivrier au Burkina: agriculture extensive et baisse de production." [The Ruin of a Food Crop System in Burkina: Extensive Agriculture and Production Decline]. *Etudes rurales,* Paris, 99–100 (1985). pp. 265–280.

———. "En Afrique des savanes, le fractionnement des unités d'exploitation rurales ou le chacun pour soi." [In the Savanas, Dividing

Farms among the Mossi of Burkina Faso, or: Each One for Himself].
Cahiers des Sciences Humaines, Paris: ORSTOM, 23, 3–4 (1987). pp.
445–454.

——. "The Evolution of Agrarian Systems: The Example of Yatenga
(Upper Volta)." *African Environment,* Dakar, 2–3 (No. 1977). pp.
73–86.

——. "Lorsque l'outil ne compte plus: techniques agraires et entités
sociales au Yatenga." [When Tools No Longer Count: Agrarian Techniques and Social Groups in Yatenga]. *Cahiers ORSTOM* (Sciences
humaines), Paris: ORSTOM, 20, 3–4 (1984). pp. 461–469.

——. "Système agraire et évolution de l'occupation de l'espace au
Yatenga (Haute Volta)." *Cahiers ORSTOM* (Sciences humaines),
Paris: ORSTOM, 14, 2 (1977). pp. 141–149.

Marchal, Monique. *Les paysages agraires de Haute-Volta: analyse
structurale par la méthode graphique.* [The Agrarian Landscapes of
Upper Volta: A Graphic Structural Analysis]. Paris: ORSTOM, 1983.
115 p.

Matlon, Peter. "Indigenous Land Use Systems and Investments in Soil
Fertility in Burkina Faso" (Survey of 6 villages in 3 regions of Burkina, 1981–1985). In *Searching for Land Tenure Security in Africa,*
edited by John W. Bruce and Shem E. Migot-Adholla, pp. 41–69.
Dubuque, Iowa: Kendall/Hunt, 1994.

McMillan, Delta E. "Distribution of Resources and Products in Mossi
Households." In *Food in Sub-Saharan Africa,* edited by Art Hansen
and Delta E. McMillan, pp. 260–273. Boulder, Colorado: Lynne Rienner, 1986.

——. "Monitoring the Evolution of Household Economic Systems
Over Time in Farming Systems Research." *Development and Change,*
Netherlands, 18, 2 (1987). pp. 295–314.

Nagy, J. G.; H.W. Ohm and S. Sawadogo. "Burkina Faso: A Case Study
of the Purdue University Farming Systems Project." In *Working Together, Gender Analysis in Agriculture,* edited by H. S. Feldstein and
S. Poats, pp. 74–106 in vol. 1 and 61–124 in vol. 2. West Hartford,
Conn.: Kumarian Press, 1989.

Ouali, Ibrahim Firmin. *Burkina Faso and the CGIAR Centers: A Study
of Their Collaboration in Agricultural Research,* Washington DC:
World Bank, 1987. 112 p.

Poats, Susan V.; Schmink, Marianne and Spring, Anita. *Gender Issues
in Farming Systems Research and Extension,* Boulder, Colo: Westview Press, 1988. 450 p.

Prudencio, C. Y. "Ring Management of Soils and Crops in the West
African Semiarid Tropics—The Case of the Mossi Farming System in
Burkina Faso." *Agriculture Ecosystems and Environment,* 47, 3
(1993). pp. 237–264.

Rasmussen, M. S. "Assessment of Millet Yields and Production in Northern Burkina Faso Using Integrated NDVI from the AVHRR." *International Journal of Remote Sensing,* Great Britain, 13, 18 (1992), pp. 3431–3442.

Reardon, Thomas; Delgado, Christopher and Matlon, Peter. "Determinants and Effects of Income Diversification Amongst Farm Households in Burkina Faso." *Journal of Development Studies,* Great Britain, 28 (Jan. 1992). pp. 264–296.

Reyna, Stephen. P. "Dual Class Formation and Agrarian Underdevelopment: An Analysis of the Articulation of Production Relations In Upper Volta." *Canadian Journal of African Studies,* Canada, 17, 2 (1983). pp. 211–253.

Savadogo, K.; Reardon, T. and Pietola, K. "Farm Productivity in Burkina Faso—Effects of Animal Traction and Nonfarm Income." *American Journal of Agricultural Economics,* St. Paul, Minnesota, 76, 3 (1994). pp. 608–612.

Speirs, Mike. "Agrarian Change and the Revolution in Burkina Faso." *African Affairs,* Great Britain, 90, 358 (1991). pp. 89–110.

Vengroff, Richard. *Upper Volta: Environmental Uncertainty and Livestock Production.* Lubbock: Texas Tech University, 1980. 147 p.

———. "The Administration of Rural Development: The Role of Extension Agents in Upper Volta and Zaire." *Rural Africana,* 18, 2 (1984). pp. 45–57.

Webley, Olivia. "Fuelwood." In *Food in Sub-Saharan Africa,* edited by Art Hansen and Delta McMillan, pp. 254–259. Boulder, Colo: Lynne Rienner, 1986.

Zongo, J. O.; Vincent, C. and Stewart, R. K. "Effects of Neem Seed Kernel Extracts on Egg and Larval Survival of the Sorghum Shoot Fly." *Journal of Applied Entomology—Zeitschrift fur Angewandte Entomologie,* 115, 4 (1993). pp. 363–369.

Agriculture: Pastoralism

Barral, Henri. *Les populations nomades de l'Oudalan et leur espace pastoral.* Paris: ORSTOM, 1977. 119 p. (Trav.–Docum. ORSTOM, no. 77.)

———. *Tiogo, étude géographique d'un terroir Léla (Haute-Volta).* [Tiogo, A Geographical Study of a Léla Territory]. Paris: Mouton, 1968. 72 p.

———. "Mobilité et cloisonnement chez les éleveurs du nord de la Haute-Volta: les zones dites 'd'endodromie pastorale'." [Mobility and separation in the society of stockbreeders in the North of the Upper Volta: the so called 'endodromie pastorale' zones]. *Cahiers ORSTOM* (Sciences humaines), Paris: ORSTOM, 11, 2 (1972). pp. 127–135.

————. "Les Populations d'eleveurs et les problèmes pastoraux dans le nord-est de la Haute-Volta (Cercle de Dori, subdivision de l'Oudalan), 1963–1964." Paris, *Cahiers ORSTOM* (Sciences humaines), 4, 1 (1967). pp. 3–30.

Benoit, Michel. *Le chemin des Peul du Boobola: contribution à l'ecologie du pastoralisme en Afrique des savanes.* Paris: ORSTOM, 1979. 208 p. (Trav.-Docum. ORSTOM, no. 101.)

————. *Introduction à la géographie des aires pastorales Soudaniennes de Haute-Volta.* [Introduction to the Geography of the Sudanese Pastoral Areas of Upper Volta]. Ouagadougou: ORSTOM, 1974; Paris: ORSTOM, 1977. 93 p.

————. *Nature Peul du Yatenga: remarques sur le pastoralisme en pays mossi.* Paris: ORSTOM, 1982. 176 p. (Trav.-Docum. ORSTOM, no. 143.)

————. *Oiseaux de mil; les Mossi du Bwamu (Haute Volta).* Paris: ORSTOM, 1982. 116 p. (Mémoires, no. 95.)

————. "Le pastoralisme en savane et la 'territorialisation' des parcours." Paris, *Cahiers ORSTOM* (Sciences humaines), 14, 2 (1977). pp. 217–219.

————. "Le pastoralisme et migration: les Peul de Barani et de Dokue (Haute Volta)." [Pastoralism and Migration: The Fulani of Barani and Dokue]. *Etudes rurales,* Paris, 70 (Apr.–June 1978). pp. 9–50.

Guillaud, Dominique. *L'ombre du mil: un systeme agropastoral sahelien en Aribinda (Burkina Faso),* Paris: ORSTOM, 1993. 321 p.

Agriculture: Drought and Desertification

"Ghana-Burkina: Food for Work and Thought." *West Africa,* London, 3529 (15 Apr. 1985). p. 716.

"Upper Volta: The Finance of Famine." *West Africa,* London, 3446 (29 Aug. 1983). pp. 1997–1999.

Ancey, G. "Recensement et description des principaux systèmes ruraux sahéliens." [Census and Description of the Principal Rural Sahelian Systems]. *Cahiers ORSTOM* (Sciences humaines), Paris: ORSTOM, 14, 1 (1977). pp. 3–18.

Baldy, Charles. *Agrométéorologie et développement des régions arides et semi-arides.* [Agrometeorology and Development in Arid and Semi-arid Regions]. Paris: Institut National de la Recherche Agronomique, 1985. 114 p.

Binns, J. A. "After the Drought: Field Observations from Mali and Burkina Faso." *Geography,* Great Britain, 71, 3 (1986). pp. 248–252.

Bovin, Mette. "Nomads of the Drought: Fulbe and Wodabee Nomads between Power and Marginalization in the Sahel of Burkina Faso and Niger Republic." In *Adaptive Strategies in African Arid Lands,* edited by Mette Bovin and L. Manger, pp. 29–58. Uppsala, Sweden: Scandinavian Institute of African Studies, 1990.

Creevey, Lucy E. *Women Farmers in Africa: Rural Development in Mali and the Sahel,* Syracuse NY: Syracuse University Press, 1986. 232 p.

Derrick, Jonathan. "The Great West African Drought, 1972–74." *African Affairs,* London, 76, 305 (Oct. 1977). pp. 537–586.

Du Bois, Victor D. "The Drought in West Africa." *American University Field Staff Reports, West Africa Series,* Hanover, N. H., 15, 1–3 (Nov. 1973–May 1974).

Forbes, Robert H. "The desiccation problem in West Africa: the capture of the Sourou by the Black Volta." *Geographic Review,* New York, 22, 1 (Jan. 1932). pp. 97–106.

Gijsbert, H. F. M.; Kessler, J. J. and Knevel, M. K. "Dynamics and Natural Regeneration of Woody Species in Farmed Parklands in the Sahel Region (Province of Passoré, Burkina Faso)." *Forest Ecology and Management,* 64, 1 (1994). pp. 1–2.

Glantz, M. H. ed. *The Politics of Natural Disaster; the Case of the Sahel Drought,* New York: Praeger, 1977. 340 p.

Grouzis, M. "Problème de désertification en Haute Volta." *Notes et documents voltaïques,* Ouagadougou, 15 (Jan.–June 1984). pp. 1–13.

Gueye, Ibrahima and Laban, Peter. *From Woodlots to Village Land Management in the Sahel,* London: International Institute for Environment and Development, 1992. 21 p. (IIED paper no. 35)

Kales, Robert W. et al. *Drought Impact in the Sahelian-Sudanic Zone of West Africa: A Comparative Analysis of 1910–15 and 1968–74.* Worcester, Mass.: Clark University Center for Technology, Environment and Development, 1981. 92 p.

Lambin, Eric F. *Spatial Scales; Desertification and Environmental Perception in the Bougouriba Region (Burkina Faso),* Boston, Mass.: Boston University African Studies Center, 1992. 17 p.

Lindskog, Per and Mando, A. *The Relationship Between Research Institutes and NGOs in the Field of Soil and Water Conservation in Burkina Faso,* London: International Institute for Environment and Development, Drylands Networks Program Issues Paper no. 39 (Dec. 1992). 17 p.

Marchal, Jean-Yves. "Facteurs climatiques limitants et calamités agricoles en regions de savane: Yatenga." [Limiting Climatic Factors and Agricultural Calamities in Grassland Regions: Yatenga]. *Herodote,* Paris, 24, 1 (1982), pp. 68–94.

McCorkle, Constance. "Foodgrain Disposals as Early Warning Famine Signals: A Case From Burkina Faso." *Disasters,* London, 11, 4 (1987). pp. 273–281.

McMillan, Della E. "The Social Impacts of Planned Settlement in Burkina Faso." In *Drought and Hunger in Africa: Denying Famine a Fu-*

ture, edited by M. H. Glantz, pp. 297–322. Cambridge UK: Cambridge University Press, 1987.

Ofori-Sarpong, E. "The Drought of 1970–77 in Upper Volta." *Singapore Journal of Tropical Geography,* 4 (June 1983). pp. 53–61.

Reardon, Thomas; Peter Matlon and Christopher Delgado. "Coping with Household-level Food Insecurity in Drought-Affected Areas of Burkina Faso." *World Development,* Oxford UK, 16, 9 (1988). pp. 1065–1074.

Reining, Priscilla. *Challenging Desertification in West Africa: Insights from Landsat into Carrying Capacity, Cultivation and Settlement Site Identification in Upper Volta and Niger.* Athens, Ohio: Ohio University Press, 1979. 180 p.

Rochette, R. M., ed. *Le Sahel en lutte contre la désertification: leçons d'expérience.* [The Sahel's Struggle Against Desertification: The Lessons of Experience]. Weikersheim, Germany: Verlag Josef Margraf, 1989. 592 p. The collection of essays includes nine on Burkina Faso.

Sharp, Robin. *Burkina Faso: New Life for the Sahel?: A report for Oxfam,* Oxford, U.K.: Oxfam, 1990. 48 p.

Skinner, Elliott P. *New Adaptive Social Mechanisms Evolving Among Three Sahelian Populations Affected by the Drought: August 1975–July 1978.* Washington DC: African-American Scholars Council, 1978. 423 p. Sections specific to Upper Volta are pp. 25–29, 178–247, 253–258.

Tengberg, Anna. *Desertification in Northern Burkina Faso and Central Tunisia: Inferred from Vegetation Cover Chanqes, Land Degradation Indicators and Local Knowledge.* Göteborg, Sweden: Earth Sciences Centre, 1995.

Weber, Fred R. and Hoskins, Marilyn W. *Fiches techniques de conservation du sol.* [Technical Data on Soil Conservation]. Ouagadougou: Office de Coopération et de Développement Internationale, 1983. 112 p.

Rural Change

Bigot, Georges and Raymond, Georges. *Traction animale et motorisation en zone cotonnière d'Afrique de l'Ouest.* [Animal Traction and Mechanization in Cotton-growing Areas of West Africa]. Montpellier, France: Cirad, 1991. 95 p.

Delgado, Christopher L. "The Changing Economic Context of Mixed Farming in Savanna West Africa: A Conceptual Framework Applied to Burkina Faso." *Quarterly Journal of International Agriculture,* London, 28, 3/4 (1989). pp. 351–364.

Ilboudo, K. Ernest. *Les inégalités de développement régional au Burkina*

Faso. [The Inequalities of Regional Development in Burkina Faso]. Ouagadougou: Université de Ouagadougou, CEDRES, 1987. 140 p.

Lambin, Eric. "L'apport de la télédetection dans l'étude des systèmes agraires d'Afrique: Burkina Faso." [The Use of Remote Sensing in the Study of Agrarian Systems in Africa: Burkina Faso]. *Africa,* London, 58, 3 (1988). pp. 337–352.

McCorkle, Constance M. " 'You Can't Eat Cotton': Cash Crops and the Cereal Code of Honor in Burkina Faso." In *Production and Autonomy: Anthropological Studies and Critiques of Development,* edited by John W. Bennett and John R. Bowen, pp. 87–103. Lanham, Maryland: University Press of America, 1988.

Nebie, Ousmane. "Evolution des systèmes agraires bwa et pougoli de Pô-Ouest, Burkina Faso." [The Evolution of the Bwa and Pougoli Agrarian Systems in Pô-West, Burkina Faso]. *Cahiers d'Outre-mer,* Bordeaux, 41, 163 (1988). pp. 259–282.

Ouedraogo, Bernard Lédéa. *Entraide villageoise et développement: groupements paysans au Burkina Faso.* [Village Mutual Aid and Development: Rural Groupings in Burkina Faso]. Paris: Harmattan, 1990. 177 p.

Reyna, Stephen P. "Donor Investment Preference, Class Formation and Existential Development: Articulation of Production Relations in Burkina Faso." In *Anthropology and Rural Development in West Africa,* edited by Michael M. Horowitz and Thomas M. Painter, pp. 223–247. Boulder, Colorado: Westview Press, 1986.

———. "Investing in Inequality: Class Formation in Upper Volta." In *Power and Poverty: Development and Development Projects in the Third World,* edited by Donald W. Atwood, et al, pp. 119–133. Boulder, Colorado: Westview Press, 1988.

Sanders, John H.; Joseph G. Nagy and Sunder Ramaswamy. "Developing New Agricultural Technologies for the Sahelian Countries: The Burkina Faso Case." *Economic Development and Cultural Change,* Chicago, 39, 1 (Oct. 1990). pp. 1–22.

Saul, Mahir. "Consumption and Intra-household Patterns among the Southern Bobo of Burkina Faso." In *The Social Economy of Consumption,* edited by Henry Rutz and Benjamin Orlove, pp. 349–378. Lanham, Maryland: University Press of America, 1987.

———. "Money and Land Tenure as Factors in Farm Size Differentiations in Burkina Faso." In *Land and Society in Contemporary Africa,* edited by R. E. Downs and S. P. Reyna, pp. 243–279. Hanover, New Hampshire: University of New England Press, 1988.

Thiombiano, T. "State Policies on Agriculture and Food Production in Burkina Faso 1960–1983." In *The State and Agriculture in Africa,* edited by Thandika P. Mkandawire and Naceur Bourenane, pp. 243–271. London: Codesria, 1987.

Vierich, Helga. "Agricultural Production, Social Status, and Intra-compound Relationships." In *Understanding Africa's Rural Households and Farming Systems,* edited by Joyce Lewinger Moock, pp. 155–165. Boulder, Colorado: Westview Press, 1986.

World Bank, *Cotton Development Programs in Burkina Faso, Côte d'Ivoire and Togo.* Washington, DC: The World Bank, 1988. 126 p.

Younger, Stephen D. and Bonkoungou, Edouard G. "Burkina Faso: The Project Agro-forestier." In *Successful Development in Africa: Case Studies of Projects, Programs and Policies,* edited by R. Bheenick, et al, pp. 11–26. Washington, DC: The World Bank, 1989.

Business, Industry, Commerce, Finance, Banking

"Burkina Faso: Programme substantiel d'action (1981–1990)." *Les plans de développement des pays d'Afrique noire,* 6th ed., Paris: Ediafric, 1986. pp. 13–19.

"Burkina Faso: Statistiques économiques et monétaires." *Notes d'information et statistiques BCEAO.* Dakar: Banque Centrale des Etats de l'Afrique de l'Ouest. Published monthly. In 1992 the Burkina section was 34 pages long.

"Buy More, Boss Less: Aid for Africa." *The Economist,* 326, 7802 (Mar. 13, 1993). pp. 51–52. On restructuring farming operations and erosion prevention in Burkina Faso.

"Haute Volta, 1971." *Europe-France-Outremer,* Paris, Aug./Sep. 1971. pp. 1–58. (Survey on Upper Volta.)

"Haute Volta 80." *Europe-Outre-mer,* Paris, 57, 600–601 (Jan.–Feb. 1980). pp. 12–50.

"Haute-Volta, un an de renouveau national." *Europe Outre-mer,* Paris, Jan./Feb. 1975. pp. 8–57. (Series of articles on the Upper Volta economy.)

"Le marché de la Haute-Volta." *Marchés tropicaux et méditerranéens,* Paris, 1118 (15 April 1967). pp. 1077–1136. (Special Number.)

"Ouagadougou, l'enclavée." *Jeune Afrique Economie* (supplément), Paris, 153 (Mar. 1992). pp. 114–151.

"The Poverty of Upper Volta. " *West Africa,* London, 3214 (19 Feb. 1979). pp. 287–289.

"Le Premier plan de développement de la Haute-Volta, 1970." *Industries et Travaux d'Outremer,* Paris, (Oct., 1967). pp. 873–880.

"Upper Volta: Widespread Poverty Makes Development Difficult, but Economy is on Right Track." *Business America,* 3 (Oct. 20, 1980). pp. 39–41.

Adams, Paul. "CFA-zone countries impose price controls (Senegal, Côte d'Ivoire, Benin, Burkina Faso)". *Financial Times,* London, 32266 (Jan. 14, 1994), p. 4.

Ancey, G. *Monnaie et structures d'exploitations en pays Mossi, Haute-Volta.* Paris: ORSTOM, 1983. 243 p.

Api, Daouda. "Burkina: Housing for the People." *West Africa*, 3637 (27 April 1987). pp. 813–815.

Asche, Helmut. *Le Burkina Faso contemporain: l'experience d'un auto-développement*, Paris: Harmattan, 1994. 288 p.

Baris, Pierre; Philippe Bonnal and Michel Pescay. *Aménagement des vallées des Volta*. Paris: Ministère des relations extérieures, coopération et développement, 1983. 226 p.

Barrier, C. "Développement rural en Afrique de l'Ouest soudano-sahélienne: Premier bilan sur l'approche gestion de terroir villageois." *Les Cahiers de la Recherche-Développement*, 25 (Mar. 1990). pp. 33–43.

Beauminy, André de. "Le pays de la boucle du Niger: Etude économique." *Revue Géographique et Commerciale de Bordeaux*, 6 (1919). pp. 71–78.

Belotteau, Jacques. "Haute-Volta: forces et faiblesses de l'économie." [Upper Volta: Strengths and Weaknesses of the Economy]. *Afrique Contemporaine*, Paris, 124 (Nov.–Dec. 1982), pp. 11–21.

Berg, Elliott, and Belot, Thérèse. *Mobilization of the Private Sector in Burkina Faso*. Ouagadougou: Ministry of Planning, 1985. 21 p.

Broekhuyse, J. *Développement du Nord du plateau mossi*, Amsterdam: Département de recherches sociales, Institute royal des tropiques, 1974. 4 vols.

Darnton, John. "A Samaritan Lightens African Women's Cross" (Moise Yameogo develops method to mass-produce fermented corn flour: product makes a type of quickly-made couscous). *The New York Times*, 143 (May 30, 1994). p. 4(N), p. 4(L).

Davies, George Ola. "The Devaluation Bombshell." *West Africa*, London, 3982 (24–30 Jan. 1994). pp. 116–117.

Dijk, Meine Pieter van. *Burkina Faso: le secteur informel de Ouagadougou*. [Burkina Faso: The Informal Sector of Ouagadougou]. Paris: Harmattan, 1986. 203 p.

———. "How Relevant is Flexible Specialisation in Burkina Faso's Informal Sector and the Formal Manufacturing Sector?" *IDS Bulletin*, Sussex UK, 23, 3 (1992). pp. 45–50.

———. "La réussite des petits entrepreneurs dans le secteur informel de Ouagadougou. " [The Success of Small Entrepreneurs in the Informal Sector of Ouagadougou]. *Revue Tiers Monde*, Paris, 21, 82 (1980). pp. 373–386.

Dumont, René. *Paysans écrasés, terres massacrées: Equateur, Thaïlande, Inde, Bangladesh, Haute-Volta*, Paris: R. Laffont, 1978. 358 p.

Economist Intelligence Unit. *Country Profile: Niger, Burkina Faso 1994–95*. London: The Unit, 1994 (annual since 1986). p. 60. Companion publication to *Quarterly Report: Togo, Niger, Benin, Burkina*.

Fall, Abdou. *Cereal Banks at your Service? The Story of Toundeu-Patar: a Village Somewhere in the Sahel*, Oxford UK: Oxfam, 1991. 52 p.

Fiedler, Dorothée, et al. *Structure et perspectives de l'artisanat et de la petite industrie du Sud-Ouest de la Haute Volta: éléments d'un programme de promotion.* [Structures and Prospects for Artisan Enterprise and Small-scale Industry in Southwest Upper Volta]. Berlin: German Institute of Development, 1978. 253 p.

Filippi-Wilhelm, L. "Traders and Marketing Boards in Upper Volta: Ten Years of State Intervention in Agricultural Marketing." In *Marketing Boards in Tropical Africa,* edited by Kwame Arhin, et al, pp. 120–148. London: Kegan Paul, 1985.

Forbes, Robert H. "The Black Man's Industries." *Geographic Review,* New York, 23, 2 (April 1933). pp. 230–247. (On local African industry in Upper Volta.)

Futures Group. *Haute-Volta: Les effets des facteurs démographiques sur le développement social et économique,* Washington DC: Futures Group, 1986.

Gigure, Pierre. "Credit rural en Afrique noire francophone: une approche à adapter." [Rural Credit in Francophone Black Africa: An Approach in Adapting]. *Canadian Journal of African Studies,* Ottawa, 21, 3 (1987). pp. 402–410.

Gosselin, Gabriel. "Travail, tradition et développement en pays bissa." *Cahiers ORSTOM* (Sciences humaines), Paris, 7, 1 (1970). pp. 29–46.

Haddad, Lawrence and Reardon, Thomas. "Gender Bias in the Allocation of Resources within Households in Burkina Faso: A Disaggregated Outlay Equivalent Analysis." *Journal of Development Studies,* Great Britain, 29, 2 (Jan. 1993). pp. 260–276.

Hannequin, Brigitte. "Etat, patriarcat et développement: le cas d'un village du Burkina Faso." *Canadian Journal of African Studies,* Toronto, 24, 1 (1990). pp. 36–49.

Hemmings-Gapihan, Grace S. "Baseline Study for Socio-economic Evaluation of Tangaye Solar Site." In *Women and Technological Change in Developing Countries,* edited by Roslyn Dauber and Melinda L. Cain, pp. 139–148. Boulder, Colorado: Westview Press, 1981.

———. "International Development and the Evolution of Women's Economic Roles: A Case Study from Northern Gulma, Upper Volta." In *Women and Work in Africa,* edited by Edna G. Bay, pp. 171–189. Boulder, Colorado: Westview Press, 1982.

Hervouet, Jean-Pierre. "La mise en valeur des vallées des Volta Blanche et Rouge: un accident historique." *Cahiers ORSTOM* (Sciences humaines), Paris, 15, 1 (1978). pp. 81–97.

Hoskins, Marilyn W. and Guissou, Joséphene. *Social and Economic Development in Upper Volta: Women's Perspective,* Ouagadougou: Société Africaine d'études et de développement, 1978. 36 p.

Kendou, Georges Kossi. "Solidarité sociale traditionnelle et promotion des structures coopératives en milieu rural africain." [Traditional Social Solidarity and Cooperative Promotion in Rural Africa: Experiences of Villager Groups in Togo and Burkina Faso]. *Cahiers des Sciences Humaines,* Paris: ORSTOM, 30, 4 (1994). pp. 749–764.

Labazée, Pascal. *Entreprises et entrepreneurs du Burkina Faso: vers une lecture anthropologique de l'entreprise africaine.* [Businesses and entrepreneurs in Burkina Faso: Towards an anthropological interpretation of African business]. Paris: Karthala, 1988. 274 p.

Lamoukry, Rita. "L'integration des femmes dans les coopératives d'épargne et de crédit au Burkina Faso." *Développement et coopération,* Paris, 2 (1992). pp. 18–20.

Maclure, Richard A. "Non-government Organizations and the Contradictions of 'animation rurale': Questioning the Ideal of Community Self-reliance in Burkina Faso." *Revue canadienne d'études du développement,* Canada, 16, 1 (1995). pp. 31–53.

Marchal, Jean-Yves. "A propos de l'amenagement des Volta et de l'encadrement sanitaire des colons (Haute Volta Centrale)." *Travaux et mémoires de l'Institut des hautes études de l'Amerique latine,* France, 32 (1979). pp. 151–159.

Mitchnik, David A. *The Role of Women in Rural Zaire and Upper Volta: Improving Methods of Skill Acquisition,* Oxford, U.K.: Oxfam, 1978. 37 p.

Nikyéma, Paul. "L'état voltaïque et les sociétés face au développement." [The Voltaic State and Societies Facing Development]. *Revue Juridique et Politique,* Paris, 32, 1 (Jan.–Mar. 1978). pp. 97–122.

OECD. *Cereals Policy Reform in the Sahel: Burkina Faso.* Paris: OECD, 1986. 129 p.

Ouali, Kamadini. "La dépendance en héritage au Burkina Faso: L'économie avant la révolution." *Africain développement,* 11, 1 (1986). pp. 5–46.

Ouedraogo, Lucie and Lent, Rebecca. *Femmes entrepreneures au Sahel.* Quebec: Université Laval, 1993. 54 p.

Pallier, Ginette. *L'artisanat et les activités à Ouagadougou, Haute Volta.* [Crafts and Activities in Ouagadougou]. Paris: Secrétariat d'Etat aux Affaires Etrangères, 1970, 1980. 363 p.

Palmer, Mariele. "Progress is Slow Towards Higher Economic Growth (Burkina Faso)." *African Business,* Great Britain, 189 (June 1994). pp. 20–21.

Pearce, Jean. "Burkina Faso Sets Stage for African Development: An Interview with H. E. Raymond Edouard Ouedraogo, Ambassador of Burkina Faso." *Japan 21st,* 40, 6 (June 1995). pp. 25–26.

Pooda, Cèsaire. "Burkina: The Kompienga Dream." *West Africa,* London, 3570 (3 Feb. 1986). pp. 239–240.

Ram, Rati and Singh, Ram D. "Farm Households in Rural Burkina Faso:

Some Evidence on Allocative and Direct Return to Schooling and Male-Female Labor Productivity Differentials." *World Development,* Washington DC, 16, 3 (1988). pp. 419–424.

Reardon, Thomas A.; Taladidia Thiombiano and Christopher L. Delgado. *La substitution des céréales locales par les céréales importées: la consommation alimentaire des ménages à Ouagadougou.* [The Substitution of Imported Cereals for Local Cereals: Food Consumption in Ouagadougou Households]. Ouagadougou: Université de Ouagadougou, CEDRES, 1988. 65 p.

Robinson, Pearl T. "Sahelian Regional Development in a Changing World Order." *Journal of African Studies,* 11, 4 (1984–85). pp. 175–181.

Rupley, Lawrence A. "Taxation of Rental Property Income in Burkina Faso." *Bulletin for International Fiscal Documentation,* Amsterdam, 40, 7 (July 1986), pp. 299, 309. And brief addendum in Nov. 1986 issue, p. 511.

Sarraut, Albert. *La mise en valeur des colonies françaises.* Paris: Payot, 1923. 659 p.

Saul, Mahir. "Beer, Sorghum and Women: Production for the Market in Rural Upper Volta." *Africa,* London, 51, 3 (1981). pp. 746–764.

———. "Development of the Grain Market and Merchants in Burkina Faso." *Journal of Modern African Studies,* Great Britain, 24, 1 (1986). pp. 127–153.

———. "The Efficiency of Private Channels in the Distribution of Cereals in Burkina Faso." In *Production and Autonomy: Anthropological Studies and Critiques of Development,* edited by John W. Bennett and John R. Bowen, pp. 105–123. Lanham, Maryland: University Press of America, 1988.

———. "The Organization of a West African Grain Market." *American Anthropologist,* Washington, 89, 1 (1987). pp. 74–95.

———. "Work Parties, Wages and Accumulation in a Voltaic Village." *American Ethnologist,* 10, 1 (1983). pp. 77–96.

Savadogo, Kimseyinga, and Wetta, Claude. *The Impact of Self-Imposed Adjustment: The Case of Burkina Faso, 1983–1989* (Structural Adjustment in Africa, no. 15). Florence, Italy: Innocenti Occasional Papers, 1990. 49 p.

Sawadogo, Mathias. "Quelques innovations et leurs divers impacts dans le milieu rural voltaïque." *Genève-Afrique,* Switzerland, 17, 2 (1979). pp. 11–17.

Sherman, Jacqueline R. *Grain Markets and the Marketing Behavior of Farmers: A Case Study of Manga, Upper Volta,* Ann Arbor, Michigan: Center for Research on Economic Development, 1984.

Sherman, Jacqueline R.; Kenneth H. Shapiro and Elon Gilbert. *The Dynamics of Grain Marketing in Burkina Faso.* Ann Arbor, Michigan:

University of Michigan Center for Research on Economic Development, 1987. 2 vols.

Singh, Ram D. and Morey, Mathew J. "The Value of Work-at-Home and Contributions of Wives' Household Service in Polygynous Families." *Economic Development and Cultural Change,* Chicago, 35, 4 (1987). pp. 743–765.

Sirven, Pierre. "Le 'secteur informel' à Fada N'Gourma." [The Informal Sector in Fada N'Gourma]. In *Pauvreté et développement dans les pays tropicaux: hommage à Guy Laserre,* pp. 541–562. Bordeaux: University of Bordeaux Institute de Géographie, 1989.

Skinner, Elliott Percival. "Trade and Markets among the Mossi People." In *Markets in Africa,* edited by Paul Bohannan and George Dalton. Evanston, Ill.: Northwestern University Press, 1962. pp. 237–278.

Slanagen, Anthony. "Burkina Faso." In *Rural Finance Profiles in African Countries,* edited by Mario Masini, Vol. 2, pp. 1–61. Milan: Finafrica, 1989.

Stamm, Volker. "Non-Commercial Systems of Land Allocation and Their Economic Implications: Evidence from Burkina Faso." *Journal of Modern African Studies,* Great Britain, 32, 4 (1994). pp. 713–717.

Stickley, Thomas and Tapsoba, Edouard. "Loan Repayment Delinquency in Upper Volta." In *Borrowers and Lenders,* edited by J. Harrell, pp. 273–285. London: Overseas Development Institute, 1980.

Taylor, Ellen. *Women Paraprofessionals in Upper Volta's Rural Development.* Ithaca NY: Center for International Studies, 1981. 56 p.

Tcha-Koura, Sadamba. *Formation d'une élite paysanne au Burkina Faso.* Paris: Harmattan, 1995.

Thiombiano, Taladidia. "Les déterminants de la consommation urbaine à Ouagadougou." [Determinants of Urban Household Consumption in Ouagadougou]. *Africa Development,* Dakar, 13, 2 (1988). pp. 77–98.

———. *Une enclave industrielle: la Société Sucrière de Haute-Volta.* Dakar: CODESRIA. 1984 (?). 192 p.

Van Dijk, Meine Pieter. "Burkina Faso: Modern Medium Scale Industries." In *Industrialization in the Third World: The Need for Alternative Strategies,* edited by Meine Pieter Van Dijk and H. Secher, pp. 102–123. London: Frank Cass, 1992.

Wilcock, David C. *Inventaire soci-économique des villages de l'est.* East Lansing: Michigan State University Department of Agricultural Economics, 1981. 110 p.

Wilcock, David and Chuta, Enyinna. "Employment in Rural Industries in Eastern Upper Volta." *International Labour Review,* Geneva, 121, 4 (Aug. 1982). pp. 455–468.

Wolfson, Margaret. *Aid Implementation and Administrative Capacity in Upper Volta: A Suggested Methodology of Assessment.* Paris: OECD, 1981. 30 p.

Wright, Peter and Bondoungou, Edouard G. "Soil and Water Conservation as a Starting Point for Rural Forestry: The Oxfam Project in Ouahigouya, Burkina Faso." *Rural Africana,* 23–24 (Fall 1985–Winter 1986). pp. 79–86.

Zuidberg, Lida. "Burkina Faso: Integrated Rural Development: For Whom and With Whom?" In *Assessing the Gender Impact of Development Projects: Case Studies from Bolivia, Burkina Faso and India,* edited by Vera Gianotten, et al, pp. 49–70. London: Intermediate Technology; Amsterdam: Royal Tropical Institute, 1994.

Labor and Migration

Adjima, G. *Migration et urbanisation au Burkina Faso.* Bamako: CILSS, Cerpod, 1989.

Agier, M.; J. Copans and A. Morice. *Classes ouvrieres d'Afrique noire.* Paris: Karthala/ORSTOM, 1987. 293 p.

Asiwaju, A. I. "Migrations As Revolt: The Example of the Ivory Coast and the Upper Volta Before 1945." *Journal of African History,* Cambridge, UK, 17, 4 (1976). pp. 577–594.

Balima, Salfo Albert. "Notes on the Social and Labour Situation in the Republic of Upper Volta." *International Labour Review,* Geneva, 1960. pp. 358–362.

Bardem, Isabelle. "L'emancipation des jeunes: un facteur négligé des migrations interafricaines." [The Emancipation of Youth: A Neglected Factor in Inter-African Migrations]. *Cahiers des Sciences Humaines,* Paris: ORSTOM, 29, 2–3 (1993). pp. 375–393.

Benoit, D.; P. Lévi and M. Pilon. *Caractéristiques des migrations et de la nuptialité en pays dagara.* [Characteristics of Migration and Marriage in Lobi Dagara Areas]. Paris: ORSTOM, 1986. 161 p.

Bonnassieux, Alain, *L'autre Abidjan: chronique d'un quartier oublié.* [The Other Abidjan: Chronicles of a Forgotten Quarter]. Paris: Karthala, 1987. 220 p. (study of Vridi-Canal, including its Mossi residents)

Boutillier, J.-L.; A. Quesnel and J. Vaugelade. "La migration de la jeunesse du Burkina." [Young Migrants from Burkina]. Paris, *Cahiers ORSTOM* (Sciences humaines), 21, 2–3 (1985). pp. 243–249.

———. "Systèmes socio-économiques mossi et migrations." Paris, *Cahiers ORSTOM* (Sciences humaines), 14, 4 (1977). pp. 361–381.

Conde, Julien. "Migration in Upper Volta." In *Demographic Aspects of Migration in West Africa,* edited by K. C. Zacharia and N. K. Nair, pp. U.V. 1–156 (Staff Working Paper No.415). Washington DC: World Bank, 1980.

Cordell, Dennis D. and Gregory, Joel W. "Labour Reservoirs and Population: French Colonial Strategies in Koudougou, Upper Volta, 1914 to 1939." *Journal of African History,* Cambridge UK, 23, 2 (1982). pp. 205–224. (Raymond Gervais's critique of this article appears as "Vérités et mensonges: Les statistiques coloniales de population." *Canadian Journal of African Studies,* Ottawa, 17, 1 (1983). pp. 101–106.)

Cordell, Dennis D.; Joel W. Gregory and Victor Piché. *Hoe and Wage: A Social History of a Circulatory Migration System in West Africa.* Boulder, Colo: Westview Press, 1995. 180 p.

Coulibaly, Sidiki; Joel Gregory and Victor Piché. *Les migrations voltaïques.* Ouagadougou: CVRS; Ottawa: CRDI (International Development Research Centre), 1980. 8 vols. (Volume 1 is titled "Importance et ambivalence de la migration voltaïque." 144 p .)

Deniel, Raymond. *De la savane à la ville—essai sur la migration mossi vers Abidjan et sa région.* [From the Savannah to the Town: Mossi Migration to Abidjan and its Region]. Paris: Aubier-Montaigne, 1968. 224 p.

Deniel, Raymond. "Mesures governementales et/ou intérêts divergents des pays exportateurs de main d'oeuvre et des pays hôtes: Haute Volta et Côte d'Ivoire." [Divergence of Interests between Labor-exporting and Host Countries, and Measures Taken by Them]. In *Modern Migrations in Western Africa,* edited by Samir Amin, pp. 215–225. London: Oxford University Press for the International African Institute, 1974.

Derrien, Jean-Maurice. "Les salariés du Burkina: faut-ils parler des classes moyennes?" [Salaried workers in Burkina Faso: can they be seen as the middle class?]. *Revue Tiers Monde,* Paris, 26, 10 (Jan.–Mar. 1985). pp. 69–78.

Du Bois, Victor D. "Ahmadou's World. A Case Study of a Voltaic Immigrant to the Ivory Coast." *American University Field Staff Reports, West Africa Series,* Hanover, New Hampshire, 8, 2 (1965). pp. 63–76.

———. "The Economic, Social, and Political Implications of Voltaic Migration to the Ivory Coast." *American University Field Staff Reports, West Africa,* Hanover, New Hampshire, 14, 1 (1972). pp. 1–9.

Gaude, J. *Phénomène migratoire et politique associées dans le contexte africain: études de cas en Algérie, au Burundi, en République Unie du Cameroun et en Haute Volta,* Geneva: International Labor Office, 1982. 298 p.

Gervais, Raymond. "Creating Hunger: Labor and Agricultural Policies in Southern Mossi, 1919–1940." In *African Population and Capitalism: Historical Perspectives,* edited by D. D. Cordell and J. W. Gregory, pp. 109–121. Boulder, Colorado: Westview Press, 1987.

Gregory, Joel W. "Development and in-migration in Upper Volta." In *Modern Migrations in Western Africa,* edited by Samir Amin, pp. 305–320. London: Oxford University Press, 1974.

————. "Migration in Upper Volta." *African Urban Notes,* East Lansing, Michigan., 6, 1 (1971). pp. 44–52.

————. "Underdevelopment, Dependence and Migration in Upper Volta." In *The Politics of Africa: Dependence and Development,* edited by Timothy M. Shaw and Kenneth A. Heard, pp. 73–94. New York: Longman; Halifax, Nova Scotia: Dalhousie University Press, 1979.

Gregory, Joel W.; Dennis D. Cordell and Victor Piché. "La mobilisation de la main-d'oeuvre Burkinabè, 1900–1974: Une vision reprospective." [Mobilization of Burkinabè Labor, 1900–74: A Retrospective View]. *Canadian Journal of African Studies,* Ottawa, 23, 1 (1989). pp. 73–105.

Hervouet, Jean-Pierre. *Peuplement et mouvements de population dans les vallées des Volta Blanche et Rouge,* Ouagadougou: ORSTOM, 1977.

International Labor Office. *Rapport sur l'éducation ouvrière en République de Haute-Volta.* Geneva, 1962.

International Labor Organization. "Le cas du Burkina Faso." [The Case of Burkina Faso]. In *Le syndrome du diplôme et le chômage des jeunes diplômés en Afrique francophone au sud du Sahara.* [Pattern of graduation and unemployment among young graduates in francophone Sub-Saharan Africa]. Addis Ababa: International Labor Organization, Employment and Technical Training Program for Africa, 1985. 5 vols.

Kabeya, Charles. "Evolution et rôle des syndicats au Burkina Faso." [Evolution and role of trade unions in Burkina Faso]. *Présence Africaine,* Paris, 2 (1987). pp. 130–147.

Kabéya Muasé, Charles. *Syndicalisme et démocratie en Afrique noire: l'expérience du Burkina Faso (1936–1988).* Paris: Karthala, 1989. 252 p.

————. "Un pouvoir des travailleurs peut-il être contre syndicats?" [Can Workers' Power Work Against the Trade Unions?]. *Politique Africaine,* Paris, 33 (1989). pp. 50–58.

Kohler, Jean Marie. *Les Migrations des Mossi de l'Ouest.* Paris: ORSTOM, 1972. 106 p. (Trav.-Docum. ORSTOM, no. 18.)

Lahuec, Jean-Paul and Marchal, Jean-Yves. *La mobilité du peuplement Bissa et Mossi.* [The Movements of Bissa and Mossi Peoples]. Paris: ORSTOM, 1979. 149 p. (Trav.-Docum. ORSTOM, no. 103.)

Laurent, Pierre-Joseph. *Migrations et accès à la terre au Burkina Faso.* Louvain-la-Neuve, Belgium: CIDEP: Academia-Eraseme; Paris: Harmattan, 1994. 136 p.

Ouedraogo, Cheikh. "Contribution à l'étude du phénomène migratoire et de la condition juridique des étrangers en Haute-Volta." [Contribution to the Study of the Migratory Phenomenon and the Legal Position of

Strangers in Upper Volta]. *Revue juridique et politique,* 34, 1 (Jan.–Mar. 1980). pp. 109–120.

Ouedraogo, Jean-Bernard. *Formation de la classe ouvrière en Afrique Noire: l'exemple du Burkina Faso.* [Formation of a Working Class in Black Africa: The Example of Burkina Faso]. Paris: Harmattan, 1989. 207 p.

Ouedraogo, O. Dieudonné. *Migration et développment en Haute Volta: l'exemple de Zogoré.* Ouagadougou: CVRS, 1976. 285 p.

Piché, Victor, et al. "Vers une explication des courants migratoires voltaïques." *Labour, Capital and Society,* Montreal, 13, 1 (April 1980). pp. 76–103.

Problems of the Sahel and Their Consequences for Workers and Peasants: Trade Union Conference, Ouagadougou, 13–15 December 1982, Brussels: International Confederation of Free Trade Unions, 1983(?). 30 p.

Psacharopoulus, George. "Returns to Education: A Further International Update and Implications." *Journal of Human Resources,* Madison, Wisconsin, 20 (1985). pp. 584–604.

Rémy, Gérard. "Les migrations de travail dans la région de Nobéré, cercle de Manga." *Cahiers ORSTOM* (Sciences humaines), Paris, 5, 4 (1968). pp. 77–91.

———. "Les mouvements de population sur la rive gauche de la Volta rouge (région de Nobéré)." *Cahiers ORSTOM* (Sciences humaines), Paris, 5, 2 (1968). pp. 45–66.

Rouch, Jean, et al. "Migrations au Ghana." *Journal de la Société des Africanistes,* Paris, 26, 1–2 (1956). pp. 33–196. Also published as book by Société des Africanistes, 1956. 175 p.

Saul, Mahir. "The Quranic School Farm and Child Labor in Upper Volta." *Africa,* London, 52, 2 (1984). pp. 71–87.

Sautter, Gilles. "Migrations, société et développement en pays mossi." [Migrations, society, and development in the Mossi region]. *Cahiers d'Etudes Africaines,* Paris, 20, 3 (1980). pp. 215–253.

Sawadogo, Filiga Michel. "Le participation des travailleurs dans les entreprises publiques burkinabé." [Worker Participation in the Burkinabé State Enterprises]. *Penant,* Paris, 95, 788/9 (July–Dec. 1985). pp. 199–218.

Sidibé, D. B. "Régime foncier et migrations: l'expérience de l'Aménagement des Vallées des Volta." [System of Land Tenure and Migration: The Land Development Experiment of the Volta Valleys Authority]. In *Espaces disputés en Afrique noire,* edited by B. Crousse, Emile Le Bris, Etienne Le Roy, pp. 187–198. Paris: Karthala, 1986.

Skinner, Elliott Percival. "Labour Migration Among the Mossi of the Upper Volta. " In *Urbanization and Migration in West Africa,* edited by Hilda Kuper, pp. 60–84. Los Angeles: University of California Press, 1965, and Westport, Connecticut: Greenwood Press, 1981.

————. "Labour Migration and its Relationship to Sociocultural Change in Mossi Society." *Africa,* 30, 4 (Oct. 1960). pp. 375–401.

Songre, A. "Mass Emigration from Upper Volta: the Facts and Implications." *International Labour Review,* Geneva, (Aug.–Sept. 1973). pp. 209–225.

Vaugelade, J. "Présentation méthodologique d'une enquête sur les migrations: 'enquête renouvelée après un intervalle pluri-annuel'." *Cahiers ORSTOM* (Sciences humaines), Paris: ORSTOM, 9, 4 (1972). pp. 455–458.

Mining and Transportation

Aziz, Christine. "Digging for Hell's Gold." *The Guardian,* London, (Dec. 10, 1994), p. 24. (Gold mining in Burkina Faso.)

Baylers, H. "Chemin de Fer du Mossi" *Encyclopédie Mensuelle d'Outre-Mer,* Paris, June, 1951. pp. 151–154.

Boulanger, Jacques J. "The Tambao Manganese Mines." *Entente Africaine,* Paris, (July 1969). pp. 68–74.

Cohn, Lynne M. "Burkina Faso Manganese Output Smooth." *American Metal Market,* United States, 101, 191 (Oct. 4, 1993). p. 4.

Cosaert, Patrice. "Les voies de communications au Burkina Faso." [Means of Communication in Burkina Faso]. *Cahiers d'Outre-mer,* Bordeaux, 43, 169 (1990). pp. 53–76.

Cuneo, Henri and Blancher, Gaston. "Les chemins de fer." *L'Encyclopédie Coloniale et Maritime, AOF,* vol. 2, edited by Eugène Guernier. Paris: Lang and Blanchong, 1949. pp. 219–228.

Furukawa, Tsukasa. "Tambao Manganese Near: Buyers Sought in Japan for West Africa Production." *American Metal Market,* 100, 237 (Dec. 9, 1992). pp. 2–3.

Grant, Sally Lyall. "A Railway by Volunteer Labour." *West Africa,* London, 3540 (1 July 1985). p. 1338.

Guerin, Bernard. "La route Ouagadougou-Bobo-Dioulasso." [The Ouagadougou-Bobo-Dioulasso Road]. *Cahiers d'Outre-mer,* Bordeaux, 145 (Jan.–Mar. 1984). pp. 5–32.

Hubner, R. "L'important project de liaison routière Lomé-Ouagadougou." *Europe-France-Outremer,* Paris, January 1966. pp. 1–41.

Japanese International Cooperation Agency. *Survey Report on Road and City Planning Related to the Tambao Manganese Mine Project.* Tokyo: Japanese International Cooperation Agency, 1976. 116 p.

Labonne, Beatrice; Guy-Bray, John and Maire, Henri. "Lead/Zinc Exploration Update: United Nations Department of Economic and Social Development" (Burkina Faso, Pakistan, Nepal). *Natural Resources Forum,* 17, 3 (1993). pp. 235–238.

Nicolas, Guy. "La mine d'or de Poura et le nombre quatre-vingts en

Afrique occidentale." *Notes Africaines,* Dakar, 161 (Jan. 1979. pp. 19–21.

Philippi, Thomas. *A Sahel Transportation Survey: A Regional Profile,* Washington DC: Office of U. S. Foreign Disaster Assistance, 1979. 137 p.

Smith, Wilbur and Associates. *Entente States Highway Reconnaissance Study: Dahomey-Upper Volta; Dassa Zoume to Fada N'Gourma.* Columbia, So. Carolina: for USAID, 1970. 143 p.

———. *Entente States Highway Reconnaissance Study: Upper Volta-Niger; Fada N'Gourma to Niamey.* New Haven, Conn.: for USAID, 1970. 409 p.

Wackermann, Gabriel. "Enclavement et mobilité en Afrique occidentale: l'exemple du Burkina Faso." [Landlockedness and Transportation Mobility in West Africa: The Example of Burkina Faso]. *Afrique Contemporaine,* Paris, 140 (Oct.–Dec. 1986). pp. 24–39.

Culture

Architecture

Barbero, L. and Savvidu, A. "On Mud-Schools in Burkina Faso" *Spazio e Societa—Space and Society,* Rome, 16, 61 (1993). pp. 60–71.

Bourdier, Jean-Paul and Minh-ha, Trinh T. *African Spaces: Designs for Living in Upper Volta.* New York: Africana, 1985. 232 p.

———. "The Architecture of a Léla Compound." *African Arts,* Los Angeles, 16, 1 (Nov. 1982). pp. 68–72.

———. "Ko Architecture: A Case Study from Koena, Upper Volta." *Tribus,* 32 (1983). pp. 113–125.

———. "Koumbili: Semi-Sunken Dwellings in Upper Volta." *African Arts,* Los Angeles, 16, 4 (Aug. 1983). pp. 40–45.

Domian, Sergio. *Architecture soudanaise: vitalité d'une tradition urbaine et monumentale.* [Sudanese Architecture: The Vitality of an Urban and Monumental Tradition]. Paris: Harmattan, 1989. 191 p.

Haberland, Erik. "West African Mud Architecture. " *African Arts,* Los Angeles, 15, 1 (1981). pp. 44–45.

Pradeau, Christian. "Etude de l'habitat en pays dagari (Haute-Volta)." *Cahiers d'Etudes Africaines,* Paris, 15, 3 (1975). pp. 501–524.

Prussin, Labelle. *Hatumere: Islamic Design in West Africa.* Berkeley: University of California Press, 1985. 448 p.

———. "An Introduction to Indigenous African Architecture." *Journal of the Society of Architectural Historians,* 33, 3 (Oct. 1974). pp. 183–205.

———. "West African Mud Granaries." *Paideuma,* 18 (Dec. 1972). pp. 144–169.

Rainer, L. "The Writing on the Wall (the Ancient Tradition of Painting Surfaces of Earthen Buildings in Burkina Faso)." *Places—A Quarterly Journal of Environmental Design,* 8, 1 (1992). pp. 42–45.

Smith, Fred T. "Gurunsi Wall Painting." *African Arts,* Los Angeles, 12, 1 (1978). pp. 78–81,

Some, Honoré P. "Habitations et occupation du sol—le yir et le village dagara: l'exemple de Tobo." [Habitations and Occupancy of the Land—The Yir and the Dagara Village: The Example of Tobo]. *Cahiers d'Outre-mer,* Bordeaux, 43, 169 (1990). pp. 77–95.

Stevens, Phyllis Ferguson. *Aspects of Muslim Architecture in the Dyula Region of the Western Sudan.* Legon: University of Ghana, 1968.

Archeology

Andah, Bassey W. "Excavations at Rim, North-Central Upper Volta: A Paleocological Study." In *West African Culture Dynamics,* edited by B. K. Swartz and R. E. Dumett. pp. 41–65. The Hague: Mouton, 1980.

———. "Excavations at Rim, Upper Volta." *West African Journal of Archaeology,* 8 (1978). pp. 75–138.

———. "The Later Stone Age and Neolithic of Upper Volta Viewed in a West African Context." *West African Journal of Archaeology,* 9 (1979). pp. 87–117.

Dupré, Georges and Guillaud, Dominique. "Archéologie et tradition orale: contribution à l'histoire des espaces du pays d'Aribinda (province de Soum, Burkina Faso)." [Archaeology and Oral Tradition: A Contribution to the History of the Aribinda Area]. *Cahiers des Sciences Humaines,* Paris: ORSTOM, 22, 1 (1986). pp. 5–48.

Labouret, Henri "Le mystère des ruines du Lobi." *Revue d'Ethnographie et des Traditions populaires,* Paris, 1920. pp.

Savonnet, Georges. "Notes sur quelques ruines situées dans la région de Léo (Haute-Volta)." *Notes Africaines IFAN,* Dakar, 71 (July 1956). pp. 65–67.

———. "Le paysan Gan et l'archéologue ou inventaire partiel des ruines de pierres du pays Lobi-Gan (Burkina et Côte d'Ivoire)." [The Gan Peasant and the Archaeologist. A Partial Survey of the Stone Ruins of the Lobi-Gan Zone]. *Cahiers des Sciences Humaines,* Paris: ORSTOM, 22, 1 (1986). pp. 57–82.

Verneau, Dr. Raymond. "Découverte de grandes ruines à Gaoua." *L'Anthropologie,* Paris, 1902. pp. 778–781.

Cinema and Theater

Bachy, Victor. *La Haute-Volta et le cinéma.* 2d ed. Paris: Harmattan; Brussels: OCIC, 1983. 86 p.

Bazie, Jacques Prosper. *Théâtre.* Ouagadougou: Ministère de la Culture, 1986. 86 p. (Volume of two plays).

Cinema, Child, and Environment: Acts of the International Symposium of Ouagadougou, Burkina Faso, 28 February 1991. Ouagadougou: FESPACO, 1991. 54 p.

Cornevin, Robert. *Le théâtre en Afrique noire et à Madagascar,* Paris: Le Livre Africain, 1970. 335 p.

FESPACO. *Cinéma et libertés: contribution au thème du FESPACO '93: essais et propos.* Paris and Dakar: Presence africaine, 1993. 125 p.

————. *L'Afrique et le centenaire du cinéma.* Dakar: Presence africaine, 1995. 412 p. (Published for Fédération Panafricaine des Cinéastes/ Panafrican Federation of Film Makers. Approximately 7 pages on Burkina Faso.)

Gauthier, G. "[African Cinema at Cannes—Burkina Faso, Mali, and Cameroon]." *Revue du cinema,* 473 (1991). pp. 13–14. (article is in French)

Guingané, Jean-Pierre. "Théâtre et développement au Burkina Faso." [Theatre and Development in Burkina Faso]. *Revue d'Histoire du Théâtre,* Paris, 40, 4 (1988). pp. 361–373.

Henderson, C. "Shining Star in the African Sky (the Film Industry in Burkina Faso)." *Index on Censorship,* Great Britain, 20, 3 (1991). 16 p.

Ilboudo, Patrick G. *Le FESPACO, 1969–1989: les cinéastes africains et leurs oeuvres.* Ouagadougou: La Mante, 1988. 499 p.

Ki, Jean-Claude. "Dix ans de théâtre: 1979–1989." [Ten Years of Theater]. *Notre Librairie,* Paris, 101 (1990). pp. 72–75.

Leroy, M. C. "Africa's Film Festival: Screenings in Upper Volta's Newly Nationalized Cinemas." *Africa Report,* Washington DC, 15, 4 (April 1970). pp. 27–28.

Olorunyomi, 'Sola. "Burkina Faso—Clash of Images." *West Africa,* London, 4042 (27 Mar.–02 Apr. 1995). pp. 458–459.

Ouedraogo, Hamidou. *Naissance et évolution du FESPACO de 1969 à 1973.* Ouagadougou: Imprimerie Nationale du Burkina, 1995. 222 p. (A collection of documents, including FESPACO prize lists from 1976 through 1993.)

Ouédraogo, Ouamdégré. *L'avare moaga: comédie des moeurs.* Ouagadougou: 1961.

Oyekunle, Segun. "Knowing Africa first hand." *West Africa,* London, 4106 (1–7 July 1996). pp. 1026–1027.

Pacéré Frédéric Titinga. *La poésie des griots.* [The Poetry of the Griots]. 2nd ed. Paris: Silex, 1983. 133 p.

Pageard, Robert. "Théâtre africain à Ouagadougou." *Présence Africaine,* Paris, 39 (1961). pp. 250–253.

Pfaff, Françoise. "Five West African Film Makers on Their Films." *Issue,* Atlanta, 20, 2 (1992). pp. 31–37.

Santos, Anoumou Pedro. *Fâsi: Pièce en cinq actes.* Dakar: Traits d'Union, 1956.

Schmidt, Nancy J. "Publications on African Film: Focus on Burkina Faso and Nigeria." *African Book Publishing Record,* London, 16, 3 (1990). pp. 153–156.

———. "Recent Films by Sub-Saharan African Filmmakers (6) (annually since 1988)." *ALA Bulletin,* Edmonton, Alberta, 19, 1 (Winter 1993), pp. 10–14.

Sowie, Moussa Théophile; Issa Nikiéma Tinga and Martin Zongo. *Pièces théâtrales du Burkina.* [Plays of Burkina]. Ouagadougou: Ministère de l'Information et de la Culture, 1983. 157 p. (Volume of three plays).

Turecamo, David. "A Celebration of Cinema" (FESPACO). *Africa Report,* New York, 38, 3 (May–June 1993). pp. 68–69.

Wright, Rob. "Africa's Film Capital" (Ouagadougou Pan-African Film Festival). *Africa Report,* New York, 40, 1 (Jan.–Feb. 1995), pp. 61–63.

Zimmer, W. "The Horses of Conversation, the Honey of Tradition and the Gold of Words: Use and Function of Proverbs in the Theater of Burkina-Faso". *Anthropos,* 89, 1–3 (1994). pp. 15–27. Article is in French.

Fine Arts

African-American Institute. *Traditional Sculpture from Upper Volta: An Exhibition of Objects from New York Museums and Private Collections.* New York: African-American Institute, 1978. 47 p.

Banaon, Kouame Emmanuel. *Poterie et société chez les Nuna de Tierkou.* [Pottery and Society among the Nuna of Tierkou]. Stuttgart, Germany: F. Steiner, 1990. 186 p.

Blegna, Domba. *Les masques dans la société marka de Fobiri et ses environs: origines, culte, art.* [The Masks in the Marka Society of Fobiri and Its Surroundings]. Stuttgart: Fran Steiner, 1990. 262 p.

Bobo, Ma-da-re. Bobo-Dioulasso: Imprimerie de la Savane, 1984?. 38 p.

Dagan, Esther A. *Man and His Vision: The Traditional Wood Sculpture of Burkina Faso.* Montreal, Canada: Galerie Amrad African Arts, 1987. 64 p.

Etienne-Nugué, Jocelyne. *Artisanats traditionnels, Haute-Volta.* [Traditional Activities of Artisans, Upper Volta]. Dakar: Institut culturel africain, 1982. 216 p.

Glaze, Anita. *Art and Death in a Senufo Village,* Bloomington IN: Indiana University Press, 1981. 267 p.

Goldwater, Robert. *Senufo Sculpture from West Africa.* New York: Museum of Primitive Art, 1964. 126 p.

Ham, Laurent van and Dijk, Robert van. *Africa: Art and Culture of the Upper Volta,* Rotterdam: R. Schuurman, 1980. 150 p.

Hinckley, Priscilla Baird. "The Dodo Masquerade of Burkina Faso." *African Arts,* Los Angeles, 19, 2 (Feb. 1986). pp. 74–77.

―――. "Street Nativities in Ouagadougou." *African Arts,* Los Angeles, 16, 3 (May 1983). pp. 47–49.

Hoskins, Marilyn W. and Charbonneau, Louise. *Bronzes de Ouagadougou,* Ouagadougou: Société africaine des affaires culturelles, 1976. 56 p.

Kaboré, Oger. "Chants d'enfants mossi." [The Songs of Mossi Children]. *Journal des Africanistes,* Paris, 51, 1–2 (1981). pp. 183–200.

Kamer, Henri. *Haute-Volta.* [Upper Volta]. Brussels: A. De Rache, 1973. 179 p.

Lallemand, Suzanne. "Symbolisme des poupées et acceptation de la maternité chez les Mossi." [The Symbolism of Dolls and the Acceptance of Maternity among the Mossi]. *Objets et Mondes,* Paris, 13, 4 (1973). pp. 235–246.

Laude, Jean and Cerulli, Ernesta. "Sudanese Cultures." In *Encyclopedia of World Art,* vol. 13, pp. 674–713. New York: McGraw-Hill, 1967.

Leuzinger, Elsy (translated by R. A. Wilson). *The Art of Black Africa.* London: Studio Vista Publishers, 1972. pp. 54–79 for material concerning Upper Volta.

Nourrit, Chantal and Pruitt, Bill. *Musique traditionnelle de l'Afrique noire: disco-graphie, no. 2: Haute Volta.* Paris: Radio-France Internationale, Centre de documentation africaine, 1978. 67 p.

Rey, Jean Dominique. *Les Lobi.* [The Lobi]. Paris: Galerie Jacques Kerchache, 1974. 61 p.

Roy, Christopher D. *Art of the Upper Volta Rivers* (Chaffin, F. Traduction et Adaptation en Francais), Meudon, France: A. et F. Chaffin, 1987. 384 p.

―――. *The Dogon of Mali and Upper Volta—Die Dogon von Mali und Ober-Volta,* Munich: Fred und Jens Jahn, 1983. 60 p.

―――. "Forme et signification des masques mossi." (Structure and Meaning of Mossi Masks]. *Art d'Afrique Noire,* Paris, 48 (Winter 1983). pp. 9–23.

―――. "Mossi Chiefs' Figures." *African Arts,* Los Angeles, 15, 4 (Aug. 1982). pp. 52–59.

―――. "Mossi Dolls." *African Arts,* Los Angeles, 14, 4 (Aug. 1981). pp. 47–51.

―――. "Mossi Weaving." *African Acts,* Los Angeles, 15, 3 (May 1982). pp. 48–53, 91–92.

―――. "Mossi zazaido." *African Arts,* Los Angeles, 13, 3 (May 1980). pp. 42–47. (A study of Mossi ceremonial headcrests.)

―――. "The Spread of Mask Styles in the Black Volta Basin." *African Arts,* Los Angeles, 20, 4 (1987). pp. 40–47.

Schweeger-Hefel, Annemarie. "L'art nioniosi." *Journal de la société des Africanistes,* Paris, 36, 2 (1966). pp. 251–332.

Segy, Ladislas. "The Mossi Doll: An Archetypal Fertility Symbol." *Tribus,* Stuttgart, 21, 1 (1972). pp. 35–68.

Skougstad, Norman. *Traditional Sculpture from Upper Volta.* New York: The African American Institute, 1978. 43 p.

Smith, Fred T. "Gurunsi Basketry and Pottery." *African Arts,* Los Angeles, 12, 1 (Nov. 1978). pp. 78–81.

Soma, Etienne Yarmon. "Les instruments de musique du pays cerma (guin), sud-ouest du Burkina Faso." [Musical Instruments of the Cerma (Gain) country, southwest of Burkina Faso]. *Anthropos,* Fribourg, 83, 4/6 (1988). pp. 469–483.

Some, R. "Les bétibé: art et pouvoir chez les Lobi et les Dagara du sud-ouest du Burkina Faso." [The Bétibé: Art and Power among the Lobi and Dagara in Southwest Burkina Faso]. In *Séminaire de recherche,* edited by L. Perrois and C. F. Bandez, pp. 137–151. Paris: ORSTOM, 1989.

Triande, Toumani. *Masques et sculptures voltaïques exposé au Festival culturel panafricain, Alger, 1969.* Ouagadougou: Musée National, 1969. 30 p.

Visages D'Afrique. Quarterly publication of the Cercle d'Activités Littéraires et Artistiques de Haute-Volta, Ouagadougou, started in 1967.

Warin, François. "La statuaire Lobi: question de style." [Lobi Statues: A Question of Style]. *L'Art d'Afrique Noire,* Arnouville, 69 (1989). pp. 11–21.

Literature and Folklore

Bakyono, Odjou Clement. *Soupir et sourire.* Bobo-Dioulasso: Imprimerie Nationale du Burkina, 1992. 43 p.

Bazie, Hubert. *Champ d'août.* [Field of August]. Ouagadougou: Imprimerie de la Presse Ecrit, 1986. 124 p.

Bazie, Jacques Prosper; Bila Roger Kabore and Hamade Y. Ouedraogo. *Poésie du Burkina.* [The Poetry of Burkina]. Ouagadougou: Ministère de l'Information et de la Culture, 1983. 149 p.

Bonnet, Doris. *Le proverbe chez les Mossi du Yatenga.* [The Proverb among the Mossi of Yatenga]. Paris: SELAF (Oralité-documents, 6), 1982. 193 p.

Bonnet, Doris. and Ouedraogo, Moussa. *Proverbes et contes Mossi,* Paris: Conseil international de la langue française, 1982. 149 p.

Canu, Gaston. *Contes du Sahel.* [Folktales of the Sahel]. Paris: Conseil International de la Langue Française, 1975. 138 p.

Cissoko, Fily Dabo. *Savane rouge* [Red Savannah]. Avignon: Presses Universelles, 1962. 139 p.

Dabiré, Pierre. *Les aventures de Dari l'Araignée,* Bobo-Dioulasso:

Imprimerie La Savane, 1972. 57 p. (The story *Sansoa* by the same author concerns the World War II period, 1969. 68 p.)

Guirma, Frederic. *Princess of the Full Moon*. Translated by John Garrett. New York: Macmillan, 1970. 32 p. (A Folktale of Upper Volta.)

————. *Tales of Mogho: African Stories from Upper Volta*. New York: Macmillan, 1971. 113 p.

Houseman, Michael. "Towards a Complex Model of Parenthood: Two African Tales." *Ethnologist,* New York, 15, 4 (Nov. 1988). pp. 658–677.

Ilboudo, Patrick; Jacques Prosper Bazie and Faustin S. Dabira. *Nouvelles du Burkina*. [Short Stories of Burkina]. Ouagadougou: Ministère de l'Information et de la Culture, 1983. 105 p.

Ilboudo, Pierre-Claver. *Adama ou la force des choses*. [Adama or the Force of Circumstances]. Paris: Dakar, 1987. 154 p.

Jahn, Janheinz; Ulla Schild and Almut Nordmann. *Who's Who in African Literature*. Tübingen, West Germany, 1972. 407 p.

Kabore, Roger Bila. *La princesse Yennéga et autres histoires*. [Princess Yennéga and other stories]. Paris: Edicef, 1983. 95 p.

Koné, Amadou. *Les fresques d'Ebinto*. [The Frescos of Ebinto]. Paris: La Pensée Universelle, 1972. 141 p.

————. *Jusqu'au seuil de l'irréel*. [To the Threshhold of Unreality]. Abidjan: Nouvelles Editions Africaines, 1976. 143 p.

Nikiéma, Roger. *L'adorable rivale*. [The Adorable Rival]. Ouagadougou: Imprimerie Presses Africaines, 1981.

————. *Dessin contraire*. [Contrary Design]. Ouagadougou: Imprimerie Presses Africaines, 1967.

————. *Mes flèches blanches*. [My White Arrows]. Ouagadougou: Imprimerie Presses Africaines, 1981. 59 p. (Volume of poetry.)

Pacéré, Frederic Titinga. *Ça tire sous le Sahel*. [It Attracts All the Sahel]. Paris: P. J. Oswald, 1976. 64 p.

————. *Du lait pour une tombe*. [Milk for a Tomb]. Paris: Editions Silex, 1984. 90 p.

————. *Quand s'envolent les grues couronnées*. [When Crested Cranes Take Flight]. Paris: P. J. Oswald, 1976. 89 p.

————. *Refrains sous le Sahel*. [Refrains beneath the Sahel]. Paris: P. J. Oswald, 1976. 89 p.

Platiel, Suzanne. *La fille volage*. [The Flighty Girl]. Paris: Armand Colin, 1984. 342 p.

Platiel, Suzy. "L'enfant, sujet du conte." [The Child, Subject of Folktales]. *Journal des Africanistes,* Paris, 51, 1/2 (1981). pp. 149–182.

Sanwidi, Hyacinthe. "Depuis le crépuscle des temps anciens: panorama du roman." [From the Dawn of Ancient Times: The Panorama of the Novel]. *Notre Librairie,* Paris, 101 (1990). pp. 48–54.

Sawadogo, Etienne. *Contes de jadis: récits de naguère*. [Tales of Long

Ago: Stories of Yesterday]. Dakar: Nouvelles Editions Africaines, 1982. 170 p.

Sidibé, Mamby. "Contes de la savane." *Présence Africaine,* Paris, 8–9 (1950). pp. 193–204.

Some, Penou-Achille and Bouygues, Claude. *Dagara-yerbie, ou, proverbes Dagara.* [Dagara-yerbie, or, Dagara Proverbs]. Paris: Harmattan, 1992. 132 p.

Language and Linguistics

Alexandre, G. *La langue möré.* 2 vols. Dakar: IFAN. 1953. 407 p., 506 p.

Alexandre, Pierre G. *Dictionnaire Möré-Française.* Maison-Carrée, Algeria: Imprimerie des Pères Blancs, 1935. 1017 p.

———. *Lexique Français-Möré.* Maison-Carrée, Algeria: Imprimerie des Pères Blancs, 1934. 263 p.

Alexandre, P. *An Introduction to Languages and Language in Africa.* Translated by F. A. Leary. London: Heinemann, 1972. 133 p.

Arnott, D. W. *The Nominal and Verbal System of Fula.* Oxford UK: Clarendon Press, 1970. 432 p.

Bazin, H. *Dictionnaire Bambara-Français.* Paris: Imprimerie Nationale, 1906 and Westmead UK: Gregg Press, 1965.

Bidaud, L. and Prost, A. *Manuel de langue peule; dialecte du Liptako, Dori, Haute Volta.* [Manual of the Fulani Language, Liptako Dialect]. Paris: Publications Orientalistes de France, 1982. 236 p.

Bonvini, Emilio. *Prédication et énonciation en kasim.* [Preaching and Articulation in Kasim]. Paris, CNRS, 1988. 198 p.

———. "La bouche: entre la parole et l'insulte: l'exemple du Kasim." [The Mouth: Between Words and Insults]. *Journal des Africanistes,* Paris, 57, 1–2 (1987). pp. 149–159.

Canu, Gaston. *Contes Mossi actuels: Etudes ethno-linguistiques.* Dakar: University of Dakar, 1966. 496 p.

———. *La langue moré: dialecte de Ouagadougou (Haute Volta): description synchronique.* [The Moré Language: The Ouagadougou Dialect]. Paris: SELAF, 1976. 421 p.

Chazal, RP. *Dictionnaire Français-Gourma.* Porto-Novo: Gouvernement du Dahomey, 1951. 139 p. (Etudes dahoméennes.)

Chéron, E. Georges. *Le dialecte Sénoufo du Minianka,* Paris: P. Geuthner, 1925. 167 p.

———. "Essai sur la langue Minianka." *Bulletin du comité d'études historiques et scientifiques de l'A.O.F.,* Paris, 1929. PP. 560–616.

Cornevin, Robert. *Littératures d'Afrique noire de langue française,* Paris: Presses Universitaires de France, 1976. 280 p.

Cremer, Jean. *Dictionnaire Français-Peul (dialectes de la Haute-Volta),* Paris: Geuthner, 1923. 109 p.

————. *Grammaire de la langue Kassena,* Paris: Geuthner, 1924. 72 p.

Delafosse, Maurice. *La langue mandingue et ses dialectes,* Paris: Geuthner, 1929. 674 p.

————. "Les langues voltaïques." *Mémoires de la Société de Linguistique de Paris,* 16 (1911). pp. 386–395.

Delplanque, Alain. "Les verbes de jugement en dagara." [Verbs of Judgment in Dagara]. *Journal des Africanistes,* Paris, 57, 1–2 (1987). pp. 133–147.

Dubois, Félix. "Vocabulaire gourma." *BCAF,* Paris, 7 (July 1898). pp. 248–249.

Ducroz, Jean Marie and Ducroz, Marie Claire. *Lexique soney (songhay) français: parler Kaado du Gouronol,* Paris: Harmattan, 1978. 285 p.

Froger, Fernand. *Etude sur la langue du Mossi.* Paris: Leroux, 1910. 259 p.

————. *Manuel pratique de langue Môré, suivie d'un vocabulaire et de textes.* Paris: Leroux, 1910. 259 p.

————. *Manuel pratique de langue Môré.* Paris: Fournier, 1923. 326 p.

Guillaud, Dominique. "Tradition orale à Koumbri (nord Yatenga)." *Notes et documents voltaïques,* Ouagadougou, 15 (Jan.–June 1984). pp. 84–109.

Haillot, J. "Etude sur la langue Dyan." *Bulletin du comité d'études historiques et scientifiques de l'Afrique occidentale française,* Dakar, 3 (1920). pp. 348–380.

Hall, H. F. *Dictionary and Practical Notes. Mossi-English Languages.* Ouahigouya: Assembly of God, n. d. (prior to 1978). 78 p.

Kédrébéogo, G. and Yaga, Z. *Langues du Burkina Faso.* [Languages of Burkina Faso]. Ouagadougou: Ministère de l'Enseignement Supérieur et de la Recherche Scientifique, 1986. 57 p.

Kenstowicz, Michael, et at. "Tonal Polarity in Two Gur Languages." *Studies in Linguistic Sciences,* Urbana, Illinois, 18, 1 (1988). pp. 77–103.

Labouret, Henri. *La langue des Peuls ou Foulbé.* Dakar: IFAN, 1952. 286 p.

Lamothe, Père Charles. *Esquisse du système grammatical Lobi.* [Outline of Lobi Grammar]. Paris and Ouagadougou: CNRS and CVRS, 1966. 168 p.

————. *Esquisse du système verbal Lobi.* Dakar: Université de Dakar, 1964. 80 p.

Lavergne de Tressan, M. de. *Inventaire linguistique de l'Afrique occidentale française et du Togo.* Dakar: IFAN, 1953. 242 p. (Mémoires de IFAN, no. 30.)

Le Bris, Pierre and Prost, André. *Dictionnaire bobo-français, précédé d'une introduction grammaticale et suivi d'un lexique français-bobo.* [Bobo-French Dictionary, Preceded by a Grammar Introduction, and

Followed by a French-Bobo Lexicon]. Paris: SELAF, 1981. 415 p. (Includes an English summary.)

Lebel, A. Roland. *L'Afrique occidentale dans la littérature française* (*depuis 1870*). Paris: Emile Larose, 1925. 279 p.

Lehr, Marianne; James E. Redden and Adama Balima. *Moré Basic Course*. Washington DC: U.S. Government Printing Office, 1966. 340 p.

Manessy, Gabriel. *Contribution à la classification généalogique des langues voltaïques*. Paris: SELAF.

—. *Les langues gurunsi; essai d'application de la méthode comparative à un groupe des langues voltaïques*. [The Gurunsi Languages]. Paris: SELAF, 1969. 2 vols.

—. *Les langues Oti-Volta: classification généalogique d'un groupe des langues voltaïques*. [The Oti-Volta Languages: Genealogical Classification of a Group of Voltaic Languages]. Paris: SELAF, 1975. 314 p.

—. "Le bwamu et les langues voltaïques." *Afrika und Übersee*, 66, 2 (1983). pp. 231–258.

—. "Les bwamu et ses dialectes." [Bwamu and Its Dialects]. *Bulletin d'IFAN*, Dakar, 23, 1–2 (Jan.–April 1961). pp. 119–178.

—. "Linguistique historique et traditions ethniques des peuples voltaïques dans l'est de la boucle du Niger." In *Zur Sprachgeschichte und Ethnohistoirie in Afrika*, edited by J. C. Wilhelm Möhlig, et al, pp. 152–165. Berlin: D. Reimer, 1977.

—. "Matériaux linguistiques pour servir à l'histoire des populations du sud-ouest de la Haute Volta." *Sprache und Geschichte in Afrika*, Hamburg, 4 (1982) pp. 85–164.

McIntosh, Mary. *Fulfulde Syntax and Verbal Morphology*. Boston, Massachusetts: KP & Ibadan University Press, 1984. 292 p.

Migeod, Frederick William. *The Languages of West Africa*. Freeport, NY: Books for Libraries Press, 1972 (Reprint of 1911–1913 ed.)

Mukosy, I. A. *A Fulfulde-English Dictionary*. Kaduna, Nigeria: Nigerian Educational and Development Council, 1991. 220 p.

Nikiéma, Norbert. *Ed gom moore: la grammaire du moore en 50 leçons*. [Ed Gom Moore: More Grammar in Fifty Lessons]. Ouagadougou: University of Ouagadougou, 1980. 2 vol.

—. *La situation linguistique en Haute Volta*. [The Linguistic Situation in Upper Volta]. Paris: UNESCO, 1980. 25 p.

Pacéré, Frédéric Titinga. *Bendrologie et littérature culturelle des Mossé. Introduction à la littérature non-écrite d'Afrique: littérature orale, langue de tam-tams, messages des masques et des danses*. [Bendrology and the Cultural Literature of the Mossi. Introduction to the Non-written Literature of Africa: Oral Literature, Tam-Tam Language, and

Messages Conveyed by Masks and Dances]. Ouagadougou: Titinga Pacéré, 1987. 6 vols.

Pageard, Robert. *Litterature Negro-Africaine. Le Mouvement littéraire contemporain dans L'Afrique Noire d'expression française.* Paris: Le Livre Africain, 1966. 138 p.

———. "Mythologie moderne: Les dieux délinquants d'Augustin Coulibaly, Haute Volta, 1974." *L'Afrique litteraire,* 54–55 (1979–1980). pp. 111–114.

Paradis, Carole. *Lexical Phonology and Morphology: The Nominal Classes in Fula.* New York: Garland, 1992. 313 p.

Platiel, Suzanne. "La formation des verbes en Sàn (Samo)." *Mandenkan: Bulletin semestriel d'études linguistiques mandé,* Paris, 2 (1981). pp. 69–83.

———. "Les procédés de formation des name en Sàn." *Mandenkan: Bulletin semestriel et d'études linguistiques mandé,* Paris, 6 (1983). pp. 75–89. (Samo language)

Prost, André. *Contribution à l'étude des langues voltaïques.* [Contribution to the Study of the Voltaic Languages]. Dakar: IFAN, 1964. 461 p. (Mémoires de l'IFAN.)

———. *Le Kusaal.* [Kusaal]. Dakar: Université de Dakar, Département de Linguistique Générale, 1979. 167 p.

———. *La langue Bisa. Grammaire et Dictionnaire.* Ouagadougou: Centre IFAN, 1950.

———. *La langue des Kouroumba ou Akurumfé.* [The Kurumba Language or Akurumfé]. Vienna: A. Schendl, 1980. 179 p.

———. "De la parenté des langues busa-boko avec le bisa et le samo." *Mandenkan: Bulletin semestriel d'études linguistiques mandé,* Paris, 2 (1981). pp. 17–29.

———. "Essai de description grammaticale du dialecte Bobo de Tansila, Haute-Volta." *Mandenkan: Bulletin semestriel d'études linguistiques mandé,* Paris, 5 (1983). pp. 3–101.

———. "Les Kamboense ou Kambense." *Notes et documents voltaïques,* Ouagadougou, 11, 2 (Jan.–Mar. 1978). pp. 51–57.

———. "Petite grammaire marka (région de Zaba)." Nouna-Dédougou: Diocèse de Nouna-Dédougou, 1977. 100 p. (multigraph)

Rennison, John R. and Staude, Wilhelm. *Textes koromfés.* [Koromfe Texts]. Hamburg, Germany: H. Buske, 1986. 125 p.

Retel-Laurentin, Anne. *Les noms de naissance, indicateurs familiale.* Paris: SELAF, 1974. 151 p.

———. "Signification des noms de naissance des Bobo-Oulé de Haute-Volta." *Notes et documents voltaïques,* Ouagadougou, 7, 3 (Feb.–Mar. 1974), pp. 1–5; 7, 4 (Apr.–June 1974), pp. 1–35; 7, 5 (July–Aug. 1974), pp. 3–31.

Rialland, Annie. "Le système tonal du gurma, langue gur de Haute-Volta." [The Tonal System of Gurma, a Gur Language in Upper Volta]. *Journal of African Languages and Linguistics,* Dordrecht, The Netherlands, 3, 1 (1981). pp. 39–64.

Socquet, P. *Manuel-grammaire Mossi.* Dakar: IFAN, 1952. 87 p. (Initiations africaines, no. 4.)

Some, Penou-Achille. *Systématique du significant en Dagara: variété Wule.* [Systemization of the Signifier in Dagara: Wule Dialect]. Paris: Harmattan,1982. 491 p.

Surugue, Bernard. *Etudes gulmance (Haute Volta): phonologie, classes nominales, lexiques.* [Gulmance Studies: Phonology, Noun Classes, Lexicon]. Paris: SELAF/CNRS, 1979. 148 p.

Tiendrébéogo, Gérard and Yago, Zakaria. *Situation des langues parlées en Haute Volta: perspectives de leur utilisation pour l'enseignement et l'alphabétisation.* Paris: ACCT; Abidjan: ILA; Ouagadougou: CNRST, 1983. 96 p.

Vallette, René. "La focalisation en fulfulde." [Focalization in Fulfulde]. *Journal of West African Languages,* Dallas, 18, 2 (1988). pp. 9–20.

————. "Un morphème de classe supplémentaire en fulfulde, dialect Jelgooji, Haute-Volta." [The Morpheme of an Extra Category in Fulfulde, Jelgooji Dialect, Upper Volta]. *Journal of West African Languages,* Cambridge UK, 15, 1 (April 1985). pp. 93–103.

Welmers, William E. *The Mande Languages.* Washington DC: Georgetown University Monograph Series on Languages and Linguistics No. 11, 1958.

Westermann, Diedrich. *The Languages of West Africa.* London: Oxford University Press, 1952. 215 p.

Zoango, Jean Bigtarma. *Dictionnaire encyclopédique moore-français.* [Encyclopedic More-French Dictionary]. Ouagadougou: Zoango, 1985. 3 vols.

The Press

Carrefour Africain. Ouagadougou. (Weekly newspaper started in 1959).

"Gouama's Gossip (Burkina Faso's Journal du Jeudi)." *Index on Censorship,* Great Britain, 21, 10 (Nov. 1992). 37 p.

Jeune Afrique. French-language weekly published in Tunis and Paris since 1947.

L'Observateur. Ouagadougou. (Newspaper founded in 1973).

Ouedraogo, M. "Jokers in the Blood (the Satirical Press in Burkina Faso)." *Index on Censorship,* Great Britain, 21, 10 (1992). p. 35.

Sidwaya. Ouagadougou. (Daily French-language newspaper started in 1984).

Thiombiano, Moustapha. "Interview: Moustapha Thiombiano, African Radio Pioneer." *Africa Report,* New York, 37, 1 (1992). pp. 10–11.

Society

Anthropology, Ethnology and Traditional Societies

Adelaja, Kola. "Traditional Power Control among the Mossi and the Yoruba: A Comparative Study." *Présence africaine,* Paris, 1 (1976). pp. 43–54.

Arnaud, Pierrette. "Expression graphique et milieu culturel: à-propos des dessins réalisés par les jeunes Kurumba." *Journal des Africanistes,* Paris, 51, 1–2 (1981). pp. 265–276.

Arozarena, P. "Sur la généalogie des Moog' Nanamse de Ouagadougou." *Notes et documents voltaïques,* Ouagadougou, 11, 3–4 (Apr.–Sep. 1978). pp. 39–42.

Bamony, Pierre. "Equilibre social et pouvoirs chez les Lyéla de la Haute-Volta." *Anthropos,* 79, 4–6 (1984), pp. 433–440.

Bernard, S. J. "Les Bissa du cercle de Garango." *Cahiers d'Etudes Africaines,* Paris, 1, 18 (1965). pp. 164–165. Also see Pegard, Odette P.

Bonnafe, P. and Fieloux, M. "Le dédain de la mort et la force du cadavre: Souillure et purification d'un meurtrier lobi (Burkina/Haute Volta)." [The disdain of death and the cadaver's power: defilement and purification of a Lobi murderer]. *Etudes rurales,* Paris, 95–96 (Jul.–Dec. 1984). pp. 63–87.

Bonnet, Doris. *Corps biologique, corps social: procréation et maladies de l'enfant en pays mossi, Burkina Faso.* [Biological Body, Social Body: Procreation and Illness of Children in Mossi Country, Burkina Faso]. Paris: ORSTOM, 1988, p. 138.

———. "Le retour de l'ancêtre." [The Return of the Ancestor]. *Journal des Africanistes,* Paris, 51, 1/2 (1981). pp. 133–147.

Brasseur, Gérard. *Notes sur les établissements humains en Oudalan,* Ouagadougou: ORSTOM, 1983. 58 p.

Brasseur, G. and Le Moal, Guy. *Cartes ethno-démographiques de l'Afrique Occidentale.* Dakar: IFAN, 1963. 29 p.

Broekhuijse, Johan Theodorus. *Notes sur les structures socio-politiques des Mossi de la région de Kaya (Haute Volta),* Amsterdam: Institut royal des regions tropicales, 1980. 103 p.

Calame-Griaule, Geneviève. *Ethnologie et langue: la parole chez les Dogons.* Paris: Gallimard, 1965. 589 p.

Capron, Jean. "Quelques notes sur la société du do chez les populations bwa du cercle de San." *Journal de la Société des Africanistes,* Paris, 27 (1957). pp. 89, 129.

————. "Univers religieux et cohésion interne dans les communautés villageoises bwa traditionnelles." [The Religious World and Internal Cohesion in Traditional Bwa Communities]. *Etudes Voltaïques,* Ouagadougou, 4, 1963 (1965). pp. 72–124. Also appears in *African Systems of Thought,* edited by M. Fortes and G. Dieterlen, pp. 291–313. London: Oxford University Press, 1965.

Cartry, Michel, ed. *Sous le masque de l'animal: essais sur le sacrifice en Afrique Noire,* Paris: Presses Universitaires de France, 1987.

Cartry, Michel. "From the Village to the Bush: An Essay on the Gourmantche of Gobnangou." In *Between Belief and Transgression,* edited by Michel Izard and Pierre Smith, pp. 210–228. Chicago: University of Chicago Press, 1982.

————. "Le lieu à la mère et la notion de destin individuel chez les Gourmantché." In *La notion de personne en Afrique noire,* pp. 255–282. Paris: Editions du CNRS, 1973.

————. "Rapport de mission 1975: structures sociales et religieuses traditionnelles des Gourmantché de Haute Volta." *Notes et documents voltaïques,* Ouagadougou, 11, 1 (Oct.–Dec. 1977). pp. 55–56.

————. "Le statut de l'animal dans le système sacrificiel des Gourmantche." [The Status of the Animal in the Sacrificial System of the Gurma]. *Systèmes de Pensée en Afrique Noire,* Paris, 2 (1976), pp. 141–175; 3 (1978), pp. 17–58; 5 (1981), pp. 195–216.

————. "Le suaire du chef." [The Chief's Shroud]. In *Sous le masque de l'animal: essais sur le sacrifice en Afrique Noire,* edited by Michel Cartry, pp. 131–231. Paris: Presses Universitaires de France, 1987.

Chamard, Philippe C. and Courel, Marie-Françoise. "De l'autochtonie des dépots superficiels du Liptako Nigero-Voltaïque." *Revue de géomorphologie dynamique,* Paris, 30, 1 (1981). pp. 11–20.

Chéron, E. Georges. *La Société noire de l'Afrique Occidentale Française,* Paris: Bonsalot-Joure, 1908.

————. "Les Bobo-Fing." *Annuaire et Mémoires du Comité d'Etudes Historiques et Scientifiques de l'Afrique Occidentale Française,* Paris, 1916. pp. 215–261.

————. "Les Minianka." *Revue d'ethnographie et de sociologie,* Paris, 4 (1913). pp. 165–186.

Collett, Peter. "Mossi Salutations." *Semiotica,* Amsterdam, 45, 3/4 (1983). pp. 191–248.

Coquet, Michèle. "Une esthétique du fétiche." [An Aesthetic of Fetish]. *Systèmes de Pensée en Afrique Noire,* Paris, 8 (1985). pp. 111–139. Concerns Bwa history.

Coulibaly, Lenissongui. *L'autorité dans l'Afrique traditionelle: étude comparative des états mossi et ganda.* Abidjan: Nouvelles éditions africaines, 1983. 239 p.

Coutouly, François de. "La famille, les fiançailles et le mariage chez les

Peuls du Liptako." *Revue d'Ethnographie et des Traditions Populaires,* Paris, 4 (1923). pp. 259–270.

———. "Les populations du cercle de Dori" *BCEHS,* 6 (1923). pp. 269–301, 471–496, 637–671.

———. "Une ville soudanaise de la Haute-Volta: Dori." *BCEHS,* 9 (1926). pp. 487–497.

Cros, Michele. *Anthropologie du sang en Afrique: essai d'hématologie symbolique chez les Lobi du Burkina Faso et de Côte d'Ivoire,* Paris: Harmattan, 1990. 297 p.

———. "Un exemple d'indépendance et de résistance religieuse: les hommes et les dieux Lobi." [An Example of Independence and Religious Resistance: The Lobi and their Gods]. *Mondes et Développement,* Paris, 17, 65 (1989). pp. 59–65.

Cros, Michele, and Dory, Daniel. "Pour une approche écologique des guerres lobi." [Toward an ecological approach to Lobi warfare]. *Cultures et Développement,* Belgium, 16, 3–4 (1984). pp. 465–484.

Dacher, Michèle. "Le deuil du père, pays Guin." [Mourning the Father among the Guin]. *Systèmes de Pensée en Afrique Noire,* Paris, 9 (1986). pp. 75–103.

———. "Genies, ancêtres, voisins. Quelques aspects de la relation à la terre chez les Ciranba (Goin) du Burkina Faso." *Cahiers d'Etudes Africain,* Paris, 24, 2 (1984). pp. 157–192.

———. "Identité de groupe et identité multiple: le cas des Goin du Burkina Faso." [Group Identity and Multiple Identity: the case of the Goin of Burkina Faso]. *Psychothérapie Psychoanalytique de Groupe,* Paris, 9–10 (1987). pp. 101–115.

Dacher, Michèle, with collaboration by Suzanne Lallemand. *Prix des épouses, valeur des soeurs; suivi de Les representations de la maladie: deux études sur la société Goin, Burkina Faso.* [Two studies of Goin society]. Paris: Harmattan, 1992. 203 p.

———. "Société lignagère et Etat: les Goin du Burkina Faso." [Lineage Societies and State: the Goin of Burkina Faso]. *Genève-Afrique,* Switzerland, 25, 1 (1987). pp. 43–58.

Delmond, Paul. "Dan la boucle du Niger. Dori, ville peul." *Mélanges ethnologiques,* Dakar: IFAN, 1953. pp. 9–109. (Mémoires de IFAN, 23.)

Delobsom, A. A. Dim. *L'Empire du Mogho-Naba, coutumes des Mossi de la Haute-Volta.* [The Mogho-Naba Empire; Mossi Customs in Upper Volta]. (Preface by Robert Randau.) Paris: Editions Domat-Montchrestien, 1932. 303 p.

Diallo, Helga. *Le chasseur lobi: une étude ethno-sociologique.* [The Lobi Hunter: An Ethno-sociological Study]. Vienna: Acta Ethnologica et Linguistica, 1978. 78 p.

Dieterlen, Germaine. "Notes sur les Kouroumba du Yatenga Septentrional." *Journal de la société des Africanistes,* Paris, 10 (1940). pp. 181–189.

Dubourg, J. "La vie des paysans mossi, le village de Taghalla." *Les Cahiers d'outre mer,* Bordeaux, 40 (Oct.–Dec. 1957). pp. 285–324.

Duval, Maurice. *Un totalitarisme sans état: Essai d'anthropologie politique à partir d'un village burkinabè,* [Totalitarianism Without a State: An Essay on Political Anthropology Based on a Burkinabè Village]. Paris: Harmattan, 1985. p. 183.

Fainzang, Sylvie, et al. *L'intérieur des choses: maladie, divination et reproduction sociale chez les Bisa du Burkina,* [The Inside of Things: Illness, Divination and Social Reproduction among the Bisa of Burkina]. Paris: Harmattan, 1986. 204 p.

Fainzang, Sylvie. "Le regard du serpent: réflexions sur la théorie de la contamination chez les Bisa de Haute-Volta." [The Eye of the Snake: Reflections on the Theory of Contamination among the Bisa of Upper Volta]. *L'Homme,* Paris, 24, 3/4 (July–Dec. 1984). pp. 23–64.

———. "Les sexes et leurs nombres: sens et fonction du 3 et du 4 dans une société burkinabè." [The Sexes and Their Numbers: The Meaning and Function of Numbers 3 and 4 in a Burkinabè Society]. *L'Homme,* Paris, 25, 96 (1985). pp. 97–109.

Fieloux, Michele and Lombard, Jacques, with Jeanne-Marie Kambou-Ferrand. *Images d'Afrique et sciences sociales: les pays lobi, birifor et dagara (Burkina Faso, Côte d'Ivoire et Ghana),* Paris: Karthala/ORSTOM, 1993. 567 p. (proceedings of a December 1990 conference in Ouagadougou)

Finnegan, Gregory A. and Delgado, Christopher L. "Cachez la Vache: Mossi Cattle, Fulbe Keepers and the Maintenance of Ethnicity." In *Image and Reality in African Interethnic Relations: The Fulbe and Their Neighbors,* edited by Emily A. Schultz, pp. 31–50. Williamsburg, VA: College of William and Mary, 1980.

Fisk, Alan Page. "Rational Self-interest or Solidarity: The Predominance of Non-economic Motives among the Moose of Burkina Faso." In *Structures of Life: The Four Elementary Forms of Human Relations,* edited by Alan Page Fisk, pp. 231–307. New York: Free Press, 1991.

———. "Relativity within Moose [Mossi] Culture: Four Incommensurable Models for Social Relationships." *Ethos,* Berkeley, Calif., 18, 2 (1990). pp. 180–204.

Froment, Alain. *Le peuplement humain de la boucle du Niger.* [Human Population in the Bend of the Niger]. Paris: ORSTOM, 1988. p. 194.

Gaalon, R. de. "Coutume peul" (Liptako). *PCEHS,* sér. A, 8 (1939). pp. 239–260.

———. "Coutume Touareg" (Udalan). *PCEHS,* sér. A, 10 (1939). pp. 217–237.

Gérard, B. "L'enfant et la hache." [The Child and the Ax]. *Cahiers*

ORSTOM (Sciences humaines), Paris: ORSTOM, 21, 2–3 (1985). pp. 237–242. (study of a village near Djibo)

———. " 'Nous, les Kurumba, nous sommes des gens à problèmes: ce que nous avons trouvé, nous ne pouvons pas le laisser'." ["We, the Kurumba, are Problem People: We Cannot Drop What We Found"]. *Cahiers ORSTOM* (Sciences humaines), Paris: ORSTOM, 21, 1 (1985). pp. 35–42.

———. "Paroles d'écriture: la lecture des traces dans des sociétés sans écriture." [Spoken Words in Writing]. *Cahiers des Sciences Humaines,* Paris: ORSTOM, 28, 2 (1992). pp. 161–186.

Goody, John R. (Jack). *Death, Property and the Ancestors: A Study of Mortuary Customs of the LoDagaa of West Africa.* Stanford, Calif.: Stanford University Press, 1962. p. 452.

———. *The Social Organization of the Lo Wiili (Lobi).* 2d ed. London: Oxford University Press for the International African Institute, 1967. 123 p. (First published, 1956.)

Griaule, Marcel. "Le Domfé des Kouroumba." *Journal de la société des africanistes,* Paris, 9, 5 (1941). pp. 7–20.

———. "Notes sur les masques des Kouroumba." *Journal de la société des africanistes,* Paris, 9, 5 (1941). pp. 224–225.

Griffith, Robert. "The Dyula Impact on the Peoples of the West Volta Region." In *Papers on the Manding,* edited by Carlton T. Hodge, pp. 167–181. Bloomington IN: Indiana University Press, 1971.

Gruénais, Marc-Eric. "Aînés, aînées, cadets, cadettes: les relations aînés/cadets chez les Mossi du centre Burkina Faso." [Eldest, Youngest: The Eldest/youngest Relationship Among the Mossi of Central Burkina Faso]. In *Age, pouvoir et société en Afrique Noire,* edited by Marc Abeles and Chantal Collard. Paris: Karthala, 1985.

———. "Du bon usage de l'autochtonie." [How to Make Good Use of Native Status]. *Cahiers ORSTOM* (Sciences humaines), Paris: ORSTOM, 21, 1 (1985). pp. 19–24.

———. "Dynamiques lignageres et pouvoir en pays mossi (Burkina Faso)." *Journal des Africanistes,* Paris, 54, 2 (1984). pp. 53–74.

Guignard, Erik. *Faits et modèles de parenté chez les Touareg Udalen de Haute-Volta.* [Facts and Kinship Models of the Odalen Tuareg of Upper Volta]. Paris: Harmattan, 1988. 259 p.

Guillaud, Dominique. "Sociogenèse et territoire dans l'Aribinda (Burkina Faso)—Le système foncier et ses enjeux." [Sociogenesis and Territory in the Aribinda: The Stakes of Landholding System]. *Cahiers des Sciences Humaines,* Paris: ORSTOM, 26, 3 (1990). pp. 313–326.

Hammond, Peter B. *Yatenga: Technology in the Culture of a West African Kingdom.* New York: Macmillan/Free Press, 1966. 231 p.

———. "Mossi Joking." *Ethnology,* Pittsburgh, 3, 3 (July 1964). pp. 259–267.

———. "Technoeconomic Innovation and Mossi Religious Change." In *African Religious Groups and Beliefs: Papers in Honor of William R. Bascom,* edited by Simon Ottenberg, pp. 225–241. Meerut, India: Archana Publications for Folklore Institute, 1982.

Haselberger, Herta. "Les anciennes constructions dans la falaise de Niansoroni." *Notes Africaines de IFAN,* Dakar, 115 (July 1967). pp. 102–103.

Haumant, Jean-Camille. *Les Lobi et leur coutumes.* Paris: Presses Universitaires de France, 1929. 178 p.

Hébert, Jean. "Esquisse de l'histoire du pays toussian." *BIFAN,* Dakar, 23, 1–2 (Jan. 1961). pp. 309–328. (Reprint under same title: Bobo-Dioulasso: CESAO, 1976. 49 p.)

Héritier-Izard, Françoise. "Univers feminin et destin individuel chez les Samo." In *La notion de personne en Afrique noire,* pp. 241–254. Paris: Editions du CNRS, 1973. (See also Izard, Françoise.)

Holas, Bohumil. *Les Sénoufo (y compris les Minianka).* Paris: Presses Universitaires de France, 1966. 184 p. (Monographies ethnologiques africaines, 5. International African Institute.)

Ilboudo, Pierre. *Croyances et practiques réligieuses traditionnelles des Mossi.* [Beliefs and Traditional Religious Practices of the Mossi]. Paris and Ouagadougou: CNRS and CVRS, 1966. 112 p. (Recherches voltaïques, no. 3.)

Imperato, Pascal James. *African Folk Medicine: Practices and Beliefs of the Bambara and Other Peoples.* Baltimore, Maryland: York Press, 1977. 249 p.

Izard, Françoise. "A propos de l'énoncé des interdit matrimoniaux." *L'homme,* Paris, 8, 3 (Jul.–Sep. 1968). pp. 5–21.

Izard, Françoise; Le Moal, Guy, et al. *Colloque sur les cultures voltaïques* (Sonchamp, 6–8 December 1965). Paris and Ouagadougou: CNRS and CVRS, 1967. 186 p. (Recherches voltaïques, no. 8.)

Izard, Michel. "Des sociétés pour l'Etat." *Cahiers ORSTOM* (Sciences humaines), Paris: ORSTOM, 21, 1 (1985). pp. 25–33.

Jacob, Jean-Pierre. "Interprétation de la maladie chez les Winyé, Gurunsi du Burkina Faso: critique d'une théorie de la contamination." [Interpretation of Illness among the Gurunsi Winyé: A Critique of a Theory of Contamination]. *Genève-Afrique,* Switzerland, 25, 1 (1987). pp. 59–88.

Kawada, Junzo. "La panégyrique royale tambourine mossi: un instrument de control idéologique." [The Mossi Royal Drums Panegyric: Instruments of Ideological Control]. *Revue Française d'Histoire d'Outre Mer,* Paris, 68, 250/253 (1981). pp. 131–153.

Labouret, Henri. *Nouvelles notes sur les tribus du rameau Lobi: Leurs migrations, leur evolution, leurs parlers et ceux de leurs voisins.* [New Notes on the Tribes of the Lobi Wedge: Their Migrations, their

Evolution, their Language, and that of their Neighbors]. Dakar: IFAN, 1958. 296 p. (Mémoires, IFAN, no. 54.)

———. *Les tribus du rameau Lobi.* [The Tribes of the Lobi Branch]. Paris: Institut d'Ethnologie, 1931. 512 p.

———. "La cérémonie du Daguéo chez les Dian de la subdivision de Diébougou." *Annales A.O.F.,* 1916.

———. "Croyances religieuses parmi les populations du Lobi." *Annales A.O.F.,* 1916.

———. "Mariage et polyandrie parmi les Dagari et les Oulée." *Revue d'Ethnographie et des Traditions populaires,* Paris, (1920). pp. 267–283.

———. "Les traveaux du Dr. Jean Cremer sur les Bobo." *Revue d'Ethnographie et des Traditions populaires,* Paris, 4 (1923). pp. 8–22.

Lahuec, Jean-Paul. *Le terroir de Zaongho: les Mossi de Koupéla.* Paris: ORSTOM, 1980. 111 p.

Lallemand, Suzanne. *Une famille mossi.* Paris: CNRS, 1977. 380 p. (Recherches voltaïques, no. 17.)

———. "Entre excision et accouchement: les scarifications des filles Mossi du Burkina." [Between Excision and Childbirth: The Scarification of Mossi Girls in Burkina]. *Archiv für Völkerkunde,* Vienna, 40 (1986). pp. 63–74.

———. "Les noms personnels traditionnels chez les Gouin de Haute-Volta." *Journal de la Société des Africanistes,* Paris, 40, 2 (1970). pp. 103–136.

———. "Pratiques de maternage chez les Kotokoli du Togo et les Mossi de Haute-Volta." *Journal de la Société des Africanistes,* Paris, 51, 1–2 (1981). pp. 43–70.

Le Moal, Guy. *Les Bobo: nature et fonction des masques.* Paris: ORSTOM, 1980. 535 p. (Trav.-Docum. ORSTOM, no. 121.)

———. "Les activités religieuses des jeunes enfants chez les Bobo." [Religious Activities of Young Bobo Children]. *Journal des Africanistes,* Paris, 51, 1–2 (1981). pp. 235–250.

———. "Code sacrificiel et catégories de pensée chez les Bobo de Haute-Volta." [Sacrificial Code and Thought Categories among the Bobo of Upper Volta]. *Systèmes de pensée en Afrique noire: Le sacrifice V,* Paris, 6, 1983. pp. 9–64.

———. "Introduction à une étude du sacrifice chez les Bobo de Haute-Volta." [An Introduction to the Study of Sacrifices among the Bobo of Upper Volta]. *Systèmes de pensée en Afrique noire,* Paris, 5, 1981. pp. 99–125.

———. "Naissance et rites d'identification." [Birth and Identification Rites]. *Archiv für Völkerkunde,* Vienna, 40 (1986). pp. 75–92.

———. "Le sacrifice comme langage." [Sacrifice as Language]. In *Sous le masque de l'animal: essai sur le sacrifice en Afrique Noire,* edited by Michel Cartry, pp. 41–87. Paris: Presses Universitaires de France, 1987.

———. "Les voies de la rupture: veuves et orphelins, face aux tâches du deuil le rituel funéraire bobo." [Making a Break: Widows and Orphans Doing Grief Work in Bobo Funerary Ceremonies]. *Systèmes de pensée en Afrique noire,* Paris, 9, 1 (1986). pp. 11–31; 10, 2 (1987). pp. 3–14.

Lebeuf, J. P. "Notes sur la circoncision chez les Kouroumba du Soudan français." *Journal de la Société des Africanistes,* Paris, 11 (1941). pp. 61–84.

Mangin, Eugène. *Les Mossi, essai sur les us et coutumes du peuple Mossi au Soudan occidental.* Paris: Augustin Challamel, 1921. 116 p., and Ouagadougou: Mission des Pères Blancs, 1960. (A reprint from "Les Mossi, Soudan Occidental." *Anthropos,* Vienna, 9, 1–2 (jan–avril 1914). pp. 98–124, 477–493, 705–736; vols. 10–11 (1915–1916). pp. 187–217.). Appears in English as *The Mossi, Essay on the Manners and Customs of the Mossi People in the Western Sudan,* translated by Ariane Brunel and Elliott P. Skinner. New Haven: Human Relations Area Files, 1959. 141 p.

Mason, Kathryn C. "Co-wife Relationships Can Be Amicable as Well as Conflictual: The Case Study of the Moose of Burkina Faso." *Canadian Journal of African Studies,* Toronto, 22, 3 (1988). pp. 615–624.

Mercier, Paul. *Cartes ethno-démographiques de l'Afrique occidentale.* Dakar: IFAN, 1954. 27 p.

Meyer, Piet. "Divination Among the Lobi of Burkina Faso." In *African Divination Systems: Ways of Knowing,* edited by Philip M. Peek, pp. 91–100. Bloomington IN: Indiana University Press, 1991.

Molex, Jules. "Le Gourma." *Journal Officiel du Dahomey,* 1 August 1898, pp. 8–10.

Ouedraogo, Joseph. "Les kinkirsi." *Notes et documents voltaïques,* Ouagadougou, 1, 2 (Jan.–Mar. 1968). pp. 3–6. (Kinkirsi are agents of female fertility.)

Ouedraogo, Joseph and Prost, André. "La propriété foncière chez les Mossi." *Notes de l'IFAN,* Dakar, 38 (Apr. 1948).

Ovesen, Jan. *Ethnic Identification in the Voltaic Region: Problems of the Perception of "tribe" and "tribal society".* Uppsala, Sweden: University of Uppsala, 1985. p. 31.

———. *The Orchestration of Lobi Funerary Ritual,* Uppsala, Sweden: University of Uppsala African Studies Programme, 1987. 35 p. Appeared also in journal: *Folk,* Copenhagen, 28 (1986), pp. 87–107.

Pageard, Robert. *Le droit privé des Mossi: tradition et évolution.* 2 vols. Paris and Ouagadougou: CNRS and CVRS, 1969. 488 p. (Recherches voltaïques, nos. 10 and 11.)

———. "Contribution a l'étude de l'exogamie dans la société mossi traditionnelle." [Contribution to the Study of Exogamy in Traditional

Mossi Society]. *Journal de la Société des Africanistes,* Paris, 36, 1 (1966). pp. 109–140.

Paternot, Marcel. *Lumière sur la Volta: chez les Dagari.* Lyon: Editions de la plus grande France; Paris: Association des missionnaires d'Afrique, 1946 (4th ed. 1953). 254 p.

Pegard, Odette P. (Soeur Jean Bernard). *Les Bissas du cercle de Garango à travers deux colonisations.* Paris: Mémoire de l'école pratique des hautes études, 6ème section, 1963. 314 p.

———. *Les Bisa du cercle de Garango.* Paris and Ouagadougou: CNRS and CVRS, 1966. 252 p. (Recherches voltaïques, no. 2.)

———. "Structures et relations sociale en pays Bisa." *Cahiers d'Etudes Africaines,* Paris, 5, 2 (1965). pp. 161–247.

Père, Madeleine. *Les Lobis: tradition et changement, Burkina Faso.* [The Lobi: Tradition and Change in Burkina Faso]. Laval, France: Siloe, 1988. 2 vols.

———. "Organisation de la société Pwo." Pt. 1. *Notes et documents voltaïques,* Ouagadougou, 14, 1 (Jan.–Mar. 1983). pp. 46–60.

Pool, D. Ian, and Coulibaly, Sidiki P., eds. *Demographic Transition and Cultural Continuity in the Sahel: Aspects of the Social Demography of Upper Volta,* Ithaca, New York: Cornell University International Population Program, 1977. 287 p.

Prost, André. "Note sur les Boussance." *BIFAN,* Dakar, 7, 1–4 (1945). pp. 47–53.

———. "Notes sur l'origine des Mossi." *BIFAN,* Dakar, 15, 3, sér. B (July 1953). pp. 1933–1938.

———. "Le pana." *BIFAN,* Dakar, 31, 3, sér. B (July 1969). pp. 886–911.

Quéant, Thierry and De Rouville, Cécile. *Etudes humaines sur la région du Gondo-Sourou.* Ouagadougou: CVRS, 1969. 295 p.

Randau, Robert S. (Robert Arnaud). "Les Yarcé." *Revue anthropologique,* Paris, 64 (1934). pp. 324–325.

Riesman, Paul. *First Find Your Child a Good Mother: The Construction of Self in Two African Communities,* New Brunswick, New Jersey: Rutgers University Press, 1992. 241 p.

———. *Société et liberté chez les Peul djelgôbé de Haute-Volta.* [Society and Freedom among the Djelgobe Fulani of Upper Volta]. Paris: Mouton and Ecole Pratique des Hautes Etudes, 1974. 261 p. Translated by Martha Fuller and subsequently published in English as *Freedom in Fulani Social Life.* Chicago: University of Chicago Press, 1977. 297 p.

———. "The Art of Life in a West African Community: Formality and Spontaneity in Fulani Interpersonal Relationships." *Journal of African Studies,* USA, 2 (Spring 1975). pp. 39–63.

———. "Love Fulani Style." *Society,* New Brunswick, New Jersey, 10, 2 (1973). pp. 27–31, 34–35.

Rohatynskyj, Marta. "Women's Virtue and the Structure of the Mossi *Zaka*." *Canadian Journal of African Affairs*, Toronto, 22, 3 (1988). pp. 528–551.

Rouch, Jean, et al. "Restes anciens et gravures rupestres d'Arbinda." [Ancient Remains and Rupestrian Engravings in Aribinda]. *Etudes voltaïques*, 2, 1963. pp. 61–70.

Rouville, Cécile de. *Organisation sociale des Lobi: une société bi-linéaire du Burkina Faso et Côte d'Ivoire*. [Social Organization Among the Lobi: A Bilinear Society in Burkina Faso and Côte d'Ivoire]. Paris: Harmattan, 1987. 259 p.

———. "Les cérémonies d'initiation du Bur chez les Lobi de la région d'Iridiaka (Burkina Faso)." *Journal des Africanistes*, Paris, 54, 2 (1984). pp. 75–98.

Samtouma, Issaka. *La métallurgie ancienne du fer dans la region de Koumbri (Yatenga, Burkina Faso)*, Stuttgart: F. Steiner, 1990. 176 p.

Sanogo, M. and Pageard, Robert. "Notes sur les coutumes des Marka de Lanfiéra (cercle de Tougan, Haute-Volta)." *Journal de la Société des Africanistes*, Paris, 32, 4 (1964). pp. 306–310.

Saul, Mahir. "Corporate Authority, Exchange and Personal Opposition in Bobo Marriages." *American Ethnologist*, Washington DC, 16, 1 (1989). pp. 57–74.

Savonnet, Georges. "Les Birifors de Dièpla et sa région, insulaire du rameau Lobi (Haute-Volta)." *Atlas des structures agraires au sud du Sahara, 12*. Paris: ORSTOM; The Hague, New York: Mouton, 1976. 170 p.

———. "Habitations souterraines bobo ou anciens puits de mines en pays wile?" *BIFAN*, Dakar, 36 (April 1975). pp. 227–245.

———. "Interrogatoire d'une défunte chez les Lobi de Pora (Haute-Volta)." *Notes Africaines IFAN*, Dakar, (Oct. 1965). pp. 119–124.

———. "Quelques notes sur les Gan et sur le rituel d'intronisation de leur chef." *Etudes voltaïques*, Ouagadougou, 4 (1963). pp. 124–132.

———. "Quelques notes sur l'histoire des Dyan (cercles de Diébougou et de Léo, Haute-Volta)." *BIFAN*, Dakar, 37, 3 (July 1975). pp. 619–645.

Schildkrout, Enid. *Children of the Zongo: The Transformation of Ethnic Identities in Ghana*. New York: Cambridge University Press, 1978. 303 p. (A study of the Mossi in the strangers' quarter of Kumasi, Ghana; comparable to Bonnassieux's study of the Mossi in Abidjan.)

Schweeger-Hefel, Annemarie. *Kinkirsi, Boghoba, Saba: das Weltbild der Nyonyosi in Burkina Faso*. [Kinkirsi, Boghoba, Saba: The Conception of the World of the Nyonyosi of Burkina Faso]. Vienna: A. Schendl, 1986. 436 p. (in German)

———. *Masken un Mythen, Sozialstrukturen der Nyonyosi und Silomse in Obervolta*. [Masks and Myths: Social Structure of the Nyonyosi and Silomse of Upper Volta]. Vienna: A. Schendl, 1980. 480 p. (in German)

————. "Approaches historiques des Nyonyosi en Haute-Volta." *Zeitschrift für Ethnologie,* Braunschweig, Germany, 108, 1 (1983). pp. 79–94.

————. "Dessins d'enfants Kurumba de Mengao." [Drawings of Kurumba Children of Mengao]. *Journal des Africanistes,* Paris, 51, 1–2 (1981). pp. 251–264.

————. "Les insignes royaux des Kouroumba." [The Royal Insignia of the Kurumba]. *Journal des Africanistes,* Paris, 32, 2 (1962) pp. 275–323.

Skinner, Elliott Percival. "The Effect of Co-residence of Sister's Sons on African Corporate Patrilineal Descent Groups." *Cahiers d'Etudes Africaines,* Paris, 4 (1964). pp. 464–478.

————. "The Mossi *pogsioure.*" *Man,* London, 60 (Feb. 1960). pp. 20–73.

————. "Processus de l'incorporation politique dans les sociétés africaines traditionnelles: le cas des Mossi." *Notes et documents voltaïques,* Ouagadougou, 1, 4 (July–Sept. 1968). pp. 29–47.

Some, B. *Famille dagara et développement destructuration et restructuration d'une société traditionnelle africaine (sud-ouest Burkina et nord-ouest Ghana).* Paris: Institut Catholique de Paris, 1986.

Some, Bozi Bernard. "Organisation politico-sociale traditionnelle des Dagara." *Notes et documents voltaïques,* Ouagadougou, 2, 2 (Jan.–March 1969). pp. 16–41.

————. "La parente chez les Dagari: appellations et attitudes." *Notes et documents voltaïques,* Ouagadougou, 1, 3 (April–June 1968). pp. 11–20.

Somé, Malidoma Patrice. *Of Water and the Spirit: Ritual, Magic, and Initiation in the Life of an African Shaman,* New York: Putnam, 1994. 311 p.

Some, Penou-Achille. *Significant en société: le cas du Dagara du Burkina Faso.* Paris: Harmattan, 1992. 271 p.

Staude, Wilhelm. "La structure de cheffrerie chez les Kouroumba de Louroum." *Anthropos,* Fribourg, vol. 57, nos. 3–6 (1962). pp. 757–778.

Swanson, Richard Alan. *Gourmantche Ethnoanthropology: A Theory of Human Being.* Lanham, Maryland: University Press of America, 1984. 464 p.

Tauxier, Louis. *Moeurs et histoire des Peuls.* [Mores and History of the Fulani]. Paris: Payot, 1937. 422 p.

————. *Le noir du Soudan: pays Mossi et Gourounsi.* Paris: E. Larose, 1912. 796 p.

————. *Le noir du Yatenga. Mossis, Nioniossés, Samos, Yarsés, Silmi-*

Mossis, Peuls. Etudes soudanaises. Paris: E. Larose, 1917. 790 p. Reprint of folklore section of this study is titled *Contes du Burkina* [Folktales of Burkina], edited by Louis Tauxier and Doris Bonnet. Paris: Conseil International de la Langue Français, 1985. 135 p.

————. *Nouvelles notes sur le Mossi et le Gourounsi.* [New Notes on the Mossi and the Gurunsi]. Paris: E. Larose, 1924. 208 p.

————. "Les Dorhosié et Dorhosié-Fing du cercle de Bobo Dioulasso (Soudan Français)." *Journal de la Société des Africanistes,* Paris, 1, 1 (1931). pp. 61–110.

————. "Les Gouin et les Tourouka, résidence de Banfora, cercle de Bobo Dioulasso." *Journal de la Société des Africanistes,* Paris, 3 (1933). pp. 79–128.

Tiendrébéogo, Yamba (Naba Agba)(Larhallé-Naba). *Contes du Larhallé suivis d'un recueil de proverbes et de devises du pays mossi.* Ouagadougou: chez le Larhallé Naba, 1963. 215 p.

————. *Les contes du Larhallé.* Ouagadougou: chez Larhallé, 1965. 212 p.

Tiendrébéogo, Yamba. *Contes de la gazelle; Contes et dictons du pays mossi.* Paris: L'Ecole, 1980. 62 p.

Tiendrébéogo, Yamba and Arozarena, Pierre. *O Mogho! Terre d'Afrique!: contes, fables et anecdotes du pays mossi.* Ouagadougou: Presses africaines, 1976. 141 p.

Zoanga, Jean Bigtarma. "The Traditional Power of Mossi *Nanamse* of Upper Volta." In *The Nomadic Alternative,* edited by W. Weissleder, pp. 215–246. The Hague: Mouton, 1978.

Zwernemann, Jürgen. "Shall we use the word 'Gurunsi'?" *Africa,* 28, 2 (April 1958). pp. 123–125.

Education

"Village Teachers for Village Schools." *The Economist,* Great Britain, 334. 7906 (Mar. 18, 1995), p. 43.

Bindlish, Vishva; Evenson, Robert and Gbetibouo, Mathurin. *Evaluation of T & V-based Extension in Burkina Faso* (training and visit). Washington DC: World Bank, 1993. 137 p.

Burkina Faso. Ministère d'Education. *Evaluation des avantages pedagogiques et économiques de l'introduction du travail productif dans les écoles primaires de Haute-Volta.* Ouagadougou, 1984.

Christol, J. "Les jeunes ruraux en dehors de l'école." [Young Rural Children Outside School]. *Carnets Enfance,* Paris, 8 (June 1968). pp. 149–160.

Dave, R. H.; D. A. Perera and A. Ouane, eds. *Stratégies d'apprentissage pour la postalphabetisation et l'education continue au Mali, au Niger, au Senegal et en Haute-Volta,* Hamburg: UNESCO Institute for

Education, 1984. 205 p. A project of UNESCO Institute for Education and German Commission for UNESCO.

Forgo, Etienne. *Education en Haute-Volta: analyse de secteur non formel,* Québec: Faculté des sciences de l'education, University Laval, 1982. 40 p.

Haddad, Wadi D. with the assistance of Demsky, Terri. *The Dynamics of Education Policymaking: Case Studies of Burkina Faso, Jordan, Peru, and Thailand,* Washington, DC: World Bank, 1994. 269 p. (pp. 178–246 concern Burkina Faso).

Lallez, Raymond. *L'innovation en Haute-Volta: éducation rurale et enseignement primaire.* [Innovation in Upper Volta: Rural Education and Primary Instruction]. Paris: UNESCO, 1976. 107 p.

Maclure, R. "Misplaced Assumptions of Decentralization and Participation in Rural Communities—Primary-School Reform in Burkina Faso." *Comparative Education,* 30, 3 (1994). pp. 239–254.

Porgo, Judicael Etienne. *Evaluation de l'influence du programme de formation des jeunes agriculteurs sur le connaissance et les pratiques des jeunes ruraux Voltaïques,* Quebec: Université Laval, 1984.

Sasnett, Martena and Sepmeyer, Inez. "Upper Volta." In *Educational Systems of Africa.* Berkeley, CA: University of California Press, 1967. pp. 738–746.

Winterbottom, Robert T. and Linehan, Peter E. "The Dinderosso Forestry School: Case Study of Extension Forestry Training in Burkina Faso." *Rural Africana,* 23–24 (Fall 1985–Winter 1986). pp. 107–114.

Religion

"L'église en Haute-Volta." [The Church in Upper Volta]. *Vivante Afrique,* Namur, Belgium, (Dec. 1962). pp. 1–60.

Baudu, Paul. *Vieil empire, jeune église.* [Old Empire, New Church]. Paris: Editions La Savane, 1956. 283 p. The story of the White Fathers in Upper Volta.

Benoist, Joseph-Roger. "Les missionaires catholiques du Soudan Français et de la Haute Volta—entrepreneurs et formateurs d'artisans." [The Catholic Missionaries of French Sudan and Upper Volta: Entrepreneurs and Mentors of Artisans]. In *Entreprises et entrepreneurs en Afrique,* pp. 249–263. Paris: Harmattan, 1983.

Benoist, Roger de. *Docteur Lumière: quarante ans au service de l'homme en Haute Volta.* [Dr. Lumière: Forty Years of Service to Mankind in Upper Volta]. Paris: Editions S.O.S., 1975. 236 p.

Ciss, Issa. "Les Medersas au Burkina: l'aide Arabe et la croissance d'un système d'enseignement Arabo-Islamique." [The Medersas of Burkina Faso: Arab Aid and the Growth of a System of Arabo-Islamic

Teaching]. *Islam et Sociétés au Sud du Sahara,* France, 4 (1990). pp. 51–272.

Clarke, Peter B. *West Africa and Islam: A History of Religious Development from the 8th to the 20th Century.* London: Edward Arnold, 1982. 275 p.

Dacher, Michele. "De l'origine et de la nature des tinni goin." [On the Origins and Nature of the Tinni Goin]. *Systèmes de Pensée en Afrique Noire,* Paris, 8 (1985), pp. 69–109.

Deniel, Raymond. *Croyances religieuses et vie quotidienne: islam et christianisme à Ouagadougou.* [Religious Beliefs and Daily Life: Islam and Christianity in Ouagadougou]. Paris: CNRS; Ouagadougou: CVRS, 1970. 360 p. (Recherches voltaïques, 14.)

Deniel, Raymond and Audouin, Jean. *L'Islam en Haute Volta à l'époque coloniale.* [Islam in Upper Volta during the Colonial Era]. Paris: Harmattan, 1978. 129 p.

Diallo, Hamidou. "Introduction à l'étude de l'histoire de l'Islam dans l'ouest du Burkina Faso: des débuts à la fin du l9eme siècle." [Introduction to the Study of the History of Islam in Western Burkina Faso: From the Beginnings to the End of the 19th Century]. *Islam et sociétés au Sud du Sahara,* Paris, 4 (1990). pp. 33–45.

———. "Islam et colonisation au Yatenga (1897–1958)." [Islam and the Colonization of Yatenga, 1897–1950]. *Le Mois en Afrique,* Paris, 21, 237/238 (Oct.–Nov. 1985). pp. 33–42.

Dieterlen, Germaine. *Essai sur la religion Bambara,* 2d ed., Brussels: University of Brussels, 1988. 264 p.

Fidaali, Kabire. *Le pouvoir du Bangré: enquête initiatique à Ouagadougou.* [The Power of the Bangré: Inquiry into Initiation in Ouagadougou]. Paris: Presses de la Renaissance, 1987. 220 p.

Froelich, Jean Claude. *Animismes, les religions paiennes de l'Afrique de l'ouest,* Paris: Editions de l'Orante, 1964. 225 p.

Hiskett, Mervyn. *The Development of Islam in West Africa,* London and New York: Longman, 1984. 353 p. (Longman Studies in African History)

Izard, Michel. "Transgression, Transversality, Wandering." In *Between Belief and Transgression,* edited by Michel Izard and Pierre Smith, pp. 229–244. Chicago: University of Chicago Press, 1982.

Kerharo, Joseph and Bouquet, A. *Sorciers, féticheurs et guérisseurs de la Côte d'Ivoire-Haute Volta.* [Sorcerers, Fetishists and Healers of Côte d'Ivoire and Upper Volta]. Paris: Vigot frères, 1950. 144 p.

Kouanda, Assimi. "Les conflits au sein de la communauté musulmane du Burkina: 1962–1986." [Conflict within the Muslim Community of Burkina Faso, 1962–86]. *Islam et Sociétés au Sud du Sahara,* France, 3 (1989). pp. 7 –26.

———. "L'état de la recherche sur l'Islam au Burkina." [The State of

Research on Islam in Burkina Faso]. *Islam et Sociétés au Sud du Sahara,* France, 2 (1988). pp. 94–105.

————. "La religion musulmane: facteur d'intégration ou d'identification ethnique. Le cas des yarsé du Burkina Faso." [The Muslim Religion: Factor for Integration or Ethnic Identification. The case of the Yarsé of Burkina Faso]. In *Les ethnies ont une histoire,* edited by J. P. Chrétien and G. Prunier, pp. 125–134. Paris: Karthala, 1989.

Mendonsa, Eugene L. "The Position of Women in the Sisala Divination Cult." In *The New Religions of Africa,* edited by Benetta Jules-Rosette, pp. 57–66. Norwood, New Jersey: Ablex Publishing, 1979.

Otayek, René. "La crise de la communauté musulmane de Haute-Volta: L'Islam voltaïque entre reformisme et tradition, autonomie et subordination." [Crisis in the Upper Volta Muslim Community: Islam Between Reform and Tradition, Autonomy and Subordination]. *Cahiers d'Etudes Africaines,* Paris, 24, 3 (1984). pp. 299–320.

Prost, André. *Les Pères Blancs en A.O.F. (1878–1940).* Ouagadougou: Pères Blancs, 1940. 179 p.

Skinner, Elliott Percival. "Christianity and Islam among the Mossi." *American Anthropologist,* Monasha, Wisconsin, 60, 6 (Dec. 1958). pp. 1102–1119.

————. "The Diffusion of Islam in an African Society." *Annals of the New York Academy of Science,* 96, 2 (Jan. 1962). pp. 659–669.

————. "Islam in Mossi Society." In *Islam in Tropical Africa,* edited by I. M. Lewis, pp. 350–373. London: Oxford University Press, 1966.

Sociology and Urbanization

Augustin, Jean Pierre. *Saponé: village mossi entre tradition et modernité,* Talence: Université Bordeaux 3, 1994. 92 p.

Baulier, Françoise. "Femmes et groupements villageois au Burkina Faso." [Women and Village Groups in Burkina Faso]. *Communautés,* Paris, 79 (Jan.–Mar. 1987). pp. 48–58.

Bohmer, Carol. "Community Values, Domestic Tranquility, and Customary Law in Upper Volta." *Journal of Modern African Studies,* Cambridge UK, 16, 2 (June 1978). pp. 295–310.

————. "Modernization, Divorce and the Status of Women: le Tribunal Coutumier in Bobo Dioulasso." *African Studies Review,* Waltham, Massachusetts, 23, 2 (Sept. 1980). pp. 81–90.

Bourgeot, A. "From Identity to Ethnicity—The Case of the Tuareg People (Some Populations in Algeria, Libya, Niger, Mali and Burkina Faso)." *Pensée,* 296 (1993). pp. 49–58. (article is in French)

Boye, Abd-el-Kader. *Synthese des études nationales et observations complémentaires sur le condition juridique et sociale de la femme dans quatre pays du sahel: Burkina Faso, Mali, Niger, Senegal,*

Dakar: CILSS, 1990. Contains 116 page chapter on the condition of women in Burkina Faso.

Brazier, Chris. "An African Village" (Sabtenga). *New Internationalist,* 268 (June 1995). pp. 1, 7–30.

Bricker, Gary and Traoré, Soumana. "Transitional Urbanization in Upper Volta: The Case of Ouagadougou, a Savannah Capital." In *Urban Systems in Africa,* edited by Robert A. Obudho and Salah El-Shaikh, pp. 177–195. New York: Praeger, 1979.

Capron, Jean and Kohler, Jean Marie. "De quelques caractéristiques de la practique matrimoniale mossi contemporaine." [On Several Characteristics of Marriage Practice among Contemporary Mossi]. In *Marriage, Fertility, and Parenthood in West Africa,* edited by C. Oppong, et al, pp. 187–223. Canberra: Australian National University, 1978.

Coulibaly, Augustin-Soudé. *Les dieux délinquants,* Bobo-Dioulasso: Editions Coulibaly Fréres, 1975. 227 p.

Etude sur la délinquance juvenile en Haute-Volta. [A Study on Juvenile Delinquency in Upper Volta]. Ouagadougou: Société Africaine d'Etudes et de Développement, 1977. 51 p.

Frenkel, R. L. *Ouagadougou Urban Masterplan,* Nijmegen, Netherlands: Haskoning, 1988. 18 p.

Ganne, B. "Le foncier et l'urbain—le cas d'une ville moyenne sahélienne: Ouahigouya." [Land Tenure and the Urban Denominator; the Case of a Medium-sized Sahelian Town, Ouahigouya]. In *Espaces disputés en Afrique noire,* edited by B. Crousse, Emile Le Bris, Etienne Le Roy, pp. 145–162. Paris: Karthala, 1986.

Gregory, Joel W. "Urbanization and Development Planning in Upper Volta: The Education Variable?" In *Urbanization, National Development and Regional Planning in Africa,* edited by Robert A. Obudho and Salah El-Shaikh, pp. 130–142. New York: Praeger, 1974.

Héritier-Izard, Françoise and Izard, Michel. *Les Mossi du Yatenga. Etude de la vie économique et sociale.* Bordeaux: Institut des Science Humaines Appliquées de l'Université de Bordeaux, 1959. 114 p.

Kaboré, Oger. "Paroles de femmes." *Journal des Africanistes,* Paris, 57, 1–2 (1987). pp. 117–131.

Launay, Robert. *Traders Without Trade: Responses to Change in Two Dyula Communities.* New York: Cambridge University Press, 1983. 188 p. (Cambridge Studies in Social Anthropology no.42.)

Lesselingue P. "Adolescents du Burkina Faso." [Adolescents of Burkina Faso]. *Cahiers ORSTOM* (Sciences humaines), Paris: ORSTOM, 21, 2–3 (1985). pp. 347–353.

McGinn, T. "Family Planning in Burkina Faso: Results of a Survey." *Studies in Family Planning,* New York, 20, 6 (1989). pp. 325–331.

Murphy, J. and Sprey, L. *The Volta Valley Authority: Socio-Economic Evaluation of a Resettlement Project in Upper Volta.* West Lafayette,

Indiana: Purdue University Department of Agricultural Economics, 1980.

Nicolas, Guy. "Communautés Islamiques et collectivité nationale dans trois états d'Afrique occidentale." [Islamic Communities and the National Community in Three West African States]. *Revue française d'histoire d'outre-mer,* France, 68, 1–4 (1981). pp. 156–194. (Examines Nigeria, Niger, Burkina Faso.)

Nikiéma, Paul. "L'enfant victime ou auteur d'infractions pénales devant la justice voltaïque." *Revue juridique et politique,* 31, 2 (Apr.–June 1977). pp. 297–316.

Père, Madeleine. "Animation féminine dans une société villageoise traditionelle; le centre de Gaoua en pays Lobi, Haute Volta." Paris: Centre de recherches coopératives, école pratique des hautes études, 1973. 264 p.

Retel-Laurentin, Anne. "Evasions féminines dans la Volta noire." [Women's absconding in the Black Volta]. *Cahiers d'Etudes Africaines,* Paris, 19, 1–4 (1979). pp. 253–298.

Savonnet, Georges. "Inégalités de développement et organisation sociale (exemples empruntés au sud-ouest de la Haute Volta." *Cahiers ORSTOM* (Sciences humaines), Paris: ORSTOM, 13, 1 (1976). pp. 23–40.

Sawadogo, Mamadou. "Le mariage en Haute Volta: option entre monogamie et polygamie." [Marriage in Upper Volta: Option Between Monogamy and Polygamy]. *Penant,* Paris, 95, 786/87 (Jan.–June 1985). pp. 53–57.

Skinner, Elliott Percival. *African Urban Life: The Transformation of Ouagadougou.* Princeton, NJ: Princeton University Press, 1974. 489 p.

———. "Intergenerational Conflict among the Mossi." In *Peoples and Cultures of Africa,* edited by Elliott P. Skinner, pp. 326–334. Garden City, New York: Doubleday/Natural History Press, 1973.

Toe, Fidele and Leplaideur, Marie-Agnes. "Burkina's Dancing Farmers Maintain 'Society's Memory'." *Ceres,* Rome, 26, 6 (Nov.–Dec. 1994). pp. 10–11.

Traore, J. M. "Aménagement urbain et pratiques fonciers coutumières en Haute Volta. [Urban Development and Customary Land Practices in Upper Volta]. In *Espaces disputés en Afrique noire,* edited by B. Crousse, Emile Le Bris, Etienne Le Roy, pp. 33–40. Paris; Karthala, 1986.

Wettere-Verhasselt, Yola Van. "Bobo-Dioulasso: le développement d'une ville d'Afrique occidentale." [Bobo Dioulasso: The Development of a West African Town]. *Les Cahiers d'Outre-Mer,* Bordeaux, 22, 85 (Jan.–Mar. 1969). pp. 88–94.

Yoon, Soon-Young. "Le barrage des femmes: les femmes mossi du Burkina Faso." [The Women's Barrage: Mossi Women in Burkina

Faso]. *Revue Tiers Monde,* Paris, 26, 102 (Apr.–June 1985). pp. 443–449.

Zoungrana, Celile Marie. *Etudes des mariages et divorces dans la ville de Ouagadougou 1980–83.* [Studies on Marriage and Divorce in the Town of Ouagadougou, 1980–83]. Ouagadougou: Institut Nationale de la Statistique et de la Démographie, 1986. 10 p.

Science

Geography: Demography

Benoit, Daniel. "Une étude démographique à partir des registres parois-saux en pays Gourounsi (Haute Volta)." *Cahiers ORSTOM* (Sciences humaines), Paris, 13, 3 (1976). pp. 297–310.

Courel, André and Pool, D. Ian. "Upper Volta." In *Population Growth and Socioeconomic Change in West Africa,* edited by John C. Cald-well, et al, pp. 736–754. New York: Columbia University Press, 1975.

Courel, M. F.; A. Courel and R. Lardinois. "La population de la Haute-Volta au recensement de décembre 1975." [The Population of Upper Volta at the December 1975 General Census]. *Cahiers d'outre-mer,* Bordeaux, 32, 125 (1979). pp. 39–65.

Fieloux, Michele. *Les sentiers de la nuit: les migrations rurales lobi de la Haute-Volta vers la Côte d'Ivoire,* Paris: ORSTOM, 1980. 199 p.

Finnegan, Gregory A. "Employment Opportunity and Migration Among Mossi of Upper Volta." In *Research in Economic Anthropology,* vol. 3, edited by George Dalton, pp. 291–322. Greenwich, Conn: JAI Press, 1980.

Gervais, Raymond. "Verités et mensonges: les statistiques coloniales de population." *Canadian Journal of African Studies,* Ottawa, 17, 1 (1983). pp. 101–103.

Livenais, P. "Déclin de la mortalité dans l'enfance et stabilité de la fe-condité dans une zone rurale mossi (Haute Volta): essai d'interpréta-tion d'un régime démographique." [Decline in Childhood Mortality and Stability of Fertility in a Mossi Rural Zone: Interpretation of a Population Pattern]. *Cahiers ORSTOM* (Sciences humaines), Paris: ORSTOM, 20, 2 (1984). pp. 273–282.

Sankara, Michel and Vaugelade, Jacques. "Evolution de la mortalité au Burkina Faso." [Changes in the mortality levels in Burkina Faso]. *Es-pace, populations, sociétés,* France, 3 (1985). pp. 619–620.

Sirven, Pierre. "Démographies et villes au Burkina Faso." [Demography of Burkina Faso Cities]. *Les Cahiers d'Outre-Mer,* Bordeaux, 40, 159 (1987). pp. 265–283.

Geography: Atlases, Maps

Atlas des villages de Haute-Volta. [Atlas of Upper Volta's Villages]. Ouagadougou: Institut National de la Statistique et de la Démographie, Ministère du Plan et de la Coopération, 1982. [n.p.]

Burkina Faso. *Carte Touristique et Routière* [Tourist and Road Map]. Ouagadougou: Institut Géographique du Burkina, 1985.

Carte des groupes ethniques de Haute Volta. Paris: Editions Ligel, 1964.

Centre voltaïque de la recherche scientifique. *Atlas de Haute-Volta,* Ouagadougou: CVRS, 1968.

Grandidier, Guillaume, ed. *Atlas des colonies françaises, protectorats et territoires sous mandat de la France.* Paris: Société d'Editions Géographiques, Maritimes et Coloniales, 1934. 236 p.

Great Britain. Naval Intelligence Division. *French West Africa.* 2 vols. London: HMSO, 1943. 436 p., 596 p. (Geographical Handbook Series, vol. 1, The Federation; vol. 2, The Colonies.)

Institut Français d'Afrique Noire (IFAN). *International Atlas of West Africa. Atlas international de l'ouest africain.* Dakar, 1965- .

Péron, Yves and Zalacain, Victoire, eds. *Atlas de la Haute-Volta.* Paris: Editions Jeune Afrique, 1975. 48 p.

Savonnet, Georges. *Atlas de Haute-Volta: Carte des densités de population.* Ouagadougou: CVRS, 1974.

Urvoy, Yves. *Petit atlas ethno-démographique du Soudan entre Sénégal et Tchad.* Paris: Larose, 1942. 48 p. (Mémoires IFAN, no. 5.)

Geography and Geology

Affaton, Pascal. *Etude géologique et structurale du nord-ouest Dahomey, du nord Togo et du sud-est Haute-Volta.* [Geological Study of Northwest Dahomey, North Togo and Southeast Upper Volta]. Marseille: Laboratoire des Sciences de la Terre, 1975. 203 p.

Bellot-Couderc, Béatrice and Bellot, Jean-Marc. "Pour un aménagement du cours moyen de la Volta Noire et de la vallée du Sourou." *Les Cahiers d'Outre-Mer,* Talence, France, 31, 123 (July–Sep. 1978). pp. 271–286.

Boulet, René. *Toposéquences de sols tropicaux en Haute-Volta: équilibre et déséquilibre bioclimatique.* [Toposequences of Tropical Soils in Upper Volta: Equilibrium and Bioclimatic Disequilibrium]. Paris: ORSTOM, 1978. 272 p.

Brown, E. T., et al. "The Development of Iron Crust Lateritic Systems in Burkina-Faso, West Africa, Examined with in-Situ-Produced Cosmogenic Nuclides." *Earth and Planetary Science Letters,* 124, 1–4 (1994). pp. 19–33.

Claude, Jacques; Michel Grouzis and Pierre Milleville, eds. *Un espace sahelien: la mare d'Oursi, Burkina Faso,* Paris: ORSTOM, 1991. 241 p.

Devillers, Carole E. "Oursi, Magnet in the Desert." *National Geographic,* Washington DC, 157, 4 (April 1980). pp. 512–525.

Diluca, C. *Etat des connaissances hydrogéologiques en Haute Volta.* [State of Hydrological Knowledge in Upper Volta]. Ouagadougou: Comité Interafricaine d'Etudes Hydrauliques, 1979. p. 75.

Dupuy, Gerard. "Ouagadougou: An African Capital." *Entente Africaine,* Paris, 1 (15 July 1969). pp. 32–37.

Gilg, J.-P. "Photographie aérienne et cartographie des structures agraires." *Cahiers ORSTOM* (Sciences humaines), Paris: ORSTOM, 9, 2 (1972). pp. 185–190.

Guitat, Raymond. "Carte et répertoire des sites néolithiques du Mali et de la Haute Volta." [Map and Inventory of Neolithic Sites in Mali and Upper Volta]. *Bulletin de l'IFAN,* Dakar, 34, 4 (1972). pp. 896–925.

Hacquard, Monseigneur. "Promenade au Mossi, relation de voyage." *Bulletin de la Société de Géographie d'Alger et de l'Afrique du nord,* Algiers, 6 (1901). pp. 76–110.

Hulugalle, N. R., et al. "Effect of Rock Bunds and Tied Ridges on Soil Water Content and Soil Properties in the Sudan Savannah of Burkina Faso." *Tropical Agriculture,* 67, 2 (June 1990). pp. 149–153.

Hulugalle, N. R. and Rodriguez, M. S. "Soil Physical Properties of Tied Ridges in the Sudan Savannah of Burkina Faso." *Experimental Agriculture,* 24, 3 (July 1988). pp. 375–391.

Huot, Daniel, et al. "Gold in Birrimian Greenstone Belts of Burkina Faso." *Economic Geology,* 82, 8 (1987). pp. 2033–2044.

Jenny, J. H. "Sols et problèmes de fertilité en Haute Volta." [Problems of Soil Fertility in Upper Volta]. *Agronomie Tropicale,* Paris, (Feb. 1965). pp. 220–247.

Kabore, J. "Prospection géochimique dans le centre et nord-centre du Burkina Faso." [Geo-chemical Prospecting in Central and North-central Burkina Faso]. *Journal of Geochemical Exploration,* New York, 32, 1–3 (1989). pp. 429–435.

Lahuec, J.-P. "Le parc d'un village mossi (Zaongho) du traditionnel au moderne." *Cahiers ORSTOM* (Sciences humaines), Paris: ORSTOM, 17, 3–4 (1980). pp. 151–154.

Marc, Lucien A. *Le Pays Mossi.* Paris: Emile Larose, 1909. 189 p.

Marcelin, Jean. *Le potentiel minier de la république de Haute-Volta.* [Mineral Potential of the Republic of Upper Volta]. Ouagadougou: Ministère du Commerce, du Développement Industriel et des Mines, 1975. 241 p.

Marchal, Jean-Yves. *Yatenga, nord Haute-Volta: La dynamique d'un espace rural soudano-sahélien.* [Upper Volta's Northern Yatenga, the Dynamics of a Sudano-Sahelian Region]. Paris: ORSTOM, 1983. 2 vols. 879 p. (Trav.-Docum. ORSTOM, no. 167.)

———. "La cartographie et ses utilisateurs en pays africains: à propos de la Haute Volta." *Cahiers ORSTOM* (Sciences humaines), Paris: ORSTOM, 16, 3 (1979). pp. 261–272.

———. "Les documents cartographiques en Haute Volta: approche historique et essai d'analyse." *Notes et documents voltaïques,* Ouagadougou, 12, 1–4 (Oct. 1978–1979). pp. 112–132.

———. "Un périmètre agricole en Haute Volta: Guiedougou, vallée du Sourou." [Reflections on an Agricultural Area of the Upper Volta: Guiedougou, Sourou Valley]. *Cahiers ORSTOM* (Sciences humaines), Paris: ORSTOM, 13, 1 (1976). pp. 57–73.

———. "Vestiges d'occupation ancienne au Yatenga (Haute Volta): une reconnaissance du pays Kibga." *Cahiers ORSTOM* (Sciences humaines), Paris: ORSTOM, 15, 4 (1978). pp. 449–484.

Moniod, F.; B. Pouyaud and P. Sechet. *Le bassin du fleuve Volta.* [The Volta River Basin]. Paris: ORSTOM, 1977. 513 p.

Nikiéma, S. et al. "Transcurrent Eburnean Tectonics in West Africa— Example of the Djibo Area (Burkina Faso)." *Comptes rendus de l'académie des sciences série II—mecanique physique chimie sciences de la terre et de l'univers,* 316, 5 (1993). pp. 661–668.

Ouattara, F. N. "Evaluation des caractéristiques climatiques sur le 13th parallèle nord en Haute-Volta." *Météorologie,* 6, 28 (1981). pp. 111–122.

Pallier, Ginette. *Géographie générale de la Haute Volta.* Limoges, France: Université de Limoges and CNRS, 1978 (2d ed. 1982). 241 p.

Pouyaud, B. *Contribution à l'évaluation de l'évaporation de nappes d'eau libre en climat tropical sec.* [Contribution to the Assessment of Evaporation of Open Expanses of Water in a Dry Tropical Climate]. Paris: ORSTOM, 1986. 254 p.

Rémy, Gérard. *Donsin: les structures agraires d'un village Mossi de la Région de Nobéré (cercle de Manga).* Paris and Ouagadougou: CNRS and CVRS, 1972. 141 p. (Recherches voltaïques, no. 15.)

———. *Enquête sur les mouvements de population à partir du pays Mossi (Haute-Volta).* Paris: ORSTOM, 1977. 159 p.

Rémy, Gérard; Jean Capron and Jean-Marie Kohler. "Mobilité géographique et immobilisme social: un exemple voltaïque." *Revue Tiers Monde,* Paris, 18, 71 (Jul.–Sep. 1977). pp. 617–653.

Roose, E. and Piot, J. "Runoff, Erosion and Soil Fertility Restoration on the Mossi Plateau." In *Challenges in African Hydrology and Water Resources,* edited by D. E. Walling, et al, pp. 485–498. Oxford, UK: International Association of Hydrological Sciences, 1984.

Savonnet, Georges. "Pina: Etude d'un terroir de front pionnier en pays dagari (Haute-Volta)." *Atlas des structures agraires au sud du Sahara, 4.* The Hague, Paris, New York: Mouton, 1976. 66 p.

Terrible, Marin. *Essai sur l'écologie et la sociologie d'arbres et arbustes de Haute Volta.* [Essay on the Sociology and Ecology of Trees and

Shrubs in Upper Volta]. Bobo-Dioulasso: Librairie de la Savane, 1984. p. 254.

Turner, Sandra. *Draft Environmental Profile on Upper Volta.* Tucson, Arizona: University of Arizona Arid Lands Information Center, 1980. 138 p.

United States Department of Interior. Office of Geography. *Upper Volta: Official Standard Names Approved by the United States Board on Geographic Names.* Gazetteer no. 87. Washington DC: GPO, 1965. 168 p.

Public Health and Medicine

"River Blindness on the Volta." *West Africa,* London, (17 and 24 May 1976) pp. 674–675 and 716–717.

Berry, Eileen; Hays, Charles and Scott, Earl. *Onchocerciasis Clearance in West Africa with Special Reference to Upper Volta.* Worcester Mass.: Clark University Program for International Development, 1978. 48 p.

Bosman, A., et al. "Further Observations on Chemoprophylaxis and Prevalence of Malaria Using Questionnaire Data in Urban and Rural Areas of Burkina Faso." *Parasitologia,* London, 30, 2–3 (1988). pp. 257–262.

Brun, T. A. "Coût énergétique comparé du puisage traditionnel de l'eau, du pompage manuel et à pied au Burkina." [Relative Energy Consumption of Drinking Water Carried on Foot, Retrieved by Pumps or Collected from Natural Rainfall]. In *Les malnutritions dans les pays du tiers-monde,* edited by D. Lemonnier and Y. Ingebleck, pp. 285–292. Paris: INSERM, 1986.

Bugnicourt, Jacques. "Views on Education and Health as Expressed by Herdsmen of the Voltaic Sahel." *African Environment,* Dakar, 14–16 (1980). pp. 449–456.

Collins, Peter. "How to Win the War on River Blindness." *West Africa,* London, 3510 (26 Nov. 1984). pp. 2389–2391.

Cousens, S., et al. "Prolonged Breast-Feeding—No Association with Increased Risk of Clinical Malnutrition in Young Children in Burkina Faso." *Bulletin of the World Health Organization,* Geneva, 71, 6 (1993). pp. 713–722.

Delnero, L., et al. "In-Vivo Sensitivity of Plasmodium-Falciparum to Halofantrine Hydrochloride in Burkina Faso." *American Journal of Tropical Medicine and Hygiene,* 50, 1 (1994). pp. 102–106.

———. "A National Survey of the Prevalence of Chloroquine-resistant Plasmodium-Falciparum in Burkina Faso." *Journal of Tropical Medicine and Hygiene,* Great Britain, 96, 3 (1993). pp. 186–190.

Frank, Odile and Dakuyo, Mathias. *Child Survival in Sub-Saharan Africa: Structural Means and Individual Capacity, A Case Study from Burkina Faso.* New York: Population Council, 1985. 76 p.

Gilles, Nadine and Ricossé, Jean-Henri. "La trypanosomiase humaine en Afrique occidentale: racines géographique d'une maladie." [Human Sleeping Sickness in West Africa: Its Geographic Roots]. *Cahiers d'études africaines,* Paris, 22, 1–2 (1982). pp. 79–100.

Gorgen, Regina; Maier, Birga and Diesfeld, Hans Jochen. "Problems Related to Schoolgirl Pregnancies in Burkina Faso." *Studies in Family Planning,* New York, 24, 5 (Sep.–Oct. 1993). pp. 283–294.

Guiguemde, T. R., et al. "Household Expenditure on Malaria Prevention and Treatment for Families in the Town of Bobo-Dioulasso, Burkina Faso." *Transactions of the Royal Society of Tropical Medicine and Hygiene,* 88, 3 (1994). pp. 285–287.

————. "10-Year Surveillance of Drug-Resistant Malaria in Burkina Faso (1982–1991)." *American Journal of Tropical Medicine and Hygiene,* 50, 5 (1994). pp. 699–704.

Hervouet, Jean-Pierre. "Organisation de l'espace et épidémiologie de l'onchocercose." In *Maîtrise de l'espace agraire et développement en Afrique tropicale: Logique paysanne et rationalité technique,* pp. 179–191. Paris: ORSTOM, 1979. (Mémoires, no. 89.)

Kabore, Abdoul Salam. "Health for Socio-Economic Development in Burkina Faso." *TransAfrica Forum: A Quarterly Journal of Opinion on Africa and the Caribbean,* Washington, DC, 3, 3 (1986). pp. 45–50.

Kambire, S. R. "Dracunculiasis in Burkina Faso: Results of a National Survey." *Journal of Tropical Medical Hygiene,* 96 (1993). pp. 357–362.

Lamontellerie, M. "Résultats d'enquêtes sur les filarioses dans l'ouest de la Haute-Volta (cercle de Banfora)." *Annales de parasitologie humaine et comparée,* 47 (1972). pp. 783–838.

Lang, T., et al. "Acute Respiratory Infections: A Longitudinal Study of 151 Children in Burkina Faso." *International Journal of Epidemiology,* Oxford UK, 15, 4 (1986). pp. 553–560.

Marchal, Jean-Yves. "L'onchocercose et les faits de peuplement dans le bassin des Volta: un objet de controverse." *Journal des Africanistes,* Paris, 48, 2 (1978). pp. 9–30.

Martin-Samos, F. *La santé publique en Haute-Volta: profil sanitaire.* [Public Health in Upper Volta: A Sanitary Profile]. Ouagadougou: CVRS, 1976. 202 p.

McMillan, Della E. *Sahel Visions: Planned Settlement and River Blindness Control in Burkina Faso,* Tucson, AZ: University of Arizona Press, 1995. 272 p.

McMillan, Della E.; Nana, Jean-Baptiste and Savadogo, Kimseyinga. *Settlement and Development in the River Blindness Control Zone: Case Study, Burkina Faso,* Washington DC: World Bank, 1993. 160 p.

McMillan, Della E.; Painter, Thomas and Scudder, Thayer. "Settlement Experiences and Development Strategies in the Onchocerciasis Control Programme Areas of West Africa. (Burkina Faso, Ghana, Mali, Togo)" *Land Settlement Review,* Binghamton, NY, (July 1990). 37 p.

Merkle, Alfred. *The Cost of Health for All: A Feasibility Study from Upper Volta,* Eschborn, Germany: German Agency for Technical Cooperation, 1982. 101 p.

Mitelberg, G. et al. "Projet de développement de la santé mentale au Burkina Faso." [A Project to Develop Mental Health in Burkina Faso]. *Psychopathologie Africaine,* Paris, 21, 1 (1986/87), pp. 19–65.

Morrison, Joy F. "Communicating Healthcare Through Forum Theater: Egalitarian Information Exchange in Burkina Faso."*Gazette: The International Journal for Mass Communication Studies,* Netherlands, 52, 2 (Sep. 1993). pp. 109–121.

Neuvy, G., "L'onchocercose, une endémie en voie de disparation au Burkina Faso." [River Blindness, an Endemic Disease about to Disappear in Burkina Faso]. *Les Cahiers d'Outre-Mer,* Bordeaux, 168 (1989). pp. 377–393.

Philippon, Bertrand. *L'onchocercose humaine en Afrique de l'ouest: vecteurs, agent pathogène, épidémiologie, lutte.* Paris: ORSTOM, 1978. 197 p.

Pilon, M. "Niveau et tendances de la mortalité dans l'enfance dans quelques régions rurales d'Afrique de l'Ouest: Kongoussi-Tikaré, Mariatang, Réo (Haute Volta), plateau de Dayes (Togo) (1950–1974)." [Levels and Trends of Child Mortality in Some Rural Zones of Western Africa (Upper Volta and Togo, 1950–1974)]. *Cahiers ORSTOM* (Sciences humaines), Paris: ORSTOM, 20, 2 (1984). pp. 257–264.

Prescott, N. "The Economics of Blindness Prevention in Upper Volta." *Social Science and Medicine,* Oxford UK, 19, 10 (1984). pp. 1051–1055.

Prost, A. "Le recensement de la cécité dans les savanes de la boucle du Niger." [The Evaluation of Blindness in Savannas of the Niger Bend]. *Cahiers ORSTOM* (Sciences humaines), Paris: ORSTOM, 19, 3 (1983). pp. 285–291. (study in Burkina Faso and Mali)

Retel-Laurentin, Anne. *Causes de l'infécondité dans la Volta noire.* [Causes of Infertility in the Black Volta]. Paris: Institut national d'études démographiques, 1980. 120 p. (Trav.-Docum. 87)

Ricosse, J. H. and Chartol, A. "Résultats de deux années d'antipaludisme dans la zône de Bobo Dioulasso." *Médecine Tropicale,* Marseille, 21 (1961). pp. 688–728.

Robert, V., et al. "Malaria Transmission in Three Sites Surrounding Bobo-Dioulasso, Burkina Faso." *Bulletin of the Society of Vector Ecologists,* London, 12, 2 (1987). pp. 541–543.

Salako, L. A., et al. "Ro–42–1611 in the Treatment of Patients with Mild

Malaria—A Clinical Trial in Nigeria and Burkina Faso." *Tropical Medicine and Parasitology*, 45, 3 (1994). pp. 284–287.

Samba, Ebrahim. M. "When the Horizon Brightens (Onchocerciasis)." *World Health*, Geneva, Switzerland, (Jan. 1983). pp. 4–7.

Sauerborn, R., et al. "The Economic Costs of Illness for Rural Households in Burkina Faso." *Tropical Medicine and Parasitology*, 46, 1 (1995). pp. 54–60.

———. "Low Utilization of Community Health Workers: Results from a Household Interview Survey in Burkina Faso." *Social Science and Medicine*, Oxford UK, 29, 10 (1989). pp. 1163–1174.

Sauerborn, R.; Nougtara, A. and Latimer, E. "The Elasticity of Demand for Health-Care in Burkina Faso—Differences Across Age and Income Groups." *Health Policy and Planning*, 9, 2 (1994). pp. 185–192.

Thierry, A., et al. "Food Consumption and Energy Expenditure among Mossi Peasants." *Africa Environment*, Dakar, 14–16 (1980). pp. 425–448.

Trussell, James, et al. "Norms and Behavior in Burkinabè Fertility." *Population Studies*, London, 43, 3 (1989). pp. 489–554.

World Health Organization. "Atlas of Onchocerciasis: Prevalence and Blindness in the Volta River Basin Area." In *Onchocerciasis Control in the Volta River Basin Area*, 30 pp. Geneva, Switzerland: WHO, 1973.

Vegetation and Flora

Dalziel, John McEwen. *The Useful Plants of West Tropical Africa*. London: HMSO, 1937. 612 p.

Hoffman, Odile. *Les plantes en pays Lobi*. [Plants in Lobi Country]. Maison-Alfort, France: Institut d'Elevage et de Médicine Vétérinaire des Pays Tropicaux, 1987. 155 p.

Kerharo, Joseph. *Plantes médicinales et toxiques de la Côte d'Ivoire-Haute Volta*. Paris: Vigot frères, 1950. 295 p.

Klintz, Danièle and Toutain, Bernard. *Lexique commenté peul-latin des flores de Haute Volta*. [Fulani-Latin Annotated List of Upper Volta Flora]. Maison-Alfort, France: Institut d'Elevage et de Médicine Vétérinaire des Pays Tropicaux, 1981. 44 p.

Marchal, Jean-Yves. "Arbres et brousses du paysage soudano-sahélien: dynamique des formations végétales au nord de la Haute Volta." [Trees and Bushes in the Sudano-Sahelian Landscape: Dynamics of Plant Formations in the North of Upper Volta]. *Cahiers ORSTOM* (Sciences humaines), Paris: ORSTOM, 17, 3–4 (1980). pp. 137–149.

Terrible, Marin. *Atlas de Haute-Volta: essai d'évaluation de la végétation ligneuse*. Ouagadougou: CVRS, 1975. 70 p.

Tiquet. J. "La flore forestière de Haute-Volta." *Etudes scientifiques,* (Sep.–Dec. 1983). 43 p.

Select List of Burkina Faso (Government) Publications

This list contains official government documents and laws, including such items occasionally published in foreign journals. The latter may be more accessible to persons working outside Burkina. It also contains quasi-official documents such as the commercial directories published by the Chamber of Commerce in Ouagadougou.

Afrique Occidentale Française, Gouvernement-Général. *Annuaire.* Since 1921.

Afrique Occidentale Française. *Bulletin Mensuel.*

Afrique Occidentale Français. *Journal Officiel, AOF.*

Afrique Occidentale Français. *La situation générale de l'Afrique Occidentale Française.* Dakar: Conseil de Gouvernement, each December.

BCEAO. *Burkina: statistiques économiques et monétaires.* [Burkina: Economic and Monetary Statistics]. Dakar: Banque Centrale des Etats de l'Afrique de l'Ouest. Quarterly. Formerly *Haute-Volta: statistiques économiques et monétaires.*

Burkina Faso. *Journal Officiel du Burkina Faso.* Ouagadougou: Imprimerie Nationale, 1984– . Weekly. Supersedes *Journal Officiel de la République de Haute Volta* which was issued 1959–84. It was preceded by the *Journal Officiel de Haute Volta,* 1919–1932 and 1953–1958. From 1948 to 1953 the official acts of Upper Volta appeared in the *Journal Officiel de la Côte d'Ivoire.*

———. *Annuaire statistique du Burkina Faso.* [Statistical Annual of Burkina Faso]. Ouagadougou: Institut National de la Statistique et de la Démographie, 1984– . Annual.

———. *Recensement général de la population, 1985: structure par âge et sexe des villages du Burkina Faso.* [The General Population Census of 1985: By Age and Sex for Villages in Burkina Faso]. Ouagadougou: Institut National de la Statistique et de la Démographie, 1988. 330 p.

———. *Analyse de résultats définitifs: deuxième recensement général de la population.* [Analysis of Final Results: Second (1985) General Population Census].

Ouagadougou: Institut National de la Statistique et de la Démographie, 1990. 318 p.

———. *Analyse des résultats de l'enquête démographique 1991.* [Analysis of Results of the Demographic Survey 1991]. Ouagadougou: Institut National de la Statistique et de la Démographie, Feb. 1994. 4 parts.

————. *Constitution du Burkina Faso*. [The Constitution of Burkina Faso]. Ouagadougou: Editions Sidwaya, 1991. 51 p.

————. *Eléments caractéristiques des entreprises du Burkina Faso*. [Typical Elements of Burkina Faso Business Enterprises]. Ouagadougou: Institut National de la Statistique, 1987. 31 p.

————. *Premier plan quinquennal de développement populaire 1986–1990*. [First Five-Year Plan for Popular Development 1986–1990]. Ouagadougou: Ministère de la Planification et du Développement Populaire, 1988. 2 vols.

————. *Deuxième plan quinquennal de développement populaire 1991–1995: programme prévisionnel des ONG*. [Second Five-Year Plan for Popular Development 1991–1995: Planned Program for Non-Governmental Organizations]. Ouagadougou, 1993. 85 p.

————. *Enquête sur les abattages domestiques*. Ouagadougou: Institut National de la Statistique et de la Démographie, 1992. 39 p.

————. *Enquête transport routier*. [Inquiry into Road Transport]. Ouagadougou: Institut National de la Statistique et de la Démographie, 1988. 107 p.

————. *Transports routiers et développement socio-économique en Haute-Volta: rapports d'enquêtes*. [Road Transport and Socio-economic Development in Upper Volta: Reports of the inquiry]. Ouagadougou: Université de Ouagadougou Groupe d'Etudes et de Recherches 'Transport et Développement', 1984. 184 p.

————. *Code des personnes et de la famille*. [Personal and Family Law]. Ouagadougou: Imprimerie Nationale, 1989. 215 p.

————. *Code de procédure pénale, suivi des décrets d'application*. [Criminal Procedure Law, Followed by Rules of Application]. Ouagadougou: Imprimerie Nationale, 1989. 328 p.

————. *La justice populaire au Burkina Faso*. [Popular Justice in Burkina Faso]. Ouagadougou: Ministère de la Justice, 1986. 99 p.

————. *Régime financier de l'Etat et des collectivités locales*. [Finance Law of the State and of Local Communities]. Ouagadougou: Ministère des Finances, 7th ed., 1988. 135 p.

————. *Réglementation des marchés administratifs*. [Regulations on Public Contracts]. Ouagadougou: Chambre de Commerce, d'Industrie et d'Artisanat, 1989. 169 p.

————. *Recueil annoté des textes applicables au droit du travail au Burkina Faso*. [Annotated Collection of Texts on Labor Law in Burkina Faso]. Ouagadougou: Chambre de Commerce, d'Industrie et d'Artisanat, 2nd ed., 1990. 465 p.

————. *Comptes nationaux de Burkina Faso 1986: méthodologie*. [National Accounts of Burkina Faso: Methodology]. Ouagadougou: Institut National de la Statistique et de la Démographie, 1990. 96 p.

————. *Recensement industriel et commercial, 1988*. [Industrial and

Commercial Census 1988]. Ouagadougou: Institut National de la Statistique et de la Démographie, 1988. 293 p. Also by same publisher, *Répertoire fichier des entreprises du Burkina Faso: 2e recensement industriel et commercial.* [File Directory of Enterprises in Burkina Faso: Second Industrial and Commercial Census]. 1988.

————. *Analyse des résultats du recensement industriel et commercial.* [An analysis of the Results of the Industrial and Commercial Census]. Ouagadougou: Institut National de la Statistique et de la Démographie, 1988. 88 p.

————. *Statut général des comités révolutionnaires.* [Status of the Revolutionary Committees]. Ouagadougou. 1989. 39 p.

Burkina Faso: Répertoire national des entreprises. [National Directory of Enterprises]. Ouagadougou: Chambre de Commerce, d'Industrie et d'Artisanat, 1992. 121 p.

Cadenat, Patrick. "La constitution de la Haute-Volta du 27 novembre 1977." *Revue juridique et politique, indépendance et coopération,* Paris, 32, 4 (Oct.–Dec. 1978). pp. 1025–1036.

France. Ministère de la Marine et des Colonies. *Annuaire,* 1898–1942.

France. Ministère de la Guerre. *Annuaire officiel des troupes coloniales,* 1894–1923.

France. Ministère de la coopération. *République de Haute Volta: économie et plan de développement.* 2d ed. Paris: Direction des affaires économiques et financieres, 1963. 66 p.

Haute Volta. "Texte de la constitution voltaïque." *Afrique Contemporaine,* (Jan.–Feb. 1978). pp. 23–31.

Haute Volta. *Bulletin Quotidien d'Information.* Ouagadougou and Bobo Dioulasso. From 1959.

Haute-Volta, Republic of. Direction du Commerce. *Commerce éxterieur et balance commerciale, 1969.* Ouagadougou: Ministère des Finances et du Commerce, Bureau d'Etudes et de Documentation, 1970. 191 p.

————. "Le premier plan de développement de la Haute-Volta, 1967–70." *Industries et Travaux d'Outre Mer,* Paris, (Oct. 1967). pp. 873–880.

————. Assemblée Nationale. *Plan quinquennal de développement économique et social, 1972–1976.* Ouagadougou, 1972.

Haute-Volta. "Haute Volta: le plan quinquennal 1977–1981." *Afrique Industrie,* Paris, 218 (Nov. 1980). pp. 60–75.

Haute-Volta, Republic of. Commission des langues voltaïques, sous-commission du Jula. *Régle de transcription et lexique de base Jula.* s.l., s.n., 1974. 97 p. (Dioula dictionary)

————. *La situation démographique en Haute-Volta. Résultats partiels de l'enquête démographique, 1960–1961.* Paris: Ministère de la Coopération et Institut National de la Statistique et des Etudes Economiques, 1962. 54 p.

————. *Enquête démographique par sondage en République de Haute-Volta, 1960–1961.* [Demographic Investigation by Opinion Poll in Upper Volta, 1960–1961]. Paris: République française, Secretariat d'état aux affaires etrangeres: Institut National de la Statistique et des Etudes Economiques, 1970. 2 vols. 466 p.

Haute Volta, Ministère des Finances et du Commerce. *Connaissance de la Haute-Volta.* Ouagadougou, 1970. 124 p.

Haute Volta. *Répertoire alphabétique des textes législatifs et règlements de la Haute Volta (1961–1973)*, Dakar: Université de Dakar, Faculté des Sciences Juridiques et Economiques, 1975. 100 p.

Haute Volta, Republic of. Ministère de la Santé Publique et de la Population. *Monographie sur le Ministère de la Santé Publique et de la Population.* Ouagadougou, 1971. 21 p.

Haute-Volta, Republic of. Assemblée Nationale. *Upper Volta Assemblée Nationale Documents for 1972 and 1973.* Bedford, NY: African Imprint Library Services, 1975. One microfilm reel.

Haute Volta, *Journal officiel de Haute Volta.* 1919–1932, 1953–1958.

Haute Volta, Republic of. Service des Liaisons Interministérielles. *Journal officiel de la République de Haute-Volta, 2e–12e année, 1960–1970,* 11 vols. Watertown, Mass.: General Microfilm Company.

Haute Volta. "Constitution de la République de la Haute Volta." *Penant,* Paris, 90 (Apr.–June 1980). pp. 221–234.

Haute-Volta, Republic of. Ministère du Plan et des Travaux Publics. *Plan-cadre de Haute-Volta: année interimaire 1971.* Ouagadougou, 1970. 111 p.

Haute-Volta, Republic of. Ministère du Développement et du Tourisme. *Situation économique actuelle de la Haute-Volta.* Ouagadougou, 1966. 63 p.

Journal Officiel de la Côte-d'Ivoire, 1895–1958.

Journal Officiel du Haut-Senegal-Niger. Koulouba: Government Printing Office, 1906–1921.

Journal Officiel du Soudan Français, 1 August 1906–November 1958.

Journal Officiel du Territoire du Niger, 1933–1958.

Journal Officiel de la République Française. Paris: National Printing Office, 1871–1940, 1943–1960.

Journal de l'Etat Français. (Official gazette of France, 1940–1944.)

Appendix A

Provinces and Their Headquarters Town
Effective April 1996

Bam	Kongoussi	Mouhoun	Dédougou
*Banwa	Solenzo	Nahouri	Pô
Bazéga	Kombissiri	Namentenga	Boulsa
Bougouriba	Diébougou	*Nayala	Toma
Boulgou	Tenkodogo	*Noumbiel	Batié
Boulkiemdé	Koudougou	Oubritenga	Ziniaré
Comoé	Banfora	Oudalan	Gorom-Gorom
Ganzourgou	Zorgho	Passoré	Yako
Gnagna	Bogandé	Poni	Gaoua
Gourma	Fada N'Gourma	Sanguie	Réo
Houet	Bobo Dioulasso	Sanmatenga	Kaya
*Ioba	Dano	Séno	Dori
Kadiogo	Ouagadougou	Sissili	Léo
Kénédougou	Orodara	Soum	Djibo
*Komondjari	Gayéri	Sourou	Tougan
*Kompienga	Pama	Tapoa	Diapaga
Kossi	Nouna	*Tuy	Houndé
*Koulpélogo	Ouargaye	*Yagha	Sebba
Kouritenga	Koupéla	Yatenga	Ouahigouya
*Kourwéogo	Boussé	*Ziro	Sapouy
*Loroum	Titao	*Zondoma	Gourcy
*Léraba	Sindou	Zoundweogo	Manga
*Les Balé	Boromo		

* New provinces as of April 1996.

255

Provinces and Their Headquarters Town
August 1983–April 1996

Bam	Kongoussi
Bazéga	Kombissiri
Bougouriba	Diébougou
Boulgou	Tenkodogo
Boulkiemdé	Koudougou
Comoé	Banfora
Ganzourgou	Zorgho
Gnagna	Bogandé
Gourma	Fada N'Gourma
Houet	Bobo Dioulasso
Kadiogo	Ouagadougou
Kénédougou	Orodara
Kossi	Nouna
Kouritenga	Koupéla
Mouhoun	Dédougou
Nahouri	Pô
Namentenga	Boulsa
Oubritenga	Ziniaré
Oudalan	Gorom
Passoré	Yako
Poni	Gaoua
Sanguie	Réo
Sanmatenga	Kaya
Séno	Dori
Sissili	Léo
Soum	Djibo
Sourou	Tougan
Tapoa	Diapaga
Yatenga	Ouahigouya
Zoundweogo	Manga

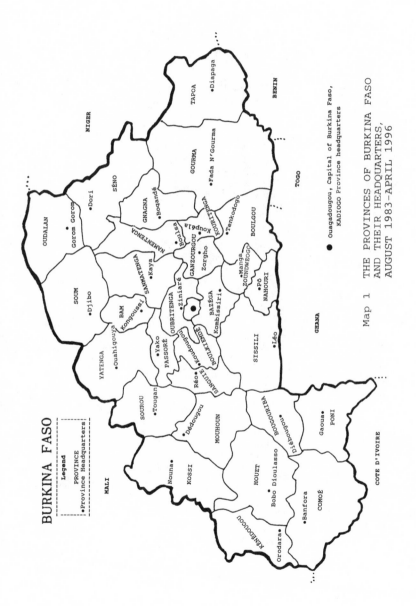

BURKINA FASO

Legend

- PROVINCE
- •Province Headquarters

Map 1   THE PROVINCES OF BURKINA FASO
AND THEIR HEADQUARTERS,
AUGUST 1983-APRIL 1996

• Ouagadougou, Capital of Burkina Faso,
KADIOGO Province headquarters

Appendix B

The Government as of 16 July 1978

President	Aboubakar Sangoulé Lamizana
Prime Minister	Joseph Issoufou Conombo

Ministers:

Interior and Security	Daouda Traore
Justice, Keeper of the Seals	Moïse Lankoandé
National Defense and Veterans' Affairs	François Bouda
Foreign Affairs	Moussa Kargougou
Finance	Léonard Kalmogo
Planning and Co-operation	Georges Sanogho
Rural Development	Issa Palé Welte
Industrial Development, Trade and Mines	Amadou Diallo
Public Works	Mahamoudou Ouédraogo
Education and Culture	Domba Konaté
Higher Education and Scientific Research	Arouna Traoré
Public Health and Population	Tinga Douamba
Civil Service and Labor	François Kaboré
Information	Edouard Tani
Posts and Telecommunications	Ismael Ouédraogo
Youth and Sports	Dramane Sanom
Environment and Tourism	Gany Tamboura
Social Affairs and Women's Affairs	Madame Moïse Alassane Traoré
Minister with responsibility to the PM for relations with Parliament	Céléstin Magnini

Source: *Africa Contemporary Record*

The Government as of 07 December 1980

Head of State, President of the
Military Committee of Redress
for National Progress (CMRPN),
President of the Council of
Ministers, Minister of National
Defense and War Veterans   Col. Saye Zerbo

Ministers:

Interior and Security	Lt-Col. Badembie Nezien
Justice, Keeper of the Seals	Bema Ouattara
Foreign Affairs and Cooperation	Lt-Col. Felix Tientarboum
Finance	Edmund Ki
Economy and Planning	Mamadou Sanfo
Rural Development	André Roch Compaore
Trade Industry and Mines	Djibrine Barry
Public Works Transport and Town Planning	Capt. Gnoumou Gaston Kani
National Education and Culture	Albert Patouin Ouédraogo
Higher Education (teaching) and Scientific Research	Faustin Sib Sie
Public Health and Social Affairs	Dr. J. M. Kielen
Civil Service and Labour	Alexandre Zoungrana
Posts Telecommunications and Information	Lt-Col. Charles Hounsouho Bambara
Youth and Sport	Lt. Moussa George Boni
Environment and Tourism	Bandre Sylvestre Ouédraogo
Social Affairs and Status of Women	Mme. Marie Madeleine Koné

Source: *Africa Contemporary Record*

The Government as of December 1981

Head of State, President of the Military Committee of Redress for National Progress (CMRPN), President of the Council of Ministers, Minister of National Defense and War Veterans	Col. Saye Zerbo

Ministers:

Interior and Security	Lt-Col. Badembie Nezien
Justice, Keeper of the Seals	Bema Ouattara
Foreign Affairs and Cooperation	Lt-Col. Felix Tientarboum
Finance	Edmund Ki
Economy and Planning	Mamadou Sanfo
Rural Development	André Roch Compaore
Trade Industry and Mines	Djibrine Barry
Public Works Transport and Town Planning	Capt. Gnoumou Gaston Kani
National Education and Culture	Albert Patouin Ouédraogo
Higher Education (teaching) and Scientific Research	Faustin Sib Sie
Public Health and Social Affairs	(Vacant)
Civil Service and Labour	Alexandre Zoungrana
Posts Telecommunications and Information	Lt-Col. Charles Hounsouho Bambara
Youth and Sport	Lt. Moussa George Boni
Environment and Tourism	Bandre Sylvestre Ouédraogo
Social Affairs and Status of Women	Mme. Marie Madeleine Koné

Source: *Africa Contemporary Record*

The Government as of February 1983

Head of State, Minister of
Defense and Veterans Affairs

Maj. Jean-Baptiste Ouédraogo

Ministers:

Interior and Security	Maj. Harouna Tarnagda
Justice	Marie-Louise Nignan
Foreign Affairs	Michael Kafando
Economy and Finance	Pascal Sanou
Planning	Eugene Dondasse
Rural Development	Edouard Tapsoba
Public Health	Alain Ouédraogo
Trade, Industrial Development and Mines	Clement Bambara
Labor and Civil Service	Jean Bado
Information and Posts	Adama Forfana
Higher Education and Scientific Research	Issa Tiendrebeogo
Education, Arts and Culture	Emmanuel Dadjaouri
Social Affairs and Women	Pauline Kambou
Transport, Environment and Tourism	Frederic Korsaga
Youth and Sport	Ibrahima Kone

Secretaries of State:

Budget	Justin Damo Barro
Civil Service	Jean-Paul Yacouba Sow
Water Resources	Benjamin Bonkoungou

Source: *Africa Contemporary Record*

The Government as of August 1983

President of the CNR, Head of State, Minister of Interior and Security	Capt. Thomas Sankara
Minister of State at the Presidency	Capt. Blaise Compaoré

Other Ministers:

Foreign Affairs	Arba Diallo
State Corporations	Capt. Henri Zongo
Justice and Keeper of the Seals	M. T. Raymond Ponda
Planning and Communications	Talata Eugène Dondasse
Equipment and Communications	Philippe Ouédraogo
Finance	Damo Justin Barro
Rural Development	Seydou Traore
Public Health	Maj. Abdou Salam Kabore
Trade, Industrial Development and Mines	Boubacar Hama
Labor, Social Security and Civil Service	Fidele Toe
Higher Education and Scientific Research	Issa Tiendrebeogo
National Education, Arts and Culture	Emmanuel Dadjaouri
Information	Adama Toure
Youth and Sport	Ibrahima Kone
Environment and Tourism	Laitar Basile Guissou
Social Affairs	Mme. Bernadette Paley
Secretary of State of Interior and Security	Nongma Ernest Ouédraogo

Source: *Africa Contemporary Record*

The Government as of 01 September 1985

Head of State, Chairman of the National Revolutionary Council (CNR) — Capt. Thomas Sankara

Minister of State at the Presidency, Minister of Justice — Capt. Blaise Compaoré

Other Ministers:

External Relations and Cooperation — Basile Guissou

Defense — Battalion Cmdr. Jean-Baptiste Boukary Lingani

Economic Promotion — Capt. Henri Zongo

Planning and Popular Development — Issouf Ouédraogo

Agriculture and Livestock — Seydou Traore

Water Resources — Michel Tapsoba

Health — Maj. Abdou Salam Kabore

Budget — Adèle Ouédraogo

Financial Resources — Damo Justin Barro

Commerce and People's Supplies — Mamadou Toure

National Education — Phillipe Somet

Higher Education and Scientific Research — Issa Tiendrebeogo

Equipment — Léonard Compaoré

Transport and Communications — Alain Koeffe

Family Welfare and National Solidarity — Mme. Joséphine Ouédraogo

Information and Culture — Ouattamou Lamien

Environment and Tourism — Beatrice Damibia

Labor and Civil Service — Fidele Toe

Territorial Administration and Security — Ernest Nongma Ouédraogo

Sport and Leisure — Sansa Dah

Secretary General to the Government and Council of Ministers — Nayatigingou Emmanuel Congo Kabore

Source: *Africa Contemporary Record*

The Government as of 29 August 1986

Head of State, Chairman of the National Revolutionary Council (CNR)	Capt. Thomas Sankara
Minister of State at the Presidency, Minister of Justice	Capt. Blaise Compaoré

Ministers:

Popular Defense	Maj. Jean-Baptiste Lingani
Economic Promotion	Capt. Henri Zongo
Foreign Relations and Cooperation	Léandre Bassole
Internal Administration	Ernest Ouédraogo
Planning and People's Development	Youssouf Ouédraogo
Peasant Affairs	Jean-Léonard Compaoré
Agriculture and Livestock	Jean-Marie Somda
Water Affairs	Michel Kouda
Budget	Adèle Ouédraogo
Financial Resources	Talata Eugène Dondasse
Information	Laitar Basile Guissou
Trade and Supplies	Mamadou Touré
Equipment	Michel Tapsoba
Transport and Communications	Alain Koeffe
Health	Azara Bamba
National Education.	Sansan Dah
Higher Education and Scientific Research	Valère Dieudonné Some
Family Affairs and Social Reform	Joséphine Ouédraogo
Environment and Tourism	Béatrice Damibia
Labor, Social Security and the Civil Service	Fidèle Toe
Culture	Bernadette Sanou
Sport	Maj. Abdou Salam Kabore
Secretary of State for Justice	Antoine Samba Komi
Secretary-General of the Government and Council of Ministers	Nayatigingou Emmanuel Congo Kabore

Source: *Africa Contemporary Record*

The Government as of 31 October 1987

Head of State, President of the
Front Populaire

Capt. Blaise Compaoré

Ministers:

Popular Defense	Maj. Jean-Baptiste Lingani
Economic Promotion	Capt. Henri Zongo
Foreign Relations	Jean Marc Palm
Health and Social Affairs	Alain Soubga
Higher Education	Clément Ouédraogo
Co-operation	Youssouf Ouédraogo
National Education	Philippe Somé
Peasant Affairs	Jean-Léonard Compaoré
Information	Sergé Théophile Balima
Tourism and the Environment	Béatrice Damibia
Trade and Supplies	Frédéric Korsaga
Territorial Administration	Léopold Ouédraogo
Justice	Salif Sampébgo
Equipment	Balao Badiel
Sport	Lt. Hein Kilimité
Labor, Social Security and the Civil Service	Albert Milogo
Finance	Guy Somé
Agriculture	Albert Guigma
Water	Alfred Nombré

Secretaries of State:

Budget Affairs	Céléstin Tiendrébéogo
Culture	Aminata Salembéré
Mining	Jean Yado Toé
Social Affairs	Alice Tiendrébéogo
Livestock	Amadou Diab
Secretary-General of the Government and Council of Ministers	Prosper Vocouma

Source: *Africa Contemporary Record*

The Government as of 23 August 1988

Head of State	Capt. Blaise Compaoré

Ministers:

Popular Defense and Security	Maj. Jean-Baptiste Lingani
Economic Promotion	Capt. Henri Zongo
External Relations	Jean Marc Palm
Higher Education and Scientific Research	Clément Ouédraogo
Health and Social Affairs	Alain Soubga
Transport and Communications	Issa Dominique Konaté
Planning and Co-operation	Youssouf Ouédraogo
Information and Culture	Sergé Théophile Balima
Primary Education and Mass Literacy	Alice Tiendrébéogo
Peasant Co-operatives	Capt. Laurent Sedgho
Finance	Bintou Sanogo
Equipment	Capt. Kambou Daprou
Labor, Social Security and the Civil Service	Naboho Kanidoua
Water Supply	Alfred Nombré
Agriculture and Livestock	Albert Guigma
Sport	Capt. Hein Kilimité
Justice	Salif Sampébgo
Territorial Administration	Jean-Léonard Compaoré
Commerce and People's Supply	Frédéric Korsaga
Environment and Tourism	Béatrice Damibia

Secretaries of State:

Housing and Town Planning	Moïse Traoré
Social Welfare	Elie Sare
Secondary Education	Jules Ouédoume Boleo
Livestock	Amadou Nori Guiao
Mines	Jean Yado Toé
Culture	Aminata Salembéré
Secretary-General of the Government and Council of Ministers	Prosper Vocouma
Secretary-General of the Revolutionary Committees	Capt. Arséne Ye Bognessan

Source: *Africa Contemporary Record*

The Government as of 25 April 1989

Head of State	Blaise Compaoré

Ministers:

Defense and Security	Maj. Jean-Baptiste Lingani
Economic Promotion	Capt. Henri Zongo
Delegate to Popular Front Co-ordinating Committee	Clément Oumarou Ouédraogo
Peasant Co-operatives	Laurent Sedgho
External Relations	Youssouf Go
Information and Culture	Beatrice Damiba
Health and Social Welfare	Naboho Kanidoua
Sport	Capt. Theodore Kilimité Hein
Labor, Social Security and the Civil Service	Salif Sampébgo
Planning and Co-operation	Pascal Zagre
Finance	Bintou Sanogo
Justice, Guardian of the Seals	Antoine Komy Sambo
Transport and Communications	Thomas Sanon
Secondary and Higher Education and Scientific Research	Mouhroussine Nacro
Primary Education and Mass Literacy	Alice Tiendrébéogo
Environment and Tourism	Maurice Dieudonne Bonane
Territorial Administration	Jean-Léonard Compaoré
Commerce and Supply	Frédéric Assomption Korsaga
Equipment	Maj. Kambou Daprou
Water Supply	Alfred Nombré
Agriculture and Livestock	Albert Guigma

Source: *Africa Research Bulletin*

The Government as of 21 September 1989

Head of State   Blaise Compaoré

Ministers:

Peasant Co-operatives	Laurent Sedgho
Environment and Tourism	Maurice Dieudonne Bonnanet
Health and Social Welfare	Naboho Kanidoua
Information and Culture	Beatrice Damiba
Foreign Affairs	Prosper Vokoumo
Sport	Theodore Kilimité Hein
Labor, Social Security and the Civil Service	Salif Sampébgo
Territorial Administration	Jean-Léonard Compaoré
Finance	Bintou Sanogo
Economic Promotion	Thomas Sanon
Planning and Co-operation	Pascal Zagre
Commerce and Consumer Supply	Frédéric Assomption Korsaga
Agriculture and Livestock	Albert Guigma
Equipment	Kambou Daprou
Transport and Communications	Roch Marc Christian Kaboré
Primary Education and Mass Literacy	Alice Tiendrébéogo
Secondary and Higher Education and Scientific Research	Mouhroussine Nacro
Justice, Guardian of the Seals	Antoine Komi Sambo
Water Supply	Sabine Koanda

Secretaries of State:

Finance in charge of Budget	Tiraogo Céléstin Tiendrébéogo
Housing and Town Planning	Joseph Kaboré
Culture	Aminata Salembéré
Social Welfare	Elie Sare
Livestock	Amadou Maurice Guiao
Mines	Aboubacar Yahya Diallo
Secretary-General of the Government and Council of Ministers	Alfred Nombré

Source: *Africa Research Bulletin*

The Government as of 18 June 1991
Transitional Government

Head of State	Blaise Compaoré

Ministers:

Minister of State responsible for co-ordinating government action	Roch Marc Christian Kaboré
Finance and Planning	Frédéric Assomption Korsaga
Industry, Trade and Mines	Thomas Sanon
Justice, Guardian of the Seals	Benoit Lompo
Defense and Security	Lassane Ouangrawa
Agriculture and Livestock	Albert Guigma
Health, Social Action and Family	Naboho Kanidoua
Foreign Relations	Prosper Vokoumo
Transport and Communications	Daprou Kambou
Employment, Labor, and Social Security	Salif Diallo
Civil Service/Modernization of the Administration	Juliette Bonkoungou
Information and Culture	Beatrice Damiba
Primary Education and Mass Literacy	Alice Tiendrébéogo
Secondary and Further Education, Scientific Research	Mouhroussine Nacro
Environment and Tourism	Maurice Dieudonne Bonnanet
Housing and Town Planning	Joseph Kaboré
Territorial Administration	Jean-Léonard Compaoré
Water Supply	Sabine Koanda
Youth and Sport Missions to the Presidency	Idrissa Zampaligre

Delegate to the Minister of:

State responsible for follow-up of economic reforms	Bissiri Joseph Sirima
State responsible for missions	Elisabeth (Ouédraogo) Yoni
Industry responsible for crafts and small/medium-size businesses	Issa Dominique Konaté
Finance, for budget	Tiraogo Céléstin Tiendrébéogo
Information, for culture	Bassie Hema
Agriculture, for livestock	Tiemoko Konaté
Transport, for landlockedness	Issa Gnanou Yao

Secretaries of State:

Planning	Haby Djiga
Energy and Mines	Aboubacar Yahya Diallo
Technical Education/Professional Training	August M'Pe Drmblele
Organization of Rural Areas	Jean-Baptiste Zongo
Social Action and the Family	Joseph Dieudonne Ouédraogo

Source: *Africa Research Bulletin*

The Government as of 26 February 1992

President, Head of State — Blaise Compaoré

Ministers of State:

Roch Marc Christian Kaboré,
Hermann Yaméogo

Ministers:

Special Duties at the Presidency and Government Spokesman	Idrissa Zampaligre
Special Duties at the Presidency	Boubacar Ouédraogo
Finance and Planning	Frédéric Assomption Korsaga
Agriculture and Livestock	Joseph Parkouda
Industry, Trade and Mines	Thomas Sanon
Equipment, Transport, Communications	Sebastien Ouédraogo
Territorial Administration	Antoine Raogo Sawadogo
Justice and Guardian of the Seals	Benoit Lompo
People's Defense and Security	Lassane Ouangraoua
Health, Social Welfare and Family	Amadou Quiminga
External Relations	Issa Dominique Konaté
Civil Service/Modernization of the Administration	Juliette Bonkoungou
Primary Education and Mass Literacy	Alice Tiendrébéogo
Secondary, Higher Education, Scientific Research	Mouhroussine Nacro
Environment and Tourism	Louis Armandouali
Water	Alphonse Ouédraogo
Information and Culture	Seck Nindou Thiam
Housing and Town Planning	Ludovic Tou
Youth and Sport	Marlene Zebango
Transport, Employment, Social Security	Arsene Armand Hein
Handicrafts and small/medium-size businesses	Mamadou Ouédraogo

Ministers Delegate to the Minister of:

Finance/Planning, for budget	Tiraogo Céléstin Tiendrébéogo
Territorial Administration, for Civil Liberties	Casimir Tapsoba
Information and Culture, for culture	Martine Bonou Houe Bationo

Equipment, Transport and Communications, for equipment	Bouraima Barry
Youth and Sports, for sports	Clement Sanon

Secretaries of State:

Planning	Haby Djiga
Animal Husbandry	Amidou Tamboura
Burkinabè Abroad	Ernest Ouédraogo
Technical Education/Professional Training	Mamadou Ganame
Social Welfare and the Family	Joseph Dieudonne Ouedraogo
Rural Organization	Alassane Sangare
Energy and Mines	Ali Coulibaly

Source: *Africa Research Bulletin*
In June 1992 Youssouf Ouédraogo became Prime Minister.

The Government as of 3 September 1993

President, Head of State — Blaise Compaoré

Ministers of State:

Relations with Institutions — Roch Marc Christian Kaboré
Finance and Planning — Ousmane Ouédraogo
Territorial Administration — Kanidoua Naboho
Minister of State — Hermann Yaméogo

Ministers:

For Presidential Mission — Salif Diallo
Defense — Yarga Larba
External Relations — Thomas Sanon
Public Works, Town Planning and Housing — Joseph Kaboré

Industry, Trade and Mines — Zéphirin Diabré
Secondary, Higher Education, Scientific Research — Maurice Mélégué Traoré
Primary Education and Mass Literacy — Alice Tiendrébéogo
Employment, Labor, Social Security — Jean-Léonard Compaoré
Environment and Tourism — Anatole Gomtirbou Tiendrébéogo
Communication, Government Spokesman — Theodore Kilimité Hein
Justice and Guardian of the Seals — Timothee Some
Civil Service/Modernization of the Administration — Juliette Bonkoungou
Transport — Idrissa Zampaligre
Agriculture and Animal Resources — Jean-Paul Sawodogo
Youth and Sport — Ibrahim Traoré
Health, Social and Family Action — Christophe Dabiré
Culture — Ouala Koutiebou
Water — Joseph Nongodo Ouédraogo

Delegate Minister:

Social and Family Action — Akila Belkemboago
Budget — Tiraogo Céléstin Tiendrébéogo
Planning — Jacques Sawadogo

Source: *Africa Research Bulletin*

The Government as of August 1994

President, Head of State	Blaise Compaoré
Prime Minister	Roch Marc Christian Kaboré

Ministers of State:

Defense	Kanidoua Naboho

Ministers:

African Integration and Solidarity	Hermann Yaméogo
Special Duties at Presidency	Salif Diallo
Economy, Finance and Planning	Zéphirin Diabré
Justice and Guardian of the Seals	Yarga Larba
External Relations	Ablasseh Ouédraogo
Territorial Administration	Vincent Te Kabré
Industry, Trade and Mines	Souley Mohamed
Secondary, Higher Education, Scientific Research	Maurice Mélégué Traoré
Primary Education and Mass Literacy	Alice Tiendrébéogo
Relations with Parliament	Thomas Sanon
Public Works, Housing and Town Planning	Joseph Kaboré
Employment, Labor, Social Security	Areuima Alphonse Ouédraogo
Civil Service/Modernization of the Administration	Juliette Bonkoungou
Agriculture and Animal Resources	Jean-Paul Sawodogo
Communications, Culture, and Government Spokesman	Nourchoir Claude Somda
Health	Christophe Dabiré
Environment and Tourism	Anatole Gomtirbou Tiendrébéogo
Water	Joseph Nongodo Ouédraogo
Youth and Sport	Ibrahim Traoré
Transport	Ouala Koutiebou
Social Welfare and the Family	Akila Belkemboago

Delegate Minister:

Budget	Tiraogo Céléstin Tiendrébéogo

Source: *Africa South of the Sahara*

The Government as of 11 June 1995

President, Head of State	Blaise Compaoré
Prime Minister	Roch Marc Christian Kaboré
Ministers of State:	
Environment and Water	Salif Diallo
African Integration and Solidarity	Hermann Yaméogo
Ministers:	
Economy, Finance and Planning	Zéphirin Diabré
External Relations	Ablasseh Ouédraogo
Defense	Col. Badaye Fayama
Justice and Guardian of the Seals	Yarga Larba
Territorial Administration	Yero Boli
Commerce, Industry, Cottage Industry	Dominique Talata Kafando
Energy and Mines	Elie Ouédraogo
Secondary, Higher Education, Scientific Research	Maurice Mélégué Traoré
Basic and Mass Education	Seydou Baworo Sanou
Public Works, Housing and Town Planning	Joseph Kaboré
Relations with Parliament	Thomas Sanon
Employment, Labor, Social Security	Areuima Alphonse Ouédraogo
Civil Service/Modernization of the Administration	Juliette Bonkoungou
Agriculture and Animal Resources	Jean-Paul Sawodogo
Communications, Culture, and Government Spokesman	Nourchoir Claude Somda
Health	Christophe Dabiré
Youth and Sport	Joseph Andre Tiendrébéogo
Transport and Tourism	Ouala Koutiebou
Social Welfare and the Family	Mme. Bana Maiga Ouandaogo
Delegate Minister:	
Budget	Tertus Zongo
Animal Resources	Alassane Sere
Water	Soma Baro
Housing and Town Planning	Viviane Compaoré

Source: *Africa Research Bulletin*

The Government as of June 1996

President, Head of State	Blaise Compaoré
Prime Minister	Kadre Desire Ouédraogo

Ministers of State:

Environment and Water	Salif Diallo
African Integration and Solidarity	Hermann Yaméogo

Ministers:

Economy, Finance and Planning	Zéphirin Diabré
External Relations	Ablasseh Ouédraogo
Justice and Guardian of the Seals	Yarga Larba
Territorial Administration	Yero Boli
Commerce, Industry, Cottage Industry	Dominique Talata Kafando
Energy and Mines	Elie Ouédraogo
Secondary, Higher Education, Scientific Research	Maurice Mélégué Traoré
Primary Education and Mass Literacy	Seydou Baworo Sanou
Public Works, Housing and Town Planning	Joseph Kaboré
Relations with Parliament	Thomas Sanon
Employment, Social Security	Souleymane Zibare
Civil Service/Modernization of the Administration	Juliette Bonkoungou
Agriculture and Animal Resources	Michel Koutaba
Communications, Culture	Nourchoir Claude Somda
Health	Christophe Dabiré
Youth and Sport	Joseph Andre Tiendrébéogo
Transport and Tourism	Viviane Yolande Compaoré
Social Welfare and the Family	Mme Bana Maiga Ouandaogo

Delegate Minister:

Budget	Tertus Zongo
Animal Resources	Alassane Sere
Water	Soma Baro
Housing and Town Planning	Issiaka Drabo

Source: *U.S. State Department Background Notes, Africa Research Bulletin*

About the Authors

Dr. Daniel Miles McFarland, a native of North Carolina, did his undergraduate studies at the University of North Carolina and his doctoral work in history at the University of Pennsylvania. He began teaching the history of Africa in 1958, with a specialty in the Volta River area of West Africa. Professor McFarland spent a year at the University of Ghana Institute of African Studies in the early 1970s, and has traveled extensively in North and West Africa. Author of many reviews and articles on West Africa, he was Professor of African Studies at James Madison University, Harrisonburg, Virginia, until his retirement.

Dr. Lawrence Rupley did his undergraduate study at Manchester College, Indiana, and received his Ph.D. in economics from the University of Illinois. After a year as a graduate fellow at University of Ibadan, Nigeria, his fourteen years of teaching included six years at Ahmadu Bello University, Nigeria, and two at the University of Nairobi, Kenya. He and his wife served as Country Representatives for the Mennonite Central Committee program in Burkina Faso from 1985–90. While living in Ouagadougou, he supervised North American volunteers in several locations in Burkina, which gave the opportunity for repeat exposure to life in small rural towns. Dr. Rupley was compiler with Tony Killick and Brendan Finucane of *The Economies of East Africa, 1974–1980: A Bibliography* (G. K. Hall, 1984) and was a correspondent for the *Bulletin for International Fiscal Documentation* (Amsterdam) for several years. His other publications include "Revenue Sharing in the Nigerian Federation," *Journal of Modern African Studies,* (1981) and numerous articles in *West Africa,* 1974–1980. In 1994–95 he served as a consultant to Mennonite Central Committee to prepare economic education materials.